STRATEGIC

—— VALUE ——

INVESTING

Practical Techniques of
Leading Value Investors

STEPHEN M. HORAN, CFA
ROBERT R. JOHNSON, CFA
THOMAS R. ROBINSON, CFA

New York Chicago San Francisco Athens London
Madrid Mexico City Milan New Delhi
Singapore Sydney Toronto

1 2 3 4 5 6 7 8 9 0 DOC/DOC 1 9 8 7 6 5 4 3

ISBN   978-0-07-178166-4
MHID   0-07-178166-8

e-ISBN   978-0-07-178167-1
e-MHID   0-07-178167-6

Library of Congress Cataloging-in-Publication Data

Horan, Stephen.
    Strategic value investing : Practical Techniques of Leading Value Investors /
Stephen M. Horan.
    - pages cm
    ISBN 978-0-07-178166-4 (hardback)–ISBN 0-07-178166-8 1. Value investing.
2. Investment analysis. 3. Securities. I. Title.
    HG4521.H7667 2014
    332.6--dc23

                                                                  2013031512

Stephen M. Horan
To Connie and Cayse and my late mentor, Jeff Peterson

Robert R. Johnson
To Heidi and my late parents, Rowena and Russell

Thomas R. Robinson
To Linda and my late father, Clarence E. Robinson

CONTENTS

INTRODUCTION

WHAT IS VALUE INVESTING?

All intelligent investing is value investing—acquiring more than you are paying for. You must value the business in order to value the stock.

—Charlie Munger

What do Benjamin Graham, Warren Buffett, Wally Weitz, and Seth Klarman all have in common? They are all value investors. What is value investing? Like beauty, it is in the eye of the beholder. Some view value investing as purchasing shares of companies that have been beaten down and are out of favor—selling at a cheap price relative to other available investments. Others may define value investing in contrast to something else—typically growth investing. Stock indices are often broken down into value and growth components, and a stock must either be classified under the value category or the growth category, but not both. In practice, however, value investing is not so limiting or narrow.

Value investing may involve any type of security or investment but is most commonly associated with the purchase of shares of stock in a company. Value investment deals with purchasing securities that are reasonably priced given their underlying fundamentals, including growth prospects. Ideally, the shares in the company should be trading at a price that is less than the intrinsic value of the shares and hence be considered a value stock. Being a value investor is no different from seeking value in the purchase of any good or service. We generally prefer to buy things when they are selling at a discount and not when they are selling at a premium.

How does price differ from value? At any point, an asset's price is subject to the economic laws of supply and demand. If demand for an asset exceeds the supply of that asset in the short run, then the price of that asset should rise and may exceed the long-term value of that asset. Prices can increase dramatically when seemingly everyone wants to buy an asset (remember the Internet bubble of the late 1990s and the more recent real estate bubble). In both cases, market prices exceeded the long-term intrinsic value of the assets, and when buyers stopped buying, prices fell dramatically (perhaps below intrinsic value in some cases). Similarly, if there is a large supply of an asset but few buyers (low demand) at any point, then the price is likely to fall, perhaps below the long-term intrinsic value. If investors recognize this value and start to buy the asset, demand increases relative to supply, and the price should rise (sometimes above intrinsic value). Value investing can be characterized by the practice of buying companies when their intrinsic value exceeds the current market price and selling companies when the current market price exceeds their intrinsic value. Some view value investing as more extreme ("deep value"), that is, buying good companies when nearly everyone else is selling and selling them when nearly everyone else is buying. At its core, value investing is indeed contrarian by nature; it does something different from other types of investing. However, value investing can also involve the practice of buying a growth stock that other investors are buying when it can be purchased at a reasonable price relative to its growth prospects. We will discuss this in more detail later in this chapter.

INTRINSIC VALUE VERSUS BOOK VALUE AND MARKET VALUE

We have mentioned *price* and *intrinsic value* thus far; before we continue, let's take a closer look at what we mean by these terms. Price and market value are one and the same. Price is what the asset is currently selling for in the marketplace—in this case, the stock market. Said another way, price is the value that the market as a whole is currently placing on the asset. The price or market value may change with each trade. If no transaction has occurred recently, we can get an idea of market value by looking at the bid and offer prices—the prices at which buyers are willing to buy and sellers are willing to sell, respectively.

Intrinsic value is what we should be willing to pay for the asset based on our assessment of its current fundamentals and long-term prospects. Intrinsic value is determined using valuation methods and estimates of the factors expected to drive value. In addition, intrinsic value is determined independently of the current market price for the stock (although it may involve the use of the market prices for similar assets, as we shall see later). Ideally, one would like to think that there is a single measure of intrinsic value that all value investors would agree upon. The truth is, however, that intrinsic value is in the eye of the beholder. Different value investors will surely use different models and different inputs and hence will not always agree as to which stocks are currently undervalued or overvalued. A single intrinsic value is rarely obtainable except with hindsight and may be unknowable even then (except perhaps when a company is liquidated). Whether a value investor purchased the stock at a good price is recognizable only as time passes.

Book value is an accounting measure that reflects the value of the assets the company holds, net of any liabilities of the company. Once upon a time, most assets held by a company were listed on the balance sheet at historical cost, and book value was therefore associated with historical cost. Historical cost represents prices paid at various times and is unlikely to have much association with what the asset is currently worth. Today, global accounting rules require that various assets be recorded at some measure of their current value, while others remain recorded at their historical cost or adjusted historical cost. Balance sheet or book value is therefore not a good measure of what the assets of the company are currently worth. Further, not all assets are reflected on a company's balance sheet (such as the value of the company's employee workforce) so book value is even further removed from the value of the company as a whole. At times, value investors may look at book value to approximate what it might cost a company to replace and rebuild or what might be obtained in an orderly liquidation. However, book value is generally not a realistic measure of the value of a company as a going concern. That said, as we shall see later, book value can be a useful benchmark against which we can measure the degree to which a stock might be considered a value stock.

INVESTING VERSUS SPECULATION?

Skeptics of equity investing claim that the stock market is simply a gamble, like trying your luck in Las Vegas. Although at times it may seem like that, nothing could be further from the truth. The underlying economics of gambling on one hand and financial markets on the other are starkly different. When we go to Las Vegas and play a fair game of chance, we cannot expect to consistently win or lose over a long time period. When we consider the house's take, we can expect to lose over repeated trials.[1] In contrast, investors can reasonably expect to earn a positive return on their investment as compensation for delaying consumption and bearing risk. Investing emphasizes the long term, and returns are derived from income and capital gains. Gambling, or speculating, is more often than not short-term oriented and is typically less focused on income and capital gains.

It should be said that speculating often gets a bad rap, and speculators are often demonized in the popular press. We do not share that view because, within certain parameters, speculators perform important economic functions in capital markets, such as providing liquidity. That said, our focus in this book is on investing. Investing involves:

1. An analysis of the current state of the economy and its future trajectory;

2. An evaluation of which industries are expected to do well in that economic environment; and

3. An evaluation of the companies within the industry that are priced below their intrinsic value given the state of the economy, the industry, and the fundamental characteristics of the company (earnings, cash flows, assets, liabilities, and the like).

Defined in this way, one could argue that all investing could be considered value investing. Too often, however, what is called investing is merely speculation.

The purchase of a security with the hope that a buyer will pay a higher price for it at a later date—perhaps because its price had been following a similar trajectory in the past—is speculation, not investing.

Unfortunately, or fortunately depending upon your perspective, hope is not a strategy. Speculation may succeed for short periods, but eventually the price of an asset should converge to its intrinsic value. At some point there may not be a subsequent investor willing to pay a higher price than that paid by the last investor. You do not want to be that last investor and end up holding the bag—or stock in this case. Many speculators learned this lesson the hard way—from buying tulip bulbs in the 1600s to Internet stocks in the 1990s to U.S. real estate or derivative debt securities in 2007.

Let's explore speculation a little further using the Dutch tulip debacle (sometimes referred to as "tulipmania") as an example. In the period from 1633 to 1637, Dutch merchants and ordinary citizens engaged in rampant speculation on the prices of tulip bulbs. Prices rose to levels never seen before, as buyers outbid each other in order to acquire tulip bulbs in the hope of turning around and selling them to others at a profit (high demand and limited supply!). At the peak of the mania, some tulip bulbs were selling at three or more times the annual salary of a typical merchant. In early 1637, liquidity in the tulip market dried up. There were no longer buyers willing to pay such high prices, and prices initially fell, then quickly plummeted as outright panic set in. In short order, tulip bulbs were selling at less than 10 percent of peak prices. The key to this mania was that buyers were buying these tulip bulbs not to plant them, but rather to turn around and sell them to someone else.

This is speculation, and it is something we would like to stress that you avoid. Again, speculation is not the subject of this book. Rather, this book is about strategic value investing: finding good companies at good prices and making a strategically oriented investment.

EFFICIENT MARKETS VERSUS IRRATIONAL MARKETS

Many finance theories are based on the notion that markets are "efficient." Market efficiency refers to the extent to which market prices fully reflect all available information. More precisely, efficient markets quickly and rationally assess and fully reflect any new information in market prices. For example, markets are said to be *strong-form* efficient when prices reflect prior price and value history; fundamental data about the company, industry, and economy; and any inside information about the company. The implication is that the current market price is correct, and no amount or type of analysis will lead to superior investment returns. *Semi-strong efficiency* exists when market prices reflect all information except for inside information—implying that neither fundamental nor technical analysis would lead to superior investment returns. *Weakly efficient* markets merely reflect prior technical data (for example, price and volume data) but not fundamental data, so fundamental analysis can lead to superior returns.

The level of efficiency in financial markets in general, as well as specific markets for shares of stock in individual companies, can be impacted by a myriad of factors; for example, the number of market participants or active investors in that stock; the availability and level of information and disclosures, including the cost to collect and process that information; any limits to trading (such as short selling or insider trading); and transaction costs. Most importantly, however, we must recognize that the market participants making investment decisions are, for the most part, individuals (whether they are retail investors or professional portfolio managers), and this can have a large impact on prices. Individuals do not always behave rationally, so information is not always reflected quickly and rationally into prices. Individuals exhibit biases, react to greed and fear, and get caught up in speculative manias such as those previously mentioned for tulip bulbs, Internet stocks, and real estate. Market efficiency requires rational economic behavior, which is something often lacking in market participants.

A large amount of research in finance has been performed on the degree to which markets exhibit "anomalies," or departures from efficiency, and the extent to which individuals and groups exhibit behavior that impacts prices—a field known as behavioral finance. There is quite a bit of evidence that these anomalies exist and that investors do not behave as rational economic units. Some markets are certainly more efficient than others. For example, a stock with a large number of analysts actively following it and evaluating its worth is likely to be more efficiently priced than one that has few analysts following it. Efficiency is a scale with a wide range. We should not expect markets to be efficient in every instance, nor at all times. In fact, we would prefer that they are not efficient. Inefficiencies create opportunities for price and value to diverge—exactly the types of opportunities value investors need to be able to exploit. So bring on the biases and anomalies!

VALUE VERSUS GROWTH INVESTING

As noted earlier, stocks are often classified as either value or growth. Value stocks are those selling at a low price relative to some underlying fundamental factor, such as earnings. Growth stocks are those whose price reflects future expectations about the company's future growth. Why might we expect to pay more for a growth stock relative to its current earnings? If earnings are expected to grow in the future, then—all else being equal—the stock should be priced higher. However, this dichotomy is arbitrary. In reality, an investment can be a "value" and "growth" stock at the same time (you may have heard the term *growth at a reasonable price,* or GARP). These terms are not mutually exclusive, although many market pundits use them in that manner. A company may be growing its revenues, earnings, and operating cash flow, and the current market price may not fully reflect that growth and future growth potential. The intrinsic value would likely be above the current market price, creating an opportunity for the value investor.

CONTRARIAN INVESTING VERSUS MOMENTUM INVESTING

As noted earlier, value investing is contrarian. A value investor perceives that the intrinsic value of a company's shares differ from the current market price—perhaps because of short-term imbalances in supply and demand, market inefficiencies, or investor behavior. A value investor never makes a decision based on price alone. Price is always compared to intrinsic value, and intrinsic value is measured (or estimated, as we shall see) based on fundamental data about the economy, industry, and company. On the other hand, momentum investing (not to be confused with growth investing although the two are often confused by market participants and pundits) involves buying shares or other securities that have exhibited strong recent increases in prices—in essence, going with the flow or investing with the crowd. Momentum investing is quite different from value investing. Value investors should not be lured into making an investment based solely on recent share price performance. It is certainly nice, however, when a value investor owns a stock that is then recognized by the crowd and exhibits strong price momentum. In this circumstance, the key for the value investor is to determine when the price has reached or exceeded fair value, given all available information, and exits the investment. The decision on when to sell is the most difficult part of investing in general, not to mention strategic value investing.

GOOD COMPANIES VERSUS GOOD INVESTMENTS

Good companies are not necessarily good investments. A company may have great products, stellar management, a spot-on brand name, healthy growth prospects, a strong balance sheet, and may be extraordinarily profitable in earnings and cash-flow terms, but in order to be a good investment, it must also be priced attractively. If the price reflects all of those attributes—or worse, if the price overvalues those attributes—then the investment itself will not offer sufficient return to compensate the investor for the possibility that expectations will not be met in the future.

Warren Buffett famously remarked that investing is like playing hockey. Players do not go to where the puck is; they go to where the puck is going to be. In the same way, a strategic value investor anticipates price changes by identifying discrepancies between price and underlying fundamentals. Strategic value investors look for good companies selling at good prices, or, in some cases, they look for companies that have poor fundamentals but some sort of impetus for change (such as change in management or where prospects look promising given the direction of the economy and industry).

A SHORT HISTORY OF VALUE INVESTING

Benjamin Graham is often referred to as the Father of Value Investing. He has also been called the Dean of Wall Street and was one of the earliest proponents of a credential for financial analysts in order to better establish security analysis and selection as a profession.[2] Graham began his career on Wall Street in 1914 at Newburger, Henderson and Loeb, where he initially summarized the details of bonds offered to the firm's clients while training to be a bond salesman. At that time, according to Graham, bonds were the only real "investment" security with common stocks being thought of as "speculative." Financial information on common stocks was just starting to become available and was largely considered only superficially. By 1920 Graham became a partner of the firm and oversaw what was then known as the "statistical" department—what we would call the investment research department today. In 1923, at the suggestion of an acquaintance interested in having Graham manage a good portion of the family's wealth, Graham amicably left Newburger, Henderson and Loeb to form a new investment firm with the family—Graham Corporation. Over the next several years the firm changed structures and became the Graham-Newman Partnership, which Graham ran for the remainder of his career. At Newburger, Graham Corporation, and the Graham-Newman Partnership, Ben Graham honed his skills as a financial analyst.

More than learning from others, Graham was creating tools and techniques for evaluating securities, including common stocks. Rather than keeping this knowledge to himself Graham shared it freely—he taught classes at Columbia University and wrote articles for periodicals such as *Forbes* and *Financial Analysts Journal*. Needing a textbook on security analysis for his course at Columbia and finding none existing at the time, Graham partnered with Columbia professor David Dodd to write *Security Analysis,* published by McGraw-Hill in 1934. This classic endures to this day, with subsequent editions published in 1934, 1940, 1951, 1988, and 2008.

The value-oriented approach of *Security Analysis* is clear from the introduction onward. In the case of bonds, the text emphasizes examining the safety of both interest and principal. For common stocks, the book eschews "speculation" and instead focuses on treating common stocks from an "investment" perspective—one that includes detailed analysis, assessment of value, and safety of principal. The first chapter introduces the concept of intrinsic value, which Graham notes is somewhat elusive, but which represents the value that is justified based on the available data. Graham was not overly concerned with obtaining a precise measure of intrinsic value. Instead, his focus was on determining whether there was adequate intrinsic value to justify the price paid for the security. A key concept presented is that of margin of safety—the analyst's estimate of how much of a discount the security is selling for relative to its intrinsic value. Margin of safety is the cornerstone of Graham's concept of value investing. A classic error among novice investors is not demanding a large enough margin of safety before investing in a security. Graham advocates a significant margin of safety—not only to enhance return but also as a risk management tool. The larger the margin of safety, the more limited an investor's downside risk.

Graham followed *Security Analysis* with another classic, *The Intelligent Investor,* first published in 1949. In the preface to the fourth edition, legendary investor Warren Buffett calls it "by far the best book about investing ever written." This text further develops the concepts presented in *Security Analysis* and describes value investing approaches to stocks adapted for different types of investors—defensive and enterprising (aggressive). Margin of safety is again emphasized as the cornerstone of investment. Beyond margin of safety, *The Intelligent Investor* stresses diversification as a key component of investment strategy, given that, even with a margin of safety, an investment in an individual security may not ultimately succeed. The emphasis on diversification seems nearly self-evident by today's standards. At the time, however, it bordered on being revolutionary. The idea of "modern portfolio theory" had not yet been developed, and conventional wisdom suggested that successful investing required focusing your efforts on a few selected securities.

Graham clearly played the preeminent role in the development of value investing, as well as in the development of security analysis as a profession. His writings and lectures influenced many of the last century's legendary value investors, notably Warren Buffett. After doing undergraduate work at Wharton and completing his undergraduate degree at the University of Nebraska-Lincoln, Buffett embarked on graduate studies at Columbia Business School in order to study under Graham. Buffett later worked with Graham at Graham-Newman before forming his own investment partnership and later running Berkshire Hathaway. Buffett has an enviable long-term track record, besting the broad market averages by a wide margin over an investing career spanning more than fifty years.

Buffett was also influenced by Philip Fisher, author of *Common Stocks and Uncommon Profits*. Buffett has stated that he is 85 percent Graham and 15 percent Fisher. Interestingly, Fisher was best classified as a growth investor with key points to investing focused on management, the business and growth prospects but not value. Fisher's son, Ken Fisher, who wrote new introductory material for the revised edition of the book, noted that Fisher's fifteen points were also relevant for value investors. In essence, value investors are primarily looking for good companies with good management—they just want to acquire them at favorable prices. When one of us (Bob Johnson) asked Buffett for recommended texts for an investments class at Creighton University in the late 1980s, he recommended *Security Analysis*, *The Intelligent Investor*, and *Common Stocks and Uncommon Profits*.

Numerous books have been written about Buffett and his investing philosophy, but none have been written by Buffett himself. Buffett has written a substantial amount of material directed to his shareholders and partners. His letters to Berkshire shareholders, annual report commentary, and "owner's manual" for shareholders (all available on the Berkshire website) contain great perspectives on his thinking. Buffett counsels the shareholders in Berkshire to regard their investment in the same way that he himself thinks about a prospective acquisition for Berkshire's portfolio—not merely as owning a "piece of paper" with a highly variable stock price but as owning part of a business. Similarly, Buffett considers the shareholders of Berkshire his business partners. Buffett always takes a long-term view and is unconcerned about daily, weekly, or monthly price fluctuations for investments he already owns. In fact, he states that he would not care if several years passed with no trading activity in an investment. On the other hand, he relishes market volatility, as it provides opportunities for the value investor, stating:

> Overall, Berkshire and its long-term shareholders benefit from a sinking stock market much as a regular purchaser of food benefits from declining food prices. So when the market plummets—as it will from time to time—neither panic nor mourn. It's good news for Berkshire.

This philosophy has served Buffett and his partners well. Berkshire has regularly stepped in during times of market turmoil to snap up bargains. During the 2008 crisis, he was sought after not only for his counsel but also to bail out overextended firms. In 2011, for example, he invested $5 billion into Bank of America after the stock had dropped to under $7 per share from over $50. As of this writing, he has doubled his money from that investment.

While Buffett is the most well known of Graham's value investing disciples, he is certainly not the only one. Most value investors trace their ancestry to Graham and Dodd's work and as a group are sometimes referred to as "residents of Graham-and-Doddsville." Buffett profiled a number of prominent value investors whose lineage can be traced to the father of value investing in a speech at Columbia, "The Superinvestors of Graham-and-Doddsville." These included Walter Schloss (who took a course from Graham), Tweedy Brown Company (whose founders took courses from Graham and Dodd), Bill Ruane of The Sequoia Fund (a classmate of Buffett's in Graham's class), Charlie Munger (now Buffett's partner at Berkshire and heavily influenced by him), Rick Guerin (influenced by Charlie Munger), and Stan Perlmeter (influenced by Buffett). Buffett noted that all of these investors had outstanding records and were value investors of the Graham and Dodd school. However, each approached value somewhat differently and held different securities in their portfolios. Buffett notes that the main commonality is the viewpoint that these investors are buying companies and not stocks, while exploiting divergences between market prices and intrinsic value.

Many other investors were influenced by Graham's writings. Max Heine, who founded Mutual Shares, was working in a department store in New York City when he discovered *Security Analysis* and began investing. Heine and his colleagues at Mutual Shares would later mentor Seth Klarman—now a renowned value investor and author of another value investing classic, *Margin of Safety*: *Risk-Averse Value Investing Strategies for the Thoughtful Investor.* The importance of margin of safety as a foundation of value investing is reflected in the title of Klarman's book. Value investors do not take investing lightly; they do their homework, only investing when there is a sufficient discount of price to intrinsic value to create an adequate margin of safety. For those of you who are sports enthusiasts, both Buffett and Klarman use a baseball analogy. Value investors do not swing at every pitch—they wait for pitches in the sweet spot. For those of you who are poker players, this is analogous to not playing every hand. You need to know when to hold them and know when to fold them.

A GUIDE TO THE REST OF THIS BOOK

This book will revisit many of the tools and techniques presented in the value investing classics, while updating them in response to the current market and economic environment. We will try to do so in a manner that makes the material easily accessible to all investors, while demonstrating how value investing can be applied in practice. We will spend more time than other books on methods by which the value investor can estimate intrinsic value—a key component for computing margin of safety. The remainder of Section 1 addresses the issues of why you should be a strategic value investor, the barriers to successful value investing, and how to assess companies as a business in the context of its industry and competitors. Section 2 presents valuation techniques through which we can estimate intrinsic value, including discounted cash flow models, asset-based models, and relative valuation models. Section 3 discusses value investing styles, including profiles of prominent value investors and techniques for applying value investing in practice.

CHAPTER TWO

WHY STRATEGIC VALUE INVESTING?

Most analysts feel they must choose between two approaches customarily thought to be in opposition: "value" and "growth." ... In our opinion, the two approaches are joined at the hip: Growth is always *a component in the calculation of value, constituting a variable whose importance can range from negligible to enormous and whose impact can be negative as well as positive.*
—Warren Buffett, 1992, Letter to Berkshire Hathaway shareholders

Now that you have a sense of strategic value investing and its variety, you may be asking yourself why this investment strategy is any better than another, particularly compared to a growth-oriented strategy. Here, we outline some of the performance characteristics of value investing that we think are particularly important. You may expect that we are going to show that value investing always produces higher returns than any other kind of investment strategy. Although we think a disciplined, long-term value investment strategy is sensible, investment performance is as much about risk as it is about return. So, we will spend some time discussing both the return and the risk profiles (and what we mean by risk) associated with these kinds of strategies.

As we said in the last chapter, value investing is in the eye of the beholder. There is no single definition or approach. Although there are various styles of value investing, it is not ill-defined. Some view value investing as purchasing shares of companies that have been beaten down and are out of favor and perhaps simultaneously selling shares of companies that have risen sharply in value. Others contrast it to growth investing. Chapters 12 through 15 are dedicated to discussing different styles and applications of the concept. In this chapter, we will confine our attention to some of the more standard and common measures of value.

PRICE REVERSALS

In the last chapter, we mentioned that a well-developed body of research documenting various market inefficiencies has spawned a new subfield of finance, called behavioral finance. One of the most important studies of purported market inefficiency was published in 1985 by Werner DeBondt and Richard Thaler in the *Journal of Finance*. Their research demonstrated that we may be able to predict future price movements simply based on past movements, which is an apparent violation of the weak form of market efficiency we described in the previous chapter, at least in the extremes. Before this time, researchers had great difficulty demonstrating that past price movements told us much about future price movements.

DeBondt and Thaler showed that if an investor were to purchase the 35 stocks that dropped the most in price over the previous three years of all the stocks on the New York Stock Exchange from 1933 to 1980, they would have outperformed the market by about 20 percent over a subsequent three-year period. If that same investor were to have purchased the 35 best-performing stocks over the previous three years, they would have underperformed the market by 5 percent over the subsequent three-year period, for a total difference between the winning and losing portfolio of about 25 percent. That's quite a difference. They also document similar results for different time horizons.

More recently, Stephen Foerster of the University of Western Ontario looked at stocks that have doubled over a four-year period. In a 2011 study, he finds that stocks that have doubled in the previous four-year period have a cumulative underperformance of 28 percent in the next four-year period. Those that double more quickly (say, in less than 12 months) underperform by 53 percent over the subsequent four-year period. All of this implies, of course, that nondoublers outperform by these margins.

Earning returns like these in the real world is very different than documenting them in a hypothetical study. For one thing, these studies ignore bid-ask spreads, commissions, market impact, and other transaction costs. It's also fair to ask whether one is really comparing apples to apples if the risk profile of the loser portfolio is different from the risk profile of the winner portfolio.

Even if these kinds of results were achievable moving forward, it would take nerves of steel and a titanium backbone to implement such a contrarian strategy. We will discuss the barriers to successful strategic value investing, some of which relate to emotional fortitude, in the next chapter. Suffice it to say for now, however, that successful value investing often requires investors to be contrarian or go against the grain of prevailing market sentiment as described in Box 2-1.

Box 2-1 People Say I'm the Life of the Party

Imagine yourself at a cocktail party in the year 2000. After a couple of drinks, people's lips start to get loose as the conversation turns toward money and investment portfolios, and a sense of bravado combined with the selective nature of our memories (both of which are likely enhanced by the cocktails) takes over. A successful doctor from down the street begins bragging about his recent purchases of medical device companies and Internet stocks. A few lawyers huddled around the cheese dip join in the chorus like boys around a campground fire. Everyone seems to be making money with ease. Out of modesty, you refrain from participating in this particular discussion topic, but not surprisingly the attention eventually turns to you. "What are you buying these days?" Dr. Frank Kelly asks.

You respond, "I am loading up on shares of WD-40 Company." An uncomfortable silence ensues, broken only by soft snickers from the successful doctor and the attorneys.

Miles Stanford, the attorney, asks "Wasn't that company trading over $30 per share in 1997?"

"It was," you respond.

"What's it trading at now?"

"Under $18 per share."

"Well, what do they do?" asks Frank.

"They manufacture the spray lubricant many of us buy at the hardware store."

"That doesn't sound very interesting. What else do they do?"

"Nothing. That is their only product," you admit.

"Well, my medical device company is using the latest technology to develop a treatment that could save tens of thousands of lives every year." And the conversation moves on to a more interesting topic.

This is the kind of embarrassing situation that strategic value investors sometimes face. It is not terribly pleasant being the butt of jokes from your peers who are boasting about the high-profile investments they have recently made. If you are patient, however, you may be able to have the last laugh.

Three years later, by the end of 2002, after the tech bubble burst, the doctors and lawyers at the cocktail party are commiserating about how much longer they will need to work before they can retire as their portfolios laden with medical device and technology stocks are decimated, with the Nasdaq 100 index down nearly 85 percent from its heyday. You, on the other hand, are deciding whether it is time to sell your shares of WD-40 Company stock because it is once again approaching $30 per share for a positive 65 percent return. Your portfolio of other value stocks, while not completely insulated from the three years of market malaise, has held up pretty nicely, as well.

So, although strategic value investing is a promising investment philosophy, it is often a contrarian strategy and not the path of least resistance.

LONG-TERM VERSUS SHORT-TERM

Nor is strategic value investing for the impatient investor. As we mentioned previously, the results of the DeBondt and Thaler study hold for different portfolio formation and holding periods. However, it is worth noting that the returns between the portfolio of winners and losers as much as 12 months after they had been chosen are virtually indistinguishable. The positive results were achieved for a three-year holding period.

In fact, once you have identified a market inefficiency and taken a position based on it, markets can often become even more inefficient before the wisdom of your analysis is finally brought to light. Many an arbitrageur has learned that sometimes markets can stay inefficient for longer than you can stay liquid.[1] This creates fundamental limits to the power of arbitrage to bring markets back to equilibrium. Fortunately, if you avoid the use of leverage, this will likely not be a risk you will need to face.

Over shorter time horizons, stocks tend to exhibit momentum rather than contrarian tendencies, which can further test the resolve of the strategic value investor. For example, Narasimhan Jegadeesh and Sheridan Titman of UCLA demonstrated in the 1990s that individual stocks that performed the best over the previous 3 to 12 months outperformed stocks that had performed the worst. The forward-looking period of outperformance is about another 3 to 12 months, and the general results have been confirmed in subsequent studies. The most pronounced effect is buying (selling) 12-month winners (losers) and holding (shorting) them for another 3 months, which produces a return of over 1 percent per month.

These types of trading strategies are often referred to as *relative strength* strategies and are not considered value strategies. Like any study of past returns, we should not be led to believe that just because they prevailed in the past that they will necessarily prevail in the future. The Jegadeesh and Titman effect is less pronounced than the long-term price reversals that DeBondt and Thaler demonstrate, but they too suggest that markets may not be efficient.

Although capitalizing on price reversals is one variety of value investing, we should not be misled into believing that value investing is necessarily predicated on this kind of technical analysis or contrarian sentiment. We mentioned growth at a reasonable price in the previous chapter as an example.

In fact, value investing (and especially "strategic" value investing) is associated much more strongly with fundamental analysis than technical analysis. Technical analysis focuses exclusively on past price and trading volume changes to predict future price changes. Fundamental analysis, on the other hand, focuses on evaluating firm, sector, and market characteristics as a means to estimate a security's intrinsic value. We believe that strategic value investing is most powerful when it is based primarily on fundamental investing, which will be the focus of this book. That said, however, an awareness of a security's past performance and an understanding of how past performance can potentially relate to future performance is a great way to augment solid fundamental analysis. In fact, value investors sometimes use technical indicators to identify entry points for companies identified as value opportunities through fundamental analysis (and subsequent exit points when it is time to sell).

PERFORMANCE CHARACTERISTICS OF VALUE VERSUS GROWTH STRATEGIES

We believe in strategic value investing because it has historically performed well as an investment strategy. That said, it is not for the faint of heart and requires a disciplined approach. To get a sense of what the historical characteristics of value investing have been, it is helpful to understand style investing.

For our purposes here, we will focus on the style metrics based on work by Eugene Fama and Kenneth French, who have been iconic leaders in our understanding of how stocks of various styles tend to perform over time. Eugene Fama, of the University of Chicago, and Kenneth French, of Dartmouth, have worked closely with Dimensional Fund Advisors to develop value-based investment strategies. Theirs is not the only framework, however. Morningstar, for example, has similar style boxes that are defined somewhat differently but get to the same idea.

We will say more about the different ways value investing is defined in Chapter 6, but suffice it to say for the time being that Fama and French focus on a stock's price-to-book (P/B) ratio. The price-to-book ratio is a stock's current price divided by the net balance sheet (book) value of the stock. Book value is the recorded accounting "value" of the firm's assets (which can either be their cost or some estimate of the value at which they could be sold) minus the accounting "value" of the firm's liabilities. In other words, the P/B ratio measures the market's perception of the stock versus what the underlying assets are "worth" from an accounting sense. Stocks with P/B ratios in the lowest 30th percentile at the beginning of a given year are considered value stocks (they are selling for a low price relative to their underlying net assets), while stocks with P/B ratios in the highest 30th percentile are considered growth stocks for that year.[2]

RETURNS

As you can see from Table 2-1, the average return on the overall stock market from 1926 to 2012 has been 11.8 percent per year. By comparison, three-month Treasury bills returned 3.6 percent, on average. The return on stocks is obviously not generated consistently one year after the next. The overall stock market is a well-diversified equity portfolio by definition. But it is still an equity portfolio and, as such, is subject to significant risk, as we have seen over the past decade. But this is nothing new. During this time, the market has dropped by as much as 44 percent in any single calendar year and gone up by as much as 56 percent. That is a range of 100 percent.

Notice that value stocks tend to outperform the overall market. Large capitalization value stocks had an average return of 14.7 percent over this period compared to 11.8 percent for the overall market. That's a difference of 2.9 percent, which is extraordinarily large and can have an incredible impact on capital accumulation over long periods of time. Value stocks have even more of a performance edge over growth stocks: 14.7 percent versus 11.2 percent for a 3.5 percent differential.

TABLE 2-1

Historical Annual Return Characteristics, 1926–2012

	Overall	Large Capitalization			Small Capitalization			
	Market	Growth	Middle 40%	Value	Growth	Middle 40%	Value	T-Bills
Arithmetic Avg.	11.8%	11.2%	12.1%	14.7%	13.9%	16.6%	18.8%	3.6%
Geometric Avg.	9.8%	9.2%	9.9%	11.2%	9.3%	12.9%	14.2%	3.5%
Median	14.9%	13.3%	13.2%	18.7%	12.5%	18.3%	20.4%	3.1%
Standard Deviation	20.3%	20.4%	21.2%	27.5%	32.9%	29.0%	32.4%	3.1%
Skewness	-0.434	-0.316	-0.0495	0.258	0.944	0.433	0.232	0.984
Excess Kurtosis	-0.031	-0.384	2.520	1.977	3.494	1.506	0.394	0.986
Sharpe Ratio	0.404	0.372	0.403	0.405	0.314	0.448	0.471	0.000

Source: Based on Kenneth French's Data Library

We see an even greater performance differential among small capitalization stocks. Small value stocks exhibited a 18.8 percent return from 1926 to 2012 compared to 13.9 percent for small growth stocks. That's a 4.9 percent differential and is not to be taken lightly.

RISK

It is foolish to talk about return without also talking about risk. With investments, risk is often measured as the variability of returns. One common way we measure this return variability is by standard deviation, a statistical measure that describes how uncertain or variable the average return has been. It incorporates more information than simply the highest and lowest values. For normally distributed returns (we will say more about what that means shortly, as well as how real life returns depart from normality), we can expect the return in any given year to fall within one standard deviation of the average about two-thirds of the time.

For example, the standard deviation for the overall market is 20.3 percent, and the average return is 11.8 percent. Therefore, we would expect the overall stock market to record a return within −8.5 percent and 32.1 percent in any given year about two-thirds of the time. We derive these figures by subtracting the standard deviation from the average return and adding the standard deviation to the average return. This range is quite large because the standard deviation is relatively high, which is an indication of risk and the overall stock market.

The range defined by adding and subtracting one standard deviation from the mean will tend to capture only about two-thirds of the returns. If we want to be more than two-thirds confident that the return in a given year will fall within a particular range, we need to widen the range to capture more of the returns. We can expect returns to fall within two standard deviations of the average about 95 percent of the time. Therefore, we would expect the overall stock market to record a return within −28.8 percent and 52.4 percent in any given year. Because this range is so wide, it is not terribly informative.

We just saw that value stocks tend to exhibit higher returns than either the overall market or growth stocks. However, they also exhibit more risk. According to Table 2-1, the standard deviation on large capitalization value stocks was 27.5 percent, compared to 20.3 percent for the overall market and 20.4 percent for growth stocks. That is a differential of more than 7 percent. Small capitalization stocks generally have higher standard deviations than large capitalization stocks regardless of whether they are considered to be value or growth. Interestingly, however, small capitalization value stocks actually have a slightly lower standard deviation than small-cap growth stocks (32.9 percent compared to 32.4 percent, respectively).

These same basic trends hold up when we look at monthly returns rather than annual returns. According to Table 2-2, monthly returns to value stocks are greater than monthly returns to growth stocks, whether they are large or small.

T A B L E 2-2

Historical Monthly Return Characteristics, 1926–2012

	Overall Market	Large Capitalization			Small Capitalization			T-Bills
		Growth	Middle 40%	Value	Growth	Middle 40%.	Value	
Arithmetic Avg.	0.93%	0.89%	0.96%	1.15%	1.03%	1.25%	1.44%	0.29%
Geometric Avg.	0.79%	0.74%	0.79%	0.74%	0.74%	1.01%	1.11%	0.29%
Median	1.27%	1.13%	1.24%	1.21%	1.21%	1.58%	1.54%	0.23%
Standard Deviation	5.38%	5.35%	5.78%	7.34%	7.74%	7.07%	8.38%	0.28%
Skewness	0.148	-0.136	1.297	1.543	0.918	1.339	1.955	1.040
Excess Kurtosis	7.290	5.276	17.192	17.802	10.014	14.870	18.878	1.260
Sharpe Ratio	0.119	0.109	0.117	0.117	0.096	0.136	0.137	0.000

Source: Based on Kenneth French's Data Library

RETURN COMPARED TO RISK

Because we should not view either return or risk in isolation, we need to come up with a way to view the two together. In the industry, a common way to do this is to look at the Sharpe ratio. The Sharpe ratio compares the average excess return on a risky investment with its standard deviation. Excess return is the average return on a risky investment (like the stock market) less what could have been earned on a risk-free investment (like three-month Treasury bills). The ratio of this excess return to the standard deviation is called the Sharpe ratio. Therefore, investments with a high standard deviation are penalized under the Sharpe ratio and investments with high return are rewarded.

The Sharpe ratio for the overall stock market was about 0.404 from 1926 to 2012. Although large capitalization value stocks were more volatile during this period, their higher average return more than compensated for the extra risk. Their Sharpe ratio was 0.405. By contrast, the Sharpe ratio for large capitalization growth stocks was only 0.372. On this basis, it seems as if the reward from value investing more than compensates for the added risk.

The risk-adjusted performance edge of value investing is even more pronounced among small capitalization stocks. Among small capitalization stocks, value stocks have a Sharpe ratio of 0.471 compared to 0.314. That is a remarkable differential.

It is important to note, as well, that this is an attractive result before we even become "strategic" about our value investing, which we will discuss in more detail in the following pages. By "strategic," we mean being thoughtful about the characteristics of a particular security rather than blindly applying some sort of trading or classification rule. If we are successful in adding a strategic element to our investing, then we can expect risk-adjusted performance to improve further.

VARIABILITY HURTS CAPITAL ACCUMULATION

It bears emphasizing that because this "average" return is not consistent, there is considerable variability around the average. We are reminded of the man who drowned crossing a stream with an average depth of six inches. All else being equal, most of us would prefer to get a consistent return rather than a variable one. You may be inclined to respond by saying, "That's all right. I'm a long-term investor and can look past short-term swings in the market. They don't bother me as long as I am confident that over a long period of time I know my average return." If that is your view, and you consider yourself to be so psychologically hardy that volatility does not matter much to you, think again.

The measure of "average" that we had been using thus far is the simple arithmetic average with which we are all familiar. The problem with this measure is that it overestimates the amount of capital we will accumulate over time. Specifically, although the stock market has an overall return of 11.8 percent per year, we cannot simply compound this return over a specified number of years to estimate how much money we are likely to have in the future.

For example, if we can earn 11.8 percent consistently each year for 10 years, we will triple our money. That is, $1,000 will grow to just over $3,000. If this average return is not consistent, however, we will accumulate less. The more volatile the returns are over this time period, the less we will accumulate. This phenomenon is called the volatility drag, which is determined in large part by the standard deviation. Most of us are familiar with the adage that if you lose 50 percent of your money one year and gain 50 percent the next year, you are not back to even. Rather, you are still down 25 percent despite our "average" return being 0 percent.[3] The reason is that volatility puts a drag on capital accumulation. If we had earned 0 percent the first and second years consistently, we would have had the same "average" return, but had a lot more money after two years: $100 versus $75.

This is not some numerical trickery. The higher the standard deviation, the higher the volatility drag. In our example in which the average return is 11.8 percent, we are more likely to double our money rather than triple it if the standard deviation is 20.3 percent. That is, half the time our $1,000 will grow to over $2,000. The other half of the time it will grow to less than $2,000.

So, we need to be just as concerned about variability of return as we are about the average returns themselves. The geometric mean allows us to incorporate both these factors. The geometric mean (or average) is the return that, if earned consistently year in and year out, would produce the same result as the arithmetic average return with variability. In Table 2-1, you can see that the annual geometric mean to large-cap value investing is two percentage points greater than the large-cap growth investing. In the small-cap universe, it's almost five percentage points greater. The greater geometric mean implies that we would have accumulated more capital with value stocks than with growth stocks over this period, even after accounting for the deleterious effect of higher volatility. We see a similar phenomenon with the monthly returns presented in Table 2-2.

WHY DO WE CARE ABOUT BEING "NORMAL"?

This performance differential can become larger when the returns are not "normal." The traditional bell curve in which observations tend to be symmetrically clustered around a central result is considered normal. In addition, bell curve observations farther away from the average are less common.

One way returns might not be normal is if they are *skewed*. In other words, they are not symmetrically distributed on either side of the average. For example, a distribution is negatively skewed when some returns below the average are more extreme than returns above the average. It is positively skewed when some returns above the average are more extreme than returns below the average. When it comes to investment returns, we like positive skewness. Negative skewness hurts us because extreme negative returns reduce the amount of capital on which we can earn future returns and reduces our compounding effect.

Unfortunately, according to Table 2-1, the stock market exhibits negative skewness. That is, some negative outcomes are more extreme than the positive outcomes. As a result, it becomes more difficult to accumulate capital over time when a few really bad years dissolve the capital base on which to earn future returns. So, skewness can really hurt (or help) our ability to accumulate capital, even when average returns and standard deviations are the same. Interestingly, value stocks do not tend to exhibit the same negative skewness that the overall market does or that growth stocks do. Managing downside risk and limiting the risk of large losses is one of the central risk control tenets of value investing.

Another way in which returns may not be "normal" is if returns farther away from the center of the distribution, or the average, are more or less frequent than the bell curve would suggest. We can measure the frequency of extreme occurrences with something called *kurtosis*. When extremely positive or negative returns are more common than the bell curve would suggest, those returns are said to exhibit excess kurtosis. As a result, the returns are more risky than a limited examination of only standard deviation would suggest. In other words, there is hidden risk that our traditional measure of volatility does not capture. So, we want to be aware of it.

Return distributions such as these are said to exhibit "fat tails."[4] They are related to what has come to be known as "black swan" events, so named by Nasim Taleb, who describes situations in which markets exhibit such unpredictable, yet catastrophic, events that they completely change the frame of reference from then on. Currencies becoming nearly worthless, the crash of tulipmania, and the unexpected default of sovereign debt can all be considered black swans. The difference between fat tails and black swans is that black swans are even rarer and more extreme than what we would normally classify as a fat tail.

To help put this concept in perspective, consider October 19, 1987, known as Black Monday. On this day, the Dow Jones Industrial Average (DJIA) declined by 22.6 percent in a single day—a very unexpected and unprecedented event. In fact, to this day that loss is still the record daily percentage loss on the DJIA. If you examine the daily stock returns on the DJIA from inception (October 1, 1928) through September 23, 2011 (20,839 days), you will find that the daily average return was 0.025 percent with a standard deviation of 1.16 percent. Extreme events, which we will define as positive or negative daily returns in excess of three standard deviations (also known as three-sigma events) away from the average, should occur only 0.27 percent of the time or on about 56 days during this time period. Unfortunately the daily returns are not strictly normal—three-sigma events occurred on 364 days, or about six and a half times more than would be expected for a normal distribution. While statistics are fine for making general observations about what is likely to happen, real life and real stock market returns are not normal. What happens is quite different from what should happen.

Returning to the data on annual returns in Table 2-1, we see that large-cap value stocks tend to exhibit some moderate excess kurtosis, and large-cap growth stocks slightly negative excess kurtosis, than a normal bell curve (i.e., the tails are thinner than normal).[5] The difference in kurtosis among value and growth for small capitalization stocks, however, is striking. Small-cap growth stocks exhibit almost 10 times more excess kurtosis than their value counterparts.

One phenomenon to be aware of is that returns over annual intervals tend to be more normal than returns over shorter intervals. In Table 2-2, for example, excess skewness is much greater than for annual returns. Further evidence is seen in the daily DJIA example above. Extreme events are much more frequent than the bell curve would suggest over short intervals than over longer intervals, and this is especially true for value stocks. This excess variability tends to dissipate over longer intervals.

PUTTING IT ALL TOGETHER

So, how do return, standard deviation, skewness, and kurtosis all pan out? What's the bottom line?

You can see how the additional return associated with value investing tends to compensate for the additional variability and, in some cases, excess kurtosis. In Figure 2-1, every dollar invested in small-cap value strategy in 1926 grew to over $89,000 in 2012 compared to only $2,100 for a small-cap growth strategy. For large capitalization stocks the differential for each dollar invested in 1926 in either a value or growth strategy was $9,200 compared to $1,900. These are huge differences. Of course, we are talking about an extraordinarily long time frame, as well.

FIGURE 2-1

Growth of $1 from 1926 to 2012.

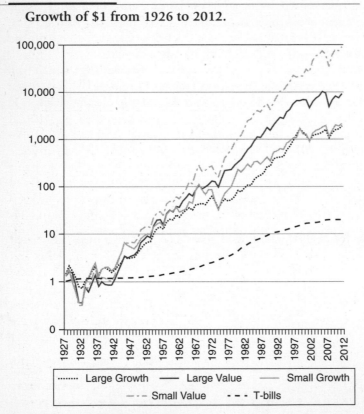

Source: Based on Kenneth French's Data Library

FIGURE 2-2

Growth of $1 from 2000 to 2012.

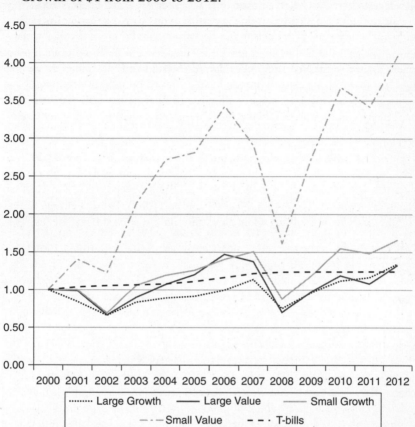

Source: Based on Kenneth French's Data Library

Therefore, the higher returns and more favorable skewness associated with value investing tends to more than compensate for its higher variability and greater incidence of extreme events (e.g., "fat tails"). In reading Figure 2-1, note that the Y-axis is logarithmic, which means that vertical increments relate to percent changes rather than absolute changes. For example, each major increment on the Y-axis relates to a tenfold increase. We do this because the numbers grow very large compared to their initial values, and a traditional scale would make it difficult to read the smaller figures.

We can also examine how value investing performed during the most recent tumultuous 12 years in which we experienced at least two severe bear markets. Here, too, value stocks tended to outperform growth stocks. In this very unfriendly period, large capitalization value stocks earned a 32.9 percent cumulative return rather than a 34.4 percent cumulative return for growth stocks. That's not a great cumulative return over that time, but small capitalization value stocks did better. In that sector, a dollar invested grew to $4.10 compared to $1.66 for small cap growth stocks.[6]

The point is that strategic value investing tends to work, but not necessarily each and every year. Although it can be variable and a bit of a roller coaster ride (note 2008 in the preceding figure), the ride is worth it. To reiterate a point we made earlier, value investing takes some fortitude and discipline, as well as a long-term mindset. Investors who are easily swayed by market sentiment have difficulty implementing true value strategies. In fact, as we will see in a later chapter, many value strategies are predicated on going against market sentiment.

Box 2-2 Market Inefficiency or Compensation for Risk

It should be clear by now that not only do value and growth stocks exhibit different return characteristics, they also have different risk characteristics. Professionals disagree about why this might be the case. One group argues that investors fundamentally underestimate the growth prospects of out-of-favor value stocks. The market is consistently surprised when things turn out better than expected. This tendency for markets to be repeatedly "fooled" would seem to indicate that markets are inefficient. That is, markets do not properly incorporate the impact of new information on security prices when the information arrives, presumably because investors let their cognitive and emotional biases get the best of them.

Another camp argues that the higher returns associated with value stocks reflect fundamentally higher risk levels associated with value stocks. Josef Lakonishok, Andrei Shleifer, and Robert Vishny (1994) try to disentangle this puzzle. They find that value stocks (defined based on price multiples) outperform glamour stocks by about 90 percent over a five-year holding period, which is consistent with what we have discussed thus far. They also find that value stocks rarely underperform glamour stocks (their term for "growth") even in extreme down markets or severe recessions, which suggests that value strategies are not fundamentally riskier than glamour strategies.

It also seems that investors extrapolate historical growth rates into their expectations about future growth rates, despite the fact that these historical growth rates tend not to continue. That is, they tend to "revert to the mean." Lakonishok, Shleifer, and Vishny (1994) show that stocks with recently low historical sales growth (i.e., value stocks) outperform stocks with recently high historical sales growth (i.e., glamour stocks) by about 50 percent over a five-year holding period. They interpret this evidence to suggest that investors are systematically fooled into believing that recent historical experience will persist into the future.

In the end, we don't really know exactly why value and growth stocks behave differently. But research on the question continues, and the more we learn about it, the more refined our strategies can become.

CORRELATION

In building a portfolio, we are not only concerned about how a security or group of securities behaves on their own. We are also concerned with how they behave in relation to other securities in the portfolios. Securities that tend to behave differently over time can smooth out our ride without necessarily decreasing our average return. The decrease in volatility can improve our capital accumulation, and our mood, even if the average return is not improved.

Table 2-3 displays correlation coefficients for various combinations of value-growth and large versus small capitalizations. A correlation coefficient measures how two securities move together. A value of positive one means that the two securities always move in the same direction, even if the magnitude of those movements is different. A value of negative 1 means that the two securities always move in opposite directions. The value of zero means they may or may not move in the same direction and that knowing the direction in which one moves does not help us predict the direction in which the other one moves.

A correlation coefficient between zero and one implies that the two securities tend to move in the same direction, but not always. A value between negative one and zero implies that the two securities tend to move in opposite directions, but not always.

As we can see, value stocks and growth stocks tend to move in the same direction, but not always. For example, large capitalization value and growth stocks tend to move together approximately 80 percent of the time. Small capitalization value and growth stocks tend to move together approximately 87 percent of the time. These are relatively high correlation coefficients, which suggests that we are not likely to diversify our portfolio by combining value and growth strategies.

That said, value and growth strategies can produce vastly different results in any given year. For example, in 2000, using the Fama-French definitions, large-cap growth stocks *fell* by 13.6 percent, while small-cap value stocks *increased* by 5.8 percent.[7] The following year small-cap value outperformed small-cap growth by a 40 percent margin. By contrast, 1999 was a favorable year for growth stocks,

T A B L E   2-3

Historical Annual Correlation Coefficients, 1926–2012

	Large			Small		
	Growth	Mid	Value	Growth	Mid	Value
Large Growth	1					
Large Mid	0.85	1				
Large Value	0.80	0.94	1			
Small Growth	0.81	0.83	0.81	1		
Small Mid	0.80	0.89	0.89	0.94	1	
Small Value	0.74	0.86	0.90	0.87	0.96	1

Source: Based on Kenneth French's Data Library

which outperformed their value brethren in the large and small size categories by 29 percent and 50 percent, respectively.

Table 2-4 displays the returns to value and growth strategies each year from 1981 through 2012 based on the definitions provided by Fama and French

TABLE 2-4

Value and Growth Performance, 1981–2012

	Large		Small	
	Growth	Value	Growth	Value
1981	−7.13	12.8	−11.53	17.68
1982	21.48	27.67	19.72	39.86
1983	14.67	26.92	22.12	47.58
1984	−0.72	16.17	−12.84	7.52
1985	32.64	31.75	28.91	32.12
1986	14.38	21.82	1.95	14.5
1987	7.43	−2.76	−12.24	−7.12
1988	12.53	25.96	16.63	30.76
1989	36.11	29.7	20.58	15.7
1990	1.06	−12.75	−17.74	−25.13
1991	43.33	27.35	54.73	40.56
1992	6.41	23.57	5.82	34.76
1993	2.38	19.51	12.64	29.41
1994	1.95	−5.78	−4.36	3.21
1995	37.16	37.68	35.13	27.69
1996	21.25	13.35	12.36	20.71
1997	31.61	31.88	15.29	37.29
1998	34.64	16.23	3.04	−8.63
1999	29.43	−0.22	54.75	5.59
2000	−13.63	5.8	−24.15	−0.8
2001	−15.59	−1.18	0.16	40.24
2002	−21.5	−32.53	−30.87	−12.41
2003	26.29	35.07	53.2	74.69
2004	6.53	18.91	12.54	26.59
2005	2.82	12.17	5.45	3.53
2006	8.88	22.61	11.67	21.76
2007	14.08	−6.45	7.36	−15.21
2008	−33.71	−49.03	−41.56	−44.39
2009	27.91	39.15	34.45	70.54
2010	15.87	21.61	30.66	33.54
2011	4.14	−9.04	−4.32	−7.04
2012	15.41	22.99	12.22	20.07

Source: Based on Kenneth French's Data Library

and highlights the strategy that performed the best in any given year. Value and growth tend to come in and out of fashion, whereby value tends to exhibit strength over a period of time followed by growth experiencing relatively good performance.

Therefore, although the correlations between value and growth strategies tend to be high, do not be fooled into believing that one is a substitute for the other. They can produce radically different results in any given year. Picking the best strategy in advance is difficult, to say the least—if not impossible—which highlights the danger for a long-term investor who loses his or her long-term focus and switches styles at precisely the wrong time.

Box 2-3 Surprise! All Information Is Not Created Equal

A recent article in the *Financial Analysts Journal* relates the value/glamour anomaly to the tendency of stock prices to react slowly to earnings surprises. This phenomenon, called "post-earnings announcement drift," is the tendency for stock prices to continue to rise after positive earnings surprises and continue to fall after negative earnings surprises over a period of months after the initial market reaction.

The *Financial Analysts Journal* study shows that the initial reaction to earnings surprises is more muted for value stocks than for glamour stocks. Moreover, subsequent returns for value stocks are better (more positive or less negative) than returns for glamour stocks. These results suggest that the information revealed around earnings surprises on value stocks is less certain than the information on glamour stocks, perhaps because glamour stocks tend to attract more media attention and analyst coverage.

Alternatively, the difference could relate to higher transaction costs associated with value stocks. Either way, we don't really know exactly why value and growth stocks behave differently. But the more we learn about what causes the differences, the more refined our strategies can become.

BETA

We can also measure risk by incorporating how our security or portfolio moves with the overall market. If a portfolio tends to exacerbate overall market movements, it would be considered relatively more risky. If it increased and decreased in value in a more muted manner than the overall market, it would be considered less risky. The measure we use to capture this phenomenon is called *beta*.[8]

A security or portfolio with a beta of one is about as risky as the overall market, assuming it is part of an otherwise well-diversified portfolio. Table 2-5 shows the data of value and growth strategies based on annual returns from 1926 to 2012. There are at least two important observations to make. First, small capitalization stocks have significantly higher betas than large capitalization stocks. This means that they are likely to increase risk when added to a well-diversified portfolio.

TABLE 2-5

Beta of Value and Growth Strategies,
Annual Data 1926–2012

	Beta
Large-cap growth	0.97
Large-cap mid	0.98
Large-cap value	1.23
Small-cap growth	1.40
Small-cap mid	1.27
Small-cap value	1.36

Second, value stocks tend to pose more market risk than growth stocks, although this is less true for small capitalization stocks. As we have seen before, this risk tends to be more than compensated in the market place. But it bears repeating that value investing is not for the faint of heart.

CONCLUSION

There is no single definition of value. Nor is there any single type of value investing. However, most value investing shares some common characteristics. It tends to be rewarded in the marketplace even before we become "strategic" about our security selection. True, volatility tends to be higher and there tend to be more extreme events than even the volatility associated with the normal bell curve would suggest. However, value investing's higher average returns and less negatively skewed distributions overcome these shortcomings. Value investing works.

Successful implementation, however, requires discipline and focus. Value strategies do poorly when many other growth investors are doing well. So one often needs to take a rather contrarian perspective when comparing a security's estimated intrinsic value to its market value. The next chapter outlines more specifically some of the barriers associated with successful value investing.

CHAPTER THREE

BARRIERS TO SUCCESSFUL VALUE INVESTING

We say that the market is a voting machine, whereon countless individuals register choices which are the product partly of reason and partly of emotion.
—Benjamin Graham and David L. Dodd,
Security Analysis
sixth edition

Even though the business ... may have economic characteristics that are stable, Mr. Market's quotations will be anything but. For, sad to say, the poor fellow has incurable emotional problems.
—Warren Buffett, 1987,
Letter to Berkshire Hathaway shareholders

The previous chapter illustrated that value investing has fairly attractive long-term prospects. If that's indeed the case, then at least some investors who follow a value investing strategy should be doing pretty well. Unfortunately, the record of the average individual investor is less than auspicious. Figure 3-1 shows the net cash flows into and out of equity mutual funds from 1996 to 2010. It shows how the global stock market performed over that time period, as well.

In the late 1990s, you can see that the stock market performed consistently well, and investors responded by consistently pouring more money into equity mutual funds. In 1997, the global stock market had a sell off even though the US stock market performed quite well. How did investors respond to the global sell off? They invested less money in equity mutual funds over the following six months. But markets rebounded nicely in 1999. Investors would have been better off if they had stayed the course and maintained their relatively high inflows into equity mutual funds.

Fool me once, shame on you; fool me twice, shame on me. Not to have the wool pulled over their eyes again, investors more than made up for the missed opportunity by doubling the rate at which they committed capital to equity funds through the end of 1999 and the beginning of 2000. In fact, we have not seen

FIGURE 3-1

Net flows to equity funds related to global stock price performance.

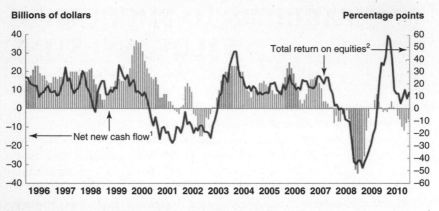

Billions of dollars   Percentage points

[1] Net new cash flow to equity funds is plotted as a six-month moving average.
[2] The total return on equities is measured as the year-over-year change in the MSCI All Country World Daily Total Return Index.
Source: 2011 Investment Company Institute Fact Book http://www.ici.org

that rate of capital commitment since then. Of course, this all happened after the market had already rebounded. We all know what happened next. The tech bubble burst, and we entered a multiyear bear market. Not only did investors reduce their rate of investment in equity mutual funds during this period when the S&P 500 lost half its value, they actually started pulling money out, especially in 2002, right before the market strongly rebounded.

As if working from a script, investors repeated this behavior during the most recent bear market and subsequent recovery, removing unprecedented amounts of money from equity mutual funds after the market had dropped in 2007 and missing the market recovery in 2009 and 2010 and beyond. Interestingly, investors have not returned to their previous levels of committing new capital to the stock market since then. In 2010, withdrawals from all equity funds amounted to $37 billion for the year, more than the $9 billion investors withdrew, on net, the previous year.

The tendency for investors to react to bull and bear markets by putting money into and taking money out of mutual funds is a widely documented, persistent phenomenon that has occurred over a long period of time.[1] In fact, some people think that past stock market performance is the most important element in explaining equity mutual fund flows.[2] And as you might infer from examining Figure 3-1, the impact of stock market declines on fund outflows is particularly pronounced during severe market declines, like the ones we saw in 2000 and 2008.

We see the same relationship between mutual fund flows and past performance in individual mutual fund flows, as well.[3] It has also been shown that investors tend to buy funds with more positive recent returns, especially if they are inattentive to macroeconomic news or vulnerable to the cognitive and emotional biases we discuss later.[4] Professional investors (as well those who have well-diversified and high-performing individual stock portfolios) tend to be less vulnerable to this return-chasing phenomenon, but as we will see they are certainly not immune.

The same general pattern holds true for individual stock investments as well. One study shows that stocks sold by individual investors perform 2.8 percent better than the stocks they purchased over the 12 months following their transactions.[5]

Individual investors ought not feel alone. Institutional investors chase returns as well. Research has found that professional investors chase past investment performance in the pension fund industry, among hedge funds, among private equity funds, between venture capital funds, and among arbitrage strategies.[6]

Investing in general requires independent thought. Strategic value investing *demands* independent thought. Blindly following the crowd will, at best, produce average results.

Does this mean you should give up, go home, and resign yourself to the fact that Mr. Market (as Warren Buffett likes to call it) will ultimately get the best of you? Absolutely not! Research has shown that better informed and more experienced investors tend to experience relatively strong performance.[7] Investors who are less vulnerable to emotional and cognitive biases are less likely to chase returns.

Understanding the tools and techniques to properly value a security is a necessary ingredient to successful strategic value investing. But investors need to recognize the many obstacles associated with successfully implementing a strategic value investment strategy. This chapter will describe them. It will also provide some techniques you can use to moderate or overcome these obstacles.

We think about the barriers to successful value investing in three general categories. The first category relates to cognitive and emotional biases that are ingrained in our DNA. We refer to these as behavioral obstacles. Unfortunately, we cannot necessarily avoid them simply because we are a little smarter than the next guy or even because we are aware of their existence. But knowing they exist can help us develop techniques to avoid succumbing to them.

The next category of obstacles is market related. Rather than residing within ourselves, these obstacles can be even more difficult to overcome because they relate to how markets function. We cannot always change these factors.

The final category relates to investment constraints that some investors may face more than others. These challenges may relate to investment mandates that restrict an investor's ability to accept investment volatility, lock up capital and illiquid investments, or make certain types of investments due to regulatory or legal restrictions.

BEHAVIORAL OBSTACLES

So why do many investors seem to get into and out of the market at exactly the wrong times? Why do they flock to mutual funds and other investments that performed well in the past but are not likely to perform well in the future?

As human beings, we are vulnerable to many cognitive and functional biases that prevent us from making rational decisions in all situations. This is not always a bad thing. In fact, these biases are often referred to as heuristics—mental shortcuts that allow us to make decisions more efficiently without having to start an analysis from first principles. The ability to take shortcuts in our decision-making processes allows us to make repeated, complex decisions more rapidly. Such shortcuts have helped us evolve as a species. Unfortunately, the very same heuristics that have served our species well in an evolutionary sense create barriers to successful investing.

Social Pressure

As we saw in the previous chapter, strategic value investing often requires a contrarian bent; that is, going against the grain of conventional "wisdom." Some of the most notorious examples of the power of peer pressure are illustrated through experiments led by Solomon Asch of Swarthmore College (See Box 3-1 for another experiment). In one experiment, Asch asked students to participate in a "vision test" in which they were asked to match two lines having the same length. One of the students was singled out as the subject, while all the other students were told to be conspiratorial and consistently and purposefully give obviously wrong answers to the vision test. When the conspirators gave the wrong answer, so did the subject, even when it was obviously wrong. And this result was independent of the level of education of the subject, which Asch thought might overcome the tendency to conform. Training is helpful, but it is not bulletproof.

Box 3-1 Yes, Sir!

Stanley Milgram also performed experiments to test people's willingness to conform. He tested a subject's willingness to inflict pain on another person at the direction of an authority figure. Subjects thought that they were participating in an experiment to determine how much electric current a person can tolerate. An experimenter asked them to apply increasing amounts of electrical shock to a person in an adjoining room. As the voltage they were asked to apply increased, so did the excruciating screams. In reality, there was no electricity and the pleas for relief from the person in the next room were feigned. But the subject who was being asked to apply the voltage did not know that. Sixty-five percent of subjects obeyed authority figures that instructed them to perform acts that conflicted with their personal conscience. Whether influence comes from peers or authority, the pressure to conform is powerful.

Researchers have proposed many explanations for the tendency to conform. Some have attributed it to the desire to preserve harmony within a group. Others have proposed that it is a way to reduce the psychological pain of making mistakes. Even if an investor knows a particular investment decision might not be optimal, they know they will be in good company if it does not pan out. Professional money managers have often said that it is better to lose money investing in IBM than in some unknown, small capitalization stock. Investors tend to be more forgiving in the first case.

Successful value investing requires independent thought. Blindly succumbing to peer pressure or the opinions of authority figures is likely to compromise your investment results.

What's on Your Mind?

Overcoming social pressures, of course, is difficult enough on its own. But we must also overcome ourselves. Not surprisingly, we tend to base decisions on information that comes to mind easily—which is sometimes called the availability or representativeness heuristic—because we tend to draw on information and data that is easily available and most well represented in our minds.

This heuristic can manifest itself in many ways. For example, recent experiences are generally more present in our minds than those in the more distant past. In essence, what have you done for me lately? It is not surprising then that when we see investments that have recently performed well, we are likely to factor their recent strong performance into our decision-making process. Box 3-2 has a noninvestments example.

Because value investing is often associated with price reversals, being aware of the undue influence of recent experiences and profound experiences is particularly important for successful strategic value investing.

Box 3-2 The Spelling Bee

Is the letter k more likely to be the first or third letter in a word in the English language? As you consider this question, you are likely thinking of words like *kite*, *king*, and *kick*, leading you to think that it is more common for the letter k to be the first letter of the word. Actually, the letter k is three times more likely to be the third letter than the first. Why do we focus on the first letter rather than third letter, on average? It is because the first letter is more prominent in our minds than the third.

Another manifestation is our tendency to emphasize anecdotes over statistics. Not only do we tend to draw on recent experience, we are much more likely to remember events with which we have a strong emotional association. Stories and personal experiences are much more alive, poignant, and present in our minds than boring tables or statistics based on the experiences of a lot of nameless and faceless investors. It is very difficult for us to identify with statistics. We are much more likely to remember our neighbor telling us about how profitable his recent investment in a medical device company is. The challenge for us is to look past these anecdotes and focus on more objective statistical data (as shown in Box 3-3), which provides a clearer sense of probable outcomes.

Extremely painful experiences tend to be more present in our minds. Investors who grew up during the Great Depression, for example, are far more conservative than baby boomers. Do your best to look past recent experiences, powerful experiences, and anecdotes to objectively analyze a company's prospects.

Box 3-3 Shh! Can You Hear the Statistics?

Are you more likely to use statistics or anecdotes in your estimates? Consider the following example from John Nofsinger (2005).

Mary is quiet, studious, and concerned with social issues. While an undergraduate at Berkeley, she majored in English literature and minored in environmental studies. Given this information, indicate which of the following three cases is most probable:

a. Mary is a librarian.

b. Mary is a librarian and a member of the Sierra Club.

c. Mary works in the banking industry.

Did you choose answer B? Most people do. After all, the anecdotes provided about Mary are most consistent with the stereotypes we have about librarians and members of the Sierra Club. Interestingly, however, answer B must be less likely than answer A because answer B is a subset of and more restrictive than answer A.

Moreover, according to the Bureau of Labor Statistics Occupational Outlook Handbook, there were almost 160,000 librarians in the United States in 2008. By contrast, there were 600,000 bank tellers and more than 327,000 loan officers, not to mention the variety of different occupations in the banking industry. It is much more likely Mary works in the banking industry. So, answer C is much more likely than answer A.

Home Sweet Home

We are always more comfortable at home because it is familiar. Our comfort with home extends to our investing habits. Investors tend to overweight their portfolios with stocks of their employer, stocks in the same industry of their employment (doctors are notorious for this), or companies that are geographically close to home. More often than not, the justification is that investors know more about these companies than other companies and therefore have an informational advantage that can be used to earn superior returns. Even Peter Lynch, the famed manager of Fidelity's mammoth Magellan Fund from 1997 to 1990, advocated that investors should invest in what they know.

Unfortunately, the evidence suggests otherwise. Investors do not seem to possess an informational advantage about their employer, the industry in which they work, or local companies. Moreover, investing in your employer's stock or in the same industry in which you are employed has significant diversification disadvantages when one considers that your labor income is likely your most valuable asset and binds you to the fortunes of your employer.

Damn, I'm Good!

The psychology literature is rife with examples demonstrating that people are generally overconfident. Students tend to overestimate their test performance. Most people tend to think they are above-average drivers. But only at Lake Wobegon can everyone be above average. In terms of investing, men tend to be more overconfident than women.[8] Their investment results, however, tend to be worse than those of women.

One of the worst things that can happen to an investor is to experience some initial success. It tends to exacerbate our overconfidence. We almost always attribute our profitable trades to our investing prowess, whether it is an accident of nature or due to an insightful, cogent, and disciplined analysis. We similarly assign blame for our unsuccessful trades to being misled by management or perhaps our inept stockbroker. Behavioral economists call this confirmation bias.

Another manifestation of confirmation bias is a tendency to focus on and highlight new information that confirms our initial prediction and to dismiss information that contradicts it. This bias is also related to a phenomenon called anchoring, in which we are slow to revise our predictions for analysis as new information comes in. As a result, we anchor on our original conviction. Some economists argue that this phenomenon causes the post-earnings announcement drift discussed in the previous chapter. At the end of this chapter, we propose investors use an investment diary to attempt to combat this bias.

Media

It is, of course, important to be armed with the latest and best information when making projections and resulting investment decisions. Properly evaluating this information is difficult, however. A common source of information is business magazines.

A recent article in the *Financial Analysts Journal* suggests that blindly investing according to magazine cover stories can also be hazardous to your wealth.[9] The authors examine almost 600 feature stories on the covers of *Forbes*, *Fortune*, and *BusinessWeek* over a 20-year period. Not surprisingly, positive cover stories tend to follow extremely positive company performance and negative cover stories tend to follow extremely negative performance. Appearing on the cover of one of these magazines, however, marks the end of the trend rather than the beginning. Although positive cover stories tend to be followed by positive stock returns, subject companies of extremely positive stories tend to underperform subject companies of extremely negative stories when compared to similar firms in the same industry and of similar size. In particular, the subject of the negative cover story tends to perform pretty well after publication. So, a negative cover story is actually a good time to cover short positions.

This phenomenon is particularly important for value investing, which often requires investing in stocks that are out of favor and eschewing the latest market trends.

Loss Aversion

It is a widely accepted tenet that investors are generally risk averse. That is undoubtedly true. Perhaps the only thing investors dislike more than risk is suffering losses. Even small losses are associated with strong negative emotional reactions. Larger losses are certainly more painful, but the incremental effect is not as severe as the initial loss, according to Nobel laureate Daniel Kahneman and Amos Tversky, who pioneered the field of what is known as *prospect theory*. The most severe emotional reactions tend to be associated with initial losses. Subsequent losses are a bit easier to tolerate.

Investors are so reluctant to suffer losses that they are sometimes willing to accept some unrewarded risk in an effort to avoid realizing them. The phenomenon of *loss aversion* leads to what many described as the *disposition effect*, which is the tendency of investors to sell winners and to hold onto losers (See Box 3-4).

Loss aversion and the disposition effect strikes investors of all shapes and sizes. Even the world's most successful investors have their fair share of investing disappointments. An old adage among the pros is that if they are right 53 percent of the time, they are doing great. So, if a stock moves against you, think honestly and critically about whether your analysis is faulty or whether its price is deviating even more from its estimated fundamental value. Do your best to not succumb to "get-even-itis," the affliction of needing to win back your losses before liquidating an investment.

Box 3-4 I *Really* Hate to Lose Money!

Imagine you are sitting in a room with dozens of people listening to a boring lecture. The lecture was free, and you ended up getting what you paid for. Suddenly, the doors to the auditorium shut and you hear the locks engage. An announcement over the loudspeaker indicates that you can leave under only two circumstances.

A. You pay the lecturer $1,000 in cash.

B. You go double or nothing on the flip of a coin. If it comes up heads, you are free to go without paying anything. If it comes up tails, the exit fee is no longer $1,000. It is $2,000.

Think about which option you would choose. If you are like 85 percent of the people one of the authors of this book surveys in his presentations, you will choose option B. This choice contradicts one of the most fundamental principles of assumed rational economic behavior. Both choices have the same expected value. On average, you will be less wealthy by $1,000 regardless of which you choose. Option B, however, is more risky. If the expected returns are the same, fundamental principles of economics says that we, as risk-averse investors, should choose the less risky proposition.

Why do people tend to choose risky option B? Losing money is almost physically painful. In addition to being risk averse, investors are also loss averse. We dislike experiencing losses so much that we are willing to accept a risky proposition on the chance that we can avoid suffering the consequences of the loss.

The disposition effect (Box 3-5) tends to encourage poor tax management strategy, as well. Selling losers and holding on to winners, all else equal, tends to accelerate our tax credits and defer our tax bills, which over time can do quite a bit to minimize our tax drag. The disposition effect has the tendency to accelerate our tax bills and defer our tax credits, which is the opposite of what we should want.

Box 3-5 The Disposition Effect

Imagine you purchased a stock last month for $20 per share, but that it is trading now for $15. You've suffered a $5 loss per share. Suppose that over the next month it will be either $10 per share or $20 per share with equal probabilities. What would you do?

a. Sell the shares now and realize your $5 loss, or

b. Hold for one more month.

Investors tend to choose option B and hold on for one more month. Next, imagine the stock you purchased for $20 per share is trading now for $25. Over the next month it will either drop back down to $20 per share or increase in value to $30 per share with equal probabilities. What would you do?

a. Sell the shares now and realize your $5 gain, or

b. Hold for one more month.

Most folks tend to choose option A and realize their gain.

There are many other behavioral biases, but it is beyond the scope of this book to address them all, much less in significant detail. Suffice it to say, however, that none of us is as rigidly rational as we would like to believe. The best approach is to be aware of our biases and to develop techniques to counteract them. We will suggest some useful techniques later in this chapter.

MARKET OBSTACLES

Yes, we must contend with our own cognitive and emotional biases, but we must also be aware of obstacles that the market puts in the way of the strategic value investor. One way to illustrate these obstacles is to show the difficulties associated with executing the most sterile forms of value investing, that is, arbitrage investing.

Arbitrage

Arbitrage involves buying an underpriced security in one market and short selling (Box 3-6) a similar overpriced security in another market in the hope that the two similar securities converge to the same, fair value. As arbitrageurs recognize and act on the price discrepancy, demand for the underpriced security will increase its price and supply from sellers of the overpriced security will decrease its price. In an efficient market this should happen fairly quickly. An arbitrageur profits when the underpriced security increases to its fundamental value and the overpriced security decreases to its fundamental value.[10] Arbitrage is pure, unadulterated value investing.

Box 3-6 Short Selling

When we sell a home or a car, we are obliged to provide proof of ownership to the buyer to prove that we have the right to sell it. That makes perfect sense. On Wall Street, however, it is not a prerequisite to own something before you sell it. It is nowhere near as nefarious as it sounds and is called *short selling*. Short sellers are able to sell shares they do not own by borrowing them from somebody who does. Short sellers are said to "cover their short" by buying back shares and returning them to their original owner.

This technique allows strategic value investors to profit from identifying overpriced securities as well as underpriced securities. If you believe the price of the stock will increase, you buy it now at its relatively low price and wait for it to increase to its fair value. But what if you think a security is overpriced and that the price will decrease? By reversing the typical buy-sell sequence, short sellers can profit from price declines. The short seller sells shares at the higher price and purchases them back later at a lower price. This practice strikes some people as untoward, but it's perfectly acceptable both legally and morally. In fact, the presence of short sellers makes a market more complete and liquid.

"Naked shorting" is the potentially dubious practice of short selling shares before the investor has properly arranged to borrow shares from somebody else. This practice puts the purchaser at risk of not receiving the shares by the time the trade settles and has been called into question by regulators and market observers.

Suppose you believe the fair value of Anheuser-Busch/In-Bev is $50 per share, but pessimistic traders have driven down its market price to $40 per share. Rational traders who see the deviation from fundamental value will buy it. Arbitrageurs will go the extra mile and hedge their positions by short selling a similar alcoholic beverage company, such as SAB Miller. The buying pressure on Anheuser-Busch/In-Bev should increase its price, and the selling pressure on SAB Miller should decrease its price. If the market for beer takes off, both companies should do well, which will help your long position but hurt your short position. If the market for beer tanks, both companies will do poorly, which will help your short position but hurt your long position. In either case, the loss on either the long or short position will be offset by a gain on the other position until their prices ultimately converge and your gains more than offset your losses.

If this example seems contrived to you, consider the possibility of a subsidiary having a market value greater than its parent company. As a subset of the parent company, a subsidiary cannot be worth more than the parent unless all the other parts of the parent company combined have a negative value.[11]

Assuming this is not the case, the arbitrage opportunity is simple and compelling. An arbitrageur would purchase shares of the undervalued parent company and sell shares of the relatively overvalued publicly traded subsidiary short.

On December 4, 1998, Creative Computers issued 20 percent of the shares of its online auction subsidiary, uBid, to the public. After the first day of trading, Creative Computer's stake in uBid was worth $351.2 million according to uBid's share price. Creative Computer's total equity market value was only about $275 million, implying the value of all of Creative Computer's other assets was negative $76 million! An arbitrageur would buy shares of Creative Computer and sell shares of uBid until the implied negative valuation disappeared. Ideally, proceeds from the short sale of uBid can be used to fund the purchase of Creative Computer so that no capital is required. Moreover, because the relative prices of the securities are determined by a mathematical relationship, it is somewhat "riskless."

It's a sure thing! What could go wrong? We will see shortly.

Limits of Arbitrage

Pristine arbitrage opportunities are extremely difficult to come by. That said, it is not uncommon for the market value of the parent company to be less than the value of one of its subsidiaries. As implausible as it seems, Mark Mitchell, Todd Pulvino, and Erik Stafford examined 82 such situations from 1985 to 2000. They show that there are many risks associated with capitalizing on this pricing even when the mispricing is obvious. It is all the more difficult for the strategic value investor who is relying on his or her analytical and economic intuition to determine this pricing.

Transaction Costs. All investors are subject to transaction costs, which include commissions, bid ask spreads, price impact, and the opportunity costs of not being fully invested 100 percent of the time. All these costs make it difficult for arbitrageurs and strategic value investors to capitalize on situations when market prices deviate from fundamental value.

Horizon Risk.   Even in the most clean arbitrage opportunities, it is unclear how long it will take for the pricing discrepancy to resolve itself. In the 82 parent-subsidiary mispricings cited in the study above, it takes 236 days on average for the mispricing to resolve. The minimum is one day, and the maximum is 2,796 days. If the resolution takes long enough, an arbitrageur can conceivably earn less than the risk-free rate.

And so it is for the strategic value investor. Many value investors believed that the dot-coms were overvalued in the late 1990s, but it took years for the results of that insight to be realized. Similarly, investors who believed that real estate was overvalued in 2005 had to wait years for that market to correct.

Funding Risk.   Not only can it take a long time for the market to correct but also price discrepancies can get much worse before they get better. In the Creative Computer/uBid example, the initial price discrepancy got much worse before it got better (see Figure 3-2). As a result, an arbitrageur attempting to profit from the discrepancy would have received a series of margin calls, which are requests from a brokerage house for an investor to put up more money when trades move against the investor so that the broker has collateral if the investor decides to renege on his obligations. If the investor refuses, the broker liquidates a portion of the position.

The Creative Computer/uBid price discrepancy resolved after six months, but the investor would have received a series of margin calls that would have depleted nearly all of his capital if he didn't put up more capital. Theoretically, an investor could have avoided all that by putting up nearly five times more capital than his long position, but that would significantly reduce his return on investment.

FIGURE 3-2

Stock prices for Creative Computers and uBid.

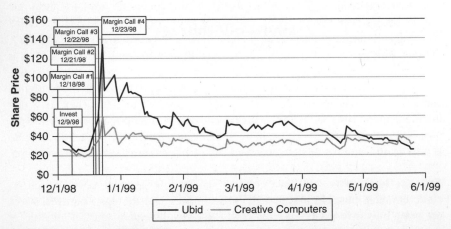

Source: Mitchell, Pulvino, and Stafford (2002)

In the previous chapter we show that, although extreme stock prices tend to reverse themselves in the long run, stock prices tend to exhibit significant momentum in the short term. That is, expensive stocks tend to get more expensive and cheap stocks tend to get cheaper in the short term. The strategic value investor then risks losing funding in the short term, especially if he or she uses leverage or is short selling shares.

Volatility Drag. In the previous chapter, we discussed the notion that earning returns in a volatile fashion over time is much worse than earning the same average return smoothly over time. Volatility puts a drag on the accumulation of capital. And so it is for the arbitrageur. The widening and narrowing of price discrepancies erodes arbitrage profits.

Other People's Money. It is one thing to manage your own money. You may be a very patient soul and have complete confidence that time will eventually reveal the wisdom of your investment decisions. Managing other people's money is an entirely different matter. Clients tend to become impatient and lose confidence if presumed arbitrage mispricings get worse before they get better.[12] As a result, they often fire a manager before prices can converge or the evidence of their investing prowess can be revealed, causing a position to be liquidated.

The same is true for strategic value investors managing other people's money. In that case, it may be even more difficult to convince a disgruntled client that a security is mispriced when there is no clear benchmark to which its value can be compared.

INVESTMENT CONSTRAINT OBSTACLES

We have seen how our own behavior and how market behavior can get in the way of successfully implementing a value strategy. There is also a third set of obstacles, called investment constraints, that can impede our success.

Investment constraints are factors that affect a particular investor and limit that investor's opportunity set in any number of ways. A reputable portfolio manager will outline these constraints in a document called an investment policy statement (IPS).

Liquidity Constraints

An IPS will outline an investor's liquidity constraints, which may represent any cash flow needs the investor has that would require a liquidation of a portion of the portfolio. Sometimes these liquidity needs are known in advance. You may need $50,000 per year over a four-year period to pay for college tuition, for example, the amount and timing of which are fairly predictable. Other times, the exact timing or amount of these cash flows is unknown (you may anticipate needing around $40,000 to pay for a daughter's wedding but not know when or even if this will actually be necessary). Either way, a portion of the portfolio must remain liquid and invested in assets with low volatility to protect against the prospect of an unexpected cash flow need.

As we saw in the last chapter, equity investing is risky in general. Value stocks are often more volatile than average. The liquidity of an investment relates to not only its price volatility but also to the ease with which a security can be sold quickly and without a significant effect on its price. Private equity investments, for example, are illiquid because there's no active market for trading in their shares. A seller must find a buyer on his own rather than go to an actively traded marketplace to find one. More often than not, an earnest seller of a private equity investment looking to satisfy a cash flow need would be forced to make a significant price concession.

Although we use an investment in private equity as an example to illustrate illiquidity, it can relate to value investments as well. Because value stocks are often low-priced or out-of-favor stocks, they are sometimes thinly traded, making the market less liquid.

Investors with significant liquidity needs are relatively ill-suited for equity investments in general and even less well suited for strategic value investing.

Time Horizon

In a similar vein, an investor's time horizon will impact his ability to accept risk as well as his tolerance for illiquidity. Significant short-term liquidity needs lead to a shorter investment time horizon. Short time horizons do not accommodate risk-taking because long time horizons often give investors the ability to recover investment losses from sources outside the portfolio.

It is rarely the case that an investor has a single time horizon. Rather, multiple investment goals lead to a series of intermittent time horizons each with their own investment implications. Time horizon is often influenced, but not fully determined by, an investor's stage of life.

Not only are investors with short time horizons relatively intolerant of price volatility, the timing of their liquidity needs is inconsistent with investment cycles characterized by price reversals that we discussed in the previous chapter. Price reversal strategies are most successful over six and 10-year periods (e.g., five years of underperformance followed by five years of overperformance according to research by Werner DeBont and Richard Thaler.

Taxes

If you are investing in a tax-sheltered retirement account, taxes will be less relevant to your investment decisions and trading style. If you are holding assets in a taxable account, however, you will want to think carefully about the impact of trading decisions on your tax bill. Articulate the salient features of your tax position in an IPS because they can affect investment strategy, security selection, asset location, and rebalancing strategies.

Tax constraints can work against the value investor in a number of ways. First, it is generally tax efficient to recognize losses as they occur, especially short-term losses that can be used to offset otherwise highly taxed short-term gains or ordinary income. The problem is that value investing does not lend itself to short-term trading strategies. Rather, it is predicated on the notion that a security's market value will ultimately converge to its fundamental value even if the process takes a long time or if the prices further diverge before they ultimately converge.

Second, it is not uncommon for investors to accumulate significant wealth by concentrating their investments in the security that substantially increases in value over a period of years. Corporate executives who are compensated with stock or stock options and entrepreneurs who sell their companies often find themselves in this position. The stock they accumulate often has a very low tax basis and hence a very large tax liability if it is sold. As a result, these wealthy investors are often loathe to sell their concentrated positions and thus incur a substantial tax liability. So, they may impose an investment constraint on their portfolio to hold these positions.

This kind of investment constraint inhibits value investing. Because the stock has appreciated significantly over the years, it is more likely to be a growth stock than it is a value stock, so the bulk of the investor's holdings is unlikely to be value-oriented. Moreover, the more capital tied up in this concentrated position, the less capital that is available for true value investing.

Legal Constraints

Some investors or portfolios are subject to legal or regulatory constraints that limit their investment behavior. If you are managing your own personal assets, there are likely no regulatory constraints. If you are managing trust assets or acting as a trustee of an estate, however, you will want to understand the Prudent Investor Rule that governs your actions. Investment managers bound by the Prudent Investor Rule are required to manage assets in a manner consistent with how people of prudence manage their own affairs and the permanent disposition of their own funds.

Conceptually, the Prudent Investor Rule accommodates a long-term investment horizon, equity investing, and even strategic value investing. Practically, however, trustees may be subjecting themselves to litigation risk at the trough of a value investing cycle because litigation is typically inspired by poor investment results rather than poor decision-making.

Similarly, pension fund managers in the United States are governed by the Employee Retirement Income Security Act (ERISA) of 1974, which subjects them to treble damages for failing to act "with the care, skill, prudence, and diligence ... that a prudent man acting in a like capacity ... would use."[13] To be sure, strategic value investing is characterized by care, skill, prudence, and diligence, but value stocks do go out-of-favor from time to time. In fact, value investing is contrarian in nature, so one could argue that they are out-of-favor most of the time. And because a lawsuit may be inspired by short-term investment results rather than a long-term investment strategy, pension fund managers may have an incentive to index rather than pursue any particular investment style. In fact, Stephen Horan (1998) shows that pension fund managers governed by ERISA are more likely to index their portfolios and more likely to take on average market risk rather than commit to a particular investment style perhaps because the law encourages them to be just like everybody else. As we have seen before, strategic and value investing requires independent thinking and going against the grain.

TECHNIQUES TO OVERCOME INVESTMENT OBSTACLES

We hope we have not discouraged you from the prospect of achieving success with strategic value investing. The purpose of the previous sections is not to dissuade but to provide a healthy dose of caution. Fortunately, there is hope. This section outlines tools and techniques you might use to overcome some of these obstacles.

Disciplined Investing

First and foremost, you must develop a disciplined approach to investing. It can be your own unique style, but you need to adhere to it doggedly. Investors get into trouble when they stray from their core investment philosophy. So, educate yourself on a company's fundamentals and the valuation framework you want to use. The following chapters will help with the latter. Stay on top of macroeconomic developments and challenge yourself by questioning your thinking, especially if you have a loss in a particular position.

Also, stay diversified. Seth Klarman, one of the great value investors, points out that successful investing is about risk management. Avoid overly concentrating your holdings in a particular stock, industry, or set of industries that are closely linked. To be sure, spreading your risk too much will make it difficult to stay focused and to capitalize on the value of your analysis. You will want to focus your efforts and end up concentrating your holdings to some extent, but we are talking about a matter of degree. Backing up the truck and loading up on a particularly good value investment may mean investing 5 or 10 percent of your portfolio in a stock, not 20 percent.

Investment Policy Statement

Draft and periodically review your investment policy statement (IPS). It will help you maintain focus during rough spells and control your impulse to overreact to experiences in your recent past. Earlier we talked about investment constraints that should be included in an IPS, but more generally an IPS is a document that outlines your risk and return objectives, as well as your investment constraints. It can also articulate your investment philosophy and asset allocation guidelines to control risk taking. As such, it serves as a reference that offers a steady hand at the helm during rough waters.

The basic IPS can be organized into three main parts:

1. Investment Objectives
   a. Return Requirements
   b. Risk Tolerance and Risk Capacity
2. Investment Constraints
   a. Liquidity Needs
   b. Time Horizon
   c. Tax Considerations
   d. Legal and Regulatory Considerations
   e. Unique Circumstances
3. Investment Philosophy and Strategies

Investment Objectives. The IPS should specify your investment goals. It should articulate the terms in which returns are denominated—nominal or real, absolute or relative, pretax or post-tax. Are you investing for retirement, using excess capital with which you can take risk, or some combination of the two? Your return requirements should distinguish between your desired return and the return necessary to achieve a particular investment goal, such as accumulating a sufficient nest egg to fund retirement.

Your return objective should be reasonable and consistent with your risk objective. Like the return objective, your risk objective should specify the method by which risk is measured and may be determined by your return objectives. For example, standard deviation may not be the best measure of risk if your primary return objective is to preserve wealth. In this case, a measure of downside risk might be more appropriate, even if expressed nonquantitatively.

You will want to distinguish between your risk tolerance and risk capacity. The former is your psychological willingness to bear risk. The latter is your objective financial wherewithal to sustain financial loss. The degree of flexibility a client has in their financial position can influence their ability to accept risk. Be honest with yourself. You may have the financial wherewithal to sustain a financial loss but not have the psychological willingness to take risk. Some pundits refer to this in colloquial terms, commenting, "You can either eat well or sleep well." If the level of volatility in your portfolio keeps you up at night, you may need to lessen the level of risk in your portfolio.

Investment Constraints. We discussed investment constraints (i.e., liquidity needs, time horizon, taxes, and legal constraints) and how they can impede successful value investing earlier in the chapter. In addition to those constraints, a section of the IPS is dedicated to unique circumstances where customization can become most apparent. This is the place where you express your preference for investment strategies that adhere to certain environmental, social, or governance agendas. This section may also list assets that are legally restricted from being sold, such as a concentrated position in a low basis stock.

Investment Philosophies and Strategies. The investment philosophy and strategies section is where you state your investment philosophy as a strategic value investor. You articulate your mandate to invest for the long term in securities with intrinsic values that exceed their market values. You can state that this sometimes means investing in securities that are out of favor and forgoing the latest investment trends. It might certainly emphasize some of the tools and techniques that we cover in the following chapters.

If you are managing a balanced portfolio of stock and bonds, you would articulate what long-term allocation of stocks, bonds, and alternative assets you want to maintain, as well as the guidelines you will use to rebalance those asset classes. These concepts are beyond the scope of this book, however.

Once you have taken the time to draft an IPS, review it periodically, especially during turbulent times. It will help you maintain a consistent investment strategy. You should also review it during more sanguine times to determine if it needs to be updated. It should not change radically (unless your personal circumstances have dramatically changed), but you may need to periodically tweak it.

Investment Diary

To help overcome investment challenges, Joachim Klement (2009) also suggests keeping a financial diary for each investment decision and comparing it to the outcome of the decision. The diary would document three things for each buy or sell investment decision, including:

1. *The investment action.* Was the intended action a buy or sell decision, and what price do you recommend? The price could be the current market price, or it could be a price limit price (e.g., a buy recommendation at a price below the current price) for a trade that may or may not occur in the future, depending on whether the price limit is reached.

2. *The investment thesis* (i.e., motivation). In a sentence, briefly articulate the reason for the trade. For a buy decision, it might be something like:
   - "The breakup value of the assets exceeds the current market price."
   - "The firm is a takeover candidate."
   - "Worst case sales growth exceeds market expectations and produces an intrinsic value in excess of the current market price."
   - "Profit margins will unexpectedly expand beyond current levels."

3. *Possible risks.* Obviously, our forecasts will sometimes be flawed. Articulate some possible scenarios that could invalidate your investment thesis. It might be something like:
   - "A developing competing product could be more of a threat than currently envisioned."
   - "The company could lose a large, key customer."
   - "Deregulation could impair margin expansion."

The diary need not be verbose. Three simple statements are all that is required. For it to be effective, however, it is important to review this periodically. We warn you, this practice is not for those with low self-esteem because it reveals the naked truth about investment performance and attribution. For example, we have a tendency to overlook our failures and focus on our successes. Or, one of our buy recommendations may have appreciated in value, but for entirely different reasons than we had envisioned. The diary removes our hindsight bias for things that have gone wrong and our attribution bias for things that have gone right.

Sunk Costs

Educate yourself about the notion that sunk costs are irrelevant (Box 3-7). Past gains or losses should be discounted. What is important is what the future looks like. There is no such thing as a hold decision, only buy and sell decisions. Each day you choose to hold onto your investment, you are in effect choosing to buy it. Ask yourself whether you would buy your investment if you did not already own it. Your decision to own it should always be based on your future expectations.

This awareness will help you overcome the tendency to hold on to losers when you have apparently made a mistake. To be effective, it requires putting it into practice in your daily life, even outside the investment arena, so that you can draw on it when it is most needed. There are many examples, including ignoring how long you've been standing in a grocery store line when deciding whether to switch to another line. Ignoring sunk costs involves simply making a judgment about which line is likely to move more quickly from this point forward.

Box 3-7 Sunk (and Drenched) Costs!

One of the authors of this book (who will go unnamed) once bought tickets to an outdoor concert for a date with his then-girlfriend. When the big day came, it was raining. He decided he didn't want to go. His girlfriend was shocked. "You paid a lot of money for those tickets!" she exclaimed. "How could you waste that money?"

The tickets were bought and paid for. Going or not going to the concert would not bring the money back. Once purchased, the marginal cost of the tickets was zero. He simply imagined what he would do if someone were to have given him free tickets to an outdoor concert on a rainy day. Would he accept? In this case, he decided he wouldn't.[14]

In the same way, when the stocks we buy go down in value, the loss is sunk (and in fact we might save taxes by selling). We need to brush it off and ignore it to make a good decision about whether to continue to hold. Instead, most of us focus on getting even. This get-even-itis needs to be consciously overcome by rational analysis.

Calming Techniques

Researchers present convincing evidence that panic reduces the brain's ability to process information clearly.[15] As a result, panicked decision makers tend to rely on flawed heuristics in such situations. Researchers recommend taking deep breaths and thinking about something else to calm reflexes. Some successful investors turn to yoga, hypnosis, and meditation to help them bring their minds to a place where heuristics cannot easily take over.

Nobel laureate Daniel Kahneman points out that our minds have two distinct cognitive systems that we use to make decisions.[16] The slow cognitive system is thoughtful, but it takes effort and time to use. The quick cognitive system is rapid and efficient because it relies on heuristics. When we focus our cognitive function and have the luxury of time to make a decision, our slow system can override what our quick system would have us do. When we get confused, overwhelmed, or panicked, however, we resort to using the system of the brain that relies on heuristics because those processes are automatic and require substantially less effort.

So do your best to avoid rash decision making by creating habits and rituals that encourage you to use your thoughtful decision-making system.

Pour Some Sugar on Me

Believe it or not, you may want to drink sweet tea or lemonade before making an important or difficult decision. Complex thought processes deplete glucose levels. When we are exhausted, our glucose levels are depleted and we are more likely to make difficult decisions using the part of our brain that relies on heuristics rather than the one that relies on the laborious analytical process.

Research describes experiments in which subjects are asked to make tough decisions after their glucose levels had been depleted.[17] Subjects who drank sweet drinks before making a difficult decision made better judgments than those who drank unsweetened or artificially sweetened drinks. It seems simple, but it works.

Leverage and Trading

Avoid excessive leverage and excessive trading. We mentioned earlier that the stocks that investors sell tend to perform better than the stocks investors buy. It stands to reason that the more they buy and sell, the worse their investment results. Brad Barber and Terrance Odean coined the phrase "trading is hazardous to an investor's wealth."[18] They examined the investment performance and trading behavior of over 13,000 households. Households that traded the least from 1991 to 1996 earned an average of 7 percent more per year than those households that traded the most.

We mentioned earlier that discrepancies between fundamental value and market value can get worse before they get better. Remember Creative Computer and uBid? If you try to magnify your returns by using leverage, you may not have the financial wherewithal to withstand the interim volatility before the wisdom of your decisions pan out. This was the case with many investors who realized that real estate was overvalued in the run-up to the financial crisis of 2008. Some investors established positions and were correct in their analyses, but didn't have the capital, or the stomach, to maintain positions until the market corrected. So, be careful with the use of leverage.

CONCLUSION

There are many barriers to successful strategic value investing. Some come from the marketplace; others reside in us or our investment constraints. Either way, they need not condemn us to a fate of lackluster investment results. The first step to overcoming them is identifying them. We can then use a series of techniques to increase the chances that we will stay disciplined, objective, and prudent in implementing our investment strategy.

CHAPTER FOUR

STRATEGIC SELECTION OF COMPANIES: ECONOMIC ANALYSIS, INDUSTRY ANALYSIS, AND SCREENING

The chief losses to investors come from the purchase of low-quality securities at times of favorable business conditions.

—Benjamin Graham

Companies do not operate in isolation, and sound investment decisions are not made in isolation. To properly evaluate the investment prospects for a particular company, an investor should assess the current economic, industry, and company environment, and, more importantly, expectations for the future on each of these dimensions. The current structure of the industry and the prospects for its future are extremely important considerations for the investor. This certainly does not mean that investors must limit their focus on industries that have bright future prospects. Well-run companies in industries with a positive future outlook do not necessarily make good investments, as they likely may be overvalued or fairly valued by the marketplace. Collectively, investors may have overly optimistic expectations for firms in industries that are currently in favor. Alternatively, firms in industries that have a poor future outlook may very well be good investments because the consensus of the market may be overly negative.

There are literally tens of thousands of companies in which you could invest. As we will see in later chapters, analysis and valuation of these companies takes time. Therefore, you need a way to strategically identify those companies for further analysis and valuation. In this chapter, we discuss alternative methods of identifying good strategic value investments. While each investor may have his own method of analysis, there are two basic styles, top-down or bottom-up, as depicted in Figure 4-1. As the titles suggest, a top-down investor first analyzes the economy as a whole, then industries, and finally tries to identify firms within the selected industry expected to outperform rivals relative to expectations. From

FIGURE 4-1

Top-down versus bottom-up analysis.

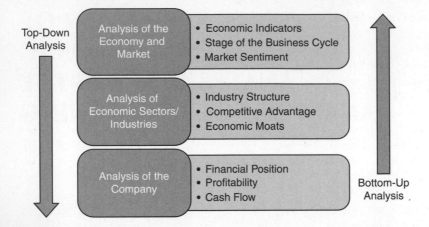

a value investor's perspective you must also determine whether these companies are a good value relative to other potential investments. A bottom-up investor first identifies companies and then considers industry and economy-wide dynamics when deciding whether or not to invest. Central to each methodology is a consideration of the broader economy and industry, as well as an analysis of the individual firm. We will provide an overview of these processes in this chapter with a primary focus on analysis of the economy and industries. We will also introduce company analysis—a topic that is critical to value investors. We will provide more details on company analysis in the next chapter.

TOP-DOWN ANALYSIS

Top-down analysis involves beginning at the highest level (the economy) and working down to the lowest level (the company). An analysis of the global/domestic economy is first performed to determine what portion of a portfolio will be allocated to international and domestic equities. This is usually followed by an analysis of which sectors (for example, consumer staples) are more attractive within the equity market. Within each sector, attractive industries (an industry in this context is defined as a subdivision of a sector, such as food and beverages) are identified. Finally, an analysis is performed to determine which companies within the industry are most attractive based on the relationship of valuation to expected performance.

In an overall portfolio management setting, top-down analysis also refers to the process of examining the interest rate, market, and economic environments to determine an appropriate allocation among available asset classes (such as cash, fixed income, and equities). This is followed by selection of sectors/industries and finally by the selection of individual securities.

BOTTOM-UP ANALYSIS

In a bottom-up analysis, the process starts at the level of individual companies. An investor begins by looking for companies that are attractive based upon some fundamental characteristics (such as return on equity (ROE), price-to-earnings (P/E) ratios, and total debt). The majority of individual investors can be characterized as bottom-up investors. Bottom-up analysis can begin by a company coming to an investor's attention for any number of reasons, such as a new product launch, a change of management, or high quality of service. On the other hand, bottom-up analysis can also involve screening on large databases of equities in an attempt to identify those firms that have attractive characteristics. Bottom-up analysis is used by both growth and value-oriented investors. A growth-oriented investor may screen for companies with high revenue or earnings growth. A value investor may screen for companies with low price multiples (for example, price-to-book and price-to-earnings) and a high return on equity. Strategies may also be combined, for example by looking for high-growth companies selling at reasonable price multiples (sometimes referred to as "growth at a reasonable price," or GARP). Screening should be considered simply a first step in making an investment decision. One should certainly not invest in all companies that pass an initial screening process. The screening process should identify those firms that warrant further attention by the investor.

OVERALL MACROECONOMIC ANALYSIS

An overall assessment of the global and domestic economy is a necessary component of the equity valuation process. In the case of an asset allocation process, a decision must be made as to the portion of a portfolio that will be invested domestically versus internationally. In evaluating cash flows, risk, and growth prospects of a company it is also necessary to assess the overall prospects of the economy. If overall economic growth is expected to be about 2 percent, this provides some insight into what industry and company growth rates are feasible. Absent evidence to the contrary, an appropriate initial assumption for sector/industry and company growth is likely to be near the overall economic growth rate (in this example, 2 percent). Overall economic growth is typically measured in terms of gross domestic product (GDP) or gross national product (GNP), discussed below.

Fluctuations in economic activity are reflected in the overall business cycle. Some industries/companies tend to perform better than others do in different stages of the business cycle. It is therefore important to examine the current stage of the economy in evaluating prospects for the sector, industry, and company.

In determining the current investment environment, the level of inflation—and most importantly, expected inflation—is also relevant, since it is an important determinant of interest rates and economic activity. That is why inflation expectations and revisions in inflation expectations have such a significant influence on financial markets.

GDP and GNP

Gross domestic product (GDP) is the total value of all final goods and services produced within a country. Nominal GDP is GDP measured in terms of current dollars. Real GDP is nominal GDP adjusted for changing prices. Table 4-1 presents nominal and real GDP for the United States from 1990 to 2012. Note that in nominal terms U.S. GDP grew by a robust 4.58 percent in 2012 relative to 2011. In real terms, however, economic growth was only 2.78 percent.

A similar measure, gross national product (GNP) is the total value of all final goods and services produced by factors of production owned by citizens of a country, regardless of where they are produced.

TABLE 4-1

Current-Dollar and "Real" Gross Domestic Product

Year	GDP in Billions of Current Dollars	Annual Growth	GDP in Billions of Chained 2009 Dollars	Annual Growth
1990	5,979.6		8,945.4	
1991	6,174.0	3.25%	8,938.9	–0.07%
1992	6,539.3	5.92%	9,256.7	3.56%
1993	6,878.7	5.19%	9,510.8	2.75%
1994	7,308.7	6.25%	9,894.7	4.04%
1995	7,664.0	4.86%	10,163.7	2.72%
1996	8,100.2	5.69%	10,549.5	3.80%
1997	8,608.5	6.28%	11,022.9	4.49%
1998	9,089.1	5.58%	11,513.4	4.45%
1999	9,665.7	6.34%	12,071.4	4.85%
2000	10,289.7	6.46%	12,565.2	4.09%
2001	10,625.3	3.26%	12,684.4	0.95%
2002	10,980.2	3.34%	12,909.7	1.78%
2003	11,512.2	4.85%	13,270.0	2.79%
2004	12,277.0	6.64%	13,774.0	3.80%
2005	13,095.4	6.67%	14,235.6	3.35%
2006	13,857.9	5.82%	14,615.2	2.67%
2007	14,480.3	4.49%	14,876.8	1.79%
2008	14,720.3	1.66%	14,833.6	–0.29%
2009	14,417.9	–2.05%	14,417.9	–2.80%
2010	14,958.3	3.75%	14,779.4	2.51%
2011	15,533.8	3.85%	15,052.4	1.85%
2012	16,244.6	4.58%	15,470.7	2.78%

Source: U.S. Department of Commerce, Bureau of Economic Analysis, www.bea.gov

As noted earlier, an important determinant of future growth for a company is the future growth prospects of the economy as a whole. The expected growth in GDP (or GNP), both long term and short term, can be used as initial estimates of a firm's growth rate. Adjustments can then be made based upon the prospects of the firm and its sector/industry relative to the economy as a whole. Suffice it to say that growth rates for GDP and GNP provide a starting point (or anchor) from which the investor can adjust individual industry and firm growth rates for the future.

Application

Value Line (www.valueline.com) is a popular equity analysis service. In forecasting industry and company sales, Value Line first forecasts GDP and subcomponents of the economy such as:

- Industrial production
- Housing starts
- Unit car sales
- Personal savings rate
- National employment

Value Line forecasts individual company sales growth based upon correlations with GDP and the subcomponents. Let's take a look at Microsoft, a once high-flying stock that has been languishing in recent years. At the time of this writing, Microsoft was selling at a price/earnings ratio of 11.6 and a dividend yield of 3.0 percent. On August 16, 2013, Value Line estimated a future short-term (five years) growth rate averaging about 9 percent per year for revenues and cash flow, and a growth rate of 8.5 percent for earnings

Business Cycle

Another useful feature of GDP is for use in measuring the business cycle and long-term economic trends. As can be seen from Table 4-1, the long-term trend in the U.S. economy has been upward. Surrounding this long-term trend line are periods of above-average economic performance and below-average economic performance. The business cycle is typically separated into the following components, depicted in Figure 4-2:

- Expansion
- Peak
- Contraction/Recession
- Trough

FIGURE 4-2

GDP over time.

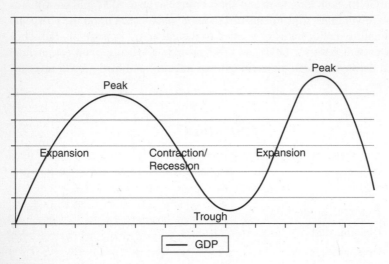

Expansion is a period of economic growth during which productive output and employment rise, leading to the highest point, the peak. Real GDP rises during the expansion. The increase in production requires additional factors of production, equipment, raw materials, and labor. This results in increased corporate purchases both of physical plant (property, plant, and equipment) and raw materials. The increased need for labor results in lower unemployment.

Recession is a period of contraction following the peak, characterized by falling productive output and employment (rising unemployment). Typically a recession is defined as two quarters of falling output, measured by real GDP. When output declines, the amount of factors of production needed as inputs declines. This results in lower purchasing of raw materials and rising unemployment. Typically, factories run at less than full capacity during a recession. Additionally, firms make fewer investments in plant and equipment. The trough is the low point following a recession. A depression is a prolonged and severe recession.

Importantly, some sectors and industries perform better in some stages of the economic cycle than in others. Under the Global Industry Classification System (GICS^{SM}) developed by Morgan Stanley Capital International and Standard & Poor's (S&P), companies are divided into 10 sectors, 24 industry groups, 68 industries and 154 subindustries. The 10 sectors and an example of an industry for each are:

Sector	Example
Energy	Energy Equipment and Services
Materials	Metals and Mining
Industrials	Aerospace and Defense
Consumer Discretionary	Automobiles
Consumer Staples	Food Products
Health Care	Pharmaceuticals
Financials	Insurance
Information Technology	Computers and Peripherals
Telecommunication Services	Wireless Telecommunication Services
Utilities	Electric Utilities

Sectors or their subcomponents (industries and subindustries) that are sensitive to the stage of the economic cycle are termed *cyclical*. An example of a cyclical sector is consumer discretionary, meaning that consumers spend less on automobiles, travel, and other discretionary expenditures during a recession.

Sectors that are less sensitive to the business cycle are *noncyclical* sectors (sometimes termed defensive sectors), such as consumer staples. Consumer expenditures for food and beverages continue through a recession (although the distribution of these expenditures within an industry may change).

Inflation

An important aspect of the analysis of the economy is an overall assessment of *expected* inflation. The risk-free rate of interest is an input into the valuation of a company's future cash flows. The nominal risk-free rate is a function of the inflation rate and the real interest rate required by investors to forgo consumption. The higher the level of expected inflation the higher the required risk-free rate of interest. Inflation impounded into the risk-free rate impacts all companies and industries. One measure of inflation is the Consumer Price Index (CPI), which measures inflation of a market-basket of consumer goods. Inflation also impacts the factors of production used by firms to create goods and services as well as the ultimate price of those goods and services. Producer price indices (PPIs) measure inflation at the wholesale level. These rates of inflation impact companies and industries differently. It is important to gain an understanding of the current level of overall inflation in an economy, as well as the relative rates of inflation impacting different sectors of the economy, in order to analyze the value of an investment in a company or industry.

Economic Indicators

In addition to GDP, a variety of economic indicators have been developed to assess the health and state of the economy and provide the investor with clues as to where the economy is heading. Leading indicators tend to move in advance of the business cycle. Lagging indicators tend to lag the business cycle. Coincident indicators move with and define the business cycle. The Conference Board compiles the Index of Leading Economic Indicators, which signal stages of the business cycle.

SENTIMENT INDICES—FEAR AND GREED

The emotions of fear and greed can be the value investor's greatest ally. While many value investors would contend that they are not market timers, it is obvious that equities are more attractively priced in some market periods than in others. In essence, all of our investment decisions involve a timing element. Certainly, investors can look at overall P/E ratios and draw inferences from where current P/E ratios are relative to historical norms to gain an appreciation of how the overall market is pricing future earnings. Warren Buffett counseled Berkshire Hathaway shareholders in his 2005 letter that "Investors should remember that excitement and expenses are their enemies. And if they insist on trying to time their participation in equities, they should try to be fearful when others are greedy and greedy when others are fearful."[1] Buffett amplified this message in his 2009 letter to shareholders by stating that "Whether we're talking about socks or stocks, I like buying quality merchandise when it is marked down."[2]

These simple, intuitive statements illustrate the contrarian nature of value investing. As with many axioms in investments, heeding this simple advice is much easier said than done. So how can we figure out if quality stocks are marked down? An investor can, somewhat objectively, determine how greedy or how fearful the general market or the market for a particular stock is by examining various market sentiment indices, several of which are described below. This is by no means meant to be an exhaustive list of sentiment indicators.

Sentiment measures are generally considered contrary indicators. When a sentiment index shows heightened fear of a market drop, one can infer that investors are concerned and nervous about the future. Thus, investors may be keeping money out of the market that can be used in the future to buy stocks and increase prices. It may seem counterintuitive, but a sentiment index that is in negative territory signals a potential buying opportunity for the value investor, as that investor is trying to go against the consensus of the market by buying low and selling high.

Suffice it to say that sentiment measures are generally in a normal range and in those circumstances the measures may offer little information to investors. Sentiment indices are most instructive to investors when they are well outside of the normal range. It is in these times that investors must trust the inclination to be greedy when others are fearful. Conversely, sentiment indicators may provide signals that market participants are understating potential risks of a bull market and encourage investors to be fearful when others are greedy. Investors can increase their success rates dramatically if they can remove some of the emotion from their investment decision-making process.

Put-Call Ratio

The Chicago Board Options Exchange publishes a daily put-call ratio (PCR), shown in Figure 4-3.[3] It is simply the ratio of put option trading volume to call option volume. A put option gives the holder the right to sell shares of stock at a specific price. Put options increase in value as share prices fall. A call option gives the holder the right to buy shares of stock at a specific price. A call option increases in value as share prices rise. A rising put-call ratio reflects concern by options traders about the potential of falling share prices. Although a value of 1.0 might seem to be a "neutral" reading (an equal number of put options and call options), historically there are more calls than puts bought on what would be considered a normal day. Thus, a PCR of approximately 0.80 is considered normal. Markets are considered strong (and contrarians would contend overbought) when the ratio falls below 0.7 since the optimists clearly outweigh the pessimists.

F I G U R E   4-3

Put-call ratio over time.

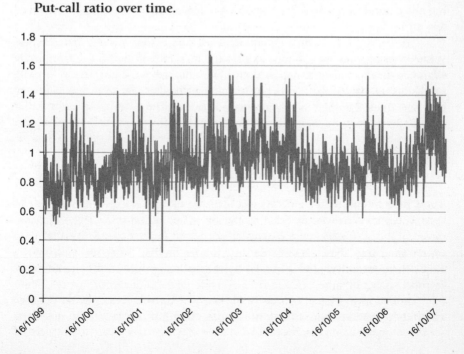

T A B L E 4-2

Put-Call Ratios for Individual Stocks
as of December 15, 2011

Symbol	Name	Ratio	52-Week Range
XOM	Exxon Mobil	1.20	0.72–2.54
AAPL	Apple	0.66	0.65–1.15
IBM	International Business Machines	1.30	0.93–2.13
MSFT	Microsoft	0.71	0.66–1.03
CVX	Chevron	1.54	0.72–2.06
GOOG	Google	0.97	0.59–1.15
WMT	Walmart Stores	1.32	0.48–1.34
PG	Procter & Gamble	1.09	0.77–2.71
GE	General Electric	1.21	0.82–1.85
JNJ	Johnson & Johnson	1.18	0.65–2.53

Source: www.schaeffersresearch.com

Markets are considered weak (and contrarians would contend oversold) when the ratio rises above 1.1 because the pessimists outweigh the optimists.

Investors may also look at put-call ratios on individual stocks, such as those in Table 4-2, as well as on the market as a whole. The put-call ratio on individual stocks varies widely, so the investor must be careful and not apply overall rules of thumb to individual stocks. This table shows the put-call ratios for 10 of the largest market capitalization firms in the United States as of December 15, 2011, as well as the 52-week highs and lows for those ratios. As one can see, the put-call ratio is near the high end of the 52-week range for Walmart stores. Since the put-call ratio is a contrary indicator, the high ratio, all else equal, would be viewed as a positive for the near term prospects for Walmart stock. On the other hand, the put-call ratio for Apple is near the low end of the range and would be viewed as negative for the near term prospects of Apple stock.

CBOE Volatility Index

The CBOE Volatility Index (VIX) is a measure of market expectations of near-term volatility conveyed by S&P 500 stock index option prices. The interpretation of the VIX is the expected volatility in the index over the next 30 days on an annualized basis. This volatility is that implied from the well-known Black-Scholes option-pricing model by the options prices in the marketplace. Introduced in 1993, the VIX has been considered an indicator of investor sentiment as well as market volatility. While the VIX is an indicator of the implied volatility in options prices (and, of course, volatility can be on the upside or

FIGURE 4-4

CBOE Volatility Index.

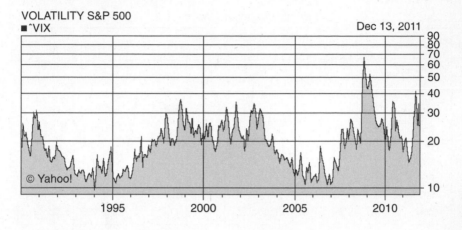

downside), many believe that a rising VIX signals growing fear and willingness to pay more for protection against falling stock prices (see Figure 4-4). As a rule of thumb, VIX measures over 30 correspond to a large amount of investor uncertainty and implied volatility, while readings under 20 are found during relatively calm periods in the market. A contrarian investor would find high VIX readings as indicators of more attractive periods to invest, as through time volatility tends to be mean reverting.

Barron's Confidence Index

The Barron's Confidence Index attempts to gauge investor confidence in the economy by dividing the average yield on high-grade bonds by the average yield on intermediate-grade bonds. Since yields on intermediate-grade bonds are higher than yields on high-grade bonds, a rising Barron's Confidence Index would indicate that the consensus of bond investors has increasing confidence in the economy as the premium for bearing higher risk is declining. That is, investors are more willing to invest in higher risk bonds, driving their yields lower relative to lower risk bonds.

As you can see from Figure 4-5, there has been a secular decline in the Barron's Confidence Index over the past 25 years. This would indicate that confidence in the economy has been steadily eroding over that time period. The contrarian investor would find periods of low investor confidence to be more attractive time periods to commit funds to the equity markets.

FIGURE 4-5

Barron's Confidence Index.

Barron's Confidence Index

Dec-08 2011 Close=69.3

world gold charts © www.sharelynx.com

American Association of Individual Investors Sentiment Index

The American Association of Individual Investors (AAII) Sentiment Survey measures the percentage of individual investors who are bullish, bearish, and neutral on the stock market over the next six months. The weekly survey of members of AAII was initiated in 1987. The results are available at no cost on the AAII website (www.aaii.com). This is not a survey of professional investment advisors, but one of serious individual investors. Since inception, the averages are 39 percent bullish, 31 percent neutral, and 30 percent bearish, respectively. Bullish sentiment reached its highest levels on January 6, 2000, (the height of the tech bubble) at 75.0 percent. Viewed as a contrary indicator, extreme bullishness would lead investors to believe that a market decline was imminent. Bearish sentiment reached a record high of 70.3 percent on March 5, 2009—near the lows of that bear market. Extreme bearishness would lead investors to believe that a market rise was on the horizon. As with other sentiment indicators, investors may want to pay particular attention when the indicator is well outside of its normal range.

SECTOR ROTATION

A common use of economic data in a top-down investment approach is sector rotation. Sector rotation involves an analysis of the current economic environment and a forecast of where the overall economy is heading. Purchases are made in those sectors expected to perform particularly well in the expected forthcoming stage of the business cycle. Economic data must be combined with other data to identify attractive sectors. Relative valuation is the most important consideration. An investor may desire to rotate out of highly valued sectors that have outperformed the broader market and into undervalued sectors that are underappreciated by the overall market. Bostian identifies six important factors in sector rotation.[4] Market (for example, relative valuation)

- Economics
- Productivity
- Profit
- Demographics
- Government policy

SECTOR/INDUSTRY ANALYSIS

In examining a sector or industry, it is important to note that a strategic value investor is primarily concerned with assessing the ability of companies within the industry to generate cash flow, the potential growth of that cash flow and the risks related to the receipt of those cash flows. The investor must assess the industry's ability to grow relative to the overall economy. Additionally, the investor should consider the stage of the business cycle. As discussed earlier, some industries tend to perform better in certain stages of the business cycle.

A first consideration when estimating the expected growth for an industry is the expected growth in the economy as a whole. Of course some industries can be expected to grow at a faster or slower rate than the overall economy. The expected relative growth of an industry is a function of the demand for the industry's goods and services. Consumer demand for goods and services is largely a function of consumer needs and tastes, demographics, and disposable income. The demand for some goods, such as automobiles, will vary with the business cycle, while the demand for other goods, such as food, will not fluctuate as much with the business cycle. The investor must gain an understanding of the demand for the goods and services of the industry under consideration and how this demand is related to the overall economic environment.

An industry's ability to generate cash flows is a function of profitability. A company makes investments in factors of production, sells goods or services (hopefully at a profit), and ultimately receives a return on its investment in cash, which can be reinvested in the business or distributed to owners. Profitability is a function of the level of competition within an industry, the demand for the industry's goods discussed above, and the price sensitivity of the consumer for the industry's goods and services. An industry that is very profitable (measured, for example, by return on equity) will attract more competitors. As competition increases, the supply of goods and services will increase relative to the demand, and prices may fall. At the very least, the overall industry sales are divided up amongst more industry participants. Conversely, if an industry is not profitable, companies will exit (through bankruptcy or otherwise). As competition declines, the industry may become profitable for the remaining participants. The ability of firms to enter or exit an industry will vary based on such considerations as barriers to entry and exit.

PORTER'S COMPETITIVE ADVANTAGE FRAMEWORK

In 1979 the *Harvard Business Review* published an article by a young and relatively unknown economist named Michael Porter.[5] The article, entitled "How Competitive Forces Shape Strategy," has become a staple of business school education and has shaped the way a generation of business strategists and financial analysts approach industry analysis. Porter's model offers the strategic value investor a framework for approaching the question of the sustainability of an industry, and, by extension, a firm's business model—integral aspects of the investment decision-making process. Although we will briefly describe the five individual competitive forces, it is incumbent upon the investor to consider them holistically and not simply focus on one or two of the individual factors. Additionally, Porter urges analysts to focus not simply on a snapshot of the industry structure in time but also on anticipated changes in the competitive forces—in Buffett's terms, skating to where the puck is going to be.

According to Porter, the five competitive forces that determine industry profitability are:

- Threat of new entrants
- Bargaining power of suppliers
- Bargaining power of buyers
- Threat of substitute products or services
- Rivalry among existing firms

Each of these competitive forces has multiple elements that determine the overall level of competition. The *threat of new entrants* is a function of capital requirements, government policy, and access to distribution (among other elements). Some industries are simply much easier to enter than other industries. Contrast, for example, the passenger airline industry and the restaurant industry. The airline industry has a much lower threat of new entrants than the restaurant industry as a result of larger capital requirements to purchase planes, government policy regarding regulation/deregulation, and higher costs to access distribution (landing and gate rights), to cite a few factors. On the other hand, the restaurant industry is relatively easy to enter—all one really needs is a location, an idea, and a knack for delivering meals that people are willing to pay for. All else equal, industries that have significant barriers to entry are more attractive. However, the fact that an industry is difficult to enter certainly does not by itself make that industry or firms within the industry good investments.

The second competitive force described by Porter is the *bargaining power of suppliers*. Supplier bargaining power is impacted primarily by supplier concentration, switching costs, and differentiation of inputs. When you look at suppliers, you are looking at suppliers of all of the factors of production. Here again, the passenger airline industry has not been very attractive. There are a limited number of airplane manufacturers (e.g., Boeing and Airbus). Typically, a supplier group is more powerful if it is more concentrated than the industry it sells to. When you couple that with the fact that many of the firms in the airline industry have employees (pilots, mechanics, and flight attendants) who are unionized—and there are no alternatives to those groups—the balance of power tips heavily with suppliers in the passenger airline industry.

The third competitive force is the *power of buyers*. Buyers are more powerful if there are a relatively few buyers or if the buyers purchase in large volumes. However, buyers are also powerful if the industry's products are considered homogeneous or standardized. An industry that has difficulty differentiating its product (in essence, a commodity business) cedes a great deal of power to buyers. The passenger airline industry is certainly not attractive on this dimension. The biggest factor dictating which airline a leisure passenger selects is price. In essence, airlines must match the price of their dumbest competitor. This issue has certainly been exacerbated in recent years by the proliferation of travel websites such as Expedia.com and Travelocity.com and the ease with which consumers can shop for flights on the basis of fare. Airlines have tried to differentiate their products by creating loyalty programs and providing frequent travelers with upgrades and other benefits. These developments have led to more loyalty on the part of business passengers. Still, the balance of power in the passenger airline industry falls on the side of buyers.

The fourth competitive force is the *threat of substitutes*. A substitute is simply another product or service that performs the same function as the industry's product but by a different means. While there are alternatives to airline travel—for instance, passenger trains, buses, and automobiles—there are few effective substitutes for airline travel. Several years ago, many contended that videoconferencing would reduce business travel substantially. Despite extensive promotion, technological advances, increased travel hassles with tighter security, and a poor economy in recent years, videoconferencing has not eroded the popularity of business airline travel.

The final competitive force cited by Porter is *rivalry among existing competitors*. Rivalry is partly a function of industry growth, barriers to exit, and current industry concentration. If industry growth is slow, then rivalry increases, as firms are battling with each other for existing market share instead of seeking to grow the overall market. High exit barriers that are due, for instance, to specialized assets result in increased rivalry among competitors. A large number of similarly sized competitors results in more rivalry, as no firm is really seen as the industry leader. The passenger airline industry is characterized by substantial rivalry among competitors and has resulted in fierce price wars, weakening market participants.

However, just because the economics of an industry appear poor doesn't mean that it is foolish to invest in firms within that industry. Nor does it mean that firms cannot create a long-term, sustainable business model. In order to prosper in a competitive industry environment, a company must engage in a well-defined competitive strategy, such as cost leadership or product differentiation. Southwest Airlines has been profitable for years pursuing a low-cost strategy. Its success is the result of entering cities and driving weaker competitors out of business on the basis of price. In essence, Southwest Airlines is the Walmart of the airline industry. It remains to be seen, however, if this strategy will continue to succeed as Southwest enters new markets and expands its flight offerings. The investor cannot be lulled into believing that the status quo in the market will extend indefinitely into the future. Other similar firms, such as Jet Blue, recognized the successful business model of Southwest and have adopted it as their own.

While the five competitive forces may simply resemble a qualitative list, an astute investor can actually quantify many of the factors. For instance, one can look at the percentage of the market controlled by the seller of a particular factor of production to understand the power of suppliers (in the case of airlines, for instance, look at the market share of Boeing or Airbus). Alternatively, one can look at the percentage of the market penetration of particular airlines to estimate rivalry among competitors. The Porter analysis need not simply be a qualitative list.

Most pundits would probably agree that Warren Buffett has made very few investment mistakes in his illustrious career. However, by his own admission, his foray into the airline industry via US Airways was ill conceived. In his annual letter to Berkshire Hathaway shareholders in 2008, Mr. Buffett lamented that "The worst sort of business is one that grows rapidly, requires significant capital to engender the growth, and then earns little or no money. Think airlines. Here a durable competitive advantage has proven elusive ever since the days of the Wright Brothers. Indeed, if a farsighted capitalist had been present at Kitty Hawk, he would have done his successors a huge favor by shooting Orville down." The futility of the airline industry was further illustrated by Jason Zweig, who commented in 2003 that "It is commonly accepted today that the cumulative earnings of the airline industry over its entire history have been negative."[6]

INDUSTRY LIFE CYCLE

Separate from the discussion of the business cycle is an analysis of the industry life cycle, that is, an analysis of the viability of an industry over time. It is informative for an investor to understand what stage of the industry life cycle characterizes a particular industry. This will allow the investor to estimate the potential future growth for the industry as a whole and for the subject firm.

The industry life cycle theory postulates that there are four phases that delineate the beginning to the end of an industry: the *pioneer, growth, mature,* and *decline* phases.

The *pioneer stage* is when the industry is attempting to establish a market for its products. This stage is characterized by venture capital financing and high failure rates. Industries in the pioneer stage are generally not profitable, as they are investing heavily and are, by nature, quite speculative. Often, market participants are overly optimistic about the prospects for industries and firms within the industry during this stage. The Internet boom of the late 1990s is a prime example of an industry in the pioneer stage. Think of how many firms failed as a truly revolutionary and successful technological innovation, the Internet, fueled rampant speculation about the potential for e-commerce. Many Internet-based firms went public and speculation sent the NASDAQ index soaring. It turns out that only a small percentage of those firms had a business model that was viable in the long term, and many investors lost substantial sums as the industry winners and losers were being identified.

In the *growth stage*, the market for the product or service being produced has been established and is well recognized. Many successful growth industries create markets for products that consumers didn't even recognize that they needed. This stage is also characterized by increasing applications of an existing product or technology. A current example of an industry in the growth stage is the Global Positioning System (GPS) industry and all of the applications that it has spawned. GPS technology has applications in the automobile, outdoor, fitness, marine, and aviation segments, to name a few. GPS technology is replacing the need for physical maps and written directions for many consumers and has become standard fare in many products (such as automobiles). In the growth stage, firms are often able to enjoy large profit margins, as it takes time for potential competitors to ramp up and participate in a burgeoning industry. Growth stock investors typically look for firms in the growth stage of the industry life cycle.

The third stage of the industry life cycle is the *mature stage.* The overall growth rate of industries in the mature stage matches that of the overall economy as a whole. The products or services produced by industries in the mature stage have become staples to consumers. Examples of industries in the mature stage are the passenger airline industry, the automobile industry, and the food service industry. Firms in industries in the mature stage of the industry life cycle can certainly grow at rates higher than the industry as a whole. The industry life cycle looks at the industry in aggregate rather than at individual firms within the industry. Firms in this situation can typically grow in two ways. First, a firm can gain market share at the expense of other competitors. For example, the passenger airline industry is in the mature stage, while a relatively recent entrant like Jet Blue has a growing market share within that mature industry. Second, a firm can gain market share by acquiring other firms within the industry via a merger or acquisition.

The final stage of the industry life cycle is the *decline stage*. Overall demand for the goods and services produced by the industry is actually falling, and firms within the industry are fighting for pieces of an increasingly smaller market pie. Profit margins tend to fall in this stage, and participants choose to exit the industry. Importantly, just because an industry is in the decline stage, it doesn't mean that there aren't potentially very good investments in that industry. In fact, this may be just the place that contrarian-oriented value investors may want to hunt for undervalued firms. Daily newspapers are an example of an industry that many market watchers believe is in the decline stage. Berkshire Hathaway purchased the Omaha World Herald Company, the publisher of the *Omaha World Herald*, the primary newspaper in Buffett's hometown of Omaha, Nebraska.

SUSTAINABLE COMPETITIVE ADVANTAGE AND ECONOMIC MOATS

What allows a firm, even in a very competitive industry, to have a business model that stands the test of time? Warren Buffett has often used imagery recalling the Middle Ages, stating that he wants to invest in businesses with economic castles protected by unbreachable moats. This is a way of describing a firm's competitive advantage and assessing the durability of that competitive advantage.

Morningstar has adopted the concept of an economic moat and classifies them into five main types: *low-cost producer, switching costs*, the *network effect, efficient scale*, and *intangible assets*.[7]

As described earlier, in the retailing industry, Walmart has adopted the *low-cost producer* strategy and has built a fairly wide moat, allowing the firm to have an astonishing market share of over 10 percent of the enormous U.S. retailing market. However, in 2010, Walmart's market share actually fell to 13.4 percent from the 2009 market share of 13.9 percent of the U.S. market. Some analysts believe that this is a signal that the Walmart economic moat is being breached by other competitors, chiefly due to the changing nature of e-commerce. Just the fact that the durability of the Walmart economic moat is being challenged by some observers should serve as a warning to investors that assuming a business model can exist forever is fraught with peril.

A firm can enjoy an economic moat by operating in an environment characterized by high *switching costs*. Switching costs are one-time inconveniences or expenses that a customer must incur in order to change from one product to another. Often, the costs are not monetary but rather involve consumer time and effort. Cell phone companies (Verizon and AT&T) have pricing models that encourage consumers to stay with their current provider by establishing high switching costs and making it difficult to switch carriers. Bundling goods and services is an effective way of increasing the switching costs and widening that economic moat.

Deep and wide economic moats can be created by firms in which a strong *network effect* is evident. A network effect occurs when the value of a good or service increases as more people use that particular good or service. FedEx is a prime example of a firm that has a strong network effect. As more and more consumers throughout the world choose FedEx as their preferred shipping firm, FedEx can, in turn, open more and more locations worldwide and provide improved service. Although there are of course other shipping firms, FedEx has been able to capitalize on this network effect and increase the size of its economic moat over time.

Efficient scale is a situation where a niche or limited market is currently served by existing players in an effective manner such that new entrants are dissuaded from entering that market. This situation includes oligopolies, in which a small number of large firms dominate the market, or niche markets, such as pipelines and airports.

The final type of economic moat is that developed by the existence of intangible assets. These assets prevent other firms from duplicating a particular good or service. Intangible assets may take the form of patents in the drug industry to brand names in the consumer products industry. When addressing a group of college students in Omaha, Nebraska, at the CFA Global Investment Research Challenge event, Warren Buffett commented that he believed that Coca-Cola is the strongest brand name in the world. Coca-Cola has built this economic moat by selling not only a product, but an image. The strength of the Coke brand is exemplified by the existence of a Coca-Cola store and a robust market in Coca-Cola memorabilia. Consumer willingness to pay for goods (shirts, signs, hats, and other paraphernalia) that advertise the brand is evidence of just how wide the economic moat for Coca-Cola has become. While it may seem easy to compete in the soft drink industry based simply upon the product produced, the economic moat created by the Coke image is difficult for competitors to penetrate.

Interestingly enough, some analysts have questioned the width of the moat of Warren Buffett's own firm, Berkshire Hathaway, contending that much of Berkshire's value is due to Mr. Buffett. In recognition of this concern, Buffett has recently made the Berkshire succession plan much clearer by naming his son, Howard, as his successor and hiring Todd Combes and Ted Weschler to manage a portion of the marketable securities portfolio.

COMPANY ANALYSIS AND BOTTOM-UP SCREENING

The predominant style of bottom-up value investing relies upon consideration of certain fundamental financial ratios. Value investors compare ratios across both time and across companies or industries to get an idea of relative under or over valuation. In the next chapter we will provide a more comprehensive discussion of analysis of a company's financials, including ratios. In the application part of this book, we will also present more screening techniques. You will see that there are a variety of ratios you can choose from, based on the company factors that most interest you, to strategically narrow down the number of companies you plan to further analyze and evaluate. For now, to demonstrate screening, we will focus on some common ratios often used by value investors.

Return on Equity (ROE)

Return on equity, or ROE, is computed by dividing net income after tax (the profits accruing to shareholders) by shareholder's equity (the shareholders' cumulative investment in the company):

$$ROE = Net\ Income/Shareholder's\ Equity$$

ROE measures the firm's ability to generate profits from capital invested by shareholders. Of course, higher ROEs are preferred to lower ROEs. Historically, ROEs in excess of 10 percent are generally considered desirable by investors. A 10 percent ROE means that each year the company is generating $10 of profits for every $100 invested in it cumulative by the owners. As with many other ratios, ROE can differ substantially across industries and stages of the business cycle. Investors place a high premium on firms that are able to generate and sustain high ROEs through time.

Long-Term Debt–to–Total Capital Ratio

Long-term debt–to–total capital (LTD/Cap) is computed by dividing a firm's long-term debt by the total capital provided to the firm by debt holders, preferred stockholders, and common stockholders:

$$Long\text{-}Term\ Debt\text{-}to\text{-}Total\ Capital = (Long\text{-}Term\ Debt)/(Long\text{-}Term\ Debt + Preferred\ Stock + Common\ Stock)$$

The long-term debt–to–total capital ratio indicates the level of financial leverage employed by a firm. Long-term debt–to–total capital ratios vary widely across industries. In general, value investors are conservative in nature and prefer firms with lower levels of financial leverage. These firms have greater financial flexibility, as they may have untapped borrowing power.

Price-to-Earnings Ratio

The price-to-earnings ratio (or P/E ratio) is simply the current stock price divided by a measure of the net income per share for a firm.

$$P/E = Market\ price\ per\ share/Earnings\ per\ share$$

The numerator of the ratio, market price per share, is simply the current market price. P/E ratios can be computed on the basis of current year's earnings per share or next year's expected earnings per share. Often, leading P/E ratios are computed, as stock prices are based largely on expectations for future earnings. A higher P/E ratio means that investors are paying more for each unit of net income. Another interpretation of P/E ratio is the number of years of current earnings the investor would need in order to get paid back for the purchase price.

Typically, stocks selling at higher P/E ratios have higher growth expectations than those selling at lower P/E ratios. In essence, investors are willing to pay a higher premium for current earnings because they expect future earnings to grow substantially. Value investors generally prefer firms selling at lower P/E ratios, as they believe there is less chance that they will be disappointed that future growth prospects will not be realized. Just because a stock is selling at a relatively low P/E ratio certainly does not mean that it is undervalued. It may sell at a low P/E ratio because investors are pessimistic regarding future earnings from the stock.

P/E ratios vary considerably through time and also across industries. When overall market sentiment is positive, P/E ratios can be very high, as investors place a high premium on future growth prospects. However, P/E ratios can also be very high when overall earnings fall considerably. For the S&P 500 Index, the P/E ratio reached a historic high of 46.5 in the early 2000s, largely due to falling earnings (see Figure 4-6). The average P/E for the past 100 years has been around 15. Firms in growth industries typically sell at much higher P/E ratios than firms in mature industries.

FIGURE 4-6

Historical P/E ratios for the S&P 500.

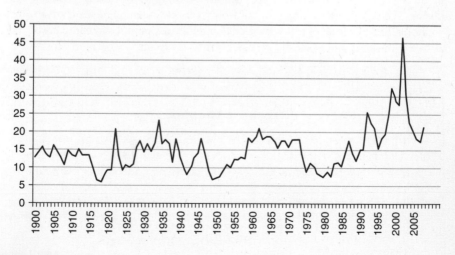

Source: Schiller

Price-to–Book Value

Price-to–book value is another ratio employed by value investors to attempt to get an idea of the relative market valuation of a company. Book value per share is the balance sheet value of all assets of the firm divided by the number of shares outstanding.

Price-to–Book Value = Market price per share/Book Value per share

Book value is computed as the balance sheet value of the company's net assets (assets net of liabilities). Most assets are listed on the balance sheet at their historical costs less some adjustment for depreciation or impairment, while some assets such as investments are listed at fair market value. Book value does not include the value of all intangible assets, such as brand names and intellectual property, but it may include their acquisition costs. Book values are more meaningful in some industries than in others. Traditionally, book values have had more applicability in the banking industry than in service industries.

Similar to how they view the P/E ratio, value investors generally prefer firms selling at lower multiples of price-to–book value than firms selling at higher multiples of price-to–book value.

Screening

Screening is the process of narrowing down a database of a large number of potential stock investments to a narrower list of companies based on factors of interest such as high profitability and low relative valuation. Screening can be performed using popular data services such as Bloomberg, Morningstar, Compustat, Reuters, or Stock Investor Pro. Data can be found in real time online or in periodic subscription services. Some screening programs are better than others. Many online screening programs only permit screening on the most recent year of a limited subset of ratios, while other databases permit screening based on a variety of ratios and past time periods.

Screening Example

To demonstrate a screening process, we will use the Stock Investor Pro database that includes Market Guide fundamental data and I/B/E/S earnings estimates. Data are presented in Table 4-3, which seeks to identify equities with high, stable returns on equity over the past five years, debt to capital below 30 percent, and a price-to-earnings multiple of less than or equal to 15 times.

TABLE 4-3

Example of a Value Investment Screening Process
as of December 22, 2011

Company Name	P/E ratio	LTD/Cap	ROE₁	ROE₂	ROE₃	ROE₄	ROE₅
Advance Auto Parts, Inc.	14.3	22.5	29.7	22.8	22.6	23.2	23.7
Aetna Inc.	8.6	26.0	18.2	14.4	15.2	19.1	17.6
Chevron Corporation	7.5	9.7	19.3	11.7	29.2	25.6	26.0
Humana Inc.	10.8	19.4	17.3	20.3	15.3	23.5	17.5
Intel Corporation	10.1	4.0	25.2	10.8	12.9	17.5	13.8
Mattel, Inc.	13.8	26.5	26.2	22.5	17.0	25.1	26.1
Microsoft Corporation	9.5	17.3	44.8	43.8	38.4	52.5	39.5
Murphy Oil Corporation	9.9	10.3	10.3	12.3	30.7	16.7	17.0
Rio Tinto plc (ADR)	5.8	18.6	27.9	15.1	16.2	34.0	44.8

Additionally, each of the firms had to have a current Value Line ranking of "1" for timeliness. In this example, we are attempting to identify companies for further analysis and valuation that are consistently profitable, have low financial risk, and are selling at reasonable prices relative to earnings. By limiting our screens to those companies ranked most highly by Value Line, we have included Value Line analyst's evaluation of these companies relative to their industry peers and the current economic environment. Note this is but one example of a value screen—others might include other factors and valuation ratios.

Stocks that meet four criteria:

1. Value Line Timeliness ranking of "1"

2. Return on equity $\geq$ 10% for each of the past 5 years

3. Long-term debt to total capital $\leq$ 30%

4. Price-to-earnings ratio $\leq$ 15

Table 4-3 presents the companies that passed all of our specified screening criteria. Note that in our screen we did not specify any criteria for industry. Our goal was to find those companies with the desired characteristics regardless of industry, but we did factor in how the companies were perceived by Value Line relative to their industry peers. Screening can also be used in top-down analysis to find companies meeting specific fundamental criteria within a selected industry.

CONCLUSION

There are a variety of ways a value investor may identify a stock for analysis. For example, he might be a consumer of the products of the company or might have read a recent earnings announcement about the company. These types of circumstances are not likely to be sufficient to identify all of the potential investment opportunities and to create a diversified portfolio (they do have merit, however, for identifying some opportunities). The strategic value investor needs a disciplined approach to narrow down the myriad investment opportunities to a subset for further analysis and valuation. The two approaches described here, top-down analysis and bottom-up analysis, are both useful and disciplined. Whichever directional approach is chosen, it is important that analysis includes the overall economy, industry, and company factors.

COMPANY ANALYSIS[1]

In the business world, the rearview mirror is always clearer than the windshield.
—Warren Buffett

In the last chapter, we discussed two strategic approaches to selecting companies for further analysis and valuation. Whether you choose the top-down or bottom-up approach, a critical step in the process is to become well-informed about the company. You need to understand the business and how profits are generated. You need to know how effective the management of the company is at operating the business and how efficiently the company converts accounting profits to cash flow. You also want to focus on how viable the company is going forward—whether they can sustain the current level of activity and can meet current and future obligations. This chapter focuses on analyzing a company's financial statements and other reported information to evaluate all of these critical dimensions. In the process, we will show you how to effectively make comparisons of the company's financial performance and financial position with their peers through ratio analysis. Ratios are also an effective tool in screening databases to narrow the field of possible companies for the detailed analysis shown in this chapter and applying the valuation models that we will present in the next part of the book.

UNDERSTANDING THE COMPANY'S
FINANCIAL SITUATION

Publicly traded companies are required to provide financial statements so that investors can evaluate how well management is operating the company. If you are a private investor in a nonpublic company with a significant ownership position, you can also compel the company to provide such financial statements (preferably ones audited by a respected accounting firm). The primary use of these statements is to evaluate the financial performance and financial position of the company. Financial performance has a couple of dimensions and hence two primary financial statements on which to focus: the income statement and the cash flow statement. On the other hand, financial position is evaluated by examining the balance sheet—not surprisingly sometimes referred to as the statement of financial position or condition.

Understanding the Income Statement

The income statement is also referred to as a statement of income, a statement of operations, a profit and loss statement, and other similar names. The income statement shows the revenues the company has generated from sales to customers and the expenses which were incurred to generate those revenues. Table 5-1 shows a recent income statement for Walmart, which we have embellished with additional information beyond that typically provided by management.

Columns one, two, and five are from the income statements provided by management. Most income statements will provide three years of financial data so that you can compare how the company is performing from year to year. For brevity we will use two years of data. However, we provide additional columns to make the comparison of data from year-over-year more illustrative. For example, when you look at the raw data provided by management in the income statement you can see that revenue has increased from $405 billion to $419 billion: Walmart sold more goods to customers year-over-year—a good thing. We also notice that net income (or profit) increased from $14.4 billion to $16.4 billion: Walmart generated higher profit year-over-year—also a good thing. However, how much of the increase in profits was due to simply selling more goods versus controlling costs or realizing economies of scale (for example, increased bargaining power or spreading out costs that are relatively fixed year-over-year across more units sold) from their operations?

In order to really assess how the company performed in generating profits, we need to remove "size" as a factor. We can do this in two different ways: We can calculate each income statement item as a percentage of revenue for the same year (analysts call this vertical common size analysis) or we can compute the year-over-year change for each item (analysts call this horizontal common size analysis). So let's look at the net profit as a percentage of revenue (we call this net profit margin) for this fiscal year versus last fiscal year. Net profit margin was 3.9 percent in the fiscal year ended January 31, 2011. The company generated 3.9 percent of profit relative to revenue or $3.9 of profits for every $100 of revenue. The higher the net profit margin, the better the company is doing at generating profits by controlling costs or achieving economies of scale. The prior year the profit margin was 3.5 percent, so Walmart did a better job at generating profits this past year, not just due to increasing the volume of products sold but also by controlling costs and generating more dollars of profit for every $100 of revenue. This is impressive given that Walmart is in the discount retail business where profit margins are notoriously low and when the firm was operating in a very difficult economic period.

TABLE 5-1

Walmart Income Statements (U.S. Dollar amounts in millions)

	FYE 1/31/2011	Percentage of Revenues	Year-Over-Year Change	FYE 1/31/2010	Percentage of Revenues
Revenues	418,952	99.3%	3.4%	405,132	99.3%
Net Sales	2,897	0.7%	(1.9%)	2,953	0.7%
Other Income	421,849	100.0%	3.4%	408,085	100.0%
Cost of Sales	315,287	74.7%	3.6%	304,444	74.6%
Gross Profit	106,562	25.3%	2.8%	103,641	25.4%
SG&A Expenses	81,020	19.2%	1.7%	79,639	19.5%
Operating Income	25,542	6.1%	6.4%	24,002	5.9%
Net Interest Expense	2,004	0.5%	6.4%	1,884	0.5%
Income Before Taxes	23,538	5.6%	6.4%	22,118	5.4%
Provision for Taxes	7,579	1.8%	5.9%	7,156	1.8%
Income from Continuing Ops.	15,959	3.8%	6.7%	14,962	3.7%
Income from Discontinued Operations	1,034	0.2%	(1408.9%)	(79)	0.0%
Consolidated Net Income	16,993	4.0%	14.2%	14,883	3.6%
Attributable to Noncontrolling	(604)	(0.1%)	17.7%	(513)	(0.1%)
Net Income Attributable to Walmart	16,389	3.9%	14.1%	14,370	3.5%

Another way of looking at the same dimension is to examine the year-over-year changes in revenue and profits. Revenue was up 3.4 percent year over year ($419 versus $405 billion), while net profit was up 14.1 percent. This tells the same story from a slightly different perspective: Walmart did a good job of increasing profits by a larger percentage than revenue increased. You do not need to do the analysis both ways because each tells you the same story. The vertical percentages are usually sufficient to determine what is going on and are often computed for you in the management discussion and analysis (MD&A) section of the company's financial reports along with an explanation for any changes. The MD&A section is a great place to start your analysis. The year-over-year changes are useful, however, for putting information together from both the income statement and balance sheet, as will be discussed further below.

We do not want to stop here and just look at the bottom line (net profits), as we want to understand what drove the increase in profit margin. We want to assess whether this is an aberration that will likely not repeat (or may even reverse) or a trend that is likely to continue. We can do that by scrutinizing the various expenses and subtotals on the common size columns of the income statement.

We should also spend a little time considering what led to the increase in revenues. Did the company sell more goods in every store, did they open more stores, or were other factors involved? In the MD&A section, the company states that same store sales in the United States actually declined year over year. In other words, revenue at stores that had been open in both years actually declined 0.6 percent. This is worrisome, but perhaps not unexpected given the poor economic environment. The majority of the increase in revenues came from the opening of new stores. In fact, the company opened 3.4 percent more square feet of store space year-over-year. The decline in same store revenues in the United States was offset by the effect of favorable exchange rate changes on non-U.S. revenue.

Now let's get back to focusing on costs and profits. Walmart's cost of sales (the amount Walmart paid to acquire or manufacture the goods which were sold to customers) as a percentage of revenues went up from 74.6 percent to 74.7 percent, meaning that the company was actually marking up products less than in the past. As a result Walmart's gross profit margin (total revenues less cost of sales) declined slightly from 25.4 percent to 25.3 percent. This is somewhat worrisome and does not help explain the increase in the company's net profit margin.

So let's take a look at Walmart's selling, general and administrative (SG & A) expenses. These represent costs other than the cost of merchandise purchased. This can include literally hundreds of expenses incurred to sell the retail merchandise such as rent expense, salary expense of store employees, insurance, and depreciation of retail stores. In this case, SG&A expenses as a percentage of revenues declined from 19.5 percent to 19.2 percent, a significant reduction. You might quibble with our use of the term *significant* for a decline of this percentage magnitude. Remember, this is a decline of 0.3 percent of revenues that are now $419 billion, representing a costs savings of $1.3 billion![2] We are well on our way to explaining the increase in the profit margin. Where did this savings come from? Walmart provides the explanation in the MD&A section of the annual report. Management notes that the savings came from higher labor productivity and lower incentive payments to employees as the result of organizational changes made during the year. While it is good that this cost is down, this tells us that future declines in this expense are not likely, and these expenses are likely to rise in the future if incentive payments increase.

Notice that net interest expense and taxes as a percentage of revenues did not change much year over year. Common size analysis allows you to focus in on important changes and you can choose where to spend your time probing further. Let's move to income from discontinued operations, which was positive this year versus negative last year. This line item represents a decision by the company to exit a particular line of business. Accounting rules require firms to report such activities separately, so you know it is not likely to recur in the future. The amount reported includes the results from the final operations of that line of business as well as any gain or loss from selling or closing down that business segment. In Walmart's case, it turns out that you have to do a little further investigation of this item. Management did not address it in the MD&A discussion, so you need to access the detailed footnotes accompanying the financial statements.[3] There you would discover that the gain in the most recent fiscal year actually relates to the 2007 sale of the company's German operations. The 2011 gain represents a settlement with the U.S. Internal Revenue Service in that year whereby the company can now deduct a loss on the prior sale of the German operations. While this tax benefit is advantageous, it will clearly not be repeated in future years and in fact resulted from prior realized losses.

So, in a nutshell, the increase in the company's profit margin from 3.5 percentto 3.9 percent of revenue is primarily attributable to a reduction in payroll costs including incentive payments and a one-time tax benefit. If we back out the one-time tax benefit from discontinued operations in 2010, profit margin increased more modestly, from 3.7 percent to 3.8 percent. The remaining reduction in payroll and incentive costs was offset by a slightly higher cost of sales. Management appears to have done a good—but perhaps not a great—job of controlling costs.

Box 5-1 Application: Comparing Company Profitability

Common size analysis is not only useful for examining changes in profitability over time for a single company but is particularly helpful in comparisons between companies. Summary common size data for Walmart and Target are provided in Table 5-2.

(Continued)

TABLE 5-2

Common Size Data For Walmart and Target

	Walmart FYE 1/31/11	Target FYE 1/29/11
Gross Profit Margin	25.3%	32.1%
Operating Margin	6.1%	7.8%
Net Profit Margin	3.9%	4.3%

Across all three measures of profitability, Target is performing better. The company is generating a higher gross profit margin than Walmart, indicating that Target is able to mark up goods more than Walmart. This is not too surprising given that Walmart's results include Sam's Club operations and Walmart has a reputation as a price leader. Similarly, Target's operating and net profit margins are also higher. From a value investor's standpoint this is certainly not a complete picture. Higher profitability does not mean a more lucrative investment. We have to consider other factors, such as how effective the company is at leveraging these profits for the stockholders (as we will see later in this chapter), as well as the relative valuation of the shares of each company.

Understanding the Cash Flow Statement

Profits are nice, but you cannot pay suppliers, employees, creditors, or the owners with profits: You need cold, hard cash. So another important dimension is how well the company does at turning these accounting profits into cash flow. Table 5-3 shows the cash flow statement for Walmart.

The cash flow statement is divided into three sections:

1. *Operating cash flows* related to running the business: cash collected from customers, cash paid to employers and suppliers, cash paid for operating expenses, and so on.

2. *Investing cash flows* related to investments the company is making for the future: cash paid to buy long-term equipment, cash paid to acquire another company, or cash paid for other long-term investments or cash received from selling any of these.

3. *Financing cash flows* related to receipts and payments of cash related to the financing of the company: cash paid or received to issue or repurchase the company's own stock, cash paid or received to issue or retire debt, and so on.

Accounting rules can vary internationally, but generally interest paid is included in the operating section, while dividends paid are included in the

TABLE 5-3

Walmart Statement of Cash Flows (Dollar amounts in millions)

	FYE 1/31/2011	Percentage of Revenue	FYE 1/31/2010	Percentage of Revenue
Revenues (from income statement)	418,952	100.0%	405,132	100.0%
Cash flows from operating activities				
Consolidated net income	16,993	4.1%	14,883	3.7%
Loss (income) from discontinued operations	(1,034)	(0.2%)	79	0.0%
Income from continuing operations	15,959	3.8%	14,962	3.7%
Adjustments to reconcile income to cash flow	7,684	1.8%	11,287	2.8%
Net cash provided by operating activities	23,643	5.6%	26,249	6.5%
Cash flows from investing activities				
Payments for property and equipment	(12,699)	(3.0%)	(12,184)	(3.0%)
Proceeds from the disposal of property and equipment	489	0.1%	1,002	0.2%
Investments and business acquisitions, net	(202)	0.0%	0	0.0%
Other investing activities	219	0.1%	(438)	(0.1%)
Net cash used in investing activities	(12,193)	(2.9%)	(11,620)	(2.9%)

(Continued)

TABLE 5-3

Walmart Statement of Cash Flows (*Continued*)

	FYE 1/31/2011	Percentage of Revenue	FYE 1/31/2010	Percentage of Revenue
Cash flows from financing activities				
Net change in short-term borrowings	503	0.1%	(1,033)	(0.3%)
Proceeds from issuance of long-term debt	11,396	2.7%	5,546	1.4%
Payments of long-term debt	(4,080)	(1.0%)	(6,033)	(1.5%)
Dividends paid	(4,437)	(1.1%)	(4,217)	(1.0%)
Purchase of company stock	(14,776)	(3.5%)	(7,276)	(1.8%)
Purchase of redeemable noncontrolling interests	0	0.0%	(436)	(0.1%)
Payment of capital lease obligations	(363)	(0.1%)	(346)	(0.1%)
Other financing activities	(271)	(0.1%)	(396)	(0.1%)
Net cash used in financing activities	(12,028)	(2.9%)	(14,191)	(3.5%)
Effect of exchange rates on cash and equivalents	66	0.0%	194	0.0%
Net increase (decrease) in cash and equivalents	(512)	(0.1%)	632	0.2%
Cash and equivalents at beginning of year	7,907		7,275	
Cash and equivalents at end of year	7,395		7,907	

financing section. Note that for the investing and financing sections the company shows the actual receipts and payments of cash, making them very easy to understand. Unfortunately, this is optional for the operating section. Most companies present that section just as Walmart does: they start with net income and adjust it to arrive at operating cash flow (we have added a line for revenue solely for the purpose of computing common size ratios, and we have lumped all of the adjustments into a single line item).

It isn't necessary to evaluate every line of the cash flow statement, although it is sometimes informative in the case of the investing and financing sections. Rather, it is generally best to start with the big picture. What are the company's major sources (and uses) of cash: operating, investing, or financing activities? Ideally, for a mature company, you will see most of the cash flows being generated from operating activities, while the company is using that cash to invest for the future (investing section) and return capital to investors and creditors (financing section). This is exactly what you see when looking at Walmart's cash flow statement. Walmart is generating about $25 billion from operating activities and spending about half of that amount on future investments and half effectively repaying investors and creditors.

For a relatively new or rapidly growing company you may see that the company is using cash rather than generating cash from operations. In that case they will likely be raising capital from investors and creditors to cover that cash outflow. If you are going to make an investment in such a company, you need to be confident that it will turn this around in the future. Many value investors prefer the certainty of companies that have already turned this corner and are generating sufficient operating cash flow to sustain themselves.

Within the operating section it is also useful to examine the relationship between net income and operating cash flow. Ideally, you would like to see operating cash flow higher than net income. In fact, over the long-term, operating cash flow should exceed net income due to noncash expenses like depreciation on equipment (remember cash paid for equipment belongs in the investing section). However, in any particular year, operating cash flow can be less than or greater than net income. For example, if the company is making a lot of credit sales to customers, the company will be generating net income but no cash flow from those sales in the current period. However, if you see that operating cash flow is consistently lower than net income, closer scrutiny of the details is warranted. The company could simply be in a growth phase, or it could be that it is having problems collecting from customers.

You can examine the investing section in more detail to determine where the company is making investments. In Walmart's case, the vast majority of investments are for property and equipment as they open new stores. A much smaller amount is used for acquisitions. As we will see later, an important concept for the value investor is free cash flow—how much excess cash flow the company generates from operations that could be used to repay owners. A simple measure of free cash flow (we will cover this concept more extensively in Chapter 8) is operating income minus capital expenditures (purchases of property and equipment). Value investors love to see companies that generate free cash flow because doing so indicates that the company can fund its own growth through operations with cash left over for the owners. It is good sign that management is avoiding unwise capital investments, choosing instead to (hopefully) return the excess cash to shareholders in the form of dividends or stock repurchases (see next paragraph). In Walmart's case, the company is generating about $11 billion of free cash flow.

Lastly, we can take a look at how the company is spending its free cash flow (or, alternatively, where it is getting financing to pay for any cash flow deficit) by examining the financing cash flow section. Walmart is spending most of its excess cash flow returning capital to shareholders through both dividends and repurchasing its own stock in the open market. This is a good sign for value investors: Investors are receiving cash flows through dividends, and the company likely views its own stock as undervalued. Interestingly, the company is also a net borrower. It is issuing more new debt than it is repaying, and this cash is supplementing the free cash flow to repurchase stock. This is very likely due to the low interest rate environment—management believes that they can earn more on borrowed funds than the cost of those funds—and we should expect to see the debt ratios on the balance sheet (see next section) increase somewhat, as well.

In a nutshell, Walmart's cash flow statement is just the type a value investor loves to see. Of course, we will still need to see if the stock is priced at an attractive level; it could be that the stock is selling at a premium due to the exceptional cash flow.

Understanding the Balance Sheet

The company's balance sheet shows the financial position at a particular point. It lists the company's assets (resources) such as cash, accounts receivable from credit sales to customers; inventory; investments; property and equipment; and intangible assets (i.e., patents). The balance sheet also shows who has claims against the resources of the company. There are two basic types of claims: liabilities and equity. Equity represents the claims of owners: common stockholders, preferred stockholders, and similar investors. Liabilities are the claims of everyone else: suppliers, banks, bondholders, and other creditors. Table 5-4 shows the balance sheet of Walmart.

The primary items you are looking for when analyzing the balance sheet are the company's liquidity and solvency. *Liquidity* is the company's ability to meet short-term obligations, while solvency is the company's ability to meet long-term obligations. Liquidity can be measured by looking the relationship between the company's current assets (those that are expected to be used up or converted into cash within a year) and the company's current liabilities (those liabilities that need to be satisfied within one year). Walmart has fewer current assets than current liabilities. This can be troubling for some companies, but in Walmart's case we saw its extraordinary operating cash flow. In essence, Walmart has strong

TABLE 5-4

Walmart Balance Sheet (Dollar amounts in millions)

Assets	FYE 1/31/2011	Percentage of Assets	Year-Over-Year Change	FYE 1/31/2010	Percentage of Assets
Current Assets					
Cash	7,395	4.1%	(6.48%)	7,907	4.6%
Receivables, net	5,089	2.8%	22.80%	4,144	2.4%
Inventories	36,318	20.1%	11.02%	32,713	19.2%
Prepaid expenses and other	2,960	1.6%	(5.37%)	3,128	1.8%
Current assets of discontinued operations	131	0.1%	(6.43%)	140	0.1%
Total Current Assets	51,893	28.7%	8.04%	48,032	28.2%
Property and equipment	148,584	82.2%	7.79%	137,848	80.9%
Less accumulated depreciation	(43,486)	(24.1%)	13.53%	(38,304)	(22.5%)
Property under capital leases	5,905	3.3%	4.16%	5,669	3.3%
Less accumulated depreciation	(3,125)	(1.7%)	7.54%	(2,906)	(1.7%)
Goodwill	16,763	9.3%	3.95%	16,126	9.5%
Other assets and deferred charges	4,129	2.3%	4.74%	3,942	2.3%
Total Assets	180,663	100.0%	6.02%	170,407	100.0%

(*Continued*)

TABLE 5-4

Walmart Balance Sheet (*Continued*)

Assets	FYE 1/31/2011	Percentage of Assets	Year-Over-Year Change	FYE 1/31/2010	Percentage of Assets
Current Liabilities					
Short-term borrowings	1,031	0.6%	97.13%	523	0.3%
Accounts payable	33,557	18.6%	10.20%	30,451	17.9%
Accrued liabilities	18,701	10.4%	(0.18%)	18,734	11.0%
Accrued income taxes	157	0.1%	(88.34%)	1,347	0.8%
Long-term debt due within year	4,655	2.6%	14.94%	4,050	2.4%
Obligations under capital leases	336	0.2 %	(2.89%)	346	0.2%
Current liabilities of discontinued operations	47	0.0%	(48.91%)	92	0.1%
Total Current Liabilities	58,484	32.4%	5.29%	55,543	32.6%
Long-term debt	40,692	22.5%	22.45%	33,231	19.5%
Long-term obligations under capital leases	3,150	1.7%	(0.63%)	3,170	1.9%
Deferred income taxes and other	6,682	3.7%	21.31%	5,508	3.2%
Redeemable noncontrolling interest	408	0.2%	32.90%	307	0.2%
Total liabilities	109,416	60.6%	11.92%	97,759	57.4%
Equity					
Common stock	3,929	2.2%	(6.03%)	4,181	2.5%
Retained earnings	63,967	35.4%	(3.60%)	66,357	38.9%
Accumulated other comp. income	646	0.4%	(1022.86%)	(70)	0.0%
Noncontrolling interest	2,705	1.5%	24.08%	2,180	1.3%
Total Liabilities and Equity	180,663	100.0%	6.02%	170,407	100.0%

cash-generating power in addition to the current assets on the balance sheet, so it is unlikely the company would not be able to meet current obligations.

We can also look at the liquidity of current assets, both in dollars and as a percentage of total assets. Cash is the most liquid current asset, whereas receivables need to be collected and inventory needs to be sold before cash is ultimately received. Overall, Walmart's current assets as a percentage of assets have increased slightly, but the increase largely came from inventory (which is not the most liquid of current assets).

In terms of *solvency* we can look at the extent of Walmart's use of debt relative to equity to finance the purchase of assets. The more debt, the more financial leverage the company is using and the less solvency it has (but not necessarily insolvency). Insolvency is a situation in which the company has large amounts of debt or other liabilities and is unable to repay those amounts. In some cases, liabilities may exceed assets (owners equity would be negative in this case). Some level of debt and liabilities is not bad. In fact, we will see later that the judicious use of leverage can help a firm generate profits and cash flow for its owners. For Walmart, current liabilities as a percentage of assets have not changed much, but total liabilities have increased quite a bit as a percentage of assets. (Recall from our earlier discussion that this resulted from the net borrowing we saw on the company's cash flow statement.) Overall, the company's financial leverage has increased, but it is not terribly worrisome because it looks to be a purposeful response to the low interest rate environment. In addition, the stability of Walmart's operations support moderate debt levels well. Over time, a little over 60 percent of the capital of the company comes from liabilities with the balance having come from the owners. The owner's investment includes both the original purchases of shares of stock, as well as the reinvestment of net profits over time that have not yet been paid out as dividends (retained earnings).

RATIO ANALYSIS

In addition to the common size analysis of individual statements, ratio analysis is useful in comparing a company's performance to itself over time (time-series analysis) or to other companies at a point in time (cross-sectional analysis). In fact, common size data is a form of ratio analysis. The financial performance or position in one period can be compared to that in prior periods to determine whether the company appears to be doing better or worse than in the past. This type of analysis is useful in identifying favorable or unfavorable trends. Additionally, we can make comparisons of a company's ratios to similar firms or to industry norms for the same time period to evaluate how the company is doing relative to peers.

A virtually unlimited number of ratios can be computed from the various available financial statements and other metrics. In this chapter we explore the most common ratios, which can be categorized as shown in Figure 5-1.

The first four categories of ratios address particular aspects of a firm's operations, investments, financing, and profitability. The fifth category is an

FIGURE 5-1

Types of ratios.

> Activity Ratios
>
> • Evaluate how efficiently the company is operating the business.

> Liquidity Ratios
>
> • Evaluate the company's ability to meet short-term obligations.

> Solvency Ratios
>
> • Evaluate the company's ability to meet long-term obligations.

> Profitability Ratios
>
> • Evaluate the ability of the company to generate profits relative to revenue, invested assets, and owners' equity investment.

> Cash Flow Ratios
>
> • Evaluate the company's ability to generate sufficient cash flow to fund growth and pay creditors and investors.

> Price Multiples
>
> • Evaluate the price of the company relative to underlying fundamentals.

alternative approach to that typically seen which considers an important factor for value investors: operating cash flow. The sixth category addresses how the market currently values the company relative to underlying factors, which is also a critical consideration for value investors. Not surprisingly, these ratios are all related; a company with poor profitability and low efficiency should trade at a low price multiple relative to peers. In this section we examine each of these categories of ratios in turn and then explore how these ratios are linked together. We have selected common ratios to represent each category. There are certainly numerous variations of these ratios, as well as other ratios that are used within each category. You should view this list as a simple sampling of potential ratios that may be applied to firms. Other ratios exist and are widely used, particularly those that are relevant to specific industries.

Activity Ratios

As a group, these ratios address how day-to-day operations function. They present information about how well the company manages inventory, collects cash from customers, and how efficient they are at managing their overall investment in assets.

Inventory Management.   The manufacturing firm has several classes of inventory, including raw materials, work in progress, and finished goods. The retail firm carries only merchandise inventory; but, depending on the type of firm, there may be hundreds or thousands of different types of merchandise that must be managed. The inventory management ratios provide one way to examine how efficiently firms manage their inventory overall. These ratios include the following:

Inventory turnover:

$$\frac{\text{Cost of Goods Sold}}{\text{Average Total Inventory}}$$

Days inventory:

$$\frac{365}{\text{Inventory Turnover}}$$

The first ratio, inventory turnover, combines an item from the income statement (cost of goods sold) with an item from the balance sheet (total inventory). The resulting number indicates how many times inventory was acquired and then sold over the year. A higher number means higher efficiency. You have to be careful comparing inventory turnover for firms from different industries. For instance, retail grocers will have much higher inventory turnover ratios than aerospace manufacturers.

Note that with this ratio, and any others that combine income statement and balance sheet items, the formulas typically indicate use of an average for the balance sheet number. This reflects the fact that the income statement number is a measure across a span of time, while a balance sheet number is a measure determined at a single point in time. Averaging the balance sheet measure over multiple points in time provides a more comparable number to the income statement number if the amounts differ significantly at different balance sheet dates throughout the reporting period. Frequently this average is calculated simply as the sum of beginning and ending inventory, divided by two. Note that you will often obtain ratios from online services and databases. Some of these services do not use this averaging convention. In fact, some databases use different formula variations for ratios. It is acceptable to use such sources, but you always want to be aware of potential differences and that ratios may be skewed for rapidly growing or shrinking firms (as year-end numbers may be dramatically different than average numbers over the year).

An easier ratio to interpret is the days inventory ratio which is computed using inventory turnover. The days inventory ratio indicates how many days, on average, inventory was held before it was sold. The longer that inventory must be held and stored before being used or sold, the greater the storage costs, likelihood of spoilage, theft, or other deterioration, and the greater overall inventory holding costs will be. A lower number means higher efficiency at managing inventory.

Receivables Management.   Operating cash is generated when inventory is sold and customers subsequently pay for their purchases. Ratios that address how well the company manages the collection of receivables include two related ratios: accounts receivable turnover and days sales outstanding.

Box 5-2 Application: Evaluating Days Inventory

Days inventory for Walmart (WMT) and Target (TGT) are presented below for three years. On average, Walmart maintains a lower level of inventory than Target (around 40 days versus around 55 to 60). Walmart appears to be more efficient at managing inventory than Target; however, some of this difference is attributable to disparities in the nature of the inventories of the two firms. Walmart has a higher proportion of grocery items, particularly in its Sam's Club segment, which turn over more rapidly. We should also look at the trend over time. Over the three-year period, Walmart has improved its management of inventory with a steadily declining ratio. Target, on the other hand, has been quite variable, and its days inventory increased in the most recent year.

Days Inventory			
	2010	2009	2008
WMT	40.0	40.3	41.8
TGT	59.0	57.5	55.7

Accounts receivable turnover:

$$\frac{\text{Credit Sales Revenues}}{\text{Average Accounts Receivable}}$$

Days sales outstanding:

$$\frac{365}{\text{Accounts Receivable Turnover}}$$

The accounts receivable turnover ratio indicates how many times over the year a credit sale is made to a customer and subsequently collected. This ratio is higher as more credit sales are made over the period. The days sales outstanding ratio (also known as the days receivable ratio) uses the calculated turnover to illustrate how many days are required to collect the average customer account. As the turnover ratio is higher, the number of days between the credit sale and collection of the cash is lower, reducing the cost of operating cash tied up in receivables from customers.

Asset Turnover.   As an owner of a business, you have an interest in how efficiently a company is using all of its investments in assets. A useful ratio is the total asset turnover ratio:

$$\frac{\text{Sales Revenues}}{\text{Average Total Assets}}$$

Box 5-3 Application: Evaluating Days Sales Outstanding

The following are days sales outstanding for Walmart and Target for three recent years. Walmart collects most of its sales immediately (in cash or credit card receipts) and as a result has very little receivables relative to sales. Target, on the other hand, issues its own credit card and as a result, on average, collects from sales in 35 to 45 days. This difference illustrates that it is important to understand the business when interpreting the ratios. Note that Target has improved its efficiency at collecting sales revenue over the three-year period.

Days Sales Outstanding			
	2010	2009	2008
WMT	4.0	3.6	3.4
TGT	35.5	42.0	45.3

This measure shows how efficient a company is at generating revenues for a given level of total assets. For example, a ratio of 1.0 would indicate that a company is generating $1 of sales for every $1 invested in total assets. A higher number is generally better than a lower number. Additionally, if this ratio is trending lower, it may indicate that the firm is making heavy investments in assets in anticipation of sales growth that has not yet materialized but should in the future.

Box 5-4 Application: Evaluating Total Asset Turnover

The total asset turnover ratio for Walmart and Target are presented below for three recent years. Walmart is very efficient in generating sales relative to assets invested with an asset turnover ratio of 2.4. Walmart generates $2.4 of revenue for every $1 invested in assets. Target is less efficient, generating $1.5 of revenue for every $1 in assets. This is in large part due to Target making credit sales through its own credit card operations and holding inventory for longer periods of time than Walmart. Both companies have been relatively stable over time.

Total Asset Turnover			
	2010	2009	2008
WMT	2.4	2.4	2.5
TGT	1.5	1.5	1.5

Liquidity Ratios

This category of ratios enables you to assess the company's ability to meet its short-term obligations. This set of ratios is based on current assets and current liabilities and, as such, is directly related to short-term operating health. These ratios are focused primarily on the short-term cash needs of the firm. Some of the ratios discussed in the section above under activity ratios, such as cash cycle, are also measures of liquidity.

Current and Quick Ratios. These ratios are measured using balance sheet numbers, so they describe the firm at the particular date of that financial statement. Therefore, no averaging is necessary. The current ratio:

$$\frac{\text{Current Assets}}{\text{Current Liabilities}}$$

indicates whether, at the balance sheet date, the company has adequate assets that are either currently cash or are readily convertible into cash over the next year to cover the liabilities that will be due over that same time period. A current ratio greater than one indicates positive working capital (defined as current assets – current liabilities).

A modification of the current ratio incorporates the fact that not all current assets are readily (or ever) converted to cash. This modification, the quick ratio (also called the acid-test ratio), removes from current assets the least liquid assets. The typical removals include inventories and prepaid expenses. Whereas accounts receivable represent a contractual claim against a customer who has already purchased goods or services from the firm, inventories must be sold before they can represent potential cash inflow. Prepaid expenses will not be converted into cash at all, but rather represent costs already paid and, therefore, not requiring further cash outflow during the period. The analyst may also remove any other specific current asset that shares these characteristics. It is useful to consider which current assets typically remain in the ratio: cash, short-term (liquid) investments, and accounts receivable. Then the quick ratio formula appears as follows:

$$\frac{\text{Cash} + \text{Short-Term Investments} + \text{Accounts Receivable}}{\text{Current Liabilities}}$$

As with the current ratio, if this ratio is greater than one, there are more than enough "quick" assets to cover the liabilities that will become due in the next year.

Box 5-5 Application: Evaluating Liquidity Ratios

The current ratio and quick ratio for both Walmart and Target are provided below for several recent years. The current ratio indicates that Walmart has less than $1 of current assets for every $1 of current liabilities whereas Target has 1.7 times as many current assets as current liabilities. The quick ratio is substantially lower for each company than the current ratio because each company has large amounts of inventory. Target, however, still has ample "quick" current assets available to pay current liabilities, while Walmart does not. This indicates higher risk/lower liquidity for Walmart. This is, however, largely mitigated by the strong cash flow Walmart has coming in from operations, funds that are also available to pay these obligations.

Current Ratio			
	2010	2009	2008
WMT	0.9	0.9	0.9
TGT	1.7	1.6	1.7

Quick Ratio			
	2010	2009	2008
WMT	0.2	0.2	0.2
TGT	0.8	0.8	0.9

Solvency Ratios

This category of ratios can be used to assess the ability of the company to meet its long-term obligations. The group also represents the relative weights of the two types of long-term financing within the firm: debt and equity. When a firm raises debt capital, it is borrowing money with a promise to repay principal and make periodic interest payments. Failure to make these payments results in default and in the extreme can result in bankruptcy and liquidation. When a firm raises capital by selling equity (stock), it typically has no such obligation—although there may be an expectation of periodic dividends (particularly in the case of preferred stock).

Higher levels of debt mean higher risk and lower solvency (the ability to meet long-term obligations). However, judicious use of debt is also advantageous. If the borrowed funds are used to support projects that are expected to earn a return greater than the borrowing costs, then that excess return accrues to the stockholders. For now, let's focus on ratios that measure how solvent a company is, and we will revisit the benefit side of borrowing later in the chapter.

Debt Ratio.   A simple debt ratio can be gleaned from a common size balance sheet by taking total liabilities as a percentage of total assets:

$$\frac{\text{Total Liabilities}}{\text{Total Assets}}$$

This ratio measures the proportion of assets financed using liabilities, that is, resources from external claimholders. This version of the ratio includes many liabilities other than pure debt (such as accounts payable) so it is a comprehensive measure of risk.

Debt-to–Total Capital

There are several variations of debt ratios, which reflect relative weights of different components of debt and equity financing. Because total liabilities includes many items such as accounts payable and accrued expenses that do not require interest payments and are a part of working capital, many analysts compute the debt ratios in a more precise fashion: They include only interest-bearing debt in both the numerator and denominator. The debt-to–total capital ratio is:

$$\frac{\text{Short-Term Debt + Long-Term Debt}}{\text{Short-Term Debt + Long-Term Debt + Equity}}$$

Short-term debt is sometimes classified as the current portion of long-term debt and represents the interest-bearing, borrowed portion of current liabilities.

Box 5-6 Application: Evaluating Solvency Ratios

The debt ratio and debt-to–total capital ratios for Walmart and Target are presented here for the last several years. The debt ratio shows that Walmart finances its assets about 60 percent with liabilities (and hence 40 percent with stockholders equity), while Target finances its assets about two-thirds with liabilities. Looking solely at interest-bearing debt, Walmart raises 40 percent of its capital from debt, while Target raises just over 50 percent from debt. Target has slightly higher risk in terms of level of debt, but both companies' debt levels are reasonable relative to other retailers.

Debt Ratio (Using Total Liabilities)			
	2010	2009	2008
WMT	60.6%	57.4%	59.0%
TGT	64.6%	65.5%	68.9%
Debt-to–Total Capital			
	2010	2009	2008
WMT	41.2%	36.3%	38.6%
TGT	50.4%	52.3%	57.8%

Coverage Ratios.   Another way of looking at level of debt, and the company's ability to repay that debt, is to compute a coverage ratio from the income statement. One such measure of how well the company can cover (or pay) its interest obligations is the interest coverage ratio, or times interest earned ratio, computed as follows:

$$\frac{\text{Earnings Before Interest and Tax Expense}}{\text{Interest Expense}}$$

In calculating this measure, interest and taxes are added back to net earnings, since interest is deductible for tax purposes, to arrive at earnings before interest and tax (EBIT). This ratio is less than one if interest expense has put the firm in the position of having a net loss. If this ratio equals one, there are just enough pretax, pre-interest earnings to cover interest. The interest deduction will then offset the pretax income and eliminate any income taxes, but no earnings are produced or retained for the stockholders. Ideally, this ratio will be much greater than one, indicating adequate coverage of these costs. Since interest payments are typically due each year (or reporting period), interest coverage can be an indicator of the firm's ability to meet these obligations.

Other coverage ratios, in which the denominator includes further desired commitments, can be used to reflect that interest costs are not the only contractual obligations. Coverage ratios, based on numbers from the income statement, can be very helpful in making projections because the balance sheet does not contain some types of obligations, such as those created by operating leases, that nevertheless require future payments. Those costs, such as rent expense, are reflected in the earnings number, providing a more precise measure of the resources that have been generated and retained in the business. A coverage ratio can be computed incorporating rent expense:

$$\frac{\text{EBIT} + \text{Rent Expense}}{\text{Interest Expense} + \text{Rent Expense}}$$

Box 5-7 Application: Evaluating Interest Coverage

The times interest earned ratio for Walmart and Target are presented here. This ratio shows that Walmart's pretax earnings cover their interest costs twelve times over. Walmart should have no problems making scheduled interest payments. Target's ratio is lower, reflecting its higher use of debt financing. However, Target can certainly more than cover its interest payments. Further Target's interest coverage has improved over the three-year period.

Times Interest Earned			
	2010	2009	2008
WMT	12.7	12.7	12.0
TGT	6.9	5.8	5.1

Profitability Ratios

Profitability ratios, also called return ratios, are a keen area of focus for value investors. Profitability or returns can be measured against revenues of the firm (as was done using common size analysis earlier in this chapter) or based on how much has been invested in the company.

Common Size Ratios.   The computation of net profit margin, also known as return on sales, is an example of a common size ratio:

$$\frac{\text{Net Income}}{\text{Sales Revenues}}$$

A common size ratio measures each item on a financial statement as a percentage of sales revenue. The following profitability ratios are found directly on the vertical common size income statement:

Gross profit margin

Operating margin

Pretax margin

Net profit margin

The analysis of these common size amounts was demonstrated earlier in the chapter.

Return Ratios.   Another method of measuring profitability is to calculate the return relative to investments in the firm. Profitability ratios that measure the return to a specified investment include return on assets and return on owners' equity. Return on assets (ROA) measures the return generated by the firm on the investment in total assets:

$$\frac{\text{Net Income}}{\text{Average Total Assets}}$$

For example, a firm with total assets of $1,000,000 that generates net income of $65,000 has a return on assets of 6.5 percent. For every $100 invested in assets, the firm generated $6.50 in net income. Obviously, a higher return is preferred to a lower return.

Since net income represents the return generated for the benefit of owners, another commonly used return measure is return on equity (ROE).

$$\frac{\text{Net Income}}{\text{Average Total Owner's Equity}}$$

Return on equity measures the return generated relative to the capital provided by the owners over time. For example, if a firm had total owners' equity of $500,000 and generated net income of $50,000, it would have ROE of 10 percent. For every $100 invested by owners, the firm is generating $10 in annual net income. Conceptually, this is a key metric for stockholders, although it is influenced by quite a few accounting conventions.

Box 5-8 Application: Evaluating Profitability Ratios

Return on assets (ROA) and return on equity (ROE) for Walmart and Target are listed on the next page. Walmart's ROA has been increasing over the three-year period and is quite good at 9.7 percent. For every $100 invested in assets, Walmart is currently generating $9.70 in profits. Target's ROA has also been increasing but substantially lags that of Walmart. Target's ROE of 18.9 percent lags Walmart's ROE of 23.6 percent, indicating that it does not do as well generating profits as Walmart relative to the investments in the company by the stockholders. Note that ROE has been increasing for both firms and that the difference between the two firms' ROE ratios is not as extreme as for ROA. This is due to Target's use of greater leverage: By borrowing more, the company increased the return to shareholders relative to what it would have been with less leverage. We will discuss this concept in more detail later.

Return on Assets			
	2010	2009	2008
WMT	9.7%	8.9%	8.5%
TGT	6.6%	5.6%	5.0%
Return on Equity			
	2010	2009	2008
WMT	23.6%	21.3%	21.1%
TGT	18.9%	17.1%	15.3%

Cash Flow Ratios

Cash flow–based ratios have become increasingly popular in recent years. While accounting profits are nice, employees, creditors, and investors prefer to get paid in cash. Additionally, some firms have been aggressive (in an accounting sense) in reporting earnings. An examination of cash flow ratios can provide insight into the quality of a firm's earnings. You can replace earnings in virtually any ratio with some measure of cash flow. In this section, we highlight some useful cash flow–based ratios.

A firm's ability to pay its obligations can be measured by the ratio of operating cash flow to liabilities:

$$\frac{\text{CFO}}{\text{Total Liabilities}}$$

CFO is cash flow from operating activities from the statement of cash flows. This ratio represents the percentage of total liabilities that can be paid with one year's operating cash flows. Keep in mind that the firm may also have assets on the balance sheet available to pay liabilities. This ratio can also be calculated considering only long-term debt in the denominator as opposed to total liabilities.

A firm's profitability on a cash flow basis relative to sales can be computed as an operating cash margin:

$$\frac{CFO}{Sales\ Revenue}$$

The ratio presents the percentage of revenue reflected in operating cash flow. A ratio of 5 percent indicates that the firm is generating $5 of cash flow from operating activities for every $100 of sales.

Similarly, we can compute a cash return on assets as:

$$\frac{CFO}{Average\ Total\ Assets}$$

A result of, say, 10 percent would indicate that the firm is generating $10 of operating cash flow for every $100 of total assets.

Taken together, the above ratios assess the company's ability to generate cash flow. Comparing these ratios to their earnings-based equivalents also provides insight into the quality of the company's earnings. For example, if the earnings-based ratios show strong profitability, but the cash flow–based ratios show an inability to generate cash flows, this could indicate poor earnings quality. However, it can also indicate a rapidly growing firm, so this analysis should serve only as a starting point. If earnings and cash flow–based ratios are out of sync, then you should take a close look at the accounting methods and estimates used by the firm. Later in this chapter, we will address this further.

Another way to examine earnings quality using cash flow is to compare cash flow from operating activities to net income. We can create a ratio to make this comparison, which we call a cash flow–earnings index:

$$\frac{CFO}{Net\ Income}$$

In any single year, this ratio can be higher or lower than one. Over the long term, however, the ratio should exceed one. This is because noncash charges (primarily depreciation) are deducted from net income but do not represent an operating cash outflow. In fact, the cash flow related to depreciable assets occurs when the asset is acquired and is classified as an investing cash outflow. As with the above discussion, if this ratio is consistently below one or declining, it is indicative of a potential problem with earnings quality. If this occurs, special attention must be paid to accounting issues, addressed later in this chapter.

A firm's operating cash flow should ideally be sufficient to pay for capital expenditures. A firm's free cash flow ratio can be computed as:

$$\frac{CFO}{Capital\ Expenditures}$$

A ratio greater than one indicates the existence of free cash flow: operating cash flows in excess of those needed to fund capital expenditures. Free cash flow is a key metric for value investors. Free cash flow can be used to pay debt and dividends. It can also be used to return cash to shareholders through stock buybacks or to acquire other companies or assets. One of the most common methods of valuing a company is to take the present value of the future free cash flow (in dollars as opposed to the ratio presented here) it is expected to generate. The more free cash flow a company can generate, the more valuable it is. This is the subject of Chapter 8.

Box 5-9 Application: Evaluating Cash Flow–Based Ratios

The following are cash flow ratios for Walmart and Target for several recent years. Walmart's cash flow is stronger on all metrics (and quite good compared to most other companies as well). The free cash flow ratio is strong for both companies: They generate more than enough operating cash flow to make needed capital expenditures, leaving plenty of cash to pay debts, pay dividends, or buy back stock.

Cash Flow–Based Ratios: CFO/Total Liabilities			
	2010	2009	2008
WMT	21.6%	26.9%	24.0%
TGT	18.7%	20.2%	14.6%
Cash Flow–Based Ratios: CFO/Sales			
	2010	2009	2008
WMT	5.6%	6.4%	5.7%
TGT	7.8%	9.0%	6.8%
Cash Flow–Based Ratios: CFO/Total Assets			
	2010	2009	2008
WMT	13.5%	15.7%	14.2%
TGT	11.9%	13.3%	10.0%
Cash Flow–Based Ratios: Free Cash Flow Ratio or Index			
	2010	2009	2008
WMT	1.9	2.2	2.0
TGT	2.5	3.4	1.2

Price Multiple Ratios

These ratios are commonly described as price multiples or market multiples. They are also useful in examining the relative valuation of the firm compared to its peers and the market as a whole. Generally speaking, as value investors we prefer to buy stocks that are inexpensive relative to other similar companies. If we were considering two companies with similar profitability, cash flow, liquidity, solvency, and efficiency we would prefer to buy the one with the lower price multiple.

Price/Earnings Ratio.   The price-to-earnings (P/E) ratio is widely used as a measure of the market's valuation of a firm's common stock.

$$P/E = \frac{\text{Share Price}}{\text{Earnings Per Share}}$$

A high P/E indicates that the firm is highly valued by the market, while a low P/E indicates that the firm is not highly valued. A low multiple might indicate that the firm is a bargain (a value stock) if the firm has strong fundamentals (for example, profitability and financial condition). A low multiple might also indicate that the firm is appropriately valued due to poor future prospects.

Overall, stocks traded at record P/E levels in the late 1990s. With the mean price/earnings ratio (P/E) on the Standard and Poor's 500 Index at over 30 and the median in the mid-twenties, some stocks were trading at multiples of 100 or more. Contrast that with a longer-term median in the mid-teens (specifically P/Es of 14 to 16). Many attributed these multiples to the "new economy" or to the high expected growth rates of the Internet-related companies. Others attributed the multiples to a "market bubble" akin to tulipmania (the Dutch bubble that occurred in 1637 for tulip bulbs, where investors were willing to pay up to a year's salary for a single tulip bulb because they hoped to sell it to someone else for more). The Internet bubble, similar to its tulip predecessor, burst in spectacular fashion. Stock prices fell dramatically in the early 2000s, although the P/E multiple of many securities and the market as a whole remained higher than the long-term average for some time thereafter. The recent market crisis has brought multiples closer to long-term historical levels. In a later chapter, we will discuss what reasonable multiples might be, considering the level of market interest rates, as well as risk and growth prospects.

Price/Book Ratio.   The price-to-book ratio (P/B) is the stock price per share divided by the book value per share. Book value per share is total common stockholders equity divided by total shares outstanding.

$$\text{Price/Book} = \frac{\text{Share Price}}{(\text{Book Value of Equity/Shares Outstanding})}$$

A high price-to-book ratio indicates that the market is valuing the firm richly compared to the accounting book value of the underlying net assets. Firms with strong profitability and growth prospects tend to have high P/B ratios. A firm with a P/B ratio of one can indicate that the firm's return on equity is equal to investor's required rate of return. The firm is not creating any value for shareholders and is selling for its underlying net asset value. The price-to-book ratio reflects the growth in the market value of the stock beyond the investment of the stockholders and the reinvestment of any earnings retained in the firm.

Price/Sales Ratio.   Another commonly used price multiple is the price-to-sales (P/S) ratio. This is computed as:

$$Price/Sales = \frac{Share\ Price}{Sales\ Per\ Share}$$

As with the P/E and P/B ratios, this ratio measures the market's relative valuation of a security. Here the value is relative to sales. This ratio is sometimes used when a firm has negligible or even negative earnings. Some caution must be applied when using this ratio in identifying securities for investment. A firm might have a low P/S ratio and poor prospects for future earnings and cash flow. The P/S ratio should be interpreted in the context of the firm's other ratios such as activity, liquidity, solvency, and profitability ratios.

Price/Cash Flow Ratio.   The price-to–cash flow measure is similar to the P/E ratio but can be used where it is desirable to evaluate firms on a cash flow rather than earnings basis. For example, this ratio might be employed if earnings quality is questionable. For example, you think the company has manipulated accounting assumptions to make earnings look better. The price/cash flow ratio has several different variations. The numerator is the price per share as in the above ratios, while the denominator can be operating cash flow per share, free cash flow per share, or some approximation of cash flow, such as earnings before interest, taxes, depreciation, and amortization (EBITDA).[4] Direct cash flow measures are generally preferable to approximations because earnings can be heavily influenced by the choice of accounting methods and assumptions.

INTEGRATION OF RATIOS

The overall return to equity holders is a function of the operating profitability, efficiency, leverage, and taxes. The relationship of ratios reflecting these components can be linked algebraically to return on equity. This process is often termed decomposition of ROE. It is also sometimes referred to as DuPont analysis, after the corporation where this method was first employed in the 1920s. In this section we first examine the relationship of ROE to ROA and leverage. We then examine the individual components driving ROE and the relationship to market value.

ROE and Leverage

Let's take a look at a basic example to examine the relationship among ROE, ROA, and the use of leverage. Consider a company, Cayse Logistics Company (CLC), which has total assets of $1,000,000, a tax rate of 30 percent, and a pretax, pre-interest (EBIT) return on assets of 9 percent (for every $100 of assets the company generates EBIT of $9). The firm is financed 100 percent with equity, so there is no interest expense. CLC's annual operating results are:

EBIT	$90,000 (9% of $1,000,000)
Taxes	(27,000)
Net Income	$63,000
ROA (net of interest and taxes)	6.3%
ROE	6.3%

Since the firm has no debt, its ROA and ROE are equal. All capital is provided by owners' equity.

What happens if we introduce leverage into the example? Assume that the company is providing a product or service with virtually unlimited demand and that the company can borrow on a pretax basis at 8 percent annually. Thus, the company can expand its sales along with its assets and continue to achieve EBIT equal to 9 percent of total assets. CLC borrows $1,000,000 and now has total assets of $2,000,000. Its financial results are:

EBIT	$180,000
Interest	(80,000)
EBT	$100,000 (Earnings before taxes)
Taxes	(30,000)
Net Income	$70,000
ROA (net)	3.5%
ROE	7.0%

Note that while the company's pretax, pre-interest ROA was constant at 9 percent, the company's net ROA has declined to 3.5 percent. This reflects the impact of interest expense on the after-tax return. While the net ROA has declined, ROE has increased. This represents a positive aspect of leverage. The company was able to borrow at 8 percent pretax and invest these funds in the business at 9 percent pretax. This added value accrues to the shareholders, resulting in the increase of ROE to 7 percent (from 6.3 percent).

Of course there can also be a negative aspect to leverage. If the firm borrowed at a cost higher than the return expected to be earned in the business, value and ROE would decline. For example, assume the same facts except that the pretax cost of debt was 10 percent. With total assets of $2,000,000 financed 50 percent with debt and 50 percent with equity, the financial results would have been:

EBIT	$180,000
Interest	(100,000)
EBT	$80,000
Taxes	(24,000)
Net Income	$56,000
ROA (net)	2.8%
ROE	5.6%

In this case, both ROA and ROE declined relative to what they would have been with no debt.

The relationship of ROE, ROA, and leverage can be depicted as:

$$ROE = ROA \times Leverage$$

or

$$\frac{Net\ Income}{Average\ Total\ Equity} = \frac{Net\ Income}{Average\ Total\ Assets} \times \frac{Average\ Total\ Assets}{Average\ Total\ Equity}$$

Leverage is measured as assets divided by equity. A ratio of one would mean that no leverage was used and that assets were financed entirely with equity. For TLC above, the leverage ratio would be 2.0. For this reason, ROE is 2.0 times ROA.

In viewing the formula decomposing ROE into two components, ROA and leverage, it is tempting to see leverage as a positive factor. Remember, however, that leverage also has an impact on ROA. Additional leverage results in additional interest expense, reducing ROA. Leverage is beneficial when the cost of borrowing is lower than the pretax, pre-interest return earned on investing the proceeds in the business. On the other hand, leverage can be detrimental when the cost of borrowing exceeds the return generated on the proceeds. This is why leverage is often referred to as a double-edged sword.

We can also use algebraic relationships to decompose ROA into two components: profit margin and turnover (the latter is sometimes called efficiency). This is the result of the following formula:

$$ROA = Profitablity \times Turnover$$

or

$$\frac{Net\ Income}{Average\ Total\ Assets} = \frac{Net\ Income}{Sales} = \frac{Sales}{Average\ Total\ Assets}$$

From this decomposition we can see that return on assets is a function of the profitability of the firm and its efficiency. A firm can increase ROA by improving profitability, improving efficiency, or both.

The underlying factors that affect ROE can be examined more precisely by decomposing the ratio into three components, using the preceding relationships. ROE is the product of profitability, efficiency, and leverage:

$$\text{ROE} = \text{Profitability} \times \text{Turnover} \times \text{Leverage}$$

or

$$\frac{\text{Net Income}}{\text{Average Total Equity}} = \frac{\text{Net Income}}{\text{Sales}} \times \frac{\text{Sales}}{\text{Average Total Equity}}$$

$$\times \frac{\text{Average Total Assets}}{\text{Average Total Equity}}$$

The first factor, profit margin, indicates the proportion of each revenue dollar that flows to income for retention in the business (or distribution to shareholders). The second factor, asset efficiency or turnover, indicates how much revenue activity is generated on the total assets acquired to run the business. The third factor, leverage, indicates the extent to which the firm has chosen to increase its asset base beyond the investment of the stockholders by using debt. Identification of these factors highlights where in the business model the firm can try to increase return on equity.

Actions taken to increase sales will increase turnover but will decrease profitability unless the sales increase also increases net income. A decrease in costs will also increase net income, leading to an increase in profitability. Improvement of the operational components, revenues and costs, improve the core business processes of the firm. The ROE can also be improved by acquiring more assets using debt (assuming the cost of borrowing is favorable relative to the return to be earned in the business).

ROE can be decomposed further by breaking down profitability into its underlying factors.

$$\text{ROE} = \text{Taxes} \times \text{Financing} \times \text{Operation Profit} \times \text{Turnover} \times \text{Leverage}$$

or

$$\frac{\text{Net Income}}{\text{Average Total Equity}} = \frac{\text{Net Income}}{\text{EBT}} \times \frac{\text{EBT}}{\text{EBIT}} \times \frac{\text{EBIT}}{\text{Sales}}$$

$$\times \frac{\text{Sales}}{\text{Average Total Assets}} \times \frac{\text{Average Total Assets}}{\text{Average Total Equity}}$$

From this decomposition we can see that there are five primary factors impacting ROE: the impact of taxes, the cost of financing, operating profitability, efficiency, and leverage. This breakdown enables you to examine which of these factors are driving ROE, both over time and in comparison to peer companies.

Box 5-10 Application: Evaluating ROE

Why did Walmart's return on equity increase from 21.1 percent to 23.6 percent over the three-year period from 2008 to 2010? Was the company more profitable, more efficient, or did it use more leverage? Below shows a breakdown of Walmart's ROE into the five factors contributing to its trend. From 2008 to 2009 Walmart's efficiency (turnover) and leverage declined slightly, but its operating profit margin more than offset this decline, increasing from 5.6 percent to 5.9 percent. As a result, there was a small increase in ROE. From 2009 to 2010 there was a larger increase in ROE coming from two factors: an increase in operating margin to 6.1 percent and a lower tax rate (the company kept 72 percent after taxes, meaning there was a 28 percent average tax rate in 2010 versus 33 percent in 2008 and 2009).

Decomposition of Walmart ROE						
	ROE	Taxes	Financing	Operating Profit	Turnover	Leverage
2010	23.6%	0.72	0.92	6.1%	2.4	2.4
2009	21.3%	0.67	0.92	5.9%	2.4	2.4
2008	21.1%	0.67	0.92	5.6%	2.5	2.5

ACCOUNTING GAMES COMPANIES PLAY

The amount of discretion that management has in how results are actually reported can have a significant impact on an evaluation of a company's performance and financial position. While there are accounting standards that companies must follow—International Financial Reporting Standards and United States Generally Accepted Accounting Standards, depending on where the securities are issued and sold—these standards permit some discretion in reporting, and quite a few estimates and assumptions are required. For example, if a company buys a machine for its factory that costs $500,000 and estimates that it will last five years under normal use of one shift per day, five days per week, it would estimate that the machine is declining in value $100,000 per year and would record depreciation expense in this amount each year on the income statement. An unscrupulous manager might manipulate the amount of depreciation by saying the machine will last 10 years, cutting depreciation expense to only $50,000 annually. Why allow management this discretion? Two companies acquiring the same machine may use it differently: One might use it six days a week for two shifts, for example, and another might only use it occasionally. Discretion exists for management to choose assumptions that match its particular circumstances.

There are quite a few areas within accounting standards that permit management to use appropriate discretion. Some managers may also simply ignore the standards and fraudulently report results that are actual departures from reality (Madoff and Enron likely come to mind). Forensic accounting is a complex topic beyond the scope of this book, but we present some warning signs you should consider. Existence of these signs may not mean the company is committing fraud, but they do mean you need to be careful and exercise due diligence or simply refrain from making the investment—there are plenty of fish in the sea![5]

- Aggressive Revenue Recognition
  - *Accounts receivable growing much faster than sales (days sales ratio increasing).* The company may be recording revenues before earned or may have substantially relaxed its credit sales policies.
  - *Positive and growing net income but persistently negative operating cash flow.* This could simply be a new start-up company where credit sales are being made, but for a company that is more mature, operating cash flow should catch up with net income. Operating cash flow is necessary to pay creditors and ultimately investors. Be wary of companies that have never generated operating cash flow or where cash flow suddenly turns negative for multiple periods.
  - *Revenues from revaluation of assets rather than sales in the ordinary course of business.* Companies simply cannot continue to revalue assets to create revenue.
- Understating Expenses
  - *Much longer depreciation and amortization periods used than peer companies.* Footnotes in financial statements list the accounting methods used and assumptions employed. Compare those for the subject company to others in the industry. More aggressive accounting treatment than industry norms may be signals of potential problems.
  - *Expenses deferred to future years.* Look for unusual assets on the balance sheet and language in the footnotes that indicate a portion of expenditures is being deferred to future years and amortized into the income statement as an expense in the future.
  - *Is inventory growing much faster than revenues (days inventory increasing)?* Overstating inventory is one method of understating expenses on the income statement. This could also indicate problems with selling inventory or the potential for later write downs if inventory becomes obsolete.
- Overstating Financial Position
  - *Does the company use significant assets that are not recorded on the balance sheet and have related obligations?* By using special purpose entities, a company can keep assets and liabilities off the

balance sheet and make its return on assets and debt ratios look discernibly better. Look for special purpose entities that are not consolidated on the balance sheet. The financial world became familiar with special purpose entities in the case of Enron, a firm that was prolific in their use.

- Related Party Transactions
  - *Did the company engage in any related party transactions: transactions with management or family members?* These transactions should be disclosed in the proxy statement. You should evaluate whether they are benefiting managers at the expense of shareholders.

OUTSIDE THE FINANCIAL STATEMENTS

In addition to the financial statements and related footnotes you should read every report issued by the company including proxy statements, prospectuses for new issues, quarterly reports, earnings releases, other SEC filings, and the like. Also listen in on analysts conference calls, where professional analysts often grill management on their performance. Not only will these documents and conference calls contain nuggets of information that may impact your view of the company but they also give you insight into the quality of management. The proxy statement and other SEC filings provide information about the backgrounds and compensation of management. If management has been in place for a while and is expected to stay, then past performance is likely a good indicator of management quality. If the executive team is new to the organization, then you should research performance at previous companies in order to project how the team members might fare at the current one. You want to see their compensation aligned with your interests, but not to exorbitant levels. Stock ownership is definitely a good indicator of close alignment. Stock options are also good, but to a limit: In the extreme, excessive stock options which do not cost management anything can encourage excessive risk taking. Lastly, when you listen to conference calls or management presentations you can get a feel for the quality of management: Are they forthcoming and transparent about both strengths and weaknesses of the company, or do they overemphasize the positives and avoid answering tough questions?

CONCLUSION

Making a strategic value investment means buying good companies at good prices. A thorough understanding of the company's past performance and current financial condition is necessary in order to determine if it is a good company. Analyzing the financial statements and related information will also help you understand what is beneath the surface—the main drivers of the company's performance. In the second section of this book we deal with the second aspect of making a strategic value investment: When is a good company selling at a good price?

MEASURING VALUE

CONCEPTS OF VALUE

We think the very term "value investing" is redundant. What is "investing" if it is not the act of seeking value at least sufficient to justify the amount paid?
—Warren Buffett, 1992,
letter to Berkshire Hathaway shareholders

One man's trash is another man's treasure. It's an old adage because it's true. Although the dichotomy between trash and treasure is a bit extreme, it does point out that not everyone has the same understanding of "value." There are many different measures of value, and it is worth taking a step back to distinguish one from another so we can speak in common terms.

This chapter discusses the meaning of value in the context of the valuation process. We discuss what is meant by different measures of absolute value. Often, financial press journalists toss around terms such as *intrinsic value* or *true value* without specifying their underlying assumptions. Understanding different measures of absolute value will help provide a benchmark against which you can measure relative value. We also clarify the methodologies that some popular financial data providers use to measure value and introduce the absolute and relative valuation models to be discussed in the remaining chapters of this section.

Upon completion of this chapter, you will have more insight about different terms you hear bandied about, understand the different valuation models you might use to assess the intrinsic value of a stock, and be better able to understand what is meant when pundits talk about "value" stocks (versus "growth" stocks).

VALUATION PROCESS

The valuation process involves five important steps. Each step follows from the one preceding it, and if you exclude one you are not really practicing value investing; you are playing a guessing game. The five steps, which are outlined in the seminal text *Equity Asset Valuation*, are:[1]

1. Understand the industry and the company
2. Forecast company performance
3. Select the right valuation model

4. Convert forecasts to valuation inputs

5. Apply and interpret the valuation model

We address each of these steps in turn.

Understand the Industry and the Company

It goes without saying that a proper analysis must be grounded in an understanding of the operating environment of the company. It involves scrutinizing the competitive forces that shape the industry, the key drivers for profitability in the industry, and the sources of competitive advantage. It also involves a familiarity with key industry metrics. Chapter 4 provides an in-depth discussion and provides examples of this kind of analysis.

In addition, the strategic value investor needs to understand the company and its position within the industry. For example, what is the company's competitive advantage or economic moat? Is the company a low-cost producer or does the company differentiate its products, enabling it to charge higher prices? These are also questions we discussed in Chapter 4.

The analyst also wants to understand and dissect the elements that have led to the company's historical financial performance. For example, if return-on-equity has been high, has that been the result of an efficient use of assets, favorable profit margins, or the magnifying effects of financial leverage? This requires an understanding of financial statements and the integrity of the information that the company provides to investors. And while we are on the issue of integrity, understanding the company involves evaluating the strengths and weaknesses of management. The discussion in Chapter 5 is a roadmap to understanding a company.

Forecast Company Performance

Although understanding the industry and the company is an evaluation of the current state of affairs, forecasting company performance is inherently forward looking. Both exercises are grounded in knowledge of the past. Although these first two steps of the valuation process are fundamentally different, they should both be placed in historical context.

We need to take our analysis in step one and apply it to the analytical models developed in Chapter 5. That is to say, we use our understanding of the company and the industry to forecast sales, expenses, earnings, dividends, and financing requirements in the years ahead. We find that translating an understanding of the industry and company into specific forecasts of company performance is the most challenging part of the process for the strategic value investor because it involves translating the subjective into the objective.

Approaches to forecasting company performance are generally classified as either *top-down* or *bottom-up*. Taking sales forecasts as an example, a value investor following the top-down approach would use macroeconomic data to estimate the future prospects for unit sales and sales price in an industry as a whole. From there, the strategic value investor might estimate a company's market share and relative pricing based on those industry forecasts.

By contrast, the bottom-up approach would involve the analyst building a sales forecast from smaller units and the company. For example, an analyst might project a manufacturer's sales based on expected increases in manufacturing capacity or a retailer's sales based on the number of retail locations that are expected to open or close. A rich forecasting analysis frequently incorporates elements of both these approaches. For example, an analyst might use a bottom-up approach to build an overall sales forecast across different product lines. The forecast within each product line, however, may be constructed using a top-down forecast.

Select the Right Valuation Model

There is no single valuation approach that is suitable for all companies. The strategic value investor selects a valuation approach that is most appropriate for the particular situation. Chapters 7 through 10 discuss a range of *absolute valuation models*, where the model arrives at an estimate of value for a particular security based on fundamental factors. Absolute value models include dividend discount models, free cash flow models, asset-based models, and residual income models. Chapter 11 discusses the class of *relative valuation models*, where the value of a stock is determined relative to the value of other securities or the market. Relative valuation models include price-to-earnings, price-to-book, price-to-sales, price-to–cash flow (P/CF), and price-to-EBIT approaches.

The best model needs to be consistent with the characteristics of the company being valued, data availability, and data quality. For example, dividend discount models, which rely on dividend forecasts, work well for utilities and other companies with stable or steadily growing dividends. Dividend discount models are not appropriate for companies that do not pay dividends, such as some technology companies or start-up firms.

Technology and start-up companies might also have negative free cash flow over a considerable forecast horizon, making a free cash flow model difficult to implement. In that situation, a residual income approach might be more appropriate because it begins with current book value and focuses on a company's ability to earn income in excess of its cost of capital. As a result, it places less emphasis on an estimate of a company's terminal value beyond an explicit forecast horizon, which tends to carry great weight in most of the other valuation models. We discuss model selection in more detail in Chapter 13.

Convert Forecasts to Valuation Inputs

On the face of it, converting forecasts to valuation inputs may seem to simply involve plugging forecasts from step two into our model from step three. For example, we can forecast sales out a number of years by applying our growth rate assumptions to the current level of sales. The sales forecast becomes an important valuation input. We can then apply forecasts of profit margins, payout ratios, and so on to forecast earnings, cash flow, and dividends. It is important to recognize, however, that even our best forecasts are inherently uncertain and not all forecasts are created equal. Sophisticated analysts humbly acknowledge this and account for it with *sensitivity analysis*.

Sensitivity analysis measures how variable our ultimate estimates of value are to changes in the assumptions we use as inputs. If a small change in one of your assumptions, such as sales growth, produces a dramatic change in your value estimate, then you know that your valuation model is extremely sensitive to sales growth. That tells you to focus special attention on the factors that affect sales growth. By contrast, other assumptions, such as interest expense, may have a much smaller impact on your value estimate. You should therefore spend less time thinking about the cost of debt and more time thinking about sales drivers.

Box 6-1 Sales Growth and Interest Expense

Your baseline forecast for sales growth for Ramsey, Ltd., is 10 percent, and your baseline forecast for interest expense is 5 percent. Your valuation model indicates that Ramsey's intrinsic value is $50 per share.

Suppose you want to tweak your sales forecast to reflect the possibility that sales growth may be only 9 percent rather than 10 percent. Independently, you tweak your forecast of interest expense to be 5.5 percent rather than 5 percent. Both scenarios are 10 percent less optimistic than the baseline and produce the results shown in Table 6-1:

TABLE 6-1

Sensitivity Analysis Example for Ramsey, Ltd.

	Sales Growth	Interest Expense
New Assumption	9%	5.5%
New Estimate of Intrinsic Value	$42	$49
% Change in Intrinsic Value	−16%	−2%
% Change in Assumption	−10%	−10%
Elasticity (% Δ Value/ % Δ Assumption)	1.6	0.2

In this case, your value estimate is much more sensitive to changes in sales growth than changes in interest expense. We measure this sensitivity by calculating the elasticity, which is the percent change in value created by an assumption change divided by the percent change in that particular assumption.

Sales growth has elasticity of 1.6, while interest expense only has an elasticity of 0.2. This means that each 1 percent change in sales produces a 1.6 percent change in intrinsic value. A 1 percent change in interest expense only produces a 0.2 percent change in intrinsic value. Therefore, you would want to focus more of your attention on factors that drive sales growth (and make sure you do all you can to estimate that accurately) rather than factors that affect interest expense.

A caveat is in order. This interpretation presumes that sales growth and interest expense are equally volatile. That is, that sales growth is as likely to vary by 10 percent as interest expense is likely to vary by 10 percent. If sales growth is likely to be more volatile or less certain than interest expense, then you would want to emphasize that input more than the elasticity alone might suggest.

Knowing how sensitive your value estimates are to different inputs will help you apply the appropriate amount of conservatism to your baseline forecasts and provide a requisite margin of error.

Apply and Interpret the Valuation Model

In some sense, applying the model is relatively straightforward. If the market price of the security is below its intrinsic value less a sufficient margin of safety, it represents a promising investment opportunity. The strategic value investor should bear in mind at least two nuances, however. First, the size of the margin of safety is not a fixed value. It depends on how confident you are in the model's inputs and how sensitive the valuation is to changes in those inputs. The less confident you are about the main value drivers and the more sensitive intrinsic value is to those inputs, the greater the required margin of safety.

Also, all investment decisions should be considered within the context of your overall portfolio, not in isolation. A series of investments that look promising on a stand-alone basis may make a highly unorthodox and unnecessarily risky portfolio when assembled together. For example, a portfolio composed of Exxon Mobil, Chevron, and British Petroleum leaves an investor exposed to a drop in oil prices. All else being equal, the strategic value investor would demand a larger margin of safety for a less diversified portfolio.

Suppose an investor decided to diversify their portfolio of oil stocks with gold, copper, and other commodity-based companies. These additions provide some insulation against oil price declines. However, oil, gold, copper, and other commodities are driven to a large extent by the same macroeconomic factors, such as inflation and the value of the U.S. dollar. So, a drop in inflation expectations or a strengthening of the U.S. dollar could damage this portfolio more than another. It is therefore important to consider risk in the context of your overall portfolio rather than on a stand-alone basis.

MEASURES OF ABSOLUTE VALUE

Until this point, we have distinguished between intrinsic (or fundamental) value and price (current market value). But value is in the eye of the beholder and is dependent upon how the assets are deployed or might be deployed. For example, a company generally has one value if it is to be immediately dissolved and another if it will continue in operation. The value of a company as a *going concern* is typically what we are estimating when we use the models in this book. If a company is in financial distress, however, its *liquidation value* can be very different. Liquidation value is the value that would be received if assets are sold individually (and often under duress).

Fair market value is similar to liquidation value in that it represents the value of what the company could receive if its assets were sold. The difference, however, is that fair market value is the price based on a transaction between a willing buyer and a willing seller, neither of whom is compelled or forced into the transaction by financial distress. Moreover, assets are often worth more when bundled together rather than sold individually. For example, a mill that supplies raw materials in a manufacturing process may be geographically proximate to a manufacturing facility. If transportation costs represent a significant portion of the cost of the raw material, then the mill may be more valuable in combination with the manufacturing facility than on a stand-alone basis. From a seller's perspective, fair market value may reflect the synergy associated with combining related assets together and does not presume assets are sold separately. Synergy implies that the same asset may have a different value to different investors. We use the term *investment value* to represent value from buyer's perspective. It also reflects synergies and situational factors.

Replacement value takes on a buyer's perspective as well. However, it only considers the cost to replace and typically overlooks potential synergies. We discuss in more detail the implications of investment value and replacement value, as well as the challenges associated with measuring them, in Chapter 9.

In most cases, we will want to determine the intrinsic value of an investment independently of the quoted market price of the company. We can do this for most securities using an absolute valuation model. Absolute valuation models include discounted cash flow (DCF) models. In a DCF model, future cash flows are forecast, and the present intrinsic value of the company is found by discounting those future cash flows back to today, using the rate of return we require to make the investment. Discounted cash flow models include dividend discount models, where the cash flows being forecast are the dividends expected to be received by the investor. Discounted cash flow models also include models where the overall cash flow of the company is forecast and discounted back to the future to ascertain the value that an acquirer would be likely to pay for the company. These models are discussed in Chapters 7 and 8, respectively.

Another absolute valuation model is an approach in which the company as a whole is valued by valuing its underlying assets: the approach commonly taken in distressed situations or similar situations where the company might be worth more broken up and sold rather than as a going concern. Asset-based approaches are discussed in Chapter 9.

For some companies, it is difficult to forecast cash flows or cash flows may be more complex than for a manufacturing company or retailer. Prime examples are financial institutions that collect cash from depositors or the insured and invest this cash to earn a premium over time. An approach that works well for such companies is another absolute valuation model: a residual income model. In a residual income model, valuation is performed based on earnings rather than cash flow. Residual income models are discussed in Chapter 10.

MEASURES OF RELATIVE VALUE

Is a share of Apple stock expensive because it trades at $500 per share? Is a share of Alcoa stock cheap because it trades at nine dollars per share? The truth is, we don't know the answers based on the information we have thus far. Apple stock would be cheap if each share entitled the investor to more than $500 of assets or a high level of predictable earnings, say, $50 per share indefinitely. Alcoa stock would be expensive if each share entitled investors to relatively few assets or a low level of earnings, say $0.25 per share.

Both Apple and Alcoa could cut their share prices in half by doubling the number of shares outstanding, but this would halve the assets and earnings to which each share is entitled. Shareholders would have twice as many shares and would be unaffected.[2] Therefore, analysts often express share price in relation to fundamental measures of value, such as earnings, cash flow, dividends, and net assets. Measures of absolute value are expressed in dollar terms. Relative value measures market value in relation to fundamental value, which can be expressed in a number of ways discussed in the following pages. Valuation of a company can then be determined relative to other companies or the overall market. For example, a company may trade at a lower multiple to earnings (P/E) than peer companies with similar risk and growth prospects, and it would therefore seem to be a better value relative to its peers.

Price-to-Earnings Ratio

Perhaps the most common measure of relative value is the price-to-earnings (P/E) ratio, which we introduced in Chapter 4. It represents the amount of money investors are willing to pay for each dollar of earnings. As we shall see, P/E is a volatile figure because both the numerator and denominator change significantly over time, and often they do not move together.

When the commentators on CNBC talk about P/E, it is important to understand precisely what they mean. The numerator is typically straightforward enough. It is the market price per share of the stock. However, the denominator, earnings, can take several forms. Most frequently, the P/E ratio is based on earnings over the trailing 12 months (TTM) in which case it is referred to as a *trailing* P/E. Alternatively, the P/E ratio may be calculated based on earnings projected over the next 12 months, in which case it is referred to as *forward P/E*. Forward-looking earnings are, of course, far more subjective and debatable than historical earnings. So, a note of caution is in order in the case of forward-looking earnings.

Because earnings may fluctuate dramatically from one quarter and one year to the next, analysts often calculate a *normalized P/E* ratio, which uses the average earnings over the most recent full business cycle in the denominator in an attempt to smooth cyclical fluctuations. As if that were not enough variations on a theme, some analysts adjust earnings for extraordinary items.

The most important point is that when you read about the P/E ratio, you understand how it is calculated. Moreover, when pundits compare it to the market or other stocks in the industry, it is important that they are comparing apples to apples and that the benchmark ratios used as a point of reference are calculated in an identical fashion. For example, comparing the forward P/E for Monsanto with the trailing P/E of the market or industry would not be meaningful and would likely make Monsanto look more attractive than it would on a more contemporaneous and comparable basis.

The strategic value investor also needs to have a sense of what constitutes a high versus a low P/E ratio. Table 6-2 displays P/E ratios based on trailing 12-month earnings as of June 2011. The median P/E ratio at that time was 17.39 for NYSE-listed stocks. Relatively less expensive stocks in the 25th percentile traded at 13.21 times earnings. Deep value stocks in the 5th percentile traded at almost half that level. By contrast, P/E ratios for growth stocks can be very high. Stocks in the 75th percentile traded at over 25 times earnings. Highflying growth stocks in the 95th percentile traded at 75 times earnings and higher, which is far greater than the median.[3]

These abnormally high P/E ratios in the upper percentiles distort the average P/E ratio for the market as a whole. The median P/E ratio (or that value at the 50th percentile) is less influenced by extreme values. Because P/E ratios on some stocks are so high, it is often better to look at the median P/E ratio rather than the average P/E

TABLE 6-2

Price-to-Earnings Ratios of NYSE-Listed
Stocks as of June 2013

Percentile	P/E Ratio
5th	6.80
25th	12.02
50th	16.37
75th	23.31
95th	78.13

Source: Calculations based on data from the Kenneth French Data Library

FIGURE 6-1

Price-to-earnings ratios of NYSE-listed stocks for various percentiles from 1951 to 2013.

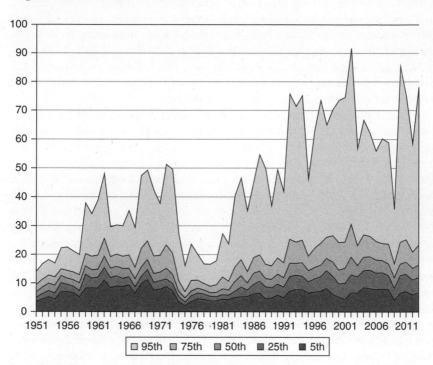

Source: Eugene Fama and Kenneth French Data Library at http://mba.tuck.dartmouth.edu/pages/faculty/ken.french /data_library.html.

ratio. We can see how large some P/E ratios can be in relation to most other stocks in Figure 6-1, which displays these P/E ratios over time from 1951 to 2011. High P/E ratios are much farther above the median than low P/E ratios are below the median.

Figure 6-1 also illustrates that the definition of a high or low P/E ratio varies considerably over time. The P/E ratio stocks in the 95th percentile are especially volatile. Therefore, measures of relative value are a moving target. They need to be placed in context of current market conditions. In general, you can see that while P/E ratios collapsed in the 1970s, they have generally increased since 1951.

Eugene Fama and Kenneth French, who compiled these data, define value stocks as those in the lower 30 percent of P/E ratios (that is, below the 30th percentile). Growth stocks have P/E ratios in the upper 30 percent of P/E ratios (that is, above the 70th percentile). Blended, or medium, stocks fall in between these two breakpoints. Although Fama and French would classify all stocks according to these breakpoints regardless of where they trade, the breakpoints themselves are determined only by NYSE-listed stocks in an effort to eliminate distortions from smaller, illiquid stocks that tend to trade off the NYSE.

Ibbotson/Morningstar measures value using the P/E ratio a bit differently. Rather that classifying all stocks according to breakpoints determined by NYSE-listed stocks, Ibbotson/Morningstar calculates a liquidity score for all stocks and eliminates those that fall into the bottom quartile (25 percent) from the analysis. They then use the remaining liquid stocks to develop "value" or "growth" classifications based on ten factors, half of which are based on historical factors (e.g., trailing 12 months earnings growth) and half of which are based on forward-looking factors (e.g., one year forward earnings). In addition to the P/E ratio, they incorporate other factors such as price-to–book value, price-to–cash flow, and the dividend yield, which we discuss in more detail below.

Both Fama and French as well as Ibbotson/Morningstar use these classification schemes to create value and growth indexes, which can be used to measure the general performance of value and growth stocks over time. We discussed some of the behavior of stocks in these indexes in Chapter 2. These different index construction methodologies most often yield very similar results. At times, however, they can lead to dramatically different indexes that can behave very differently from each other.

In the year 2000, for example, which saw a collapse in the stock market, the Fama-French large-cap growth index fell by 13 percent, but the comparable Ibbotson Associates index fell by 22 percent, an enormous 9 percent difference. Similarly, the Fama-French large-cap value index increased almost 6 percent, while the Ibbotson Associates index declined by 3 percent, another 9 percent difference. The small-cap value index had an even greater differential of over 23 percent! The main point here (and the main theme for this chapter) is that there is no single, uniform way to measure value. The value investor should be aware of the differences and make the necessary adjustments. Judgments should be based on a variety of factors rather than rely on a single factor.

Average P/E ratios and other measures of relative value vary from one industry to another. For example, stocks in the computer software industry generally have much higher P/E ratios than utility stocks because their growth prospects are generally more promising. Therefore, most analysts look at P/E ratio and other measures of relative value in relation to other stocks in the same industry rather than simply the market as a whole. The idea is that direct competitors and other stocks in the same industry are more comparable.

Annual Return in the Year 2000

	Large		Small	
	Growth	Value	Growth	Value
Fama-French	−13.63	5.80	−24.15	−0.80
Ibbotson Associates	−22.01	−3.00	−22.60	22.69

So, the P/E takes on meaning and significance when we understand how it compares to that of other stocks (especially comparable firms that might be in the same industry) and how it has varied through time. We will see some examples of this later in this chapter.

Market-to-Book Ratio (Price-to-Book)

The next most common measure of relative value is the market-to-book ratio. When market value and book value are expressed on a per-share basis, the ratio is referred to as price-to-book (P/B). Either way, we're talking about the same figure.

Book value is equal to the sum of the accounting book value of stockholders equity, preferred stock, deferred taxes, and any investment tax credits reported on the balance sheet. The P/B ratio expresses market price of a share in relation to the accounting value per share in the balance sheet.

Book value is generally much more stable over time than earnings. So, P/B is less vulnerable to statistical noise than P/E. In addition, book value is far less likely to be negative than earnings. For example, 202 of the 1,242 stocks listed on the New York Stock Exchange (NYSE) reported negative earnings as of December 2011. In 2009, over a third of NYSE-listed stocks reported negative earnings. A negative figure in the denominator distorts the interpretation of the ratio rendering it useless. Therefore, P/B has some advantages over P/E.

Although book value is more stable and more likely to be positive than earnings, it is a very crude measure of value. Table 6-3 displays P/B ratios for NYSE-listed stocks as June 2011. The median P/B ratio is 1.73, meaning that investors are willing to pay $1.73 for every dollar of book value. Value stocks can trade at a fraction of book value, whereas growth stocks can trade at several multiples above book value. Like the P/E ratio, the P/B ratio can get fairly high relative to the median, which can skew the calculation of the average. So, as with P/E ratios, analysts often focus on the median value.

TABLE 6-3

Price-to-Book Ratios of NYSE-Listed Stocks as of June 2013

Percentile	P/B Ratio
5th	0.61
25th	1.06
50th	1.65
75th	2.73
95th	7.04

Source: Calculations based on data from the Kenneth French Data Library

FIGURE 6-2

Price-to-book ratios of NYSE-listed stocks for various percentiles from 1951 to 2013.

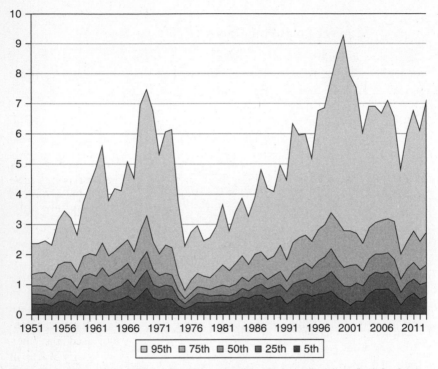

Source: Eugene Fama and Kenneth French Data Library at http://mba.tuck.dartmouth.edu/pages/faculty/ken.french /data_library.html.

Figure 6-2 shows how P/B varies over time. Like P/E ratios, P/B ratios have generally increased since the 1950s, spiking in the early 1970s and late 1990s. Fama and French classify stocks in the lower 30 percent of P/B ratios (that is, below the 30th percentile) as value, and stocks in the upper 30 percent of P/B ratios (that is, above the 70th percentile) as growth. So, classifying a stock as value or growth based on P/B requires knowing where other stocks are trading. As with the P/E ratio the P/B method of valuation looks at price relative to some underlying fundamental factor (book value in this case) and relative to other securities.

We mentioned earlier that Fama and French might use a variety of measures to classify stocks as either value or growth. It is important to emphasize, however, that the P/B is the measure that they would emphasize mostly because they believe it does a better job of predicting future return than any of the other measures. Ibbotson/Morningstar, on the other hand, weight forward P/E much more heavily. Although we believe having understanding of a variety of valuation measures is helpful for analysts to develop a complete picture of the stock's investment opportunity, we place heavy weight on the price-to-book ratio because of its historically stronger predictive properties.

Price-to–Cash Flow

We mentioned earlier that the P/E ratio is a noisy measure of value because earnings can fluctuate substantially over time. Another weakness of the P/E ratio is that earnings are subject to manipulation through different accounting treatments. Ultimately, the investor is interested in the cash flows to which they are entitled as a shareholder. Therefore the price-to–cash flow ratio is intended to remove distortions that might be caused by alternative accounting conventions and potential earnings manipulation.

Table 6-4 shows the price-to–cash flow ratios of stocks on the New York Stock Exchange as of June 2011. Figure 6-3 shows how these breakpoints have varied over time from 1951 to 2011. Because earnings and cash flows tend to correlate over time, these figures and trends look similar to those for the P/E ratio. Specifically, the median stock trades at about 12 times cash flow. Deep value stocks in the 5th percentile trade at less than half that at five times cash flow. Highflying growth stocks can trade at over 40 times cash flow.

Because some stocks trade so far above the median, the average price-to–cash flow ratio for the market tends to be distorted and biased upward. So, a good measure of the market's price-to–cash flow that is less influenced by these extreme values is the median rather than the average ratio. Like P/E ratios, price-to–cash flow ratios collapsed in the 1970s and have steadily increased since then as interest rates have declined. Again, Fama and French would classify stocks in the bottom 30 percent of price-to–cash flow ratios (that is, below the 30th percentile) as value stocks, and stocks in the upper 30 percent of price-to–cash flow ratios (that is, above the 70th percentile) as growth stocks.

TABLE 6-4

Price-to–Cash Flow Ratios of NYSE-Listed
Stocks as of June 2013

Percentile	P/CF Ratio
5th	4.82
25th	8.01
50th	11.68
75th	16.56
95th	46.95

Source: Calculations based on data from the Kenneth French Data Library

FIGURE 6-3

Price-to–cash flow ratios of NYSE-listed stocks for various percentiles from 1951 to 2013.

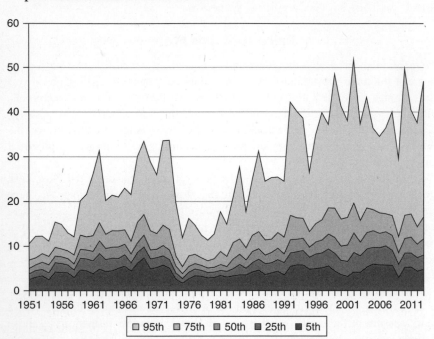

Dividend Yield

Dividends are much more stable than either earnings or cash flow. Most companies that pay dividends want to gradually increase their dividend payments over time. Companies rarely decrease a dividend payment, as that is interpreted by the market as a strong signal that the firm is having financial difficulties. Therefore, many analysts look at the dividend yield as an indication of value because it highlights changes in price and eliminates much of the noise associated with changes in earnings and cash flow. It is, however, a crude measure in part because management, rather than markets, determines dividend policy. That said, it is nonetheless an important tool in the strategic value investor's toolkit.

Unlike the measures of relative value that we have discussed thus far, dividend yield places market value in the denominator rather than the numerator. It is calculated as the annual dividend divided by the current market price, which is often expressed as D/P. Table 6-5 shows dividend yields of New York Stock Exchange listed stocks as of June 2011. The median dividend yield at that time was just over 1.5 percent. A few stocks in the 95th percentile had dividend yields above 6 percent. These are considered deep value stocks.

TABLE 6-5

Dividend Yields of NYSE-Listed Stocks
as of June 2013

Percentile	D/P
5th	0.31
25th	1.19
50th	2.03
75th	3.31
95th	8.43

Source: Calculations based on data from the Kenneth French Data Library

A classic trading strategy, known as *the Dow Theory*, is to buy a few stocks in the Dow Jones Industrial Average that have the highest dividend yield. As the stock price increases and the dividend yield falls, the strategy directs investors to sell those stocks with falling yields and buy those with the next highest dividend yield.

Figure 6-4 shows dividend yields over the last 60 years. Dividend yields have generally declined over that time. Rather than paying out earnings to investors, firms have increasingly reinvested those earnings into their businesses. This trend can be either good or bad depending on how the earnings are invested. If management has promising and profitable investment opportunities, then investors will want them to forgo paying dividends and instead invest the earnings into the promising growth opportunities which will translate into future capital gains. If management, however, has exhausted most of the profitable investment opportunities, investors are much better off having earnings distributed as dividends lest they be wasted by management.[4]

Again, if we were to use dividend yield as a barometer for value or growth, Fama and French would consider stocks in the upper 30 percent of dividend yields (above the 70th percentile) to be value stocks, and those in the lower 30 percent of dividend yields (below the 30th percentile) to growth stocks.

Other Measures of Relative Value

The list of relative value metrics, or market multiples, is quite lengthy. Although the P/E ratio, P/B ratio, P/CF ratio, and dividend yield are staples, a few others deserve mention. The price-to-sales ratio, for example, is commonly used by analysts who want to eliminate some of the distortions that can result in arriving at earnings. In some instances, accounting policies provide a lot of discretion about how to treat expenses, and these alternative treatments can skew earnings. Stock-based compensation, for example, is often not expensed despite the fact that it represents a true economic cost borne by existing stockholders. Likewise, a first-in-first-out (FIFO) inventory accounting convention can deflate cost of goods sold compared to last-in-first-out (LIFO).

FIGURE 6-4

Dividend yields of NYSE-listed stocks for various percentiles from 1951 to 2013.

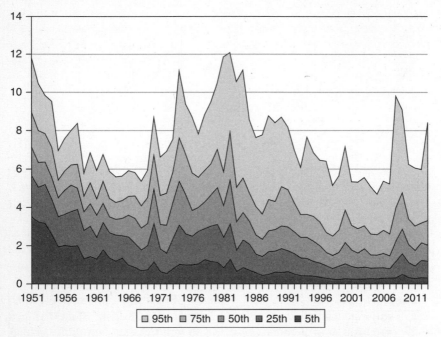

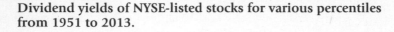

Source: Eugene Fama and Kenneth French Data Library at http://mba.tuck.dartmouth.edu/pages/faculty/ken.french /data_library.html.

The price-to-sales ratio is not affected by these accounting choices and can provide a more reliable comparison across firms. That said, it is possible to manipulate sales figures with aggressive revenue recognition policies. The Internet bubble in the late 1990s provided a plethora of examples of firms using questionable practices concerning revenue recognition.[5] Moreover, focusing on sales to the exclusion of expenses fails to account for the significance of margins. Nonetheless, price-to-sales is a useful tool that can provide additional insights when used in combination with the other market multiples.

Price-to-EBIT is intended to express value in relation to operating income, or earnings before interest and taxes (EBIT). By excluding the impact of interest and taxes, EBIT focuses on earnings associated with current operations.

A related figure is operating cash flow, estimated earnings before interest, tax, depreciation, and amortization. Removing noncash expenses, like depreciation and amortization, from the earnings figures produces a measure of cash flow—operating cash flow, in particular. Operating cash flow focuses on cash flow derived from ongoing operations and excludes the cash flow effects associated with investing and financing activities. Focusing just on cash flow removes distortions associated with ramping up capital expenditures or issuing stock.

Each of these market multiples has advantages and disadvantages. It is imprudent to use any single measure as a definitive measure of value or growth or as an estimate of intrinsic value. We examine the use of relative valuation models to make investment decisions and estimate intrinsic value more fully in Chapter 11. But for now, understanding these ratios helps us gauge whether a particular stock is more likely to be a value stock or growth stock. Here are some examples that help pull all these measures of relative value together.

Box 6-2 Xerox: Value or Growth?

Xerox is an interesting case of a company that transitions between value and growth. Figure 6-5 displays relative valuations of Xerox according to Morningstar.com. Recently, Xerox's P/E ratio and price-to–cash flow ratios place it solidly in the value category according to Fama and French percentiles (see Tables 6-2 and 6-6, respectively). Interestingly, the P/E ratio was much higher in the early part of the 2000s, even though its other multiples

FIGURE 6-5

Relative valuation of Xerox.

Valuation History XRX

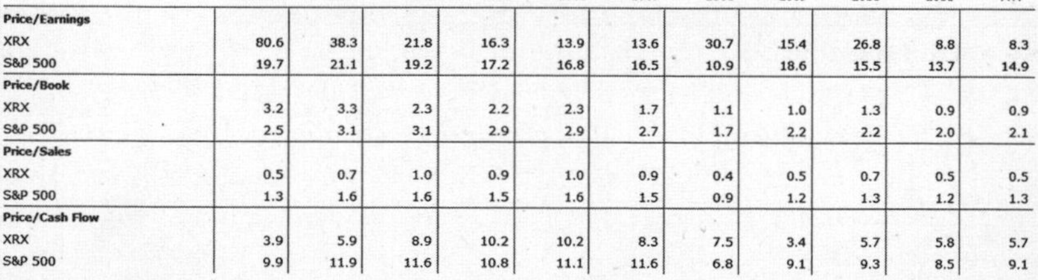

| Price/Earnings | Price/Book | Price/Sales | Price/Cash Flow |

• XRX   • S&P 500

History	2002	2003	2004	2005	2006	2007	2008	2009	2010	2011	TTM
Price/Earnings											
XRX	80.6	38.3	21.8	16.3	13.9	13.6	30.7	15.4	26.8	8.8	8.3
S&P 500	19.7	21.1	19.2	17.2	16.8	16.5	10.9	18.6	15.5	13.7	14.9
Price/Book											
XRX	3.2	3.3	2.3	2.2	2.3	1.7	1.1	1.0	1.3	0.9	0.9
S&P 500	2.5	3.1	3.1	2.9	2.9	2.7	1.7	2.2	2.2	2.0	2.1
Price/Sales											
XRX	0.5	0.7	1.0	0.9	1.0	0.9	0.4	0.5	0.7	0.5	0.5
S&P 500	1.3	1.6	1.6	1.5	1.6	1.5	0.9	1.2	1.3	1.2	1.3
Price/Cash Flow											
XRX	3.9	5.9	8.9	10.2	10.2	8.3	7.5	3.4	5.7	5.8	5.7
S&P 500	9.9	11.9	11.6	10.8	11.1	11.6	6.8	9.1	9.3	8.5	9.1

Source: Morningstar.com

(*Continued*)

remained modest, suggesting that earnings were severely depressed during this period.

Its recent price-to-book and price-to-sales ratios are also below the average for the S&P 500, and its price-to-book ratio puts it solidly in value territory according to a Fama and French classification scheme (see Table 6-3). Similarly, its higher-than-average dividend yield inches it toward value, as well, although it does not reach the 70th percentile (see Table 6-5). Taken as a whole, most investors would classify Xerox as a value stock.

The strategic value investor can validate this further by comparing Xerox to industry (rather than market) averages and the average over the last five years (see Figure 6-6). Here, too, its market multiples are below and its dividend yield higher than its peers in the industry. Moreover, all of its multiples are below the averages, and the dividend yield is above the five-year average.

FIGURE 6-6

Industry and time comparison of Xerox.

Valuation   Wall Street Estimates

Current Valuation XRX

	XRX	Industry Avg	S&P 500	XRX 5Y Avg*
Price/Earnings	8.3	11.2	14.9	19.1
Price/Book	0.9	1.4	2.1	1.2
Price/Sales	0.5	0.7	1.3	0.6
Price/Cash Flow	5.7	6.7	9.1	5.0
Dividend Yield %	2.2	1.1	2.2	1.6
Price/Fair Value	▣ Premium	—	—	—

Data as of 09/21/2012, *Price/Cash Flow uses 3-year average.

Forward Valuation XRX

	XRX	Industry Avg	S&P 500
Forward Price/Earnings	6.6	—	14.1
PEG Ratio	6.9	—	—
PEG Payback (Yrs)	5.5	—	—

Data as of 09/21/2012.

Source: Morningstar.com.

Box 6-3 Google: Value or Growth?

Figure 6-7 displays relative valuations of Google according to Morningstar .com.

Back in 2004, Google was clearly a growth stock. Its P/E ratio was over 100, its price-to-book ratio was 18, its price-to-sales and price-to–cash flow ratios were well above the average for the S&P 500, and it didn't pay a dividend. Over time, these valuation ratios have declined dramatically. Although they remain much higher than the average for the S&P 500, they are much more in line with that average.

Because of this compression of multiples, the classification of Google as a growth stock is less clear than it was in 2004, but it is still a growth stock. The P/E ratio in 2011 was 21.7, which puts it close to the 70th percentile that Fama and French would use to classify it as a growth stock (see Table 6-2). Similarly, the price-to–cash flow ratio of 17.3 is very close to the 70th percentile breakpoint for a growth stock (see Table 6-4). Moreover, the price-to-book ratio of 3.6 is above the 70th percentile that Fama and French would use to classify it as a growth stock (see Table 6-4). The price-to-sales ratio is also well above market norms.

FIGURE 6-7

Relative valuation of Google.

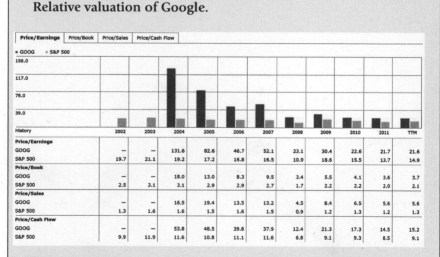

Price/Earnings	Price/Book	Price/Sales	Price/Cash Flow

● GOOG   ● S&P 500

History	2002	2003	2004	2005	2006	2007	2008	2009	2010	2011	TTM
Price/Earnings											
GOOG	–	–	131.6	82.6	46.7	52.1	23.1	30.4	22.6	21.7	21.6
S&P 500	19.7	21.1	19.2	17.2	16.8	16.5	10.9	18.6	15.5	13.7	14.9
Price/Book											
GOOG	–	–	18.0	13.0	8.3	9.5	3.4	5.5	4.1	3.6	3.7
S&P 500	2.5	3.1	3.1	2.9	2.9	2.7	1.7	2.2	2.2	2.0	2.1
Price/Sales											
GOOG	–	–	16.5	19.4	13.5	13.2	4.5	8.4	6.5	5.6	5.6
S&P 500	1.3	1.6	1.6	1.5	1.6	1.5	0.9	1.2	1.3	1.2	1.3
Price/Cash Flow											
GOOG	–	–	53.8	48.5	39.8	37.9	12.4	21.3	17.3	14.5	15.2
S&P 500	9.9	11.9	11.6	10.8	11.1	11.6	6.8	9.1	9.3	8.5	9.1

Source: Morningstar.com

All in all, Google is still a growth stock despite the compression of its valuation multiples. It is worth noting that, although Google's price

(Continued)

multiples have fallen dramatically since 2004, the share price did just the opposite. Because earnings, book value, and sales grew more quickly than the multiples declined, Google's share price has risen from $132 per share to $897 per share. Not a bad performance.

CONCLUSION

No single, authoritative method for measuring value exists. Everyone, it seems, has a different notion of value. That is part of the art of investing. In this chapter, we showed that the concept of value can have several dimensions: replacement value, market value, and liquidation value, for example. Similarly, distinguishing between value stocks and growth stocks is not a straightforward exercise. It is a judgment informed by a variety of different metrics. A preponderance of indicators pointing in the same direction, however, can give the strategic value investor confidence in his or her assessment. The following chapters present the various absolute and relative valuation methods in more detail, including examples of how to calculate intrinsic value using these models.

CHAPTER SEVEN

DIVIDEND DISCOUNT MODELS

The stock market is filled with individuals who know the price of everything, but the value of nothing.

—Phil Fisher

At the heart of value investing is the application of financial models for determining the worth (or intrinsic value) of an investment. If the intrinsic value is substantially higher than the market price, you are on to something. Investors are generally an unemotional lot concerning how they earn their returns. Unlike car owners, for instance, who may derive psychic income from driving an expensive sports car versus a more pedestrian family sedan, the typical investor is indifferent when it comes to owning shares of IBM versus shares of Apple. Investors typically select the investment that provides them with the highest expected return after taking into account the risk of the investment. The models presented in this chapter are all mathematically based and unemotional in nature.

Lest you fear that this chapter will devolve into complex formulas and a plethora of Greek symbols, let us assure you that the quantitative proficiency required to understand this exposition is no more than a junior-high school level of mathematical expertise. While at first glance, the equations may look a bit daunting for readers with math phobia, in reality the calculations are very simple and straightforward. One of our pet peeves in the investment management field is over-complicating what, in essence, is a very simple idea: You want to buy something for less than it is "worth." "Keep it simple, stupid" is the mantra that we follow.

This chapter will present a very basic valuation model (and variations on that model) founded on the concept of present value or discounted cash flow. This basic model is applied by many professional investors, both from the value and growth camps. It is also the model that forms the basis for valuation as taught in undergraduate and graduate business programs throughout the world, as well as in the Chartered Financial Analyst (CFA) Program.

What you will discover is that this basic model is quite simplistic. The application of the model, specifically estimating the parameters, is what leads some investors to be successful and others to struggle and make regrettable decisions. The model is sound, both theoretically and practically. But, a sound model with poor estimates of inputs is subject to the old saying "garbage in, garbage out."

PRESENT VALUE

Central to the concept of investing is the most basic concept of finance: present value. Simply stated, present value is the fundamental principle that a dollar received today is worth more than a dollar received tomorrow. Likewise, a dollar to be received tomorrow is worth more than a dollar received in two days. The rationale is that a dollar received today can be invested to earn interest and will be worth more at a later date. Mathematically, the present value of an amount of money to be received at a future point—let's say a year from now—if the appropriate interest rate is r (more about that later) is:

$$Present\ Value = \frac{Future\ Value}{(1+r)}$$

So, the present value of one dollar to be received one year from today if the appropriate interest rate is 3 percent is:

$$Present\ Value = \frac{\$1.00}{(1+.03)} = \$0.9709$$

What this means is that if the appropriate interest rate is 3 percent, an investor should be indifferent to receiving $0.9709 today or $1.00 a year from today. This simple idea is the basis of all discounted cash flow models.

Further extrapolating the concept, the value of a dollar to be received in two years is discounted (the opposite of compounded) for two periods:

$$Present\ Value = \frac{Future\ Value_2}{(1+r)^2} = \frac{\$1.00}{(1.03)^2} = \frac{\$1.00}{1.0609} = \$0.9426$$

If that dollar were to be received 10 years from today, the present value is:

$$Present\ Value = \frac{Future\ Value_{10}}{(1+r)^{10}} = \frac{\$1.00}{(1.03)^{10}} = \frac{\$1.00}{1.3439} = \$0.7441$$

So, the general formula for the present value of a lump sum to be received in the future at time n is:

$$Present\ Value = \frac{Future\ Value_n}{(1+r)^n}$$

Box 7-1 An Historical Anecdote

The idea of present value can be traced to Irving Fisher and his seminal works *The Rate of Interest* (1907) and *The Theory of Interest* (1930). Although Fisher is considered one of the giants in investment history, his ability to forecast market activity was less than stellar. A scant one week before the stock market crash of 1929, Fisher proclaimed that the U.S. economy was on a "permanently high plateau." But don't let his lack of forecasting ability cloud your judgment of the concept of present value's validity. In golf parlance, we will give Fisher a mulligan (a second chance).

The critical concept to present value is that once dollars to be received in the future are discounted back to a present value, they can be added together to determine the value of a series of future cash flows (CF). Finance professionals would say that adding together dollars in hand today and dollars to be received at some time in the future is akin to adding U.S. dollars and euros. You can certainly add dollars and euros together, but you have to convert them into the same currency first.

In its most basic form, the value of any investment (stock, bond, real estate, etc.) is simply the future value of all the cash flows discounted back to the present time (or put in present value terms). The general formula for the value of any investment is:

$$Value = \frac{Cash\,Flow_1}{(1+r)^1} + \frac{Cash\,Flow_2}{(1+r)^2} + \cdots + \frac{Cash\,Flow_N}{(1+r)^N}$$

Note that these cash flows can be dividends, interest payments on a bond, rent flows on a real estate investment, or any other payout from an investment. As you will see, the valuation model is simple. The art of investing comes with estimating both the magnitude of the future cash flows and the appropriate interest (or discount) rate.

Box 7-2 Application: "NEW ECONOMY" Warning

If anyone tries to convince you that there is a new paradigm and that present value doesn't matter anymore, then run away as fast as you can. This actually happened during the Internet bubble of the late 1990s when some market pundits claimed that we needed to develop metrics such as "click-throughs" or "eyeballs" to value firms in the so-called "*new economy*." These firms weren't

(Continued)

making money—in fact, they were bleeding cash—yet investors bid the stocks up on expectations that they would revolutionize the economy and create a new business model. One of the authors of this text encountered this thinking in a presentation to a group of analysts in the late 1990s. Bob Johnson was presenting the CFA Program to a group of investment professionals (mind you, this wasn't a crowd of unsophisticated investors) when an audience member, and apparently a skeptic of the traditional valuation models promulgated in the CFA Program, stated, "These traditional models are antiquated because they don't explain the valuations of companies like Value America and Pets.com." Dr. Johnson responded by saying that perhaps the valuations the market is providing to some of those firms are not warranted and that we are witnessing something of a "bubble" in asset valuation. Soon thereafter, NASDAQ crashed and that index is still well below the frothy valuation levels of the late 1990s. Suffice it to say that all investment valuation models have at their nexus the concept of present value. Remember that the four most dangerous words in the English language just might be *"This time, it's different."*

So, for a bond that pays the holder $50 annual interest and a lump sum of $1,000 in three years, if the appropriate interest (discount rate) is 7 percent, the present value is found as:

$$Present\ Value = \frac{\$50}{(1.07)} + \frac{\$50}{(1.07)^2} + \frac{\$50}{(1.07)^3} + \frac{\$1,000}{(1.07)^3} = \$947.51$$

Likewise, for a stock that pays the holder a dividend of $3 annually and is estimated to be sold for $50 in three years, if the appropriate discount rate is 7 percent, the present value is found as:

$$Present\ Value = \frac{\$3}{(1.07)} + \frac{\$3}{(1.07)^2} + \frac{\$3}{(1.07)^3} + \frac{\$50}{(1.07)^3} = \$48.69$$

That is really as complicated theoretically as discounted cash flow models get. Now, clearly, firms generally pay dividends quarterly, and the majority of bonds pay interest semiannually. But, assuming annual payments does not invalidate the model. In fact, we would argue that for the value investor the convention of adopting any payment convention other than annual is unwarranted. Remember, these models are meant to provide an approximation of value and not a precise value to the penny. Often, when models are made more complicated it gives the user the illusion of precision. The value investor is looking for the opportunity to buy something for $50 that is worth $80 or to buy something for $20 that is worth $40.

GORDON CONSTANT GROWTH DIVIDEND DISCOUNT MODEL

The only cash flows received by the investor from owning a share of stock are dividend payments (D) plus whatever the investor can sell the share for at the end of his holding period. To the ultimate investor, a series of dividend payments is the only cash flow stream paid to investors. Thus, the value of any share of stock is equal to:

$$Share\ Value = \frac{D_1}{(1+r)^1} + \frac{D_2}{(1+r)^2} + \cdots + \frac{D_n}{(1+r)^n} + \cdots$$

where D_n is the dividend in a given period. The above equation has an infinite number of terms and would seem impossible to apply, but if we make a simplifying assumption about the growth rate of dividends being constant through time, that equation simplifies into the following:

$$Share\ Value = \frac{D_0(1+g)}{r-g}$$

In this model, g is the growth rate of the dividends. This formula is known as the constant growth dividend model, or the Gordon model (named after Professor Myron Gordon, who originally published it in 1959).[1] It is the most widely used stock valuation model and it is taught in business schools throughout the world as well as in the CFA Program.

To apply the model, look up what the last full year's dividend payments were and provide estimates of two variables: (1) the appropriate discount rate (or interest rate) and (2) the future growth rate of dividends. We can estimate the value of General Electric (GE) common stock by applying the formula in Box 7-3.

Box 7-3 Application: Value of GE Stock Using Gordon Constant Growth Model

Data:

Current (2012) dividend = $0.70
Appropriate interest or discount rate = 11%
Growth rate of future dividends = 7%

$$GE\ Stock\ Value = \frac{D_0(1+g)}{r-g} = \frac{\$0.70(1.07)}{.11 - .07} = \$18.73$$

(Continued)

Thus, the Gordon constant growth model assumes that a fair valuation for GE stock is $18.73 if the appropriate discount rate is 11 percent and the growth rate of future dividends is a constant 7 percent.

But note how sensitive the estimate of value is to the selection of inputs. If we assume a slightly higher growth rate of dividends, 8 percent, and maintain the appropriate discount rate at 11 percent, the value estimate is $25.20.

Likewise, if we assume an appropriate discount rate of 12 percent and keep the growth rate of future dividends at 7 percent, then the value estimate is $14.98. This example illustrates that it is a good idea for an investor to perform a sensitivity analysis—in essence, varying the inputs to determine how sensitive the valuation is to small changes in inputs.

The bottom line is that the mathematics of the model is simple. The art of asset valuation comes in estimating the inputs.

TWO-STAGE DIVIDEND GROWTH MODEL

Assuming a constant growth rate in dividends "forever" seems, and is, unrealistic in the majority of cases. A more realistic assumption for most firms is to assume an "abnormal" growth rate in the short term and then a "normal" growth rate in dividends thereafter. As was shown in Chapter 4 in the discussion on the industry life cycle, industries and firms typically go through four different stages of growth: pioneer, growth, mature, and decline. Firms likely aren't publicly traded in the pioneer stage and the discounted cash flow models generally aren't applicable to firms in the pioneering or venture capital stage. However, once firms have advanced into the growth and mature stages, the models are wholly appropriate.

The two-stage dividend growth model is theoretically the same as the constant growth model: The value of a share of stock is equal to the sum of the discounted value of all future dividends. But we can think of it as two separate streams of cash flows: (1) the present value of the dividends during the abnormal growth period, and (2) the present value of the dividends during the normal growth period.

If we assume a firm will have a higher growth rate in dividends for three years and then the dividend growth rate will revert to a normal, long-term rate, we can value the stock as follows:

Stock Value = PV of dividends during abnormal growth
+ PV of dividends during normal growth

In our case of abnormal growth for three years, the equation becomes

$$Stock\ Value = \frac{D_1}{(1+r)^1} + \frac{D_2}{(1+r)^2} + \frac{D_3}{(1+r)^3}$$
+ PV of all dividends from year 4 onward

Since the dividends are assumed to grow at a constant rate after three years, we can apply the Gordon constant growth model to find the stock value at that time. In other words, the stock value at time 3 is equal to the following:

$$Stock\ Value_3 = \frac{D_3(1+g)}{r-g}$$

But remember that this stock value at time 3 is a value in terms of time 3 (future value) dollars. We need to discount this value back to the present to be able to add it to the present value of the dividends during the first three years. This is shown as:

$$Stock\ Value = \frac{D_1}{(1+r)^1} + \frac{D_2}{(1+r)^2} + \frac{D_3}{(1+r)^3} + \frac{Stock\ Value_3}{(1+r)^3}$$

Or,

$$Stock\ Value = \frac{D_1}{(1+r)^1} + \frac{D_2}{(1+r)^2} + \frac{D_3}{(1+r)^3} + \frac{\frac{D_3(1+g)}{(r-g)}}{(1+r)^3}$$

This formula looks messy, but the calculations are really quite simple. To apply the two-stage dividend discount model, simply look up what the last full year's dividend payments were and provide estimates of three variables: (1) the appropriate discount rate (or interest rate), (2) the future growth rate of dividends during the near term, and (3) the long-term growth rate of dividends. We can estimate the value of General Electric (GE) common stock by applying the formula in Box 7-4.

Box 7-4 Application: Value of General Electric Stock Using Two-Stage Dividend Growth Model

Data:

Current (2012) dividend = $0.70
Appropriate interest or discount rate = 11%
Growth rate of future dividends during years one through three = 12%
Growth rate of future dividends after year three = 7%

$$GE\ Stock\ Value = \frac{D_1}{(1+r)^1} + \frac{D_2}{(1+r)^2} + \frac{D_3}{(1+r)^3} + \frac{\frac{D_3(1+g)}{(r-g)}}{(1+r)^3}$$

(Continued)

$$GE\ Stock\ Value = \frac{\$0.70(1.12)}{(1.11)^1} + \frac{\$0.70(1.12)^2}{(1.11)^2} + \frac{\$0.70(1.12)^3}{(1.11)^3} + \frac{\dfrac{\$0.70(1.12)^3(1.07)}{(.11-.07)}}{(1.11)^3}$$

$$GE\ Stock\ Value = \$0.71 + \$0.71 + \$0.72 + \$19.23 = \$21.37$$

Thus, the two-stage growth model assumes that a fair valuation for GE stock is \$21.37 if the appropriate discount rate is 11 percent and the growth rate of future dividends is assumed to be 12 percent for the next three years and a constant 7 percent thereafter.

Again, we note how sensitive the estimate of value is to the selection of inputs. If we assume a slightly higher growth rate of dividends thereafter, 8 percent, and maintain the appropriate discount rate at 11 percent and the first three years growth rate at 12 percent, the value estimate is \$28.03.

Likewise, if we assume an appropriate discount rate of 12 percent and keep the growth rate of future dividends for three years at 12 percent and at 7 percent thereafter, then the value estimate is \$17.08.

Again, the mathematics of the model is fairly straightforward. The art of asset valuation comes in estimating the inputs.

There is certainly nothing magical about assuming a three-year abnormal growth period versus a two-year or a five-year abnormal growth period. The model can be modified to fit any proposed dividend growth pattern. An Excel spreadsheet can be used to take into account different lengths of abnormal growth periods and also changes in growth rates and discount rates. Doing this sort of sensitivity analysis helps the analyst realize how sensitive estimated value is to changes in inputs and helps the value investor determine the margin of safety of any proposed investment. A bigger margin of safety allows us some cushion if we are incorrect and are overly optimistic when determining the cash flow stream, or if we underestimate the risk of the investment and apply a discount rate that is too low.

This particular valuation model is obviously only relevant—and can only be employed—to value firms that pay dividends. Firms like 3M, United Technologies, Johnson Controls, Abbott Labs, and Coca-Cola are examples of firms that have paid dividends without interruption for many, many years and closely fit the parameters of this model. Many of the largest and most successful firms cannot be valued by using a dividend discount model. Firms like Berkshire Hathaway, DirecTV, eBay, Google, and Amazon.com pay no dividends and simply cannot be valued using a dividend discount model. They are candidates for income-based, asset-based, or free cash flow models, which are detailed in the other chapters. However, the wide applicability of dividend-based models is illustrated by the fact that as of mid-March 2013 there were only 90 stocks in the S&P 500 that did not pay dividends. Further buttressing the point, at the time of the writing of this book, all 30 stocks in the Dow Jones Industrial Average pay dividends and are candidates for valuation using a dividend discount model. In Chapter 12 we will discuss further how to select the appropriate valuation model for a company.

In the following sections we will focus on the estimates of the dividend cash flows (the values in the numerator of the models) and then turn our attention to that pesky "appropriate" discount rate (the key input in the denominator of the models).

ESTIMATES OF CASH FLOWS

While the discounted cash flow models may be mathematically simple, estimating future dividends with any degree of accuracy is quite challenging for some firms. First, analysts rarely estimate future dividends directly. Most often, analysts will estimate earnings per share and assume a fixed dividend payout ratio (dividends per share/earnings per share) to obtain a dividend estimate. If one assumes that the dividend payout ratio is constant through time, then the earnings growth rate and dividends per share growth rate are identical. However, with some firms—those that have consistently paid and consistently increased dividends through time—one can examine the history of dividend payments and extrapolate that payment history into the future and infer a dividend growth rate.

Second, as shown in the previous section, dividends (and earnings) typically don't grow at a constant rate forever. Estimating growth rates of earnings and dividends, particularly many years in advance, is fraught with peril, and the further out in time one goes, the less accurate are the estimates. Some solace can be drawn, however, from the fact that near-term cash flows generally represent a greater portion of the value of a firm, due to present-value considerations.

In this section, we will describe a method for estimating a dividend growth rate for Johnson & Johnson, a firm that is a perfect candidate for the constant growth dividend model, as it has consistently increased dividends annually for a long period of time. In fact, 2012 represented the fiftieth consecutive year that Johnson & Johnson has raised its dividend payments to shareholders. Box 7-5 provides the dividend history of Johnson & Johnson since 1997.

Box 7-5 Application: Valuation of Johnson & Johnson Using Constant Growth Dividend Model

Data:

Current (2012) dividend = $2.40

Constant dividend growth rate = 8.17%

Appropriate interest (discount rate) = 12%

(Continued)

$$Value = \frac{D_0(1+g)}{r-g} = \frac{\$2.40(1.0817)}{.12-.0817} = \$67.78$$

This compares to a market price at mid-March of 2013 at around $75 per share.

Another way to apply the dividend growth model and compare your assessment of Johnson & Johnson's growth prospects to the market's assessment is to solve for the growth rate using the market price. For example, the growth rate that justifies a market price per share of $75 is equal to:

$$g = r - \frac{D_0(1+g)}{Market\ Value} = .12 - \frac{\$2.40(1.0817)}{\$75} = 8.54\%$$

The second term in this expression is called the expected dividend yield. Therefore, the implied growth rate is equal to the discount rate less the expected dividend yield. In this case, the market price of $75 per share implies that other investors are assuming a dividend growth rate of 8.54 percent compared to your estimate of 8.17 percent. It does not seem like a big difference in future growth rates, but it leads to a pretty big difference in the estimate of value.

Firms like Johnson & Johnson, Abbott Labs, Pitney Bowes, PPG Industries, and Automatic Data Processing are examples of stocks that some analysts refer to as "ruler stocks." This term refers to the fact that if you placed a ruler from the starting point in the series to the ending point in the series on a graph, most of the points would be very close to the ruler. Ruler stocks are ideal for the constant growth dividend model.

Valuing Johnson & Johnson using the constant growth dividend model requires an estimate of the dividend growth rate and the appropriate interest rate to apply. As shown in Figure 7-1, the current (end of year 2012) dividend was $2.40. To compute a historical growth rate of dividends for the past 5 years, we need to simply calculate the compound annual growth rate that equates a value of $1.62 at time 0 to a value of $2.40 at time 5 (in five years). That calculation yields a growth rate of 8.17 percent. You might ask why we didn't go back to 1997 and compute a 15-year growth rate. There certainly is no magical number of years on which to base an assumed growth rate. But for Johnson & Johnson, the 15-year compound annual dividend growth rate is 12.15 percent, a growth rate that will not necessarily continue into perpetuity (more on long-term sustainable growth rates below). So, applying the constant growth dividend model for Johnson & Johnson, assuming a dividend growth rate of 8.17 percent and an appropriate discount rate of 12 percent yields a value of $67.78, as shown in Box 7-5. As of

FIGURE 7-1

Annual dividend history of Johnson & Johnson since 1997.

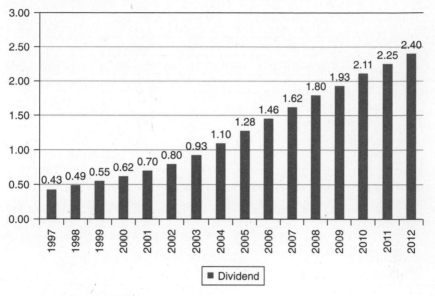

Source: Compiled from U.S. SEC filings

mid-March 2013, Johnson & Johnson was selling at a little over $75 per share. The constant growth dividend model indicates that at that time the stock was fairly valued to slightly overvalued. Certainly there is no margin of safety for a value investor purchasing the stock at a price of around $75 per share.

Let's spend a little more time on long-term sustainable growth rates. How much can a company grow internally by reinvesting its profits? Recall from Chapter 5 that an overall measure of profitability for investors is return on equity (net income divided by average stockholders' equity). If a company reinvests all of these profits by choosing not to pay a dividend, then its equity (book value) will grow by the same amount. So if ROE is 15 percent, book value would grow by 15 percent. Assuming the profits can be deployed in a similar manner next year to increase sales, then earnings should grow by 15 percent. Conversely, if a company pays out all profits as a dividend, then book value will not grow nor will earnings (or dividends). A measure of a long-term sustainable growth rate in earnings (and hence dividends) is:

LT Sustainable Growth Rate in Earnings = Return on Equity
$$\times (1 - Dividend\ Payout\ Rate)$$

So for a return on equity of 15 percent (which is quite good) and a dividend payout rate (dividends/earnings) of 60 percent the sustainable growth rate would be 6 percent.

Box 7-6 Application: Long-Term Sustainable Growth Rate for Johnson & Johnson

Johnson & Johnson's return on equity for recent years was:

2008	30.2%
2009	26.4%
2010	24.9%
2011	17.0%
2012	17.8%

Johnson & Johnson has been paying out about 62 percent of its earnings each year as dividends. The lower ROE in recent years can be attributed to the sharp economic downturn. On the other hand, the very strong ROE in earlier years may not be sustainable indefinitely. If we estimate that Johnson & Johnson can sustain an ROE of 20 percent and will pay out 60 percent of earnings as dividends going forward, then the long-term sustainable growth rate in earnings and dividends would be 8 percent.

Investors certainly don't have to estimate their own dividend growth rates. There are many published sources of growth rates in earnings and dividends available to investors (some at no charge and others on a subscription basis). Table 7-1 provides several dividends and earnings growth estimates for Johnson & Johnson as of mid-March 2013.

Individuals certainly don't need to be tied to the constant growth dividend model. Suppose you forecast a dividend growth rate of 12.15 percent (the 15-year compound growth rate of Johnson & Johnson) over the next three years and then assume that dividend growth rate will fall to 8 percent thereafter. We can apply the two-stage growth model to estimate a current stock value for Johnson & Johnson, as shown in Box 7-7.

TABLE 7-1

Earnings or Dividend Growth Rates for Johnson & Johnson Stock

Source	Estimated Growth Rate	Earnings or Dividends and Time Period
Yahoo! Finance	6.35%	Earnings for next five years
Value Line	6.50%	Dividends for next seven years
Thomson Reuters	6.4%	Consensus LT growth rate (five years)
Zacks Investment Research	6.22%	Earnings for next five years

Box 7-7 Application: Value of Johnson & Johnson Common Stock Using a Two-Stage Dividend Growth Model

Data:

Current (2012) dividend = $2.40
Dividend growth rate for first three years = 12.15%
Dividend growth rate for years four and after = 8%
Appropriate discount rate = 12%

$$Value = \frac{D_1}{(1+r)^1} + \frac{D_2}{(1+r)^2} + \frac{D_3}{(1+r)^3} + \frac{\frac{D_3(1+g)}{(r-g)}}{(1+r)^3}$$

$$Value = \frac{\$2.40(1.1215)}{(1.12)^1} + \frac{\$2.40(1.1215)^2}{(1.12)^2} + \frac{\$2.40(1.1215)^3}{(1.12)^3}$$

$$+ \frac{\frac{\$2.40(1.1215)^3(1.08)}{(.12-.08)}}{(1.12)^3} = \$72.28$$

The two-stage dividend growth model yields a slightly higher valuation than the constant growth dividend model in this case. However, with a market valuation of slightly higher than $75 per share, the model indicates that the stock is fairly priced.

ESTIMATES OF THE APPROPRIATE DISCOUNT RATE

One of the most important inputs to estimate in order to apply the dividend discount model is the appropriate discount rate or interest rate. To be clear, it is an interest rate, but it is referred to as a discount rate because it is used to convert (or discount) future dollars into today's dollars. We cannot specify one discount rate to use for all investments at a particular point. In addition, discount rates for all securities will vary through time as market conditions change. Specifically, the discount rate will vary according to several conditions, including the returns (or yields) on other investments in the marketplace, as well as the perceived riskiness of the dividend stream being analyzed. The basic principle is that the discount rate should be higher for riskier dividend streams, and it should be higher when the yields on other investments—namely, riskless U.S. government securities— are higher.

The basic concept is that the discount rate should take into account both the pure time value of money (that a dollar to be received in a year is worth more than a dollar today) as well as the riskiness of that dollar. In other words, if we can be certain (or fairly certain) that we will in fact receive that dollar in a year, then we can use a lower discount rate than the case where there is uncertainty regarding our receipt of that dollar. And we should use a higher discount rate the higher the uncertainty level.

Despite the recent downgrade of the U.S. debt, and the specter of default that was raised during the hubbub of the debt ceiling crisis, the debt of the U.S. government is still considered the most risk-free investment in the financial markets. Payment is backed by the full faith and credit of the U.S. government. Thus in finance when we talk about the risk-free rate, we are generally referring to the yield on U.S. government securities; however, we must acknowledge that no investment, including U.S. government securities, is truly risk free.

When we are figuring out a discount rate, we begin with that risk-free rate and add to it a risk premium that takes into account (or compensates) the investor for the risk of that particular investment. One of most common methods of determining the risk premium is to use the capital asset pricing model (CAPM). CAPM is an asset pricing model developed by (among others) Nobel Laureate and Stanford Professor William Sharpe in 1964[2] and built on the seminal work on modern portfolio theory by Nobel Laureate Harry Markowitz.[3] CAPM states that the appropriate discount rate (or required rate of return on an investment) can be found by the following equation:

$$r = r_{rf} + \beta \, (r_m - r_{rf})$$

where r_{rf} = risk-free rate
         β = beta (a measure of the risk for a particular security relative to the market based on stock price volatility)
         r_m = return on the market (or return on a broad market index)

Now, here is where both the disagreement and the art of investing play major roles. Even professional investors who employ the CAPM to determine their discount rate estimates will disagree on the specific values for the inputs. Some choose to use historical values, while others use their own estimates of current values. Ideally, we would like to know the risk of a security in the future relative to the market, but that is not knowable with certainty. The term in the preceding equation that is in parentheses $(r_m - r_{rf})$ is referred to as the *market risk premium*. Instead of trying to estimate a current *market risk premium*, many analysts use long-term historical averages. For example, from 1926 through 2010, the average annual return on large company stocks (the S&P 500) was 11.9 percent, and the average return on long-term U.S. government bonds was 5.9 percent. A reasonable long-term estimate of the market risk premium is therefore 6.0 percent. On average, investors in a diversified index of common stocks earned 6.0 percent more annually than investors who kept their money in Treasury bills.[4] See Box 7-8.

Box 7-8 Ibbotson Index Series: Summary Statistics of Annual Total Return, 1926–2010

	Arithmetic Mean Return	Standard Deviation
Large Company Stocks	11.9%	20.4%
Long-Term Government Bonds	5.9%	9.5%
U.S. Treasury Bills	3.7%	3.1%
Inflation	3.1%	4.2%

Source: Ibbotson® SBBI®, 2011 Classic Yearbook: Market Results for Stocks, Bonds, Bills, and Inflation, 1926–2010 (Chicago: Morningstar, 2011).

There is certainly no requirement to use an historical market risk premium. Some professional investors choose to provide estimates of what they believe the market risk premium will be. Professionals tend to widely disagree about the appropriate forward-looking equity risk premium. In a survey of 19 professional investors, as of 2001 the average equity risk premium was estimated to be 3.7 percent.[5] The estimates ranged from a low of 0 percent to a high of 7 percent. The survey of professional investors actually overstated the equity risk premium for this time period, as the 10-year compound return on the S&P from 2001 through 2011 was around 2.7 percent. Once you subtract out the risk-free rate, the equity risk premium was virtually zero.

Even if an analyst uses the historical market risk premium, there is a strong likelihood that the same individual will use a current value of the risk-free rate in the CAPM equation. To find the risk-free rate, one simply needs to see what the current yield is on long-term government bonds. As of mid-March 2013, the yield on 30-year U.S. Treasury bonds was approximately 3.2 percent.

It is quite likely that the market risk premium changes over time. The difference between yields on high-risk bonds and government bonds (another form of risk premium called the default risk premium) tends to increase dramatically in periods of market crisis when fear is prevalent. This was certainly the case in 2008 and 2009 at the depths of the financial crisis. In bull markets, the default risk premium tends to be very thin. You may want to factor an estimate of this time variability into your calculation, or you may choose to assume such variations are likely to smooth out over time as investors' "animal spirits" ebb and flow. This approach can help maintain a constant investing discipline that insulates the strategic value investor from the emotional whims of "Mr. Market."

We have all of the variables we need to calculate the discount rate except for β, or the beta on the investment. Beta is a risk measure and is calculated by comparing the return on a particular investment against the return on a broad market index (like the S&P 500).[6] The beta of the market is 1.0. Investments with a beta greater than 1.0 are said to be riskier than the market, while stocks with a beta of less than 1.0 are less risky than the market. The intuition is that, on average, when the market is up, stocks with a beta of greater than 1.0 are up more than the market. Likewise, when the market is down, stocks with a beta of greater than 1.0 are, on average, down more than the market.

Carrying the intuition a bit further, you would be correct in assuming that investors would demand a higher return for investing in a more risky (or a higher β) investment. Thus, you see that in the CAPM equation, as β increases, the appropriate discount rate increases. And as the appropriate discount rate increases, the present value of the cash flows declines. When you apply the CAPM equation to determine a discount rate, the risk-free rate and the market risk premium will be identical for all stocks at a particular point. What will differ from stock to stock is the estimate of beta.

There are many sources for β, including Yahoo! Finance, Morningstar, ValueLine, and Standard & Poor's. One of the most popular is Yahoo! Finance. You will get very different estimates of β for the same stock depending on your source. It can vary dramatically depending on the time period, market proxy, and return interval used to estimate it. In fact, some data providers, such as Bloomberg, incorporate a smoothing technique to balance out extreme results. If this poses a problem, you might take an average of more than one source. Text Box 7-9 shows the Yahoo! Finance estimates of β for many well-known securities as of mid-March 2013.

Box 7-9 Application: Estimates of β from Yahoo! Finance and the Resulting Discount Rate

	Beta
3M	1.07
Apple	0.74
Berkshire Hathaway	0.25
Boeing	1.07
Coca-Cola	0.38
Exxon	0.86
General Electric	1.47
IBM	0.61
Johnson & Johnson	0.45
Pfizer	0.74

So, for General Electric, the appropriate discount rate to be used in the dividend discount model (estimated by using the CAPM) is:

$$r = r_{rf} + \beta(r_m - r_{rf}) = 3.2\% + 1.47\,(6.0\%) = 12.02\% \approx 12\%$$

Note that the discount rate for Johnson & Johnson, a stock with a much lower β at 0.45, is estimated to be:

$$r = r_{rf} + \beta(r_m - r_{rf}) = 3.2\% + 0.45\,(6.0\%) = 5.9\% \approx 6\%$$

All else equal, the cash flows expected from Johnson & Johnson will equate to a higher present value than identical cash flows from General Electric because they are considered less risky.

The capital asset pricing model and beta are far from perfect. They are based on many assumptions, such as the assumption of rational behavior by investors. Anyone who has watched recent market bubbles and crashes can see that greed and fear often rule markets more than rationality. Further, although what we really want to know is the risk of a security going forward that has many components (financial risk, business risk, size factors, purchasing power risk, and the like), beta is a single factor that may not capture all of these future risks. Professional investors use other multifactor models, but rather than make things more complicated, let's make them simpler.

The *build-up method* is an approach used in valuing private companies for acquisitions or other purposes. It starts with the risk-free rate and adds additional required returns to this amount based on risk factors:

Risk-Free Rate	Amount to compensate for the pure use of money, which effectively includes inflation.
Plus: Equity Risk Premium	The additional return that should be required for an investor to purchase a stock rather than invest at the risk-free rate. This is a premium for the market as a whole (generally for large stocks). This can be determined using historical comparisons (for example the 6 percent discussed previously) or forward-looking forecasts (such as the 3.7 percent survey of professional investors mentioned previously).
Plus: Size Premium	Small stocks are typically considered riskier than large stocks, and, correspondingly, they have exhibited higher historical returns than large stocks over time. Historically, mid-cap stocks have had a long-term risk premium of about 1 percent, low cap about 2 percent, and micro-cap about 4 percent.
Plus: Specific Premium	Judgmentally determined based on the individual stock under consideration. For example, if the company is highly leveraged relative to other companies, you might add a bit. If the company is illiquid or non-public, you might add a larger amount for this illiquidity.

The total of these factors gives you the required rate of return for the investment (desired return or discount rate). As you can see from the table, while there is historical data on which you can at least partially rely, there is also an enormous amount of judgment required. As a value investor, you want to only buy securities with a sufficient margin of safety, so it is generally best to be conservative in your assumptions and specifically err on the side of overestimating risk premiums.

Box 7-10 Application: Required Rate of Return for Mitcham Industries

Mitcham Industries (MIND) provides seismic equipment for geological surveying both onshore and offshore. It has a market capitalization of about $200 million (micro-cap). The following table provides one estimate of a required rate of return for an investment in Mitcham Industries:

Risk-Free Rate	3.2%
+Equity Risk Premium	6.0%
+Size Premium	4.0%
+Specific Premium for a company in a cyclical industry, judgmentally determined	3.0%
Total Required Return	16.2%

These models should give you ideas for how to determine the rate of return that you and other investors might seek from investing in a security. However, ultimately, you are the investor (and we hope a value investor at that!). You should therefore use a required rate of return (discount rate) that will make you happy by compensating you for the risk you are assuming, even if it is beyond these models. For example, if you feel that, going forward, large stocks in general are only expected to offer single digit returns of 7 percent (about 3 percent for risk-free rate and 4 percent for a modest equity risk premium), then you should feel free to use a higher required rate of return (but not lower) to ensure a sufficient margin of safety. For some of you, that may mean 10 percent or even 15 percent.

WHAT WOULD WARREN BUFFETT DO?

Warren Buffett has been quoted many times on the subject of what discount rate he uses in evaluating an investment. He is not known to use models such as the CAPM. He takes the simpler approach. At his annual meetings in the late 1990s, Buffett stated that he typically uses a long-term U.S. Treasury rate (then around 7 percent) to get a preliminary value but then will only buy if he can do so at a significant discount to that value. For example, he once stated he might like to see at least a 10 percent discount rate relative to a 7 percent Treasury rate, but the distance away from the Treasury rate is a function of how comfortable he is with the company—how certain he thinks its estimates of future cash flow are.

CONCLUSION

The many varieties of dividend discount models are standard fare among professional analysts. In fact, they are typically the first models that students are exposed to when studying valuation in undergraduate business programs. While these models can be modified to fit nearly all patterns of expected future dividend growth rates, they are built on the premise that the firm is indeed properly valued by looking at the future dividend stream. Some firms simply cannot be valued by this methodology, leaving you to use a free cash flow, residual income, or asset-based model to obtain an estimate of intrinsic value.

The strategic value investor must recognize that the accuracy of the valuation is a direct function of the accuracy of the inputs to the model. Different investors can apply the same models yet ascertain wildly different intrinsic value estimates, due to differences in assumed dividend growth rates or differences in required rates of return. In fact, one value investor may apply the model and determine that the security is undervalued and purchase it from another value investor who applies the same model and determines that it is overvalued. That is the essence of what makes investment markets function and why many investors are fascinated by them.

CHAPTER EIGHT

FREE CASH FLOW MODELS

'The number one idea is to view a stock as an ownership of the business and to judge the staying quality of the business in terms of its competitive advantage. Look for more value in terms of discounted future cash-flow than you are paying for. Move only when you have an advantage.'

—Charlie Munger

In Chapter 7 you were introduced to dividend discount models, one class of models that is based upon estimating the present value of all future cash flows to value a security. Dividend discount models are appropriate for valuing firms that pay a significant amount of their earnings out as dividends to shareholders. But how should you value firms that pay no dividends or firms in which the dividends paid differ significantly from the company's capacity to pay dividends? For instance, in fiscal year 2012, Apple had $41.7 billion in net income yet only paid dividends of $2.5 billion, which is a dividend payout ratio of a little under 6 percent. Contrast that with Johnson & Johnson's $10.8 billion in net income and dividend payout of $6.6 billion in 2012. You certainly could value Apple using a dividend discount model, but it is readily apparent that the value of Apple is better assessed by its ability to generate cash flow being retained in the firm rather than its ability to pay dividends. In fact, some analysts have criticized Apple for its huge cash hoard. On the other hand, Johnson & Johnson is characterized as a firm paying out a significant portion of its earnings as dividends, so a dividend discount model seems perfectly appropriate for valuing that firm.

Estimating the present value of all future dividends is one way to determine the value of a security. Later chapters show you how to use asset-based models and value the firm according to the assets on its balance sheet. The focus of this chapter is on free cash flow models, and it illustrates how to arrive at an estimate of value based on a firm's sustainable cash generating capability. The models presented in this chapter are applicable to valuing a wide variety of companies: those that pay dividends and those that don't. We introduced the concept of free cash flow in the context of ratio analysis in Chapter 5. This chapter shows that in addition to providing a means of *relative* valuation, you can estimate the intrinsic value of a firm through an analysis of free cash flow. Specifically, we show that the value of a firm can be estimated by computing the present value of all future free cash flows to the firm. Likewise, we can estimate the value of a share of common stock in the firm by computing the present value of all future cash flows that accrue to stockholders whether or not these cash flows are distributed to shareholders year to year.[1]

In the following sections, we introduce the concept of free cash flow and show how to value a firm based on free cash flow to the firm (FCFF) and free cash flow to equity (FCFE). Unlike dividends, FCFF and FCFE are not readily available metrics that one can simply find on published financial statements. Free cash flow models require you to provide estimates of a number of variables and involve more calculations than the much simpler dividend discount models presented in the previous chapter. The presentation here is designed to provide you with a flavor of free cash flow models. Readers interested in a more detailed, robust and calculation-intensive treatment should refer to Pinto, Henry, Robinson, and Stowe (2010).

WHAT IS FREE CASH FLOW?

Free cash flow is not a formal accounting concept and therefore is sometimes defined differently by different people. In its simplest form, free cash flow is the amount of operating cash flow (cash flow from operating activities or CFO) left over after paying for any needed capital expenditures (whether for replacement or future growth), and it can be measured as:

$$Free\ Cash\ Flow = CFO - Capital\ Expenditures$$

We have to be a bit more precise when computing free cash flow for valuation purposes. There are two definitions of free cash flow that are relevant to the valuation process: free cash flow to the firm and free cash flow to equity. We distinguish between the two concepts below and show how you can use the concepts to estimate the value of a share of stock.

Free cash flow to the firm is the cash flow available to a firm's suppliers of capital after all operating expenses (including taxes) have been paid and all necessary investments in working capital (think inventory) and fixed capital (think plant and equipment) have been made. Free cash flow to the firm is:

$$Free\ Cash\ Flow\ to\ the\ Firm\ (FCFF)$$
$$= CFO + Interest\ Expense\ (1 - Tax\ Rate) - Capital\ Expenditures$$

The firm's suppliers of capital include common stockholders, preferred stockholders, and bondholders. Simply put, free cash flow to the firm is that cash flow available after everyone but the suppliers of capital have been paid and necessary investments have been made to ensure the proper functioning of the firm, both now and in the future.

The analogy is to that of running a household. Cash flow to a household is what is left after all routine expenses (groceries, mortgage, fuel, etc.) have been paid. But to maintain a household, one must periodically spend money on maintenance and upkeep or the home will decline in value. Think about a situation where a homeowner does not perform routine upkeep on the house—paint, replace the furnace and appliances. The value of the house will erode. In the same way, all of the cash flow from operations is not freely available to claimants. Some portion of cash flow must be spent to maintain and improve the business.

A firm must replace machinery; invest in new property, plant, and equipment; and invest in research and development to remain viable in the long term and maximize the long-term free cash flow from operations. We also need to provide a caveat to the FCFF equation above. This is the equation you would use in most circumstances. Under U.S. accounting standards, interest expense is deducted on the cash flow statement in order to arrive at cash flow from operations. Because FCFF is free cash flow available to all capital suppliers (including debt holders) and interest flows to those debt holders, it needs to be added back (net of taxes) when computing FCFF. However, under International Financial Reporting Standards (IFRS) companies are permitted so show interest expense in either operating cash flow or financing cash flow. If a company is using IFRS and chooses to deduct interest expense from financing cash flows, then the interest adjustment is not necessary and the formula becomes:

Free Cash Flow to the Firm (FCFF) = CFO − Capital Expenditures

When we are trying to value a share of the firm's common stock, we must recognize that all free cash flow does not accrue to stockholders. There are other suppliers of capital—namely, bondholders—who must also be paid. When valuing equity, we are interested in only that portion of free cash flow that is the "property" of stockholders. Free cash flow to equity (FCFE) is the cash flow available to the company's common stockholders after all operating expenses, interest, and principal payments have been paid and after all necessary payments to fixed capital have been made. Free cash flow to equity is:

Free Cash Flow to Equity (FCFE)
= CFO − Capital Expenditures
+ Net Borrowing from Debt Holders

We saw in Chapter 5 that a publicly traded company is required to report cash flow from operations (CFO) on its statement of cash flows. But as you can see in both the equations above, CFO needs to be adjusted to arrive at FCFF and FCFE.

Calculating FCFF and FCFE for past years is not difficult. All you need to do is access the statement of cash flows to obtain the necessary inputs. However, forecasting these amounts for future years is much more problematic and requires several simplifying assumptions. You will find that using spreadsheet models makes this process manageable. Additionally, when you employ spreadsheet models you can perform a sensitivity analysis by altering the various inputs. We show how to forecast free cash flow in a later section of this chapter.

Box 8-1 Application: Computing FCFF and FCFE for Walmart

Refer to Table 5-2 for the statement of cash flows for Walmart. The following values are provided for the year ended January 31, 2011 (amounts are in $ millions):

Cash flow from operations	$23,643
Payments for property and equipment	($12,699)
Proceeds from the disposal of property and equipment	$489
Investments and business acquisitions, net	($202)
Short-term borrowing	503
Long-term borrowing	11,396
Payments of long-term debt	($4,080)
Payment of capital lease obligations	($363)

Additionally, from supplemental disclosures we can determine that Walmart paid $2,163 of interest to debt holders and had an average tax rate of 32 percent.

Free cash flow to the firm (FCFF) is computed as:

Cash flow from operations	$23,643
Plus: After-tax interest ($2,163 * 0.68)	1,471
Less: Payments for property and equipment	($12,699)
Plus: Proceeds from disposal of property and equipment	$489
Less: Investments and business acquisitions, net	($202)
Equals: Free cash flow to the firm (FCFF)	$12,702

Note that we are including as capital expenditures investments in businesses as well as net investments in property and equipment (sales net of payments). This is appropriate when computing past FCFF, but when we are forecasting future FCFF we typically just forecast net investments in property and equipment and consider potential acquisitions, if any, separately.

Free cash flow to equity (FCFE) is computed as:

Cash flow from operations	$23,643
Less: Payments for property and equipment	($12,699)
Plus: Proceeds from disposal of property and equipment	$489
Less: Investments and business acquisitions, net	($202)
Less: Short-term borrowing	503

Plus: Long-term borrowing	11,396
Less: Payments on long-term debt	($4,080)
Less: Payment of capital lease obligations	($363)
Equals: Free cash flow to equity (FCFE)	$18,687

Note that in computing FCFE from an historical perspective we are including borrowings from debt holders. This may seem odd, as it implies that borrowing could increase FCFE and somehow increase the value of the firm, as well. We do not use historical FCFE for valuation—we want to forecast future average FCFE, which includes borrowing to the extent that it pays for some portion of capital expenditures. This means it does not have to be paid for by the equity holders. The repayment of borrowing in subsequent years will reduce FCFE.

THE FREE CASH FLOW TO THE FIRM (FCFF) MODEL

The FCFF valuation model estimates the value of the firm (debt and equity) as the present value of future FCFF estimates discounted at a rate known as the weighted average cost of capital (WACC). We show how to compute the WACC in a section below. So, the market value of the firm using the FCFF model is:

$$Value \ of \ the \ Firm = \frac{FCFF_1}{(1+WACC)^1} + \frac{FCFF_2}{(1+WACC)^2} + \cdots \frac{FCFF_n}{(1+WACC)^n} + \cdots$$

If this equation looks familiar, it is identical in form to the basic dividend valuation model presented in the previous chapter. The only differences in the formulas are that the numerator in this case involves free cash flow estimates (while in the dividend model the cash flows were estimated dividends) and the denominator in this case involves a discount factor determined as the WACC (while in the dividend model, the denominator was a discount rate determined by the riskiness of the firm's equity).

As potential shareholders, we are ultimately interested in the market value of the equity rather than the market value of firm. Because FCFF involves the cash flow available to all suppliers of capital (both debt holders and equity holders), the market value of equity can be approximated as the market value of the firm less the market value of debt:

Equity Value = Value of the Firm − Value of Debt

To determine the share value, you simply need to divide the equity value by the number of shares outstanding.

Determining the Weighted Average Cost of Capital (WACC)

Simply put, the WACC is the overall average rate of return of a company's suppliers of capital. For simplicity's sake, we will assume that there are two classes of suppliers of capital: debt holders and stockholders. However, the WACC framework can easily be expanded to include preferred stockholders.

The formula for WACC is straightforward. The component costs—cost of debt and cost of equity—are simply weighted by the amount of debt and equity, respectively, in the capital structure of the firm. The amount of debt and equity is determined by market values of each component, not book values. Thus, the WACC formula is:

$$\text{WACC} = \frac{MVD}{MVD + MVE} k_d + \frac{MVE}{MVD + MVE} k_e$$

where: MVD = Market value of debt
MVE = Market value of equity
k_d = After-tax cost of debt
k_e = Cost of equity

In many jurisdictions, most notably the United States, corporations are allowed to deduct net interest expense from income in calculating taxes owed. Dividend payments to shareholders (including preferred shareholders) do not receive such a favorable tax treatment. Thus, we say that corporate debt has a tax shield—in effect, lowering the cost of debt financing by a factor equivalent to the tax rate. The before-tax cost of debt for a corporation can be approximated by the yield to maturity on a corporation's long-term debt. If several debt issues are outstanding, you can use some sort of average yield to maturity on the issues. Remember, WACC is an input to a valuation model and involves several simplifying assumptions. Getting exact estimates down to the basis point is unnecessary. The goal of the value investor is to identify investments that are significantly misvalued in the marketplace.

If the before-tax cost of debt capital is 6 percent and the tax rate is 30 percent, the after-tax cost of debt (k_d) is determined as:

After tax cost of debt = Before Tax Cost of Debt

$$\times (1 - Tax\ Rate)$$
$$= 6\% \times (1 - 0.3) = 4.2\%$$

The cost of equity (k_e) can be determined in a number of ways, including the capital asset pricing model and build-up methods outlined in Chapter 7. In Box 8-2 we provide an estimate of the WACC for Walmart.

Box 8-2 Application: WACC Estimate for Walmart as of Mid-March 2013

Average yield to maturity for Walmart debt	= 3.5%
Income tax rate	= 32%
Market value of debt	= $54.230 billion
Market value of equity	= $255.143 billion
Beta of WMT equity	= 0.41 (from Yahoo! Finance)
Market risk premium	= 6.0%
Risk-free rate	= 3.2%

First, we compute the after-tax cost of debt capital:

$$After\ Tax\ Cost\ of\ Debt = Before\ Tax\ Cost \times (1 - tax\ rate)$$
$$= 3.5\% \times (1 - 0.32) = 2.38\%$$

Next, we compute the cost of equity capital:

$$Cost\ of\ Equity = r_{rf} + \beta(r_m - r_{rf}) = 3.2\% + 0.41(6\%) = 5.66\%$$

The WACC is estimated as:

$$WACC = \frac{MVD}{MVD + MVE}k_d + \frac{MVE}{MVD + MVE}k_e$$

$$= \frac{54.230}{54.230 + 255.143}(2.38\%) + \frac{255.143}{54.230 + 255.143}(5.66\%) = 5.09\%$$

This is an extremely low estimate for the cost of capital for a firm. The low estimate is due to three factors:

1. Walmart is a very strong credit risk, thus the yield to maturity on its bonds is extremely low;

2. This estimate was made in a very low interest rate environment; and

3. The beta of Walmart is substantially less than the market.

We do not believe that this is a long-term sustainable WACC. In your valuation models, you should use your desired rate of return for the cost of equity. If you feel you would like to get an 8 percent rate of return, for example, based on your comfort level with Walmart, then you should use it in the model—and not use what some financial model would indicate. Using a higher rate is conservative, as it will result in a lower intrinsic value that may result in your passing on some marginal investment opportunities. Using 8 percent as the cost of equity for Walmart would yield a WACC of 7 percent.

FORECASTING FREE CASH FLOW
TO THE FIRM (FCFF)

All valuation models require that the investor have a thorough understanding of the company. The free cash flow models presented in this chapter are no exception, and they required a detailed analysis of the firm's financial statements. In this section we show you how to develop estimates of free cash flow to the firm (FCFF).

Although you can compute historical free cash flow directly from the cash flow statement, you likely do not want to simply extrapolate those numbers forward. The operating cash flow achieved last year was a function of last year's revenue, profit margin, collection of receivables, purchases of inventory, and so on. In forecasting, we prefer some flexibility to adjust those parameters going forward, so we use a model that forecasts revenue, then operating income, then operating cash flow, and finally forecasts free cash flow to the firm:

Revenue

Operating profit before tax (and before interest expense)

Less: Taxes

Operating profit after tax (and before interest expense)

Plus: Depreciation and amortization

Less: Additional working capital

Operating cash flow (excluding interest expense)

Less: Capital expenditures

Estimated Free Cash Flow to the Firm

This model gives you flexibility to change inputs based on what you believe will occur in the future, such as higher or lower profit margins, higher or lower taxes, higher or lower capital expenditures.

Box 8-3 Application: Forecast of Walmart FCFF

You would like to compute a forecast of Walmart's FCFF for next year (assuming it is currently early April 2013). You collect the following historical data provided in Table 8-1 for Walmart to help you assess reasonable inputs in forecasting FCFF. Note that the 2013 fiscal year for Walmart ended January 31, 2013. We will use revenue of $469,162 million as the base year to forecast FCFF for FYE January 31, 2014. We estimate the inputs to the model as:

Inputs		
Sales for base period	469,162	Most recent 12 months
Sales growth rate	4.00%	Our estimate of the future
Operating profit margin	5.90%	Our estimate of the future
Depreciation and amortization (percent of revenues)	1.80%	Our estimate of the future
Additional working capital investment (percent of increase in revenues)	4.00%	Our estimate of the future
Capital expenditures (percent of revenues)	2.90%	Our estimate of the future
Tax rate	32.00%	Our estimate of the future

The future estimates we show here are our judgments based on historical information, the current economic and tax environment, and what we think the future holds for Walmart. This may make you uncomfortable versus just inserting historic averages, but judgment is needed: You cannot assume the past will extrapolate into the future. Valuation is as much an art as it is a science!

Based on these inputs we can forecast future revenue, operating income, operating cash flow, and free cash flow to the firm as:

Amounts in $ Millions	Forecast
Revenue	487,928
Operating profit before tax (and before interest expense)	28,788
Less: Taxes	(9,212)
Operating profit after tax (and before interest expense)	19,576
Plus: Depreciation and amortization	8,783
Less: Additional working capital	(751)
Operating cash flow (excluding interest expense)	27,608
Less: Capital expenditures	(14,150)
Estimated free cash flow to the firm	13,458

So, we are forecasting that next fiscal year's free cash flow to the firm as $13,458. As shown in the next section, we can use this estimate to value the firm.

Optimists are tempted to underestimate the capital expenditures necessary to sustain a reasonable growth rates. Pessimists may overestimate capital expenditures necessary for future growth. It is important to recognize that there is a link between the two, and that it is inconsistent to estimate high future growth (which increases future free cash flow) and low capital expenditures (which also increases future free cash flow). We shall see the importance of growth in the next section.

TABLE 8-1

Selected Financial Statement Data for Walmart

Amounts in Millions	Source	2013	2012	2011	2010	2009
Revenue	Income statement	469,162	446,950	421,849	408,085	404,254
Operating profit	Income statement	27,801	26,558	25,542	24,002	22,767
Depreciation and amortization	Cash flow statement	8,501	8,130	7,641	7,157	6,739
Working capital investments						
(Increase) or decrease in accounts receivable	Cash flow statement	(614)	(796)	(733)	297	(101)
(Increase) or decrease in inventory	Cash flow statement	(2,459)	(3,727)	(3,205)	2,213	(220)
Increase or (decrease) in accounts payable	Cash flow statement	1,061	2,687	2,676	1,052	(410)
Increase or (decrease) in accrued liabilities	Cash flow statement	1,252	59	(433)	1,348	2,036
Total working capital adjustment to net income		(760)	(1,777)	(1,695)	4,910	1,305
Capital expenditures (net)	Cash flow statement	12,366	12,930	12,210	11,182	10,785
Tax rate	Footnotes or computed	31.0%	32.6%	32.2%	32.4%	34.2%
Revenue increase (percent)	Computed	5.0%	6.0%	3.4%	0.9%	
Revenue increase (dollars)	Computed	22,212	25,101	13,764	3,831	
Operating margin	Operating profit/revenue	5.9%	5.9%	6.1%	5.9%	5.6%
Depreciation and amortization as a percent of revenue	Computed from above	1.8%	1.8%	1.8%	1.8%	1.7%
Additional working capital investment	Minus total WC adj/revenue	3.4%	7.1%	12.3%	(128.2%)	
Capital expenditures as a percent of revenue	Computed from above	2.6%	2.9%	2.9%	2.7%	2.7%

162

VALUATION USING FREE CASH FLOW
TO THE FIRM

As with the dividend discount model, we can use an FCFF model that assumes a constant future growth rate in FCFF into perpetuity. The formula for the value of the firm under this model is:

$$Firm\ Value = \frac{FCFF_1}{WACC - g}$$

In this model we discount next year's FCFF by our weighted average cost of capital minus the future growth rate (note that we have already forecast next year's FCFF in the numerator, so we do not need to grow it by g as we did for the dividend discount model in Chapter 7). The result is the value of the firm (debt plus equity), therefore we need to subtract the value of debt to get the value of the equity:

Equity Value = Value of the Firm – Value of Debt

Lastly, if we desire a value per share, we simply divide the estimated equity value by the number of shares of stock outstanding.

Box 8-4 Application: Valuation Using Forecasted FCFF

We will use our forecast for Walmart's FCFF for 2014 of $13.458 billion, our estimate of a WACC of 7 percent (the conservative amount previously discussed) and assume Walmart will continue to grow at a modest 3 percent per year after next year.

Value of the Firm = $13.458/(.07 – .03) = $336 billion

Walmart currently has about $54 billion of debt, so the value of the equity is about $282 billion. With 3.34 billion shares outstanding, this means the value per share is $84.43 per share.

At the time of this writing, Walmart is currently trading at around $76 per share, or about a 10 percent discount to the intrinsic value we calculated. The current market price is only a modest discount from the calculated intrinsic value—not enough to attract the attention of most value investors. This discount represents the "margin of safety" that Ben Graham emphasized and that Warren Buffett and Seth Klarman adopted.

MULTISTAGE FREE CASH FLOW TO THE FIRM

The model presented above is a single-stage model. You are assuming constant growth and that all of your inputs are the same every year. A multistage model allows you to vary inputs for some years, although at some point you have to simplify things and assume the future is constant. In a multistage FCFF model, you explicitly forecast FCFF for a number of years and then assume the constant growth formula to determine the terminal value—the value in the last year of the forecast. This is analogous to the multistage dividend discount model presented in Chapter 7. Most commonly, investors forecast five years into the future, but you can use any number of years you are comfortable with. Forecasting involves estimating the future and forecasting beyond five years in a changing economic environment is problematic and likely won't be worth the additional effort.

We use the same forecasting approach we used for FCFF previously, but we employ a model that allows us to adjust individual inputs year-over-year if we so desire.

Box 8-5 Application: Multistage FCFF Valuation Model

Table 8-2 presents the inputs and model for a multistage FCFF model for Walmart. In this multistage model you can adjust each input separately for each year, if so desired. We have left most inputs the same as in our single-stage model presented earlier except that we assume the operating margin will continue to be compressed and will decline from 5.9 percent to 5.5 percent over the five-year period. Note we are also growing revenues by 4 percent in the first five years but then only 3 percent into perpetuity to estimate the terminal value.

For years one through five, we are forecasting out FCFF for each year and then discounting it back to today at the WACC. Year one is discounted back one year; year two is discounted back two years, and so on. The terminal value represents the value of the firm at the end of year five. It is computed by forecasting the FCFF for year six, then applying a single-stage constant growth model to determine the value at the end of Year five. This value is then discounted back five years at the WACC. This model results in an intrinsic value for Walmart of about $81 per share. This is slightly below our single-stage model due to the declining operating margin.

The free cash to the firm model is very flexible. For Walmart we used its current capital structure—about 17.5 percent debt and 82.5 percent equity. However, you can also change the capital structure assumptions in the model. For example, if you thought that Walmart was an attractive takeover candidate and that the acquirer would employ a different capital structure (for example, more debt) then you can simply change that assumption. For this reason, the FCFF model is quite commonly used in acquisitions and leveraged buyouts to determine the price that could reasonably be paid for the target company.

TABLE 8-2

Discounted Free Cash Flow to the Firm Model

Walmart			4/5/2013			
Inputs	Year 1	Year 2	Year 3	Year 4	Year 5	Terminal Value
Sales growth rate	4.00%	4.00%	4.00%	4.00%	4.00%	3.00%
Operating profit margin	5.90%	5.80%	5.70%	5.60%	5.50%	5.50%
Depreciation and amortization (percent of revenues)	1.80%	1.80%	1.80%	1.80%	1.80%	1.80%
Additional working capital investment (percent of increase in revenues)	4.00%	4.00%	4.00%	4.00%	4.00%	4.00%
Capital expenditures (percent of revenues)	2.90%	2.90%	2.90%	2.90%	2.90%	2.90%
Tax rate	32.00%	32.00%	32.00%	32.00%	32.00%	32.00%
Sales for base period—TTM or forecast adjusted for first-stage growth	469,162					
Cost of debt	3.00%					
Cost of equity	8.00%					
Total debt	54,230					
Nonoperating assets	0					
Current price per share	76.39					
Shares outstanding	3,340					
Computed below here						
Market value of equity	255,143					
Percentage of debt	17.53%					
Percentage of equity	82.47%					
Weighted average cost of capital (Computed do not input)	6.96%					
Sales	487,928	507,446	527,743	548,853	570,807	587,932
Operating profit before tax	28,788	29,432	30,081	30,736	31,394	32,336
Taxes	(9,212)	(9,418)	(9,626)	(9,835)	(10,046)	(10,348)

(Continued)

TABLE 8-2

Discounted Free Cash Flow to the Firm Model (*Continued*)

Walmart			4/5/2013			
	Year 1	Year 2	Year 3	Year 4	Year 5	Terminal Value
Operating profit after tax	19,576	20,014	20,455	20,900	21,348	21,989
Plus: Depreciation and amortization	8,783	9,134	9,499	9,879	10,275	10,583
Less: Additional working capital	(751)	(781)	(812)	(844)	(878)	(685)
Operating cash flow	27,608	28,367	29,143	29,935	30,745	31,886
Less: Capital expenditures	(14,150)	(14,716)	(15,305)	(15,917)	(16,553)	(17,050)
Estimated free cash flow	13,458	13,651	13,838	14,019	14,191	14,836
Terminal value						375,105
Present value	12,583	11,933	11,310	10,713	10,139	268,005
Total firm value	324,683					
Plus nonoperating assets	0					
Less debt	(54,230)					
Equity value	270,453					
Current intrinsic value per share	80.97					

Another feature of the model presented in Table 8-2 that we left blank for Walmart is the possibility that the company has significant nonoperating assets that provide additional value. For example, if a company has accumulated large amounts of cash (Apple, for example) or investments that are not needed for operational purposes (working capital), then these can be added to the model and will increase the estimated value.

Forecasting Free Cash Flow to Equity (FCFE)

We can use a similar process to forecast free cash flow to equity. We start with a forecast of revenue and operating cash flow and then adjust for capital expenditures, after-tax interest expense, and net borrowing:

Revenue
Operating profit before tax (and before interest expense)
Less: Taxes
Operating profit after tax (and before interest expense)
Plus: Depreciation and amortization
Less: Additional working capital
Operating cash flow (excluding interest expense)
Less: Capital expenditures
Plus: Net borrowing (Capital expenditures times % debt)
Less: After-tax interest expense
Estimated free cash flow to the firm

Box 8-6 Application: Forecast of 2014 FCFE for Walmart

Using similar assumptions to those used earlier with the addition of an assumption as to the portion of capital expenditures that will be financed with debt and how much interest expense will be each year, we forecast Walmart's FCFE as:

Inputs	
Sales for base period	469,162
Sales growth rate	4.00%
Operating profit margin	5.90%
Depreciation and amortization (percent of revenues)	1.80%
Additional working capital investment (percent of increase in revenues)	4.00%
Capital expenditures (percent of revenues)	2.90%
Tax rate	32.00%
Percentage of debt in capital structure	17.50%
Interest expense as a percentage of revenues	0.50%
Forecast	
Revenue	487,928
Operating profit before tax (and before interest expense)	28,788
Less: Taxes	(9,212)
Operating profit after tax (and before interest expense)	19,576
Plus: Depreciation and amortization	8,783
Less: Additional working capital	(751)
Operating cash flow (excluding interest expense)	27,608

(Continued)

Less: Capital expenditures	(14,150)
Plus: Net borrowing (capital expenditures times % debt)	2,476
Less: After-tax interest expense	(1,659)
Estimated free cash flow to equity	14,275

Relative to the forecast of FCFF, this forecast of FCFE has two additional components: the amount of borrowing to support capital expenditures (reducing the cash outflow for equity holders) and the amount of interest that was paid to the debt holders (which flows to the debt holders) adjusted for taxes saved. As a result, we estimate Walmart's FCFE as $14.275 billion.

VALUATION USING FREE CASH FLOW TO EQUITY

Once again, our valuation model for FCFE is very similar to that of a dividend discount model. In this case, a forecast of next year's FCFE is discounted at the return desired by you as an equity investor minus the future expected growth rate of free cash flow to equity:

$$Equity\,Value = \frac{FCFE_1}{r - g}$$

The only difference from the dividend discount model presented in Chapter 7 is that we replace dividends per share with total free cash flow to equity. To get intrinsic value per share, take the total equity value divided by the number of shares outstanding.

Box 8-7 Application: Valuation Using Forecasted FCFE

With a forecast of FCFE for Walmart of $14.275 billion, a desired rate of return of 8 percent (for an equity investor based on our assessment of risk), and a future growth rate of 3 percent, the total value of equity is estimated at:

Equity Value = $14.275/(.08 − .03) = $285.5 billion

With 3.34 billion shares outstanding, the intrinsic value per share for Walmart is $85.50 per share. Note that this is very close to the value we received using the single-stage FCFF model—as it should be, as long as we were consistent with our assumptions (within some tolerance for rounding of computations). Again, it shows that Walmart is currently trading at a slight discount to intrinsic value.

MULTISTAGE FREE CASH FLOW TO EQUITY

The single-stage model is easy to apply but lacks flexibility if you feel growth and other inputs will not be constant over the next few years. We can create a spreadsheet for a multistage FCFE model in which inputs for each year in the early stage can be adjusted individually, as with our earlier FCFF model. Similar to the FCFF model, this model involves forecasting for an explicit number of years and then computing a terminal value at the end of that period using the single-stage model. All free cash flow to the firm is then discounted back to today to get the intrinsic value in today's dollars. The inputs are similar to those for the FCFF model, with the addition of required information on the amount of interest expected to be paid.

Box 8-8 Application: Valuation of Walmart Using a Multistage FCFE

Table 8-3 presents the inputs and model for a multistage FCFE model for Walmart. We have left inputs identical, as in our multistage FCFF model presented earlier, except that we add an input for interest expense because this flows to the debt holders rather than the equity holders and must be subtracted in determining FCFE. Some other inputs are rounded. Although we definitely want to be careful with our assumptions and inputs, we don't want to give ourselves a false sense of precision. Do we really know whether the percentage of debt going forward is 17.5 percent or 17.53 percent? Many analysts fall prey to the illusion of precision and lose sight of the fact that their goal is to determine a rough estimate of value. Our resulting intrinsic value is intended to give us an idea of the margin of safety we have when making this investment at the current price: We hope to buy at a significant discount to the intrinsic value.

The FCFE model presented in Table 8-3 results in an intrinsic value for Walmart of about $82 per share. This is slightly below our single-stage model due to the declining operating margin and is very close to the value we derived using the multistage FCFF model. At a current market price of $76.39, we have a margin of safety of only about 7 percent.

As with the free cash to the firm model, this model is very flexible. For Walmart, we used its current capital structure, which is about 17.5 percent debt and 82.5 percent equity. However, we can change the capital structure going forward for valuation purposes and vary other inputs year over year. We can shorten the model to forecast fewer years or lengthen it if we are confident in our ability to forecast longer periods. As with the FCFF model, we also have the ability to incorporate any significant nonoperating assets that may provide additional value.

TABLE 8-3

Discounted Free Cash Flow to Equity Model

Walmart				4/5/2013		
I	Year 1	Year 2	Year 3	Year 4	Year 5	Terminal Value
Sales growth rate	4.00%	4.00%	4.00%	4.00%	4.00%	3.00%
Operating profit margin	5.90%	5.80%	5.70%	5.60%	5.50%	5.50%
Depreciation and amortization (percent of revenues)	1.80%	1.80%	1.80%	1.80%	1.80%	1.80%
Additional working capital investment (percent of increase in revenues)	4.00%	4.00%	4.00%	4.00%	4.00%	4.00%
Capital expenditures (percent of revenues)	2.90%	2.90%	2.90%	2.90%	2.90%	2.90%
Tax rate	32.00%	32.00%	32.00%	32.00%	32.00%	32.00%
Sales for base period: TTM or forecast adjusted for first stage growth	469,162					
Percentage of debt in capital structure	17.50%					
Interest expense as a percentage of revenues	0.50%					
Cost of equity	8.00%					
Nonoperating assets	0					
Shares outstanding	3,340.00					

	Year 1	Year 2	Year 3	Year 4	Year 5	Terminal Value
Sales	487,928	507,446	527,743	548,853	570,807	587,932
Operating profit before tax	28,788	29,432	30,081	30,736	31,394	32,336
Taxes	(9,212)	(9,418)	(9,626)	(9,835)	(10,046)	(10,348)
Operating profit after tax	19,576	20,014	20,455	20,900	21,348	21,989
Plus: Depreciation and amortization	8,783	9,134	9,499	9,879	10,275	10,583
Less: Additional working capital	(751)	(781)	(812)	(844)	(878)	(685)
Operating cash flow	27,608	28,367	29,143	29,935	30,745	31,886
Less: Capital expenditures	(14,150)	(14,716)	(15,305)	(15,917)	(16,553)	(17,050)
Plus: Net borrowing (capital expenditures times % debt)	2,476	2,575	2,678	2,785	2,897	2,984

Less: After-tax interest expense	(1,659)	(1,725)	(1,794)	(1,866)	(1,941)	(1,999)
Estimated free cash flow to equity	14,275	14,501	14,722	14,938	15,147	15,821
Terminal value						316,424
Present value	13,218	12,432	11,687	10,980	10,309	215,353
Total firm value	273,979					
Plus nonoperating assets	0					
Equity value	273,979					
Current intrinsic value per share	82.03					

APPLYING FREE CASH FLOW VALUATION

Which model should you use: FCFF or FCFE? There are definitely some guiding principles. If you think the capital structure is going to remain relatively constant and the borrowing is going to occur smoothly to support capital expenditures, then the FCFE model works well. If, however, borrowing and repayment vary year to year, then in reality FCFE will fluctuate widely over time and your forecast will likely be inaccurate (but the valuation may not be far off). In cases where capital structure is changing—such as in a leveraged buyout—the FCFF works well. In fact, we believe that FCFF can be used in most circumstances, making it a pretty safe bet. You should, however, get similar results by employing either model. The estimated margin of safety likely won't be dramatically different from one model to the other.

The "art" of valuation is easy to see in the amount of judgment required to generate assumptions for the inputs into these models. You should not just extrapolate the past. You may feel that the company is overly aggressive in reporting their earnings and therefore may want to adjust assumed margins downward. Further, the past is fine to start with, but then you have to look at trends, the current state of the economy, and changes in the industry and business model of the company. Some companies have drastically different business models that can have major influences on valuation. For example, most companies need to invest in working capital (inventory, receivables, etc.). Note that we assumed this to be the case for Walmart, even though in some years (see Table 8-1 2009 and 2010) it actually generated cash from working capital. Dell, on the other hand, is an example of a company that has a business model that collects payments quickly from customers, and they only build a computer once is it ordered. This business model allows Dell to carry lower inventories than other similar firms. In addition, Dell takes their time paying suppliers (accounts payable). As a result, they have pretty consistently generated cash from working capital. We would input this as a negative investment—accretive to cash flow—in our models.

CONCLUSION

Free cash models provide a way to estimate intrinsic value when dividends are low or nonexistent or when they are unreliable. They represent a helpful discipline for the strategic value investor, as well, because they require the analyst to consider carefully the factors that will impact sales, margins, capital expenditure, and growth in the future. These models are therefore well-structured mechanisms to learn the company.

CHAPTER NINE

ASSET-BASED APPROACHES

*We believe this margin-of-safety principle, so strongly emphasized by Ben Graham,
to be the cornerstone of investment success.*

—Warren Buffett, 1992,
Letter to Berkshire Hathaway shareholders

In previous chapters we have largely focused on the ability of firms to generate
and increase future earnings and cash flows as the primary element in valuation. Most investors purchase stocks because they believe that these investments will generate substantial future cash flows and earnings. But there are
reasons other than ability to generate earnings and cash flows that warrant
the strategic value investor to consider purchasing or short selling the stock
of a firm. Some firms may be good investments because the net assets (assets
less the liabilities) held by the firm are, for whatever reason, undervalued or
underappreciated by the market. These firms are purchased primarily based
on the value of their underlying assets.

Asset-based approaches sometimes have the advantage of providing clar-
ity and objectivity in an otherwise ambiguous setting. Estimating future cash
flows can be a subjective process subject to tremendous uncertainty. Suppose,
however, a firm is trading at a value that is less than the net cash on its balance
sheet (i.e., cash less current liabilities and other debt). In theory, an acquirer
could purchase the firm, pay off the debt, and still have money left over
before he or she even started liquidating the other assets on the balance sheet.
Although such deep value circumstances are rare, and a strategic value investor would want to perform a more thorough analysis that included the quality
of management, contingent liabilities, and off-balance-sheet liabilities, these
types of situations do happen and make a compelling case for a strategic value
investing play.

How do you value a gold mining stock? It is purported that Mark Twain
once said that "a gold mine is a hole in the ground owned by a liar." It is difficult
to use standard discounted cash flow models for firms that don't have well-
defined cash flows or good estimates of future cash flows, especially when it is
so difficult to predict future commodity prices. The value of a mining company

is really the value of the natural resources in the ground today less the cost of extracting those resources. So, asset-based approaches are commonly used to value natural resource firms. An oil firm such as Exxon Mobil or Petrobas, for instance, can be valued on the basis of the value of proven oil reserves less extraction costs.

Similarly, a timber firm such as Weyerhauser might be valued on the basis of the number of board meters of timber it controls. But, even then, one must be cognizant of the other potential uses of the land a timber firm controls.[1] The underlying land value should be considered, including the hunting and mineral rights that add value to the land without interfering with timber management. In addition, the land may have potential parcelization and development value. Thus, the analyst considering timber firms may need to consider two potential avenues of value: the timber value and the real estate value. The values of each of these components need not move in tandem and may not be properly recognized by Mr. Market.

Valuing natural resources firms can get quite complicated, and market prices can be quite volatile when there is general disagreement concerning the amount and value of assets a firm controls. In early June 2011, shares in Sino Forest, one of the leading commercial forest plantation operators in China, plummeted following the release of a negative research report by Carson Block of Muddy Waters Research. The report claimed that Sino Forest had overstated its timber holdings and claimed that Sino Forest was a "multibillion-dollar Ponzi scheme" that was "accompanied by substantial theft."[2] Hedge fund manager John Paulson, made famous by his bet against the subprime mortgage market (and the subject of Gregory Zuckerman's book *The Greatest Trade Ever*), along with former American International Group Chief Executive Officer Maurice "Hank" Greenberg suffered substantial losses investing in Sino Forest.[3] Shares in Sino Forest fell by over 80 percent following the publication of the research report, and the firm filed for bankruptcy in March of 2012. Paulson suffered a loss of approximately $720 million on his stake. Needless to say, this didn't rival his bet against the subprime market as the greatest trade ever!

In this chapter we look at asset-based approaches based on book value, replacement cost, and sum of the parts. We also look at a special case of value investing that identifies firms that are selling at such a significant discount from asset value that it provides the strategic value investor with a very large margin of safety. These deep value situations exist where firms can be purchased at a price that is less than net current assets less long-term debt. Essentially, investors can have the long-term assets (plant, equipment, land, etc.) for free!

One may wonder how such undervaluations can exist in the market. Aren't market prices arrived at by the interaction of many buyers and sellers acting on the latest and best information? Aren't there an army of analysts in Wall Street firms and hedge funds pouring over complex models? The answer to these questions is a resounding yes; but undervalued (in reality, misvalued) firms do exist and have over the years. These situations reinforce the notion that markets are not solely quantitatively focused and purely rational. Investor sentiment and psychology play a large role in ensuring the inefficiency of market pricing—a situation that is a boon to the disciplined strategic value investor. In terms we all understand, one man's junk is another man's treasure. Asset-based approaches can help us identify the situations where treasure exists.

BOOK VALUE

As introduced in Chapter 4, book value is computed as the balance sheet value of the company's net assets (assets net of liabilities). Most assets are listed on the balance sheet at their historical costs less some adjustment for depreciation or impairment, while some assets, such as investments, are listed at fair market value. Book value does *not* include the value of all intangible assets, such as brand names and intellectual property, but may include their acquisition costs. Book values are more meaningful in some industries than others. Traditionally, book values had more applicability in the banking industry than in service industries or in industries where much of the value is in brand names, patents, and intellectual property.

Book value per share simply takes the total value of a company's net assets and divides it by the number of shares outstanding. Along with companies selling at low P/E ratios, companies with relatively high book value to market value (BV/MV)[4] ratios are synonymous with value investing in many academic studies of investment returns. When the performance of value versus growth stocks is examined, the typical proxies for value stocks are some combination of low P/E stocks and high BV/MV stocks. Studies documenting this apparent market inefficiency began appearing in the finance literature in the mid-1980s and various iterations of the so-called book-to-market effect are still being published today.

There are no rules of thumb when examining book-to-market ratios or its inverse price-to–book value ratios. Certainly an investor is wise to consider the market context when looking at a firm's price-to–book value. As the chart, of the price-to–book value ratio on the S&P 500 index shows (Figure 9-1), there is considerable variation in absolute level of the ratio over time. Over the 12-year period from 2000 through 2011, the price-to–book value ratio of the S&P 500 ranged from a high of over 5.0 in early 2000 to a low of 1.75 in early 2009. These levels clearly reflect the prevailing market sentiment at the time. The high of over 5.0 coincided with the height of the speculative dot.com bubble in March of 2000. At this time the NASDAQ index peaked at over 5,132 in intraday trading, a level that hasn't been reached again. The low of less than 1.75 was realized at the height of the financial crisis in early 2009. The fact that over a 12-year time period price-to-book ratios from the low to high were at levels of approximately 2.85 times shows how market sentiment can influence valuation levels.

We discuss the price-to-book ratio, other measures of absolute and relative value, how they are calculated, and how we might use them to distinguish value stocks from growth stocks in more detail in Chapter 6. Here, we focus on how to use them to estimate intrinsic value.

FIGURE 9-1

S&P 500 Price-to–book value ratio since 2000.

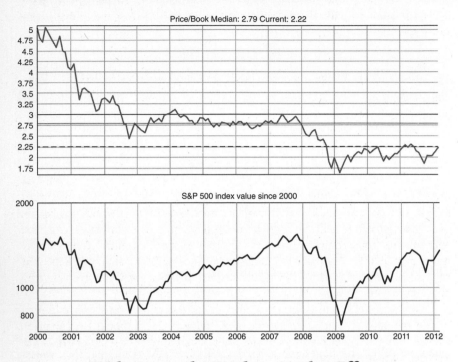

Evidence on the Book-to-Market Effect

The evidence that high BV/MV stocks outperform low BV/MV stocks is quite pervasive. Starting with Rosenberg, Reid, and Lanstein (1985), many research-ers have documented that even after controlling for many other variables (risk, in particular), firms with high BV/MV ratios outperform stocks with low BV/MV ratios. One of the most widely referenced studies was coauthored by none other than Dr. Eugene Fama, the academic who developed the efficient market hypothesis (EMH).[5] In a seminal academic paper entitled "The Cross Section of Expected Stock Returns," Fama and French (1980) found evidence that firms with high book-to-market ratios outperform firms with low book-to-market ratios on a consistent basis. These findings have stood the test of time. Very few relationships are as strong and persistent as this so-called book-to-market effect.[6]

The evidence of a book-to-market effect is not limited to U.S. equity markets. Fama and French (1998) found that over a 21-year time period from 1975 through 1995, sorting on book-to-market equity, value stocks outperformed growth stocks in 12 of 13 major developed global markets. The difference between average returns on global portfolios of high and low BV/MV stocks was an impressive 7.68 percent per year. As you would expect, researchers have examined whether a book-to-market effect exists in emerging markets. Notably, van der Hart, Slagter, and van Dijk (2003), using data from 1982 to 1999 and in a study of nearly 3,000 firms from 32 emerging markets, find that high BV/MV stocks outperform low BV/MV stocks by approximately 10 percent annually. Thus, the book-to-market effect appears to be pervasive across the global investment landscape.

Why Does the Book-to-Market Effect Exist?

What insight does the book-to-market ratio provide an investor? Stocks may have a high book-to-market ratio for a couple of reasons. First, they may simply be undervalued or neglected by the marketplace. Second, their future prospects may not be good: They may be selling at a high BV/MV ratio for sound reasons, such as poor future growth prospects or inept management. Often, it is very difficult to discern which of these two explanations is correct for a given firm. Lakonishok, Shleifer, and Vishny (1994) and Haugen (1995) argue that this "value premium" arises because the market systematically undervalues distressed stocks and overvalues growth stocks. In essence, the behavioral bias of investors is to both overestimate troubled firms' problems and to overestimate trendy growth stocks' future prospects. When reversion to the mean takes place—that is, when the market realizes the error of its ways—the distressed (value) stocks have relatively high returns and growth stocks have relatively low returns.

In a case of "things are not always as they seem," upon closer examination of the book-to-market effect one of the authors of this book, Bob Johnson, teamed with two other researchers and found that the book-to-market effect varied according to the economic environment. Jensen, Johnson, and Mercer (1998) indicated that both the size and the book-to-market effect were prevalent only during periods of expansive Federal Reserve monetary policy. Specifically, these effects were only significant (in both an economic and statistical sense) when the interest rate environment was one characterized by declining rates.

Taking Advantage of the Book-to-Market Effect: "Top Down" or "Bottom Up"

As discussed in Chapter 4, strategic value investors can take a top-down perspective or bottom-up perspective, and this can be performed in conjunction with a consideration of book value.

The bottom-up investor would start at the individual firm level and perform a screen on all firms in a particular database based upon price-to–book value. For instance, Table 9-1 shows the top 20 stocks sorted on BV/MV in a database of all NYSE, AMEX, and NASDAQ stocks.[7]

As you can see, there are some fairly high BV/MV (low P/B) ratios. There is some industry diversity, but you will notice that 8 of the 20 stocks are in financially oriented industries. This is a critical element of the discussion of BV/MV as a screening tool. You will find fairly high concentrations of certain industries,

T A B L E 9-1

Top 20 Stocks with Highest Book Value to Market Value
(Lowest Price-to–Book Value)

All Companies on NYSE, AMEX, and NASDAQ, Minimum $5/Share
Price, as of February 28, 2012

Ticker Symbol	Company Name	Industry	BV/MV Ratio	P/B Ratio
HCMLY	Holcim Ltd (ADR)	Construction— Raw Materials	15.16	0.07
DWRI	Design Within Reach, Inc.	Furniture & Fixtures	10.07	0.10
BCDS	BCD Semiconductor Manufacturing	Semiconductors	9.39	0.11
KLMR	KLM Royal Dutch Airlines (ADR)	Airline	8.90	0.11
XAND	Xanadoo Company	Computer Services	8.07	0.12
OSG	Overseas Shipholding Group, Inc.	Water Transportation	5.45	0.18
AORE	American Overseas Group Ltd.	Insurance (Property & Casualty)	5.42	0.18
SVIN	Scheid Vineyards, Inc.	Crops	5.03	0.20
AFLYY	Air France—KLM (ADR)	Airline	4.87	0.21
GNK	Genco Shipping & Trading Limit.	Water Transportation	4.64	0.22
WCSTF	Wescast Industries, Inc.	Auto & Truck Parts	4.17	0.24
RAS	RAIT Financial Trust	Real Estate Operations	4.02	0.25
DFR	CIFC Corp	Investment Services	3.88	0.26
GNW	Genworth Financial, Inc.	Insurance (Life)	3.69	0.27
AKPB	Alaska Pacific Bancshares, Inc.	Regional Banks	3.58	0.28
MCPH	Midland Capital Holdings	S&Ls/Savings Banks	3.55	0.28
FAVS	First Aviation Services, Inc.	Aerospace and Defense	3.53	0.28
FFKT	Farmers Capital Bank Corp	Regional Banks	3.49	0.29
AEG	AEGON N.V. (ADR)	Insurance (Life)	3.43	0.29
SRNN	Southern Banc Company, Inc.	S&Ls/Savings Banks	3.36	0.30

Source: American Association of Individual Investors, Stock Investor Pro Database, February 28, 2012.

with financially oriented firms being most prevalent. Any investor who would simply invest on the basis of the BV/MV metric would find his portfolio concentrated in a very few industries. Such a strategy is perilous, as many of the firms within those industries will have very highly correlated returns.

The industry effect in BV/MV ratios can be reinforced by looking at all 30 of the components of the Dow Jones Industrial Average sorted by BV/MV from highest

TABLE 9-2

Book Value to Market Value and Price-to–Book Value of the 30 Component Stocks of the Dow Jones Industrial Average as of February 28, 2012

Ticker Symbol	Company Name	Industry	BV/MV Ratio	P/B Ratio
BAC	Bank of America Corp	Money Center Banks	2.61	0.38
AA	Alcoa	Metal Mining	1.24	0.81
JPM	JPMorgan Chase & Co.	Money Center Banks	1.21	0.83
TRV	Travelers Companies, Inc.	Insurance (Property & Casualty)	1.04	0.96
HPQ	Hewlett-Packard Company	Computer Hardware	0.74	1.35
T	AT&T Inc.	Communications Services	0.59	1.69
GE	General Electric Company	Consumer Financial Services	0.57	1.75
PFE	Pfizer Inc.	Major Drugs	0.56	1.79
CVX	Chevron Corporation	Oil & Gas–Integrated	0.56	1.79
KFT	Kraft Foods	Food Processing	0.55	1.82
DIS	Walt Disney Company	Broadcasting & Cable TV	0.50	2.00
MRK	Merck & Co, Inc.	Biotechnology & Drugs	0.47	2.13
CSCO	Cisco Systems, Inc.	Communications Equipment	0.46	2.17
XOM	Exxon Mobil Corporation	Oil & Gas—Integrated	0.37	2.70
WMT	Walmart Stores, Inc.	Retail (Department & Discount)	0.35	2.86
INTC	Intel Corporation	Semiconductors	0.34	2.94
PG	Procter & Gamble Company	Personal & Household Products	0.34	2.94
JNJ	Johnson & Johnson	Biotechnology & Drugs	0.34	2.94
VZ	Verizon Communications	Communication Services	0.33	3.03
AXP	American Express Company	Regional Banks	0.31	3.23
UTX	United Technologies Corporation	Aerospace and Defense	0.29	3.45
HD	Home Depot, Inc.	Retail (Home Improvement)	0.25	4.00
MMM	3M Company	Construction–Supplies & Fixtures	0.25	4.00
MFST	Microsoft Corporation	Software & Programming	0.24	4.17
KO	Coca-Cola Company	Beverages (Non-Alcoholic)	0.20	5.00
DD	E I Du Pont De Nemours and Co	Chemical Manufacturing	0.18	5.56
CAT	Caterpillar, Inc.	Construction & Agricultural Machinery	0.17	5.88
MCD	McDonald's Corporation	Restaurants	0.13	7.69
IBM	International Business Machines	Computer Services	0.09	11.11
BA	Boeing Company	Aerospace and Defense	0.06	16.67

Source: American Association of Individual Investors, Stock Investor Pro Database, February 28, 2012.

to lowest (Table 9-2). As is seen from the table, the industries in the DJIA with the highest BV/MV ratios are financially oriented firms. Four of the top seven ratios are financial firms, representing all of the financial firms in the DJIA. As expected, firms in which intellectual property and brand names are important assets (i.e., Microsoft, Coca-Cola, McDonald's, and IBM) have comparatively low BV/MV ratios.

The top-down investor would examine future prospects for the economy and specific industries to identify potential investment opportunities. Suppose, for instance, that the economy was in a recession and that through a top-down analysis, the strategic value investor forecast a strong economic recovery with rising levels of consumer disposable income. An industry that typically benefits from such an economic situation is specialty retailers. At this point, the top-down strategic value investor might benefit from running a screen on the specialty retailing industry to determine which retailers are selling at relatively high multiples of book-to-market

TABLE 9-3

Book Value to Market Value of Specialty Retailers as of February 28, 2012 (Minimum Price of $5/Share)

Ticker Symbol	Company Name	BV/MV Ratio	P/B Ratio
TA	Travel Centers of America LLC	2.18	0.46
BBW	Build-A-Bear Workshop, Inc.	1.34	0.75
BKS	Barnes & Noble, Inc.	1.08	0.93
UNTD	United Online, Inc.	1.02	0.98
IEP	Icahn Enterprises, L.P.	1.00	1.00
HZO	Marine Max, Inc.	1.00	1.00
WMAR	West Marine, Inc.	0.96	1.04
HVT	Haverty Furniture Companies, Inc.	0.93	1.08
BGFV	Big 5 Sporting Goods Corporation	0.82	1.22
GPI	Group 1 Automotive, Inc.	0.71	1.41
PBY	Pep Boys—Manny, Moe & Jack	0.64	1.56
PERF	Perfumania Holdings, Inc.	0.63	1.59
KAR	KAR Auction Services, Inc.	0.61	1.64
LAD	Lithia Motors, Inc.	0.58	1.72
SAH	Sonic Automotive, Inc.	0.58	1.72
PAG	Penske Automotive Group, Inc.	0.52	1.92
SIG	Signet Jewelers Ltd.	0.52	1.92
AUTCF	Auto China International Limited	0.50	2.00
CAB	Cabelas, Inc.	0.48	2.08
TGT	Target Corporation	0.43	2.33
ARCI	Appliance Recycling Centers of America, Inc.	0.43	2.33

TABLE 9-3

(Continued)

Ticker Symbol	Company Name	BV/MV Ratio	P/B Ratio
AN	Auto Nation, Inc.	0.40	2.50
CRMT	America's Car-Mart, Inc.	0.40	2.50
ABG	Asbury Automotive Group, Inc.	0.40	2.50
KMX	CarMax, Inc.	0.39	2.56
KIRK	Kirkland's, Inc.	0.37	2.70
COST	Costco Wholesale Corporation	0.33	3.03
DG	Dollar General Corp.	0.32	3.13
BID	Sothebys	0.32	3.13
DKS	Dicks Sporting Goods, Inc.	0.29	3.45
TIF	Tiffany & Co.	0.28	3.57
BBBY	Bed Bath & Beyond	0.27	3.70
UGP	Ultrapar Participacoes SA (ADR)	0.27	3.70
ORLY	O'Reilly Automotive, Inc.	0.26	3.85
BIG	Big Lots, Inc.	0.26	3.85
PIR	Pier 1 Imports, Inc.	0.21	4.76
CPWM	Cost Plus, Inc.	0.20	5.00
TRS	TriMas Corp.	0.20	5.00
PETM	PetSmart, Inc.	0.19	5.26
PSMT	PriceSmart, Inc.	0.19	5.26
FDO	Family Dollar Stores, Inc.	0.18	5.56
HIBB	Hibbert Sports, Inc.	0.15	6.67
AAP	Advance Auto Parts, Inc.	0.14	7.14
WINA	Winmark Corporation	0.10	10.00
ULTA	Ulta Salon, Cosmetics & Fragrances	0.10	10.00
NILE	Blue Nile, Inc.	0.07	14.29
MFRM	Mattress Firm Holding Corp.	0.00	773.75

Source: American Association of Individual Investors, Stock Investor Pro Database, February 28, 2012.

value within that industry (see Table 9-3, for example). In other words, the top-down investor isn't looking at all firms and determining which are selling at attractive book-to-market multiples. This investor is identifying the industry first and then comparing firms within that industry on the basis of book-to-market.

Of all firms on the NYSE, AMEX, and NASDAQ markets, there were 48 specialty retailers with a minimum stock price of $5. As you can see, there is a wide range of BV/MV ratios within the specialty retailing industry, but the ratios at the high end of the industry are nowhere near the ratios seen in the market as a whole. This is to be expected, as much of the value in a specialty retailer is in the brand name. The BV/MV ratios ranged from a high of 2.18 in the case of Travel Centers of America to a low of 0.0 for Mattress Firm Holding Company. Additionally, the median BV/MV ratio for the specialty retailing industry was 0.40. This screen would provide the investor with several potential companies to investigate further. Screening on BV/MV ratio is just that—a screen. Further investigation is warranted before any investment should be considered.

Strategic value investors can use price-to-book ratios (and any relative valuation metric for that matter) to estimate intrinsic value. For example, suppose your other fundamental analysis (such as an evaluation of management, a closer examination of the financial statements, and footnotes) made you more interested in Travel Centers of America (ticker: TA). On February 28, 2012, TA was trading at $5.21 per share and its book value per share was $11.33 per share, making its price-to-book ratio 0.46. The median price-to-book ratio for specialty retailers was 2.50. If we believe that TA's price-to-book ratio will increase from the lowest among specialty retailers to just the median among specialty retailers and that its book value per share will remain at about $11.33 per share, then we might estimate that its intrinsic value will be $28.25 per share (i.e., 11.33×2.50). As of March 22, 2013, TA was trading at $9.55 per share. Although this is not equal to $28.25, it represents a nice return of 83 percent.

Part of the reason for the price increase is that TA's price-to-book ratio increased to 0.79. In this case, the price increase was driven not by an increase in earnings or both value per se, but rather by increases in the multiples that the market assigns to these value metrics. Although this illustrates how relative value can be used to estimate intrinsic value, a couple of caveats are in order. First, the price of TA did not increase steadily over that time period. It dropped to a low of $4.18 in December 2012, illustrating once again the fortitude that value investors must have to successfully implement their strategies. Second, much of that price increase occurred in March 2013. The share price on February 28, 2013 was $6.88 per share. Still a nice return, but not as dramatic.

The top-down methodology is an example of the aphorism first attributed to John F. Kennedy, "a rising tide lifts all boats." The logic is that if the market recognizes that an industry is prospering, then valuations will improve. If an investor can identify securities that are more undervalued in an industry than others, then these valuations should improve more than average.

REPLACEMENT VALUE

In principle, valuing a firm via replacement value is a simple, useful concept. An investor would indeed find it attractive to be able to purchase a firm's assets at a discount to the cost to replace those assets. This idea is straightforward in concept, but, unfortunately, in practice it is much more difficult for the investor to estimate this seemingly straightforward metric.

Tobin's *q*

James Tobin, Nobel Laureate in economics from Yale University, developed Tobin's *q*.[8] He hypothesized that the combined value of all companies in the stock market should have a value roughly equal to their replacement costs. Specifically,

Tobin's q is the ratio of the market value of debt and equity to the replacement cost of total assets:

Tobin's q = (Market value of debt and equity)/(Replacement cost of total assets)

This is similar to MV/BV explained in the previous section, but there are obvious differences. The numerator for Tobin's q includes the market value of total capital (debt as well as equity). The denominator uses total assets rather than equity. Most importantly, assets are valued at replacement cost rather than at historical accounting cost (or book value). Most analysts contend that replacement cost is a much more accurate determination of value, largely because replacement cost takes into account the effects of inflation since the assets were initially acquired.

The logic behind Tobin's q is that, all else equal, the ratio is expected to be higher the greater the productivity of the company's assets. In fact, Tobin himself theorized that q would average 1.0 for all companies because economic rents or profits earned by assets would average to zero. From an investor's standpoint, a high Tobin's q signals a possible overvaluation and high level of market risk. Conversely, a low Tobin's q indicates that the market may be undervalued and investors have less risk in the market at that time.

While Tobin's q certainly *can* be estimated for individuals stocks, the general feeling in the investment community is that it is most useful for determining the overall valuation level of the market. The main difficulty in computing Tobin's q is the lack of reliable information on the replacement cost of assets. As you can imagine, calculating the replacement value of corporate assets for individual firms is fraught with great difficulty and will necessarily involve many assumptions and estimates. Unlike book value, where there can be no disagreement among investors, rational investors are likely to disagree on the replacement value of Microsoft. This disagreement reflects the reality that rational investors will have divergent views on the value of the brand equity inherent in the firm.

The general market, however, is a different story for investors. The Federal Reserve provides estimates of most of the variables needed to estimate Tobin's q in a publication labeled the *Flow of Funds* report.[9] Other variables must be estimated or proxied via financial modeling.

As shown in Figure 9-2, over the past 60 years, Tobin's q for the S&P 500 has ranged from a low of 0.3 to a high of over 1.8.[10] The lowest reading was achieved during the recession and high interest rate environment of the early 1980s and coincided with the low point of that market correction. The high reading, similar in timing to the high reading of the MV/BV ratio, was in early 2000 at the height of the dot.com bubble.

The takeaway for the strategic value investor on the discussion on replacement value in general and Tobin's q specifically, is that it gives you an idea of the general valuation level of the market. A quick perusal of the chart indicates that Tobin's q frequently drops to low levels during cyclical lows in the equity market. These low levels indicate that the strategic value investor should consider

FIGURE 9-2

Tobin's q for S&P 500 since 1950.

a heavier weighting of equities. Conversely, a high Tobin's q level suggests cyclical highs in the equity markets, signaling that perhaps equity weightings should be trimmed. Unquestionably, an occasional monitoring of the level of Tobin's q is warranted.

SUM OF THE PARTS VALUATION

Two plus two equals four—except when it doesn't. This captures the essence of the sum of the parts valuation method. Since many businesses are extremely complex enterprises (composed of several distinct, and often dramatically different, business lines) the valuation placed by the market on the combined enterprise may be significantly different from the sum of the parts. Specifically, there are instances where the combined value placed by the market on the firm is markedly less than sum of the parts, a case in which two plus two equals three—or even two plus two equals two. The value derived using this methodology is sometimes called the breakup value. However, don't let the name fool you. Such a valuation approach doesn't assume or necessitate that any future restructuring will actually occur.

A case of sum of the parts valuation was provided in Chapter 3 in the arbitrage discussion of Creative Computers and uBid. Recall that Creative Computers issued 20 percent of the shares of its online auction subsidiary, uBid, to the public. Creative Computer's remaining stake in uBid was worth $350 million according to uBid's share price. But Creative Computer's total equity market value was only about $275 million, implying that the rest of the firm was worth a negative $75 million. Either Creative Computers is undervalued or uBid is overvalued, or some combination of the two. A sum of the parts valuation can provide the strategic value investor with such insight.

Many prominent investors try to unlock the hidden value in a company by acquiring a large position and then attempting to convince management to break the company into two or more component parts. By mid-February 2012, hedge fund manager John Paulson had acquired approximately 8.4 percent of the Hartford Financial Services Group. According to data compiled by Bloomberg, at that time Hartford was selling for less relative to net assets than comparable U.S. insurers. Paulson started acquiring shares of Hartford in mid-2009 and established this position because he believed that the insurer was substantially undervalued by the market.[11] Paulson believes that by splitting the firm into separate property-casualty and life-insurance businesses, the firm could be worth $32 per share, a 50 percent premium over the $21 per share that Hartford was selling for in mid-February.

Sum-of-the-parts valuation is commonplace in conglomerate enterprises— firms with many divisions that produce and sell unrelated goods and services. Firms such as General Electric, Procter and Gamble, Johnson Controls, Time Warner, and Walt Disney are complex multinational enterprises with multiple divisions and extremely diverse product lines. General Electric, for instance, is composed of four main operating segments: Energy, Technology Infrastructure, Capital Finance, and Consumer and Industrial. The Walt Disney Company also has four operating segments: Studio Entertainment, Parks and Resorts, Disney Consumer Products, and Media Networks.

Conglomerates became very popular in the 1960s as firms sought to continue to exhibit a growing return on equity that was highly valued by the investment community. The easiest way to accomplish this was through acquisitions, and many large conglomerates were created. As is the case with almost any fad, a reversal took place. In the 1970s many of these conglomerates were broken up as firms sought to focus on their core competencies.[12] In addition to providing a growing return on equity, the formation of conglomerates was thought to provide investors with diversification, resulting in more stable earnings and less fluctuation in value. In addition, the theory was that conglomerates would realize synergies in management and marketing.

The reality was often just the opposite: Firms experienced difficulties managing diverse enterprises, and the combined organizations often underperformed expectations. Additionally, diversification at the firm level really doesn't benefit investors, as they could achieve that diversification on their own. In fact, diversification at the firm level limits the ability of investors to invest in businesses that they like without forcing them to invest in business lines that they don't like. For instance, an investor in Walt Disney that is bullish on the parks and resorts business but is bearish on the other three business lines cannot take a position in the parks and resorts business without also taking a position in the other three business lines. This illustrates why two plus two may equal three (or even two).

Spin-Offs and Carve Outs

If the current management is underutilizing the assets of one of its business lines, or has some unprofitable operating units, then a spin-off or equity carve out of the business may be warranted to unleash some of the earning power and realize the true value of the businesses. A spin-off is a divestiture of assets by a firm through the creation of an independent company. An equity carve out can be thought of as a partial spin-off. An equity carve out occurs when a parent company sells a minority stake in a subsidiary through an IPO or a rights offering. In the example cited here, uBid was an equity carve out from Creative Computers.

The performance of spin-offs and carve outs over time has been quite remarkable. The mere announcement of a spin-off or carve out is generally positively received by the market (see Hite and Owers [1983], Schipper and Smith [1983], Miles and Rosenfeld [1983], and Schipper and Smith [1986]), as the market anticipates improved operating performance by the parent company. These studies find a mean abnormal (that is, above the market and adjusted for risk) spin-off announcement return of approximately 3 percent.

More importantly, there is considerable research that suggests that spin-offs and carve outs outperform the general market by a considerable margin in the months and years following the event (see McConnell and Ovtchinnikov [2004], and Hite and Owers [1983]). Anslinger, Klepper, and Subramaniam (1999) find that restructuring through spin-offs and equity carve outs can create substantial shareholder value. In a study covering 1988 through 1998, equity carve outs easily outperformed the Russell 2000 index, with an average annual total return to shareholders in the two years after issue of 24 percent as compared to 11 percent for the index. Spin-offs also subsequently outperform the market, showing a two-year annualized return of 27 percent compared with 14 percent for the index.

The most interesting finding of the study of spin-offs and carve outs, however, is that, on average, investors who purchased stock of the *parent* companies also did quite well. Anslinger, Klepper, and Subramaniam found that the average improvement in the P/E multiple of the consolidated parent and subsidiary outperformed the market by 21 percent. Cusatis, Miles, and Woolridge (1993) find significantly positive abnormal returns for spin-offs, their parents, and the spin-off–parent combinations. These results certainly provide an economic rationale for firms to consider spin-offs and provides evidence that strategic value investors should consider spin-offs (and their parents) as potential investments.

But investors need to exercise caution when considering any investment strategy. While on average spin-offs and equity carve outs do quite well, remember that you can drown in a river with an average depth of six inches. A high-profile spin-off occurred in 1996 when AT&T spun off a division called Lucent Technologies. Lucent was trading at $27 per share on the day of the spin-off and three years later was trading at over $230 per share on a split-adjusted basis. Investors who purchased the stock on the first trading day and held it for three years had a return in excess of 780 percent! Although not as spectacular a return as Lucent, the parent company, AT&T, earned around 92 percent over those same three years. That all sounds well and good, but you need to hear (as Paul Harvey would say) the rest of the story. In January of 2000, Lucent made the first in a series of announcements that it had missed its quarterly earnings targets. It was later revealed that it had used questionable accounting and sales practices to boost its quarterly numbers. By October 2002, its stock price had fallen to 55 cents per share. Lucent has since merged with French company Alcatel and the combined firm, Alcatel-Lucent, continues to have problems.

Sum-of-the-Parts Valuation Example: Berkshire Hathaway

One of the most successful conglomerate enterprises is the investment vehicle used by the world's greatest value investor, Warren Buffett. Berkshire Hathaway was a New England–based textile manufacturer in the early 1960s. But Buffett didn't make his fortune in textile manufacturing. In fact, the textile operations were an underperforming part of Buffett's operations in the early days of his involvement, and Buffett acknowledges that his investment in Berkshire Hathaway was one of the least savvy investments in his distinguished career.

How does an investor go about valuing a complex organization like Berkshire Hathaway? Tom Gayner, value investor and president and chief investment officer of Markel Corporation advocates employing the sum-of-the-parts valuation method.[13] He contends that Berkshire Hathaway has evolved into a company with three major business lines: an investment portfolio, insurance operations, and non-insurance operating businesses. The basis of applying a sum-of-the-parts valuation to Berkshire Hathaway involves making certain assumptions (estimates) about each of the business lines and aggregating the results. Bear in mind that an analyst can make things as easy or as complicated as need be. However, increased complexity does not necessarily equate into greater precision or better estimates of value.[14]

Greg Speicher is an Ohio-based value investor who followed Gayner's general approach to estimate the value of both the A and B shares of Berkshire Hathaway.[15] While Berkshire Hathaway is a complicated enterprise with many moving parts, Speicher's model is relatively simple. It separately determines the net profit from each of the three business components by making some assumptions about performance of each business line and also assumptions about market multiples (P/E ratios) to be applied to the aggregated earnings. Specifically, for the insurance division Speicher considers a low case where Berkshire does not earn any underwriting profit, a middle case where it earns a 4.5 percent profit, and a high case where it earns 9 percent. For the investment portfolio, he considers a range of values: On the low end he assumes the portfolio will earn 3 percent, the middle case is 7 percent, and the high end is 11 percent. Speicher used Berkshire's investment portfolio value from the 2011, first quarter 10-Q. To calculate the insurance premiums earned, Speicher used Berkshire's 2010 insurance premiums. For normalized operating earnings, drawing upon Buffett's own estimate of normalized earnings given in the 2010 shareholder letter, Speicher used an estimate of $9 billion as his normalized after-tax earnings for the non-insurance operating businesses. He then sums the earnings from the three parts and applies a 10x, 14x, and 18x multiple. This gives him a range for his estimate of Berkshire's intrinsic value, much as we did for Travel Centers of America earlier in this chapter.

Speicher's calculations are detailed in the Box 9-1. He arrives at an average value of the A and B shares of $191,336 and $128, respectively. These valuations are dramatically different than the prices of $175,825 and $117.17 for the A and B shares on the date of the writing of this book. This model would also allow the user to do a sensitivity analysis by varying each of the critical variables and seeing how that effects estimated share value. Putting this data into an Excel spreadsheet would allow for this type of sensitivity analysis.

Box 9-1 Berkshire Hathaway Sum of the Parts Valuation

Case	Low Case	Middle Case	High Case
2010 Insurance Premiums Earned	$30,749	$30,749	$30,749
Net Profit Margin	0%	4.5%	9
Net Insurance Profit	$0	$1,384	$2,767
Investment Portfolio (Q1, 2011 10-Q)	$153,000	$153,000	$153,000
Points Earned	3%	7%	11%
Net Investment Profit	$4,590	$10,710	$16,380
Operating Businesses Net Profit	$9,000	$9,000	$9,000
Total Net Profit	**$13,590**	**$21,094**	**$28,597**
Shares	1.648	1.648	1.648
EPS	$8,246	$12,800	$17,353
P/E Multiple	10x	14x	18x
Intrinsic Value of A shares	$82,464	$179,194	$312,350
Intrinsic Value of B shares	$54.98	$119.46	$208.23
Average Value A Shares	$191,336		
Average Value B Shares	$128		

DEEP VALUE STOCKS: THE CASE OF LONG-TERM ASSETS FOR FREE

Deep value investors look for situations with a profound undervaluation, a large margin of safety. One of the most striking examples of a methodology to detect deeply undervalued companies was outlined by Benjamin Graham in his classic book on investing, *The Intelligent Investor.* He referred to this as one of his two classes of the "purchase of bargain issues." The first class of undervaluation involves firms that have currently disappointing results and are expected to rebound—a more traditional, value investing approach. The second class and one that we shall discuss is a special situation, involving identifying stocks that, on a per share basis, sell for less than the company's net working capital alone after deducting all debt.[16] See Box 9-2 for an explanation of how net working capital less debt is calculated. In essence, these firms are selling at a price that enables the investor to pay nothing for the fixed assets (any buildings, machinery, land, etc.) and any goodwill items that appear on the balance sheet.

Box 9-2 Net Working Capital Less Debt

Net Working Capital = Current Assets − Current Liabilities

Current Assets are those assets held for the purpose of trading or expected to be sold, used up, or realized in cash within one year. Examples are cash, trade receivables, inventories, and marketable securities.

Current Liabilities are those liabilities expected to be settled within one year. Examples are trade payables, tax liabilities, short-term bank loans, and accrued expenses.

To compute net working capital less debt per share, the investor takes the balance sheet value for current assets less the balance sheet value for current liabilities and long-term debt and divides that value by the number of shares of common stock outstanding. If this exceeds the market value of the common stock, the investor has identified a potential deep value investment.

Finding stocks that sell at such a low price relative to net working capital less debt is rare. In fact, Graham himself notes that firms selling for less than net working capital less long-term debt are truly an exceptional circumstance. Yet in 1957 he found that about 150 stocks met that criterion. Graham also tracked the performance of those firms over the following couple of years and found that a diversified portfolio of these firms outperformed the broader markets. Perhaps more importantly, and quite remarkably, *none* of those firms identified by Graham showed significant losses—a true indication of the margin of safety involved in this investment strategy that demonstrates the inextricable link between value and risk management.

Market sentiment definitely plays an important role in determining how many deep value investment opportunities exist at a given time in the marketplace. As one would expect, more deep value investments typically exist during periods of negative market sentiment than during periods of positive market sentiment. Box 9-3 provides a listing of the nine firms selling for less than net working capital less debt per share as of January 27, 2012.[17]

Box 9-3 Deep Value Screen
Firms Selling at Less Than Net Working Capital Less Long-Term Debt as of January 27, 2012

Ticker	Name	Net Working Capital Per Share	Long-Term Debt Per Share	Short-Term Debt Per Share	NWC— LTD Per Share	Market Price
BSHI	Boss Holdings, Inc.	11.90	0.50	1.10	10.30	8.00
CXS	Crexus Investment Corp.	12.00	0.00	00.0	12.00	11.06
FLXS	Flexsteel Industries, Inc.	14.10	00.0	00.0	14.10	14.03
GENC	Gencor Industries, Inc.	9.40	00.0	00.0	9.40	7.17
MRINA	McRae Industries	14.80	00.0	00.0	14.80	13.05
MPAD	Micropac Industries, Inc.	6.50	00.0	00.0	6.50	5.10
OPST	OPT-Sciences Corp.	13.50	00.0	00.0	13.50	11.80
PARF	Paradise, Inc.	26.00	00.0	1.10	24.90	14.60
TNRK	TNR Technical, Inc.	12.70	00.0	00.0	12.70	10.79

Source: American Association of Individual Investors, Stock Investor Pro Database, February 28, 2012.

Why would a situation exist in which firms were selling for less than net working capital minus long-term debt? Is this yet another indication that stock markets are not efficient? Stocks in this category are often stocks that are out of favor with the general marketplace. They may be out of favor for good reason. Perhaps the management of the firm is inept, and continued mismanagement may result in continued losses and falling valuations. Remember, the investor cannot force the company to liquidate and realize that valuation differential.

Neglect by the investing marketplace may be another reason that these extreme undervaluation situations exist. The types of firms in this category are certainly not the "sexy" type of investments that make for good cocktail party conversation and may lack compelling stories to create interest by investors.

This is not an endorsement that you immediately call your broker or logon to your online account and purchases these equities. Any screening process issimply a method to identify securities that you may want to further investigate.

CONCLUSION

Forecasting earnings is not the only way to estimate intrinsic value. In some situations, estimating the value of the assets directly is a more effective and straightforward approach. In this chapter, we present different approaches to estimating the value of those assets. Even if not used in isolation, these measures can help provide a reasonableness check on the results from earnings-based approaches.

RESIDUAL INCOME MODELS

It is easy to forget why senior management's most important job must be to maximize the firm's current market value. ... A quest for value directs scarce resources to their most promising uses and most productive uses.

—G. Bennett Stewart III

In the preceding chapters we presented two models for valuing firms involving discounting future cash flows: a dividend approach and a free cash flow approach. These models are appropriate when a company pays dividends and when current operating cash flows can be readily forecast into the future. However, some companies do not pay dividends, and others may not yet have positive operating cash flow. Still other firms may have cash flows that are earned in a manner that is quite different from other companies—for example, financial companies like banks. Banks have fundamentally dissimilar business models and types of cash flows from manufacturing companies, retailers, and the like. They collect cash from customers and use this cash to make loans. They earn a spread on the difference in interest rates between borrowed and lent funds. True operating cash flow can be difficult to determine for these types of firms. Fortunately, another approach exists that focuses on book value and earnings. This method is called a residual income[1] model and is quite effective for valuing many companies, particularly those in the financial industry.

WHAT IS RESIDUAL INCOME?

Recall our example of Cayse Logistics Company (CLC) from Chapter 5. Cayse has $2,000,000 of assets, financed $1,000,000 with debt and $1,000,000 with shareholders equity. Book value of the company is the amount of shareholders equity as recorded on the balance sheet, so it is also $1,000,000 (book value is just another term for shareholders' equity). The debt pays interest of 8 percent annually. The $1,000,000 was raised by issuing 10,000 shares of common stock at $100 per share. CLC generates $180,000 of earnings before interest and taxes based on the $2,000,000 investment in assets and has a 30 percent tax rate. For simplicity, let's assume that the company intends to pay out all earnings as dividends with no reinvestment in the company. It is therefore not expected to grow in the future. CLC's traditional income statement would be:

Earnings Before Interest and Taxes	$180,000
Interest	(80,000)
EBT	$100,000
Taxes	(30,000)
Net Income	$70,000
ROA	3.5%
ROE	7.0%

How did the company perform for shareholders? Although the company generated a 3.5 percent return on assets, it effectively used leverage to magnify those returns and create return on equity of 7 percent for shareholders. They did this by borrowing funds at 8 percent and investing in assets that earned 9 percent before taxes and interest. The question is whether this is a sufficient return for the owners. If the owners desire a 7 percent rate of return on their investment (the discount rate described in Chapters 7 and 8), then the company earned exactly what the owners require (for that level of risk).

One deficiency with the traditional income statement presented here is that while the cost of debt (interest) is reflected on the income statement, the cost of equity (the discount rate investors want) is not. We can extend the traditional income statement to show the desired cost of equity as follows:

Earnings Before Interest and Taxes	$180,000
Interest	(80,000)
EBT	$100,000
Taxes	(30,000)
Net Income	$70,000
Desired Cost of Equity ($1,000,000 * 7%)	(70,000)
Residual Income	0

Residual income is the amount of net income remaining after subtracting the required cost of equity capital. For Cayse, it is zero. The company earned exactly what shareholders required for the risk they assumed, so the residual income is zero.

So what is this company worth? Using the dividend discount model and assuming no future growth, the company would be worth $1,000,000 ($70,000 of dividends divided by a discount rate of 7 percent or 0.07). The price-to-book ratio of this company should be 1.0 (value of $1,000,000 divided by the book value of equity of $1,000,000). This is logical given that the company is earning exactly the rate required by shareholders. Another way of looking at the value under the residual income method without looking at dividends is the company should be worth its book value ($1,000,000 in this case) plus the present value of the future residual income it is expected to generate ($0 in this case).

Now let's change the facts slightly. Assume the company can earn EBIT of $220,000 with its asset investment of $2,000,000. The residual income would be:

Earnings Before Interest and Taxes	$220,000
Interest	(80,000)
EBT	$140,000
Taxes	(42,000)
Net Income	$98,000
Desired Cost of Equity ($1,000,000 * 7%)	(70,000)
Residual Income	$28,000

Now the company has positive residual income of $28,000. Because the company is earning more than the return required by shareholders, it is adding value to shareholders and should be worth more than book value. How much more? The additional value is the future residual income discounted at the required rate of return—assuming here a perpetuity[2] of residual income that is not growing. The present value of this infinite series of cash flows is $28,000/0.07 = $400,000. The total value of the company should be the book value of $1,000,000 plus the present value of future residual income of $400,000 or $1,400,000. Dividing that total by 1,000 shares, the value (price) per share should be $140, and the price-to-book ratio would be 1.4.

A firm can also have negative residual income and would therefore be worth less than book value. Returning to our original example, assume that our investors demand or require a return of 10 percent to invest in Cayse and they purchased the stock for $1,000,000:

Earnings Before Interest and Taxes	$180,000
Interest	(80,000)
EBT	$100,000
Taxes	(30,000)
Net Income	$70,000
Desired Cost of Equity ($1,000,000 * 10%)	(100,000)
Residual Income	(30,000)

The shareholders will be quite disappointed. If these results are expected to continue indefinitely, the value of their stock would drop dramatically to $700,000 (book value of $1,000,000 less the present value of future *negative* residual earnings of $300,000, or −$30,000/0.10). There is another way to look at this scenario. Let's say that the investors knew in advance that the company would generate net income of $70,000 each year and they desired a 10 percent rate of return on their investment. How much would they be willing to pay for that stream of income? The answer is $700,000 because at this amount of investment $70,000 of income would provide them with a 10 percent return on their equity.

Residual Income in Perpetuity

Based on the dividend discount model presented in Chapter 7 and normal relationships between earnings and dividends we can develop a valuation formula for the residual income approach when that residual income is expected to continue indefinitely:

$$Company\ Value = B_0 + \frac{B_0(ROE - r)}{r - g}$$

B_0 is the current book value (stockholder's equity) of the company as a whole; ROE is the expected future return on equity; r is the discount rate or required return; and g is the expected future growth rate in residual income (if any).

Let's apply this model for two of our examples above. In the first example, book value was $1,000,000, ROE was 7 percent, the discount rate was also 7 percent, and there was no growth. The value of the company would be $1,000,000 ($1,000,000 plus $0). In the second example, book value was $1,000,000, ROE was 9.8 percent ($98,000 of net income divided by $1,000,000 of equity), the discount rate was 7 percent, and there was no growth. The value of the company would be $1,000,000 + ($1,000,000*0.028)/(.07) = $1,400,000. In the third example, ROE was 7 percent, the discount rate was 10 percent, and there was no growth. So, the value of the company would be $1,000,000 + $1,000,000*(0.07 − 0.10)/(.10) = $700,000.

Box 10-1 Application: Valuation Using a Perpetual Residual Income Model

A fellow value investor calls you and tells you he has found a classic Graham and Dodd value stock that is currently selling for substantially less than book value. He tells you the stock is Citigroup (NYSE -C). You decide to perform a residual income analysis to determine whether the stock is indeed a bargain, given that it is selling less than book value. You access a ValueLine report dated February 15, 2013, which provides a one-page summary of the company including information on return on equity and book value going back for more than 10 years and also provides forecasts for the next several years. You find the following information:

Current Price	$42.92
Current Book Value	$61.57
ROE 2002 to 2006	About 18%
ROE 2007 to 2009	Losses
ROE 2010 to 2012	4 to 6.5%
ROE Projection 2013	7.5%
ROE Long-Term Projection	10%

The stock is indeed selling for less than book value. The P/B ratio is about 0.70, so the firm is selling for about a 30 percent discount to book value. Does this discount from book value make it a bargain?

It depends on how you feel about the future ROE prospects and what rate of return you require to make this investment. Let's say that given the recent volatility in financial stocks and the current market environment you require a 10 percent return to invest in Citigroup's stock and you feel that the ROE projection of 7.5 percent is about all that you can expect from Citigroup going forward. Further, you assume a very modest future growth rate of 3 percent. What is the value of Citigroup's stock using a perpetual residual income model?

Current Value = $61.57 + $61.57 ((0.075 − 0.10)/(0.10 − 0.03)) = $39.58

It turns out that given your assumptions the stock is not undervalued at all. In fact, it is slightly *overvalued*. What if Citigroup can indeed achieve a 10 percent ROE in future years? Since you have a required rate of return of 10 percent, the residual income would be zero, but the good news is that the stock should then trade at book value of $61.57.

FORECASTED RESIDUAL INCOME MODEL

Many companies can be expected to have a return on equity that varies over time. In fact, there is substantial evidence that ROEs are mean reverting: Companies or industries that have higher ROEs to others generally see their ROEs decline over time, while companies or industries with very low ROEs likely see theirs increase over time. Let's say that you identify an industry within which only a few companies compete and virtually all of these companies have high returns on equity. If there are not significant entry barriers to this industry, there are likely to be new entrants over time. The arrival of new entrants will increase competition and likely decrease margins and ROEs for all industry participants. Conversely, if there is an industry that is crowded and very competitive and has poor ROEs among its companies, some firms will likely exit over time (both voluntarily and involuntarily!). This would decrease competition and likely increase ROE.

A forecasted residual income model involves forecasting out future residual income and then discounting it back to the present to combine with current book value to determine the current value:

$$Value = B_0 + \frac{RI_1}{(1+r)^1} + \frac{RI_2}{(1+r)^2} + \cdots + \frac{RI_N}{(1+r)^N} + \cdots$$

Note that this looks very much like the dividend discount and free cash flow formulas presented in Chapters 7 and 9 except that we start with book value then add the present value of the future residual income each year rather than some measure of cash flow. This is an earnings-based model. An attractive feature of the residual income model is that in actuality you don't need to forecast residual income out very far into the future. A reasonable assumption is that a company cannot maintain a high return on equity forever. At some point, competition or new products will enter the market and drive return on equity down to be equal to the return desired by the owners. Hence, residual income eventually declines to zero in competitive markets.

This model is best implemented using a spreadsheet approach (Excel is a wonderful tool for this type of financial analysis). This can be done using either total company information (e.g., total book value) or per share data (book value per share, earnings per share, etc.). We will demonstrate this using per share data.

Free Union Enterprises has a current book value per share of $10, a current return on equity of 15 percent, and a dividend payout ratio of 40 percent (the company pays out 40 percent of earnings each year as dividends). Based on current interest rates and the risk of Free Union Enterprises, you have determined that you have a desired rate of return for this investment of 10 percent. You expect that over the next 10 years the company's ROE will decline from 15 percent to 10 percent. A forecast of book value per share, earnings per share, dividends, and residual income is provided in Table 10-1.

Let's review how each cell was calculated:

Forecast ROE—Given for the first year and declining by 0.5 percent per year thereafter

Discount Rate—Given. The rate you desire from this investment

Beginning Book Value Per Share—Given for Year 1 and calculated based on the prior year each year thereafter

Forecast Earnings Per Share—Beginning book value per share times return on equity

Forecast Dividends Per Share—40 percent of forecast earnings per share

Ending Book Value Per Share—Beginning book value per share + earnings per share – dividends per share

Residual Income Per Share—Beginning book value per share times (ROE – r)

Present Value of Residual Income—Present value of residual income discounted at 10 percent using the number of years in the first column.

The total value of Free Union Enterprises using this model is $12.39.

TABLE 10-1

Residual Income Valuation for Free Union Enterprises

Year	Forecast ROE	Discount Rate [r]	Beginning Book Value Per Share	Forecast Earnings Per Share	Forecast Dividend Per Share	Ending Book Value Per Share	Residual Income Per Share	Present Value at 10%
1	15.0%	10%	$10.00	$1.50	$0.60	$10.90	$0.50	$0.45
2	14.5%	10%	10.90	1.58	0.63	11.85	0.49	0.41
3	14.0%	10%	11.85	1.66	0.66	12.84	0.47	0.36
4	13.5%	10%	12.84	1.73	0.69	13.88	0.45	0.31
5	13.0%	10%	13.88	1.80	0.72	14.97	0.42	0.26
6	12.5%	10%	14.97	1.87	0.75	16.09	0.37	0.21
7	12.0%	10%	16.09	1.93	0.77	17.25	0.32	0.17
8	11.5%	10%	17.25	1.98	0.79	18.44	0.26	0.12
9	11.0%	10%	18.44	2.03	0.81	19.65	0.18	0.08
10	10.5%	10%	19.65	2.06	0.83	20.89	0.10	0.04
11	10.0%	10%	20.89	2.09	0.84	22.15	(0.00)	0.00

Total PV of RI   2.39
Beginning Book Value   10.00
Value Per Share $12.39

Box 10-2 Application Using a Forecasted Residual Income Model: Rising ROE

Continuing with the Citigroup example, let's assume that you believe the 2013 ROE forecast of 7.5 percent is accurate, and you feel Citigroup will achieve a 10 percent ROE in five years and ROE will remain at that level. Citigroup has not been paying dividends recently, and you predict the firm will not initiate a dividend payment during that five-year period. A forecast of residual income and current value would be:

Year	Forecast ROE	Discount Rate [r]	Beginning Book Value Per Share	Forecast Earnings Per Share	Forecast Dividend Per Share	Ending Book Value Per Share	Residual Income Per Share	Present Value at 10%
1	7.5%	10%	$61.57	$4.62	–	$66.19	($1.54)	($1.40)
2	8.0%	10%	66.19	5.30	–	71.48	(1.32)	(1.09)
3	8.5%	10%	71.48	6.08	–	77.56	(1.07)	(0.81)
4	9.0%	10%	77.56	6.98	–	84.54	(0.78)	(0.53)
5	9.5%	10%	84.54	8.03	–	92.57	(0.42)	(0.26)
6	10.0%	10%	92.57	9.26	–	101.83	0.00	(0.00)

Total PV of RI	(4.09)
Beginning Book Value	61.57
Value Per Share	$57.48

In this case, if you are confident in Citigroup's ability to increase ROE to 10 percent over five years and are comfortable with a 10 percent required return, then you would conclude that there is sufficient margin of safety to make this investment (a purchase price of $42.92 compared to an intrinsic value of $57.48).

Box 10-3 Application: Declining ROE

You are interested in an investment in Aflac Inc. (NSYE – AFL), so that the stock will pay you in the future when you can't work (or perhaps you are interested because you like ducks). Alfac's current book value is about $30, and its ROE is estimated to be 16.5 percent next year. Alfac's historical ROEs have typically ranged between 15 and 20 percent, but you feel that ROE will gradually decline to a desired rate of return of 10 percent over a 20-year period. You assume the company maintains its historical dividend payout ratio of a little more than 20 percent. What is the intrinsic value today of Alfac's stock using a forecasted residual income model?

Year	Forecast ROE	Discount Rate [r]	Beginning Book Value Per Share	Forecast Earnings Per Share	Forecast Dividend Per Share	Ending Book Value Per Share	Residual Income Per Share	Present Value at 10%
1	16.500%	10%	$30.00	$4.95	$1.11	$33.84	$1.95	$1.77
2	16.175%	10%	33.84	5.47	1.23	38.08	2.09	1.73
3	15.850%	10%	38.08	6.04	1.36	42.76	2.23	1.67
4	15.525%	10%	42.76	6.64	1.49	47.90	2.36	1.61
5	15.200%	10%	47.90	7.28	1.64	53.54	2.49	1.55
6	14.875%	10%	53.54	7.96	1.79	59.71	2.61	1.47
7	14.550%	10%	59.71	8.69	1.95	66.45	2.72	1.39
8	14.225%	10%	66.45	9.45	2.13	73.77	2.81	1.31
9	13.900%	10%	73.77	10.25	2.31	81.72	2.88	1.22
10	13.575%	10%	81.72	11.09	2.50	90.32	2.92	1.13
11	13.250%	10%	90.32	11.97	2.69	99.59	2.94	1.03
12	12.925%	10%	99.59	12.87	2.90	109.57	2.91	0.93
13	12.600%	10%	109.57	13.81	3.11	120.27	2.85	0.83
14	12.275%	10%	120.27	14.76	3.32	131.71	2.74	0.72
15	11.950%	10%	131.71	15.74	3.54	143.91	2.57	0.61
16	11.625%	10%	143.91	16.73	3.76	156.87	2.34	0.51
17	11.300%	10%	156.87	17.73	3.99	170.61	2.04	0.40
18	10.975%	10%	170.61	18.72	4.21	185.12	1.66	0.30
19	10.650%	10%	185.12	19.72	4.44	200.40	1.20	0.20
20	10.3%	10%	90.32	9.33	2.10	97.55	0.29	0.04

Total PV of RI	20.43
Beginning Book Value	30.00
Value Per Share	$50.43

With an intrinsic value of $50.43 and a current price (at the time of this writing) of $53.12, not only is there no margin of safety but also the stock is currently overpriced. It is certainly not a value investment, given your assumptions.

THE RESIDUAL INCOME MODEL AND THE PRICE-TO–BOOK VALUE RATIO

In previous chapters we have talked about the price-to–book value ratio (P/B) as an important relative valuation ratio. In the next chapter we will show how the P/B ratio can be used in a relative valuation model to assess whether a stock is currently over- or undervalued relative to peers. Interestingly, there is a close relationship between the price-to–book value ratio and residual income valuation.

In fact, a formula for a justified P/B ratio can be derived from the perpetual residual income model. Recall our earlier formula:

$$Company\ Value = B_0 + \frac{B_0(ROE - r)}{r - g}$$

If we replace company value with the current price, we get:

$$Price = B_0 + \frac{B_0(ROE - r)}{r - g}$$

Now let's divide both sides by book value:

$$\frac{Price}{B_0} = 1 + \frac{(ROE - r)}{r - g}$$

So, we have developed a formula for what a company's P/B ratio should be, given its return on equity, growth rate, and investor's desired return. With some arithmetic manipulation we can rearrange this formula to get a shorter form of a justified P/B ratio:

$$\frac{Price}{B_0} = \frac{ROE - g}{r - g}$$

Let's see how this works. Assume you desire a rate of return of 10 percent for a stock that has a 15 percent return on equity and this is a no-growth company ($g = 0$). What P/B would you be willing to pay? Given the assumptions, P/B should be 1.5. If the company is currently trading at a P/B over 1.5, then it is overpriced. If it is trading at a P/B under 1.5, then you may have just identified a bargain, given your assumptions and desired rate of return.

Box 10-4 Application: Justified Price-to–Book Value Ratio

Bank of America (NYSE – BAC) is currently trading at $12 per share and has a book value of about $20 per share, so it has a current P/B ratio of 0.60. If you feel that the company's long-term ROE will remain about 7.5 percent, its growth rate around 2.5 percent, and you desire an 11 percent rate of return for an investment in Bank of America, what is its justified P/B ratio?

Justified P/B = (.075 − .025)/(.11 − .025) = 0.59

Given your assumptions, it appears that Bank of America is properly valued (and hence would not currently be considered a value stock).

ACCOUNTING GAMES AND RESIDUAL INCOME

A downside to a residual income model is that it is earnings based, and earnings can easily be manipulated by unscrupulous management. You should exercise caution in simply taking historical company data and ratios such as ROE and plugging them into a residual income model. If you do this, you are assuming that these historical values were accurate and will continue into the future. It is better to use your own conservative forecasts of the inputs. Also exercise extra caution with companies with warnings signs concerning quality of earnings (see Chapter 5). Of course, you may simply want to avoid these kinds of companies altogether. To quote a baseball analogy used by Warren Buffett, you may want to take a few pitches.

CONCLUSION

Residual income models are one of several types of valuation models available to strategic value investors. Although not applicable in all situations, residual income is a very useful framework because it simply and powerfully lays out the notion that managers need to do more than report positive net income. They need to also compensate stockholders for the risk they bear, and failing to do so will drive down the stock price. Residual income is a convenient way to illustrate what management needs to deliver to justify the current price or P/B ratio. That can highlight home runs as well as strikeouts.

CHAPTER ELEVEN

RELATIVE VALUATION

But a pin lies in wait for every bubble. And when the two eventually meet, a new wave of investors learns some very old lessons: First, many in Wall Street, a community in which quality control is not prized, will sell investors anything they will buy. Second, speculation is most dangerous when it looks easiest.

—Warren Buffett

One of the most common valuation methods and one often cited in the financial press and on financial television shows is relative valuation. In fact, nearly everyone practices relative valuation in his or her daily life. Let's say you're driving home from work and need gasoline and come across two gas stations next to each other and you know both brands well. You are confident that the quality of each is identical and both provide the same discounts for the credit card you carry but one is priced by a few cents less per gallon. Unless you have money to waste, you are likely to choose the lower-priced gasoline. Now let's change the scenario. If one is a brand-name gas station and the other is a brand you have never heard of, you may stop at the brand-name station even if the gasoline is selling for a few pennies more per gallon. In this scenario, the off-brand station would likely have to offer a more substantial discount to get you to try it and test its quality. Price per gallon is a relative valuation metric. It is the price of something divided by some underlying fundamental.

In the investing world, the most common valuation metrics are price-to-earnings, price-to-book, price-to–cash flow, price-to-sales, and dividend yield ratios. Less common metrics, such as enterprise value–to-EBITDA, include the value of the firm in the numerator. All of these measures take the price of equity or the price of debt plus equity divided by some underlying fundamental value. You can certainly create others. During the Internet frenzy of the late 1990s, we frequently heard about such unique measures as price per click or price per eyeball. New companies with no earnings or cash flow, some without revenues, were selling at outrageous prices, and the media and others created new metrics in an attempt to justify the prices. That is, until the pin burst the bubble. In this chapter we will focus on the traditional relative valuation metrics that have withstood the test of time.

RELATIVE TO WHAT?

We have already mentioned that relative valuation metrics use some measure of current price divided by (relative to) some underlying fundamental value. However, we must take *relative* a step or two further. Relative value is different from the absolute valuation methods we discussed in the last few chapters. Relative valuation requires that you compare a relative value metric for one company to something else: the same metric for peer companies, the industry, or the market. As value investors, we are looking to buy companies that are selling at a lower multiple relative to other companies of similar quality and similar risk. (We will define what we mean by quality with regard to companies in the next section.)[1] Alternatively, we could be looking to buy companies that are trading at a lower multiple than their historical norms, assuming the fundamental value drivers have not substantially changed.[2] By comparing one company's price multiples to its peers, you are likely assuming that the comparable firms or market are fairly valued and you are looking to identify a bargain. We would urge you to make such assumptions carefully. For example, recall the long-term chart of P/E ratios presented in Chapter 4 and replicated in Figure 11-1.

Let's say it is early in the year 2000, and you are looking at buying a stock that has a P/E ratio of 20 when other peer companies and the market are selling at multiples above 30. It would have looked like an attractive value relative to the others, but in reality the subject stock was not such a bargain in the context of the historical P/E ratio of approximately 15 for the market.

FIGURE 11-1

Historical P/E ratios for the S&P 500.

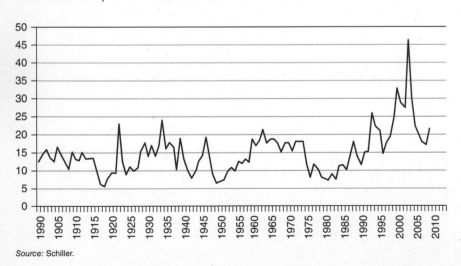

Source: Schiller.

This example illustrates the value of both comparison to peers and comparisons over time. You should take some time to consider the overall valuation of the market before rushing to judgment on the relative value of an individual security. You can do this by looking at the historical context: What multiple has the company traded at over time, and where is the market multiple relative to its history?

WHAT FACTORS DRIVE PRICE MULTIPLES?

Most investors use price multiples without spending any time thinking about what underlying factors drive them. This is the case because multiples are easy to use, widely available, and are known by some as the tool of the armchair analyst. Some investors use them without reference to any underlying factors. We hope that this is not you—at least, not after you have read this book. As with any valuation method, you need to thoroughly research the company you want to own before you consider the price that you are willing to pay. You want to buy a good company at a good price, so you also need to understand what quantitative and qualitative factors (quality mentioned in the introduction above) should make a company sell at a higher or lower multiple than others.

So let's take a look back at one of our absolute valuation methods. The constant growth dividend discount model introduced in Chapter 7 can help us discern these factors:

$$Share\ Value = \frac{D_0(1+g)}{r-g}$$

Let's assume a stock is fairly valued; that is, its current price equals its intrinsic value. This formula would then be:

$$Price = \frac{D_0(1+g)}{r-g}$$

Now let's divide both sides by last year's earnings, E_0:

$$\frac{Price}{E_0} = \frac{(D_0/E_0)(1+g)}{r-g}$$

We now have a formula for *justified P/E ratio*, which is the P/E ratio at which the company should sell, given its payout ratio (D/E), its projected future dividend growth rate (g), and your desired rate of return (r). Now don't rush off and start applying this formula to companies. At this point, that would be a waste of your time. The formula is derived from the dividend discount model and will give you the same results. We present it here to get you thinking about what factors should drive P/E ratios.

Let's make things even simpler for a minute. Let's take a company that pays out all of its earnings in dividends and therefore has an expected future dividend growth rate of zero. The formula simplifies to:

$$\frac{Price}{E_0} = \frac{1}{r}$$

The P/E ratio for a no-growth stock should be 1 divided by your required rate of return. If you desire a rate of return of 10 percent, then a fair price to pay for the company is 10 times earnings. If you desire a rate of return of only 5 percent, then a fair price would be 20 times earnings. If you desire a rate of return of 20 percent, then a fair price would be only 5 times earnings. As you can see, there is an inverse relationship between desired rate of return and a fair price: The higher your desired return, the lower the price you should be willing to pay.

So what factors influence your required rate of return? Recall from Chapter 7 that these include the risk-free rate, the equity risk premium, a size premium, and a risk premium specific to a company. These are summarized in Table 11-1.

The first two factors affect all companies equally. In a low interest rate and low inflation environment you should be willing to pay higher P/E multiples for investments in stocks in general. Conversely, in a high interest rate and high inflation environment you should be willing to pay lower P/E multiples. In periods of higher risk for equity markets in general, you would be willing to pay lower P/E multiples. Conversely, in period of low risk for equities (stable economy, good employment, etc.) you would be willing to accept higher P/E multiples.

The last two factors influencing your desired return are factors specific to individual companies: size and specific risk. The higher the risk you see in a given

TABLE 11-1

Factors Influencing Your Desired Return

Risk-Free Rate	Amount to compensate for the pure use of money which effectively includes inflation.
Plus: Equity Risk Premium	The additional return that should be required for an investor to purchase a stock rather than invest at the risk-free rate. This is a premium for the market as a whole (generally for large stocks).
Plus: Size Premium	Small stocks are typically considered riskier than large stocks, and correspondingly they have exhibited higher historical returns than large stocks over time.
Plus: Specific Premium	Judgmentally determined based on the individual stock under consideration. For example, if the company is highly leveraged relative to other companies you might add a bit. If the company is illiquid or nonpublic, you might add a larger amount for this illiquidity.

company, the lower the P/E ratio you should accept. Here are some factors you might look at including size:

- Size: Smaller companies tend to be riskier.
- Tenure: Newer, unproven companies are likely riskier.
- Nature of the business: Some businesses are inherently riskier than others. For example, a company that makes consumer nondiscretionary goods like food staples is generally less risky than a biotechnology company.
- Leverage: While leverage can have its benefits, including higher returns to equity if used appropriately, having more leverage is riskier and should command a higher desired return and result in a lower P/E multiple.
- Consistency of results: How stable are the company's profits and cash flows? The more volatile they are, the riskier they are.

Now let's return to the P/E formula introduced above:

$$\frac{Price}{E_0} = \frac{(D_0/E_0)(1+g)}{r-g}$$

What is the relationship of growth to P/E? Growth has a positive relationship with P/E, with the greater influence from the denominator of the relationship. Since growth is subtracted from the desired return in the denominator, a higher growth rate will result in a lower denominator and, therefore, a higher justified P/E. Now you know why growth stocks typically trade at high P/Es.

The remaining factor in the right-hand side of the formula is the dividend payout ratio. This factor is not easy to generalize. Not all companies pay dividends. When they do, the dividends are typically related to the company's ability to generate and sustain profits and cash flow. Further, the dividend payout is inversely related to growth: The higher the dividends paid out, the lower the growth (because less of the earnings are being retained in the firm and invested to fuel future growth). So don't worry about this factor, other than to recognize that the higher the profits and cash flow the company can generate in the future, the more likely it is that they will be able to reward shareholders through dividends or stock buybacks.

We have demonstrated the important factors here using a formula for the P/E ratio; however, we could have just as easily done so using price-to–book value, price-to-sales, or some other multiple. Regardless of method, we would reach the same conclusions. There are three main factors that should influence all multiples:

- Risk: inversely related to multiples
- Growth: positively related to multiples
- Profitability: positively related to multiples

Now comes the fun part. We will show how to apply relative valuation in practice using the most common price and enterprise value multiples.

PRICE-TO-EARNINGS APPROACH

Price-to-earnings multiples are readily available on financial websites and in financial databases. What most people do not realize, however, is that not all sources calculate P/E ratios in an identical manner. Here is a sampling of just a few of the common methods (price is always the current price):

- Historical P/E based on the last full fiscal year's earnings (also known as a trailing P/E).
- Historical P/E based on the last 12 months of earnings (commonly known as trailing 12 months, but practically speaking it is really the last four quarters); also referred to as a trailing P/E. This is the method used by Yahoo! Finance.
- Leading P/E based on a forecast of the next fiscal year's earnings.
- Leading P/E based on a forecast of the next four quarters' earnings.
- P/E based on a combination of the last two historical quarters plus the next two forecast quarters. This is the method used by *Value Line*.

Are you confused or befuddled? Which one is right? In a sense, they all are reasonable measures. On one hand, historical P/E ratios can fluctuate wildly due to transitory impacts on earnings such as one-time gains or write downs. Leading P/E ratios are inherently more stable because they typically use a consensus of analysts' forecasts that focus only on normal earnings and ignore transitory effects. But some transitory effects are indeed real, and the forecasts are just that—forecasts.[3] You can use any of these P/E ratios, but consistency is paramount. Do not mix and match P/E ratio methods or data sources. When you are performing a relative valuation, try to draw all of your data from the same source and at the same time (even P/E ratios drawn a single day apart from each other will vary due to market movements).

The first step in performing a relative valuation is to identify peer companies for comparison. You want companies as close as possible in terms of many factors: product lines, geographic dispersion of sales, size, and so forth. Sometimes, however, you will not find perfect matches and may have to select less than perfect peers. That is fine, as long as you consider their differences in assessing relative risk, growth, and profitability. Sources such as Yahoo! Finance and *Value Line* make the selection of peers relatively easy to accomplish. On Yahoo! Finance, for instance, you can run a competitors' report for any company, and it will identify three competitors and show aggregate industry data (including P/Es and other data). *Value Line* is organized by industry, and you can select peers from within the subject company's industry group.[4]

Once you have selected peers, you need to collect data on their multiples (P/E in this case), as well as other data that will help you assess relative profitability, risk, and growth.

Box 11-1 Application: Relative Valuation Using P/E Ratios

Suppose you are interested in purchasing a consumer products company for your portfolio and have decided to select from among those covered by *Value Line* since it performs some analysis for you and provides a good one-page summary of important data. You are interested in purchasing the company that appears to provide the greatest value for its price. You have selected the following peer companies from *Value Line*:

Company	Ticker Symbol	P/E Ratio at 3/29/2013
Clorox Company	NYSE – CLX	19.1
Colgate Palmolive	NYSE – CL	23.1
Kimberly-Clark	NYSE – KMB	19.6
Procter & Gamble	NYSE – PG	18.8

Without considering other factors, Procter & Gamble is the least expensive based on its current P/E ratio, while Colgate Palmolive is the most expensive on that basis. We should note that as of this date the median P/E ratio of all stocks covered by *Value Line* (which had earnings) was 16.7, which was up from 15.2 26 weeks earlier. The previous market high P/E for *Value Line* stocks was 19.7 in mid-2007. Let's look at some historical context for the peers.

Ticker	Average P/E 2008	Average P/E 2009	Average P/E 2010	Average P/E 2011	Average P/E 2012
CLX	18.5	14.5	14.4	31.9	16.7
CL	19.8	16.1	18.6	17.3	19.6
KMB	15.2	12.2	14.1	16.9	18.2
PG	18.6	16.4	17.0	16.0	16.7

Note the very high P/E for Clorox in 2011. This was not a result of a spike in the stock price, but rather was due to a substantial decline in earnings from recognition of an impairment loss. It appears that, for all four of these companies, current P/E ratios are high relative to history and relative to the market. As value investors, we might stop here and decide that a consumer products company is not attractively priced right now. It appears that over this time period the consumer products industry was in favor with investors. Perhaps we should look to an industry that is out of favor in order to identify a candidate for a strategic value investment. We will look at some out of favor companies later in this chapter, so let's continue to identify which of these four peers in the consumer products industry is likely the greatest value. Let's examine some risk and profitability factors.

(Continued)

Ticker	Value Line Safety Rating	Beta	Market Capi-talization	Leverage (% of Debt)	Business
CLX	2	0.60	$11.1 billion	97%	Somewhat limited household products
CL	1	0.60	$52.6 billion	69%	Broad selection of household products
KMB	1	0.55	$36.4 billion	50%	Personal care products with an emphasis on paper goods
PG	1	0.60	$211 billion	26%	Broad selection of consumer goods

Ticker	ROE 2008	ROE 2009	ROE 2010	ROE 2011	ROE 2012	ROE Forecast 2013	ROE Forecast 2014
CLX	NMF	NMF	NMF	NMF	NMF	NMF	NMF
CL	NMF	NMF	NMF	NMF	NMF	NMF	NMF
KMB	43.8%	34.9%	31.1%	30.3%	35.1%	39.0%	40.0%
PG	17.4%	17.9%	17.8%	17.3%	17.7%	18.5%	19.5%

NMF = Not meaningful. CLX had negative or very low book value of equity in these years, while CL had very low book value.

From a value perspective, our relative risk assessment is becoming clear. CLX and CL are quite risky. CLX is the most risky. It is relatively small, has high debt, a poor safety rating, and sells a limited product portfolio. Based on P/E and risk alone, why pay 19.1 times earnings for CLX when you can get PG for 18.8 times earnings? PG is the least risky of the bunch because it has low debt, large size, a broad product portfolio, and stable profitability (although not as profitable as KMB).

Now let's get an idea about these firms' growth prospects. *Value Line* provides the following data on earnings growth:

Ticker	Past 10 Years Growth (Annual)	Past 5 Years Growth (Annual)	Forecast Growth 5 Years (Annual)
CLX	8.0%	3.0%	10.5%
CL	9.5%	10.0%	10.5%
KMB	2.5%	1.5%	9.5%
PG	9.0%	6.5%	8.5%

Now we can get a better idea as to why CLX and CL have high P/E ratios in spite of their high risk levels. They have the highest expected future earnings growth, and, as we learned earlier, higher growth is associated with a higher P/E ratio. The market will pay a premium for growth (and sometimes will overpay). Combining risk and growth, our choice for the value investor comes down to KMB or PG. PG is the lower-risk stock, but KMB has higher growth prospects.

We can also use this data to estimate an intrinsic value and margin of safety. Let's say that you would like to make an investment in PG and that you feel it should be trading at the average P/E multiple of its peer companies, which is 20.6. PG's current price and earnings used in computing its P/E were $77.11 and $4.10, respectively. A P/E multiple of 20.6 times $4.10 of earnings would imply a fair valuation of $84.46. Given that two of the three companies appear overvalued based on our analysis above, we might more conservatively assume PG deserves a similar multiple as KMB of 19.6, implying a valuation for PG of $80.36. With a current price of $77.11, the margin of safety is only about 4 percent. If you really are set on owning a consumer products company in your portfolio, the next step should perhaps be to use an absolute valuation model on KMB and PG to ascertain whether there is more intrinsic value and margin of safety than this crude relative valuation might suggest. Otherwise it might simply be time to look for some other securities that are not currently market favorites.

THE PEG RATIO

An extension of a P/E approach is the PEG ratio. The PEG ratio is the P/E ratio relative to growth prospects. Recall that higher growth typically implies a higher P/E multiple. Dividing the P/E ratio by the growth rate (ignoring the percent sign) attempts to adjust for this. The idea is that a lower PEG ratio means a lower P/E relative to expected growth and connotes greater value.[5] We can compute a PEG ratio for Kimberly-Clark and Procter & Gamble from our previous example:

Company	P/E	Growth	PEG
Kimberly-Clark	19.6	9.5	2.06
Procter & Gamble	18.8	8.5	2.21

It appears that Kimberly-Clark is a more attractive value investment on a relative basis. You should interpret PEG ratios cautiously, however. The PEG ratio assumes a linear (or a one-to-one) relationship between growth and P/E ratios, meaning it is OK to divide the two. In reality, the relationship is more complex—certainly nonlinear. In this case, the growth period forecasted is the same length of time, which certainly helps. You would not want to compute PEG ratios using different time lengths of growth for your comparison companies. You will hear many value investors say an ideal PEG ratio is one or less; that is, the P/E ratio should be lower than the growth rate. Although we do not hold to the one threshold, lower is definitely better and both of these companies appear pretty richly priced on a PEG basis—another reason for us to take a more contrarian approach and look for something cheaper.

Box 11-2   Application: PEG Approach to Relative Valuation

It is April 5, 2013, and you have decided to seek out companies in an industry that is not currently in favor with the marketplace and have identified manufacturers of hard drives. In particular, you are interested in whether Seagate Technology (STX) or Western Digital Corporation (WDC) is a better value based on the future growth prospects of each and that they each have a P/E ratio close to 7.0.

Both companies have market capitalizations of around $12 billion and *Value Line* safety ratings of 3. STX has more debt (43 percent of capital) than WDC (18 percent). Their products and customers are similar. Data on their P/E ratios and growth prospects are:

	P/E	Sales Growth Forecast	Earnings Growth Forecast	PEG Ratio (based on earnings)
STX	7.0	5%	11%	0.63
WDC	6.5	6%	6.5%	0.92

Both companies have attractive P/E ratios relative to the broader market P/E of 16.7 and have PEG ratios less than 1.0. STX has the lower PEG ratio, indicating it is more attractively priced based solely on its future growth prospects. Note, however, that the higher earnings growth rate is not the result of a higher sales growth forecast. WDC actually has a higher sales growth forecast. The higher debt of STX leads to greater leverage and greater earnings growth than sales growth. Both companies appear to be classic value stocks. The question is whether they will keep pace with technology changes and the movement toward newer solid state technology.

PRICE-TO-BOOK APPROACH

The price-to-book ratio is another popular price multiple for assessing the relative value of stocks (although no other multiple is as popular as the price-to-earnings ratio). The price-to–book value multiple has tremendous flexibility and can be used in some circumstances in which the price-to-earnings measure cannot be used, such as when companies have negative earnings. The price-to–book value multiple is also significantly less variable than the price-to-earnings measure, as book value is a cumulative amount whereas earnings (estimated or actual) is for a single year. Lastly, as we saw in the residual income chapter, there is a direct relationship between residual income and the price-to-book ratio. Thus, it is appropriate to use the price-to-book approach in circumstances similar to the residual income model, such as for financial companies.

Computing the price-to-book ratio is relatively straightforward. Book value is equal to the sum of the amounts reported on the most recent balance sheet for total stockholders equity. Book value per share is this amount divided by the number of shares of common stock currently outstanding. For valuation purposes, if the company has preferred stock, this must be treated separately: You must subtract the book value of preferred stock from stockholders equity before dividing by the number of common shares outstanding.

The price per common share is divided by the book value per share to obtain the P/BV ratio. The P/BV ratio therefore expresses the market price of a share in relation to the accounting value per share on the balance sheet. A P/BV relative valuation approached is applied in the same manner as a P/E approach. Peer companies are selected for comparison, and data is collected on their relative profitability, risk, and growth.

Box 11-3 Application: P/BV Relative Valuation

Recall that in Chapter 10 we determined that Aflac was currently fully valued by the market using the absolute valuation method based on residual income. You would like to see how Aflac stacks up compared to its peers in the insurance industry on a relative basis. You collect the following information from the April 12, 2013, issue of *Value Line* (ranked by P/BV ratio):

Company	Ticker	Price	Book Value Per Share	Price/ Book Value
Aflac	AFL	52.90	34.16	1.55
Torchmark Corp	TMK	59.62	46.57	1.28
Manulife Financial	MFC	14.82	14.28	1.04
Unum Group	UNM	27.98	31.92	0.88
Prudential Financial	PRU	59.04	83.31	0.71
Metlife, Inc.	MET	38.16	58.94	0.65
Reinsurance Group	RGA	58.83	93.47	0.63
Protective Life Corp	PL	35.71	59.06	0.60
Lincoln National	LNC	32.60	55.17	0.59
Aegon	AEG	6.18	17.04	0.36
Genworth Financial	GNW	9.79	33.61	0.29
The Phoenix Companies	PNX	29.99	193.67	0.15

(Continued)

This listing presents all companies classified as operating in the life insurance industry covered by *Value Line*, although these firms certainly have varying amounts of life insurance exposure (versus medial insurance, investments, etc.). Note that Aflac is the most expensive on a relative basis, and there is a broad range of P/BV ratios for the industry. Don't assume the lowest P/BV ratio is necessarily the best value or represents a value stock. Some stocks, like The Phoenix Companies, are trading at a low multiple because they have earned it: Phoenix announced in late 2012 that it was going to reissue the past three years of financial reports due to errors in their accounting reports—never a good sign.

Take note of the following additional information extracted from *Value Line*. Alfac has similar risk to the other companies listed here on most measures. It is ranked 3 for safety by *Value Line*, has 21 percent debt and consistent profitability. One area of higher risk is that Alfac has substantial operations in Japan and is subject to yen exposure, meaning that currency fluctuations between the dollar and yen can impact the earnings of the firm. On the other hand, Alfac's expected earnings growth rate is at the high end of the peer companies. We would likely conclude that Aflac is a good, solid company—it has good profitability, good products, and even entertaining commercials—but the stock does not appear to be attractively priced from a value investor's standpoint. Aflac is expensive on a relative basis using a P/B approach. We could compute an implied price and margin of safety using the average P/B of an appropriate subset of the peer companies; however, no matter what subset we use, we would find an intrinsic value below the current price for Aflac and a negative margin of safety.

PRICE-TO-SALES APPROACH

Price-to-sales is a metric that can be used regardless of whether a company has earnings, cash flow, or positive book value. This is true since sales (or revenue) is always a positive number. As such, it is frequently used (and, unfortunately, frequently misused). The price-to-sales ratio is quite commonly applied in valuing service businesses, such as professional firms in the context of a potential merger or acquisition. In these circumstances, an acquirer often cares most about the revenue stream it is acquiring and not as much about the business models and expense levels of the target company (since after the acquisition it probably would apply its own business model). Even though you are likely an individual investor and therefore unlikely to acquire the entire company, it is of keen interest that you know what an acquirer might be willing to pay. The price-to-sales ratio can be misused when applied to companies and industries that do not have positive earnings and cash flows and may have no prospects to generate them in the future. A good example is the Internet bubble of the late 1990s. Some Internet companies were trading at huge multiples to sales but had no earnings or cash flows. In fact, some of the revenues being reported were inflated barter arrangements with other Internet companies.

The price-to-sales approach is applied in the same manner as the P/E approach discussed earlier. In fact, in working through the formula for a theoretically justified value of P/S, we would find that a key driving factor here is profitability—more so than in the case of P/E. A P/S approach is appropriately used when earnings are currently negative (but you should have confidence in a future return to profitability in order to use it).

Box 11-4 Application: Relative Valuation Using Price-to-Sales

In a recent article in *Barron's*, restaurant chain Ruby Tuesday was profiled as being a good value investment with strong upside potential. Unfortunately, Ruby Tuesday had negative earnings recently. Fortunately, *Value Line* forecasts a return to profitability and a return on equity of 11 percent several years into the future. You may therefore choose to assess Ruby Tuesday's relative value using a P/S approach. You collect the following information on casual dining restaurants from *Value Line*:

Company	Ticker	Price ($)	Sales 2012 ($millions)	Shares Outstanding (millions)	Sales Per Share ($)	P/S Ratio
BJ's Restaurants	BJRI	33.10	708.30	28.02	25.28	1.31
Cheesecake Factory	CAKE	33.32	1,809.00	53.67	33.70	0.99
Brinker International	EAT	32.02	2,843.70	71.89	39.55	0.81
Darden Restaurants	DRI	45.25	8,220.00	129.36	63.54	0.71
Red Robin Gourmet	RRGB	43.33	977.20	14.25	68.57	0.63
Bloomin' Brands	BLMN	18.61	3,945.40	121.10	32.58	0.57
Ruby Tuesday	RT	7.55	1,325.10	61.70	21.48	0.35

We see from this table that Ruby Tuesday has the lowest P/S ratio of these casual dining restaurants. Excluding Ruby Tuesday, the mean P/S ratio of the group is 0.84, while the median is 0.76.

Ruby Tuesday, BJ's, and Red Robin, are all small cap companies and should have similar risk premiums. They have similar profitability prospects

(Continued)

with forecast ROEs as follows: Ruby Tuesday, 11 percent; BJ's, 13 percent; and Red Robin, 9 percent. Forecasted long-term earnings growth rates are: Ruby Tuesday, 17 percent; BJ's, 20.5 percent; and Red Robin, 15 percent. It would appear that Ruby Tuesday should warrant a P/S ratio at least at the level of Red Robin, which is 0.63.

With sales per share of $21.48 and a justified P/S of 0.63, Ruby Tuesday would have an intrinsic value of $13.53, which would yield a substantial margin of safety and imply terrific upside potential.

PRICE-TO–CASH FLOW APPROACH

A price-to–cash flow (P/CF) ratio is an attractive measure in that cash flow is one of the most important drivers of firm value. Companies not only need to generate earnings but also need to turn these earnings into cash flows in order to have a long-term and sustainable business model. As we saw in previous chapters, a common absolute valuation method is to discount future cash flows. Applying a price-to–cash flow approach therefore makes good sense. Unfortunately price-to–cash flow ratios are not readily available in databases or on most financial Internet sites. Even when these ratios are available, they are often not based on "true" cash flow measures. Instead, they often use crude approximations, such as earnings per share plus deprecation per share. We prefer to compute a price-to–cash flow ratio using operating cash flow from the firm's cash flow statement:

$$Cash\ Flow\ Per\ Share = \frac{Annual\ Operating\ Cash\ Flow}{Number\ of\ Common\ Share\ Outstanding}$$

The P/CF ratio can then be computed as follows:

$$\frac{P}{CF} = \frac{Price\ Per\ Share}{Cash\ Flow\ Per\ Share}$$

We should note that we could use a measure of free cash flow (usually free cash flow to equity) rather than operating cash flow (a price-to-free-cash-flow ratio). This is also very useful and is sensible, as free cash flow is available to shareholders. However, free cash flow can fluctuate substantially year-over-year due to increased borrowing, higher than normal capital expenditures, and the like. Operating cash flow is typically much more stable. We can also invert this ratio to create a ratio called cash flow yield (we can do the same thing for a P/E ratio to compute earnings yield). A yield measure avoids problems of ranking stocks when one has negative cash flow (or earnings) and in the case of cash flow can be thought of as the return an investor is getting on a cash basis by buying the stock at its current price. For example, if cash flow yield is 15 percent (a price-to–cash flow ratio of 6.7), then the company is generating a cash flow return of 15 percent on the current price. Cash flow yield computed as:

$$Cash\ Flow\ Yield = \frac{Cash\ Flow\ Per\ Share}{Price\ Per\ Share}$$

A price-to–cash flow or cash flow yield relative valuation is performed using the same approach outlined above with P/E. From a value investing perspective, you are looking for companies selling for a lower P/CF ratio (higher cash flow yield) than peers with similar risk, profitability, and growth prospects. Cash flow yield can also be used as a screen to identify companies with strong cash flow for which you can then perform an absolute valuation using a discounted cash flow model.

Box 11-5 Application: Relative Valuation Using Cash Flow Yield

You have an interest in identifying a semiconductor company to add to your portfolio based on a belief that, while they are currently out of favor, the industry valuations will recover as the economy recovers. You subscribe to a database of historical financial data that allows you to create your own ratios. You run a screen to identify large (we will use over $1 billion market cap) companies in the semiconductor industry with cash flow yields in excess of 15 percent (a high number if you would be satisfied with a 9 percent return on equity investments at this time but appropriate for the risk of the industry and your desire to find companies with a good margin of safety). You also screen for price per share of at least $5 (very low priced shares are often considered more speculative and sell for a low price for a good reason). You find that there are 214 semiconductor companies in the database with only four meeting your cash flow yield, price, and size criteria.

Company	Price ($)	Cash Flow Yield (%)	Market Cap (millions)
First Solar, Inc.	26.44	33.08	2,304
Flextronics International Ltd.	6.66	26.21	4,368
Intel Corporation	20.94	18.21	103,673
Vishay Intertechnology	12.29	16.31	1,762

This narrows down the population of attractive semiconductor companies to a number for which you can do a more detailed free cash flow valuation. Note that while all four firms have a market capitalization in excess of $1 billion, Intel has a market cap that is nearly 24 times that of the next largest firm identified in the screen. Are these companies truly comparable? That is where the art of investing comes in, as different investors would answer that question differently.

DIVIDEND YIELD APPROACH

Similar to a cash flow yield or earnings yield measure mentioned in the previous section, dividend yield is the inverse of a price-to-dividend ratio. For relative valuation, a dividend yield format is almost always used, and dividend yield is readily available in financial publications, websites, and databases. Dividend yield represents the current yield a stock investor is receiving from his or her investment in a stock. Dividend yield is computed as:

$$Dividend\ Yield = \frac{Annual\ Dividend\ Per\ Share}{Price\ Per\ Share}$$

Seeking companies with a high dividend yield (low price-to-dividend ratio) is definitely considered a value approach. However, you should exercise caution when using this measure. Some investors seek current income over capital gains and hence purposely seek out high dividend yielding stocks. You should consider any favorable tax treatment of long-term gains over current income: In some tax environments the latter may be more desirable, and you can achieve the same current income by periodically pruning long-term gains. Additionally, high dividend paying stocks tend to be those that do not have opportunities to invest in new projects internally, and so you may bias your portfolio to stocks that will not be able to significantly grow their dividends in the future. You may also concentrate your portfolio in a few industries (for example, utilities that pay high dividends) and end up with an underdiversified portfolio. Lastly, some companies continue to pay high dividends in spite of declining business prospects and earnings. This situation cannot continue forever. You should consider a company's ability to continue its current dividend yield by examining its ability to generate earnings and cash flow to maintain and support those dividends.

Box 11-6 Application: Selecting Value Stocks Using Dividend Yield

Suppose you would like to apply a "dogs of the Dow" value approach to the S&P 500 universe using dividend yield (i.e., buying the least expensive companies within the index). You screen the S&P 500 stocks in a financial database for stocks with the highest dividend yield (which indicates they are less expensive).

Ticker	Company	Price ($)	Dividend Yield (%)	Earnings Yield (%)	Cash Flow Yield (%)
WIN	Windstream Corporation	8.87	11.30	7.69	26.35
PBI	Pitney Bowes, Inc.	15.09	9.90	14.29	28.20

FTR	Frontier Communications Corp	4.22	9.50	3.08	34.66
CTL	CenturyLink, Inc.	37.22	5.80	3.36	17.75
EXC	Exelon Corporation	36.22	5.80	3.86	17.49
LO	Lorillard, Inc.	41.56	5.30	6.76	7.18
GRMN	Garmin Ltd.	34.72	5.20	7.94	11.21
RAI	Reynolds American, Inc.	46.18	5.10	4.85	5.12
MO	Altria Group, Inc.	35.91	4.90	5.75	4.74
POM	Pepco Holdings, Inc.	22.05	4.90	5.62	13.68
ETR	Entergy Corporation	69.70	4.80	6.85	26.89
FE	FirstEnergy Corp.	45.72	4.80	4.03	14.72
PBCT	People's United Financial, Inc.	13.30	4.80	5.41	6.91
TE	TECO Energy, Inc.	18.45	4.80	6.17	18.32
LMT	Lockheed Martin Corporation	97.18	4.70	8.62	10.22
NEM	Newmont Mining Corp	36.37	4.70	10.42	16.82
T	AT&T, Inc.	38.59	4.70	3.13	16.66
PPL	PPL Corporation	31.99	4.60	8.13	13.09
TEG	Integrys Energy Group, Inc.	60.45	4.50	6.06	14.18
AEE	Ameren Corp	35.49	4.50	NM	20.87
COP	ConocoPhillips	59.36	4.40	10.00	23.23
GAS	AGL Resources, Inc.	43.50	4.30	5.32	12.93
HCN	Health Care REIT, Inc.	71.11	4.30	0.69	3.20
DUK	Duke Energy Corp	72.97	4.20	4.20	8.70
INTC	Intel Corporation	21.68	4.20	9.80	17.51
STX	Seagate Technology PLC	36.09	4.20	20.83	16.16

Source: American Association of Individual Investors, Stock Investor Pro database at 4/14/2013.

Listed here are the top 26 companies ranked in order by dividend yield. Note that we have shaded the yield of a number of companies, indicating that their current earnings are not sufficient to cover the dividend. Fortunately, all but one of these does have sufficient operating cash flow. If you desire to invest in any of the shaded companies you should first ascertain their ability to maintain current dividend levels (they may need the operating cash flow to cover replacement of property, plant, and equipment).

ENTERPRISE VALUE APPROACH

In Chapter 8 we presented a free cash flow to the firm (FCFF) approach to absolute valuation. Recall that free cash flow to the firm is a valuation approach that values the firm as a whole rather than just the equity and then subtracts out the value of debt and preferred stock to estimate the value of equity. Such an approach is very useful in acquisition situations when the acquirer may significantly change the capital structure for the acquired firm, such as in a leveraged buyout. An enterprise value multiple is the relative valuation equivalent of a FCFF absolute valuation approach. It is an effective way to assess what an acquirer might be willing to pay, which is relevant for all investors. There are several variations to this multiple, but the most common is the enterprise value (EV)–to–earnings before interest, taxes, depreciation, and amortization (EBITDA) multiple.

$$Enterprise\ Value\text{–}to\text{-}EBITDA = \frac{Value\ of\ Debt + Value\ of\ Equity}{EBITDA}$$

The numerator is the value of all debt and equity securities including preferred stock. The denominator is basically operating earnings with depreciation and amortization added back and is an approximation of the operating cash flow available to all of the capital providers: both debt holders and equity holders. The application of this multiple is similar to those presented above except that an extra step is required to determine the implied value of equity per share.

Box 11-7 Application: Using an EV/EBITDA multiple

You are interested in determining which pharmacy companies are trading at the most attractive valuation levels. You find that four companies you have identified as peers have dramatically different capital structures, and you decide to use the EV/EBITDA multiple. You collect the following data from Yahoo! Finance:

Ticker	Company	Value of Common Equity	Value of Debt	Enterprise Value	Percentage of Debt	EV/ EBITDA
RAD	Rite Aid Corp	2.06	6.29	8.35	75%	7.38
CVS	CVS Care-mark	70.82	8.65	79.47	11%	8.85
WAG	Walgreen Co.	46.21	3.91	50.12	8%	10.88
ESRX	Express Scripts	46.08	13.12	59.2	22%	11.22

Source: Yahoo! Finance at 4/14/2013. Dollar amounts in billions.

Rite Aid is clearly the least expensive based on the ratio of enterprise value to EBITDA, but it has likely earned the lowest multiple given the high amount of risk (very high debt levels) in the firm's capital structure. On the other hand, CVS looks attractive relative to its peers. Additional work should be done investigating the future prospects of CVS relative to the others. Let's say that you determine that CVS deserves a similar multiple to WAG of 10.88. The value of the firm and equity would be determined as follows:

EBITDA from Yahoo! Finance (you can imply from data above)	$8.98 billion
Assessed EV/EBITDA multiple	10.88 times
Implied value of enterprise	$97.70 billion
Less value of debt	$8.65 billion
Implied value of equity	$89.05 billion
Number of shares outstanding from Yahoo! Finance	1.23 billion
Implied value per share (intrinsic value)	$72.40
Current price per share from Yahoo! Finance	$57.52
Margin of safety	20%

ACCOUNTING ADJUSTMENTS

The current price used in price multiples is not controversial; however, the other data used are typically based on reported accounting numbers. As we noted in Chapter 4, some companies may select accounting methods that make earnings appear higher than they should be, making the P/E ratio appear more attractive. You should review the accounting warning signs presented in Chapter 5. If any of these signs exist, you should consider making adjustments to the reported data for that company or should consider avoiding the firm altogether. Some additional readings on accounting problems are listed in the Resources section at the end of this book.

CONCLUSION

Price multiples are both readily available and easy to apply in order to ascertain the relative value of stocks. They are especially useful in screening large databases of stocks to identify *potential* value opportunities. However, as noted at the beginning of this chapter, you are ascertaining value relative to peer companies or the market and would be wise to combine a relative valuation approach with an absolute approach. Remember, Warren Buffett dissolved the Buffett Limited Partnership in 1969 because he "didn't have any first class ideas" and felt that the market as a whole was so overvalued that he characterized his continued involvement in the market as "trying to play a game I don't understand." In retrospect, Mr. Buffett was prescient, as the 1970s are considered a lost decade for equity investors.

VALUE INVESTING STYLES AND APPLICATIONS

CHAPTER TWELVE

VARIATIONS ON A THEME: VALUE INVESTING STYLES

Value stocks are about as exciting as watching grass grow. But have you ever noticed how much your grass grows in a week?

—Christopher H. Browne

In this chapter, we examine the styles of nine of the most prominent value investors. This is not meant to be an exhaustive list, but rather a representative sample of some of the most acclaimed value investors. The intention is not to describe each style in great detail, but instead to provide a flavor of each approach and show how they relate to, and differ from, one another. This will help the reader to fashion his or her own distinctive investment style, the subject of Chapter 13.

BENJAMIN GRAHAM

Any examination of the great value investors begins with Benjamin Graham, who is often referred to as the "father of value investing." While an impressive title, that moniker actually understates Graham's contribution to the world of investing. He is perhaps, more aptly referred to as the founder of a profession—financial analysis.[1] Graham is credited with applying the scientific method and quantitative study to the investment process, which led to the creation of the field we now know as financial analysis. Prior to Graham's contributions, stock market participants were referred to as speculators and not investors. Bonds were seen as the purview of true investors, while stock market activity was viewed as speculation.

For decades, Graham managed investment funds for the Graham-Newman partnership, and his approach was always to look for companies that sold at a large discount to intrinsic value. He survived the Crash of 1929 and had fabulous success over the decades that he managed money. Reports vary, due to the time period in question as well as the calculation methods used, but John Train reported in his book *The Money Masters* that the Graham-Newman Corporation earned 21 percent annually over 20 years.[2] In addition to managing money, Graham taught investments for many years at his alma mater, Columbia University.

Graham's contributions to investing in general, and value investing in particular, cannot be overstated. His thinking and writing influenced many of the leading value investors, including Bill Ruane, John Bogle, John Neff, Seth Klarman, Wally Weitz, and of course, most famously, Warren Buffett. In fact, noted investors Buffett, Ruane, and Walter Schloss all worked for Graham at Graham-Newman. Graham described his investment philosophy in two of the most popular investment books of all time, *Security Analysis* and *The Intelligent Investor*. *Security Analysis* is frequently referred to as the "bible of investing." Buffett famously described *The Intelligent Investor* as "by far the best book on investing ever written." Both books, and the investment principles described within them, have stood the test of time. The first edition of *Security Analysis* was published shortly after the stock market crash in 1934. It has been updated several times, most recently in 2008 with commentary by some leading value investors, including Seth Klarman, as well as a foreword by Warren Buffett.

Graham made a strong argument for including a substantial position in common stocks in investment portfolios. He made the argument based on two principles. First, he argued that common stocks provided investors with some protection against the erosion of the value of the dollar caused by inflation. Second, combining both the dividend yield on common stocks and the increase in market value, Graham believed that, on average, common stocks would provide a higher return than bonds in the long run.

Graham coined the phrase "margin of safety" and built an investment philosophy around this simple concept. In fact, he stated that the secret of sound investing is a large margin of safety. Simply put, Graham's concept of margin of safety is the difference between an asset's price and its intrinsic value. If you can purchase an asset at a substantial discount from its intrinsic value, then you have a margin of safety available for absorbing the effect of miscalculations or worse than average luck. Graham believed that in order for an investment to be a true one, there must be a true margin of safety.

Graham applied the scientific method to investment analysis and described seven quality and quantity criteria (although, when closely examined, they are all quantitatively oriented) for the selection of common stock for inclusion in a defensive investor's portfolio. Graham defines a defensive investor as one who ". . . will place his chief emphasis on the avoidance of serious mistakes or losses." The seven criteria are:

1. Adequate Size of the Enterprise: In 1973 dollars, Graham stated that a minimum of $100 million in annual sales for an industrial company and not less than $50 million in total assets for a public utility is needed.
2. A Sufficiently Strong Financial Condition: For industrial companies, the current ratio (current assets divided by current liabilities) should be at least two. In addition, long-term debt should not exceed net current assets (current assets minus current liabilities). For public utilities, the debt should not exceed twice the stockholder's equity.

3. Earnings Stability: Positive earnings for the common stock in each of the past 10 years.

4. Dividend Record: Uninterrupted payments for at least the past 20 years.

5. Earnings Growth: A minimum increase of at least one-third in per share earnings in the past 10 years using three-year averages at the beginning and end.

6. Moderate Ratio of Price to Earnings: Current price should not be more than 15 times average earnings of the past three years.

7. Moderate Ratio of Price to Assets: Current price should not be more than 1 ½ times the book value last reported. Graham did qualify this by stating that a multiplier of earnings below 15 could justify a higher multiplier of assets. He suggested a rule of thumb that the product of the multiplier times the ratio of price to book should not exceed 22.5.

WARREN BUFFETT

Warren Buffett is inexorably linked to Benjamin Graham. Graham was Buffett's mentor at Columbia University. In fact, when Buffett graduated from Columbia University in 1951 after earning the only two A+ grades that Graham ever awarded, he offered to work at Graham-Newman for free. Graham turned him down. Buffett remarked that after he had volunteered, "Ben made his customary calculation of value to price and said no."[3] In 1954, Graham reconsidered and hired Buffett at an annual salary of $12,000.

Buffett is effusive in his praise of Graham's work. In particular, he has been quick to compliment as "true north" two chapters in the *Intelligent Investor*: Chapter 8: "The Investor and Market Fluctuations" and Chapter 20: "Margin of Safety as the Central Concept of Investment." But Buffett's value investing style deviates from Graham's on a number of important counts. Buffett contrasts Graham's style of investing with his own:

> Ben was looking for the used cigar butt. That is, he bought crummy companies, but they were so cheap that they had one puff left in them. On the other hand, I buy into very big, well run operations—companies that I would be very happy to leave the country for ten years and come back to. Ben had a quantitative approach. Qualitative aspects are harder to teach and emulate.[4]

Graham and Buffett fish in slightly different ponds: Buffett measures Berkshire against the most widely referenced, large cap index, the S&P 500. In his 2010 letter to shareholders, Buffett stated, "In Berkshire's case, we long ago told you that our job is to increase per-share intrinsic value at a rate greater than the increase (including dividends) of the S&P 500."[5] Given the sheer size of Berkshire Hathaway's pool of capital, Buffett must deal in large firms in order for his investment decisions to have an impact on Berkshire's bottom line.

Buffett has been enormously successful in beating the S&P 500. From 1965, Berkshire has averaged a 19.8 percent per share book value compound annual growth rate while the S&P has returned 9.2 percent annually over the same time period. Note that Berkshire's returns are after tax, while the S&P numbers cited are before tax.

While Graham focused almost entirely on quantitative factors, Buffett places great importance on more qualitative elements when considering investment opportunities. Two aspects that Buffett emphasizes that are not central to Graham's writings are quality of management and the economic pricing power of a business. It is not surprising that Buffett places a premium on quality of management when making investments, as he is in the business of taking large, often majority control positions in companies. However, he would argue that what he does is not different from a small investor purchasing 100 shares of a company. Buffett is not in the business of shareholder activism; that is, seeking changes in management. Buffett looks for companies that are already well run, not companies in need of a management makeover:

> We tend to let our many subsidiaries operate on their own, without our supervising and monitoring them to any degree. That means we are sometimes late in spotting management problems and that both operating and capital decisions are occasionally made with which Charlie and I would have disagreed had we been consulted. Most of our managers, however, use the independence we grant them magnificently, rewarding our confidence by maintaining an owner-oriented attitude that is invaluable and too seldom found in huge organizations. We would rather suffer the visible costs of a few bad decisions than incur the many invisible costs that come from decisions made too slowly— or not at all—because of a stifling bureaucracy.[6]

It is certainly a difficult task for the average value investor to evaluate the quality of management of a publicly traded firm. In response to a student question on that dimension, Buffett responded:

> Evaluate management by what they do and not what they say. Believe your eyes, not your ears. In 52 years, I've probably owned 300 to 500 stocks. In 90 percent of them I haven't had any contact with the management. Smart management will get out of a lousy business. It took us 22 years, but we finally got out of the textile business.[7]

Buffett is on record that the single most important factor in evaluating a business is pricing power. In an interview with the Federal Crisis Inquiry Commission he stated, "You've got the power to raise prices without losing business to a competitor, and you've got a very good business. And if you have to have a prayer session before raising the price by a tenth of a cent (laughs), then you got a terrible business. And I've been in both and I know the difference."[8] He has a history of investing in firms in industries with significant pricing power, such as railroads and electricity producers, whose pricing power is the result of a lack of competitive options available to consumers. Buffett has also built large stakes in publicly traded firms like Coca-Cola, Gillette, Anheuser-Busch, and Procter & Gamble, which rely on the appeal of their brands (their franchise power) to attract and retain customers. In fact, despite the importance Buffett places on management, he has stated "The extraordinary business does not require good management."[9]

Benjamin Graham believed in diversification and felt that margin of safety and diversification are highly correlated. In essence, Graham believed that even with a large margin of safety, an individual investment may not work out in the investor's favor. However, Graham believed that if the investor made a large number of commitments with a margin of safety, ultimate success was more likely. Buffett is not a big advocate of diversification. In fact, he has been quoted as saying that "wide diversification is only required when investors do not understand what they are doing." He has also said, "Diversification is a protection against ignorance. It makes very little sense for those who know what they're doing." Buffett practices what he preaches: An academic study showed that over the period from 1976 to 2006, Berkshire Hathaway's portfolio was concentrated in relatively few stocks, with the top five holdings averaging 73 percent of the portfolio value.[10]

Furthermore, Buffett actually argues that portfolio concentration (i.e., the opposite of diversification) can actually *reduce* risk by focusing efforts on analyzing fewer opportunities. In his 1993 letter to shareholders, he stated:

> We believe that a policy of portfolio concentration may well decrease risk if it raises, as it should, both the intensity with which an investor thinks about a business and the comfort-level he must feel with its economic characteristics before buying into it. In stating this opinion, we define risk, using dictionary terms, as "the possibility of loss or injury."[11]

While Buffett believes in holding concentrated positions, he doesn't suggest that diversification is necessarily a bad idea for the average investor:

> [A] situation requiring wide diversification occurs when an investor who does not understand the economics of specific businesses nevertheless believes it in his interest to be a long-term owner of American industry. . . . By periodically investing in an index fund, for example, the know-nothing investor can actually out-perform most investment professionals. Paradoxically, when "dumb" money acknowledges its limitations, it ceases to be dumb.[12]

SETH KLARMAN

Seth Klarman is the Boston-based CEO of the nearly $30 billion and ninth largest hedge fund in the world, the Baupost Group. It has been a remarkably successful fund, having only two negative years (in 1988 and 2008) since its inception in 1982. Since 2007, in a tough environment in which many funds have floundered,

Baupost's assets have more than tripled.[13] Klarman started the firm in 1982 with $27 million and has averaged 20 percent annual gains ever since. In 2007, amid the depths of the credit crash, Baupost had its best year, gaining 52 percent.[14] Lest you should contemplate investing in Baupost, the fund has been closed to new investors for quite some time. Large endowments such as Harvard, Yale, and Stanford have positions in Baupost.

Perhaps the greatest compliment paid to Seth Klarman was in response to a question posed to Warren Buffett by a student in Bob Johnson's portfolio practicum course at Creighton University in fall 1992. When asked which young investment professionals he was impressed with and who he felt might be the next Warren Buffett, Mr. Buffett replied without hesitation, "Seth Klarman."[15] Following this meeting, Dr. Johnson assigned Klarman's *Margin of Safety* as required reading to class. This ended up being one of the best investments that he ever made. The book originally sold for $19.95 and became a cult classic. Used copies in excellent condition were quoted on the web as selling for approximately $2,500 in the fall of 2012. Someone who purchased the book for around $20 in 1992 and sold it for $2,500 twenty years later would have earned a compound annual return of over 27 percent!

Klarman's style is distinguished from the other value investors profiled in this chapter largely on two counts. First, he often has a large percentage of his portfolio in cash. Secondly, he looks for value investments throughout the investment landscape and does not focus merely on traditional stocks and bonds.

In July of 2012, Klarman's portfolio had 30 percent in cash, and he has been known to have in excess of 50 percent of his portfolio in cash. In the hedge fund world, holding copious amounts of cash is highly unusual. In fact, most hedge funds use a high degree of leverage in order to magnify returns. Klarman cites two reasons for his propensity to hold cash: his risk averse nature and the ability to buy when others are forced to sell.

As the title of his book indicates, Klarman is a firm believer in the Graham concept of margin of safety. He believes that that avoiding loss should be the primary goal of every investor. In *Margin of Safety*, Klarman wrote:

> A loss-avoidance strategy does not mean that investors should hold all
> or even half of their portfolios in U.S. Treasury bills or own sizable
> caches of gold bullion. Investors must be aware that the world can
> change unexpectedly and sometimes dramatically; the future may be
> very different from the present or recent past. Investors must be prepared
> for any eventuality.[16]

To Klarman, margin of safety simply means buying securities at such a significant discount from their current underlying values that the odds are very much in favor of realizing value over an extended holding period. Klarman looks for bargains and is very willing to hold large amounts of cash until those bargains appear in the marketplace. His success is driven by both his ability to uncover undervalued assets and the discipline to buy only when a sufficiently large margin of safety is present.

According to Klarman, the problem that many individual investors have in applying a value investing approach is the patience and discipline *not* to commit capital when compelling valuation discounts are unavailable. He cites the baseball analogy popularized by Warren Buffett:

> A long-term-oriented value investor is a batter in a game where no balls or strikes are called, allowing dozens, even hundreds, of pitches to go by, including many at which other batters would swing. Value investors are students of the game; they learn from every pitch, those at which they swing and those they let pass by. They are not influenced by the way others are performing; they are motivated only by their own results. They have infinite patience and are willing to wait until they are thrown a pitch they can handle-an undervalued investment opportunity.[17]

Klarman believes that most institutional investors believe that balls and strikes are being called (and in the short-term nature of the institutional investment landscape, they may very well be judged by many in that fashion) and that they must swing at many pitches. Even if an asset is selling at less than its intrinsic value, it is not necessarily a compelling buy. Instead of purchasing an asset at a modest discount from intrinsic value, Klarman would rather wait and purchase an asset at a substantial discount. What that means is that he is willing to forgo some returns in the short-run to wait for the big opportunities.

Klarman's large cash hoard becomes his distinct advantage in uncertain times. In 2008, Baupost was one of the few firms that had the scale and the available capital to buy up lots of assets from distressed sellers. According to Klarman, "The ability to be one-stop shopping for an urgent seller is very advantageous."[18]

Whereas Graham generally limited his investments to more traditional stock and bond instruments, Klarman invests in a wide variety of assets, ranging from traditional common stocks and government bonds to more esoteric investments at times when investors are unwilling to embrace them, such as securitized debt, private commercial real estate, and liquidations during the recent credit crisis.[19] As the credit crisis evolved, he put more than a third of his assets into high-yield bonds and mortgage-related securities.[20] At the end of 2012, his largest distressed debt position was in Lehman Brothers.[21] In essence, Klarman looks for value in many disparate parts of the investment landscape at times when entire markets are out of favor, and he doesn't limit his search to traditional investment instruments.

Klarman also takes positions in derivative securities. He is particularly concerned with the potential for inflation, given the government's high rate of borrowing to bail out the financial system. He has purchased out-of-the-money puts on bonds to hedge inflation risk, and he characterizes this move as "cheap insurance" for tail risk. The puts will expire worthless even if long-term interest rates rise to 6 or 7 percent. But if rates rise to 10 percent, Baupost would make large gains. If rates were to exceed 20 percent the firm could make 50 or 100 times its outlay.[22]

BILL RUANE

Bill Ruane was a classmate of Buffett's in Graham's investments course at Columbia. Ruane's distinction in the world of investing is that he was the only person that Buffett recommended to his investors when the Buffett Limited Partnership was closed. Ruane set up the Sequoia Fund in 1970 to handle these investors. The fund was so successful in attracting capital that it closed its doors to new investors in 1982. Sequoia was reopened to new investors in 2008, not because of capital withdrawals due to poor performance, but because it realized that its original client base from the 1970s was aging and, in some cases, dying. Ruane himself passed away in 2005, but the fund is still run by the same value investing principles followed during his lifetime.

Ruane is linked to Buffett not only because of the referral at the closure of the Buffett Limited Partnership but also because the fund, since first buying Berkshire Hathaway stock about 20 years ago, has made it a major holding. At one point Berkshire Hathaway was nearly 30 percent of the portfolio. When Ruane spoke to Bob Johnson's portfolio practicum course, he told the students that one of the great things about the investing industry was that you can get great ideas from your competitors.[23] The fund has recently trimmed its holdings in Berkshire to about 10 percent. The reason provided for the sale is a value investing reason: Sequoia's current managers believe the stock isn't as inexpensive as it used to be.[24]

Ruane's philosophy involved looking for high-quality investments; that is, companies that dominate their sectors and have strong revenue growth and improving margins.[25] He also focused on larger capitalization firms. Ruane didn't look for the cigar butts that Graham focused on. He felt that even if a company trades at a steep premium to the overall market, Sequoia will still consider buying it as long as its management is excellent and the prospects for its business are strong. In essence, Ruane focused on quality at the right price.

He also didn't mind taking a large position in a particular investment (witness the Berkshire position) if he felt strongly about the firm's prospects. Ruane was more akin to Buffett in his stance on diversification than to Graham. Even today, the Sequoia Fund is a heavily concentrated portfolio with only around 30 holdings. Normally Sequoia won't hold more than 15 percent of its assets in a single stock.[26]

JOHN NEFF

John Neff, CFA, is one of the true mutual fund manager superstars. He managed the behemoth Vanguard Windsor Fund, a fund that started with $75 million in 1964 and grew to over $11 billion in assets by the time he retired in 1995. The fund was so successful that it was closed to new investors in the late 1990s. His performance managing such a large pool of capital was nothing short of incredible. During his tenure, the compounded annual return of the Windsor Fund was

13.7 percent compared to 10.6 percent for the S&P 500 over that roughly 31-year time period from 1964 to 1995. To put this into perspective, $10,000 invested in the Windsor Fund would have grown to $564,637. $10,000 invested in the S&P 500 would have grown to $232,974.[27]

Neff was a notorious contrarian and value investor, following a consistent investment style over his years in the industry. Like Graham, Neff cited seven principal elements of his strategy. Fortunately, he clearly spelled these out in his book *Neff on Investing*, written following his retirement:[28]

1. **Low price-to-earnings (P/E) ratio.**

   A low P/E ratio was the cornerstone of Neff's strategy. In fact, when asked about his investment style, Neff said he preferred to be referred to as a "low price-earnings investor. It describes succinctly and accurately the investment style that guided Windsor while I was in charge." Neff looked for out-of-favor stocks with good prospects and avoided the popular growth stocks.

   The P/E ratio is critical because it is all about expectations. A stock typically sells at a high P/E ratio because the consensus of the market is that firm will grow at a very high rate. On the other hand, if a stock has a low P/E ratio, investors aren't expecting much growth from it. If expectations are already low, there is less risk of a downside earnings surprise from a low P/E stock. However, the risk of a negative earnings surprise from a high P/E stock is both significant and the consequences are dramatic. This line of thinking is consistent with what many investors have witnessed in the market. You often see a high P/E stock get pummeled after a quarterly earnings shortfall of a couple of pennies.

   The typical Windsor stock had P/E ratios that were 40 to 60 percent below the market. Neff believed that these P/E ratios represent the best of both worlds as they provide upside potential (when the market recognizes their merits) and downside protection (because expectations are so low).

2. **Fundamental growth in excess of 7 percent.**

   Coupled with a low P/E ratio, firms with an expected earnings growth rate of over 7 percent signaled to Neff that a firm was underappreciated by the market. He also indicated that he steered clear of firms with growth rates less than 7 percent or exceeding 20 percent. Firms with growth rates lower than 7 percent didn't show enough promise. Firms with growth rates above 20 percent were too risky for Neff. Those firms had the potential to disappoint. The relevant term for earnings growth projections at Windsor was five years.

3. **Yield protection (and enhancement, in most cases).**

   A low P/E strategy often results in firms with high dividend yields (annual dividend/price). Return on any common stock investment consists of two components: dividend yield and change in share price (which is related both to growth in earnings and the earnings multiplier).

Neff agreed with the assessment by Graham and Dodd that the dividend yield was the more assured part of growth and thus favored stocks with higher yields. However, by his own admission, Neff did not insist on yield. He would invest in less-recognized growth firms with 12 to 15 percent growth rates and little or no yield. This was, however, the exception rather than the rule.

Neff believes that many investors value stocks strictly on the basis of their price appreciation potential and neglect dividend payouts when valuing securities. He estimated that about two-thirds of Windsor's 3 percent per year market outperformance during his tenure came from dividends.[29]

4. Superior relationship of total return to P/E paid.

Neff developed a simple, yet elegant metric he called "total return ratio" to measure the attractiveness of a potential investment. Total return is defined as the sum of the dividend yield and the expected earnings growth rate. Total return is then divided by the P/E ratio, which represents the "richness" of the price. Thus, total return ratio is:

Total Return Ratio = (Earnings Growth + Dividend Yield) ÷ (P/E Ratio)

He looked for total return ratios that exceeded market or industry averages by 2 to 1. This is simply a measure of how cheaply he could acquire expected returns. He found it difficult to identify firms that met this metric in some frothy markets, but to Neff that was a signal that the market was overvalued.

5. No cyclical exposure without compensating P/E multiple.

Neff did not shy away from cyclical firms (see Chapter 4 for a discussion of cyclical firms). In fact, cyclical stocks normally constituted about one-third of the holdings of the Windsor Fund. However, Neff did recognize that his total return ratio could be misleading for cyclical firms and that some adjustments were necessary. The issue is that growth stocks are expected to increase earnings steadily, while earnings growth rates for cyclical stocks will vary according to where we are in the business cycle. In place of five-year growth rates, Neff would substitute an estimate of normal earnings growth. Normal earnings growth merely represented a best estimate of earnings at more fortuitous points in the business cycle.

The key to cyclical firms was not to overpay for peak earnings. In fact, in contrast to the buy-and-hold philosophy advocated by many value investors, including Buffett, Neff believed that timing was everything with respect to cyclical stocks. The strategy was to purchase them when prospective P/E ratios were very low and to sell them when the market was overly optimistic on the prospects of the firm. Such a philosophy led Neff to buy the same companies over and over. For instance, in 1994 he purchased Atlantic Richfield and took a 5 percent position in the firm.

This represented the sixth time that he had bought and sold Atlantic Richfield in the three decades that he managed the Windsor Fund.[30]

6. **Solid companies in growing fields.**

The previous five criteria were all very quantitatively oriented. While one can have differing opinions on expected future earnings growth rates or normalized earnings, one cannot quibble about P/E ratios or dividend yields. The sixth criterion is all qualitative and involves identifying solid companies in growing fields. Neff typically didn't invest heavily in the great, recognizable companies, the industry leaders.[31] He preferred to fly a little under the radar and believed that good, solid companies were more vulnerable to mispricing due to investors' whims than were the recognized industry leaders. His strategy was to try to buy these good companies when the markets were most pessimistic about them. That certainly doesn't mean that he wouldn't purchase the industry leaders if the prices came down to levels where he was comfortable.

The strategy of identifying solid companies in growing fields led Neff to have holdings of vastly different sized firms. In essence, he applied his low P/E style across the entire capitalization spectrum.

7. **Strong fundamental case.**

John Neff is a CFA charter holder and is a strong advocate of fundamental analysis. He believes that no single measure or pair of measures should dictate a decision to buy or sell a stock. In other words, the strategic value investor needs to get behind the numbers and discern their reliability. The idea is to develop credible estimates of earnings growth rates. Thus, a strong fundamental case must be made to justify estimates used in valuation models.

Neff tries to identify firms that produce excess cash flow and believes that retained earnings plus depreciation is a sufficient proxy for cash flow. Excess cash flow can provide capital for dividend increases, stock repurchases, acquisitions, or reinvestment.

Like Buffett, Neff believes that return on equity (ROE) is a critically important metric by which managements should be measured. Firms that consistently earn high ROEs are making good use of stockholders' equity and providing value for shareholders.

Neff also looks behind the earnings growth numbers, seeking firms that have sustainable earnings growth rates in excess of 7 percent. Sustainable growth rates are those driven by sales and not by cost-cutting measures or other one-time events. To Neff, not all earnings growth is created equally.

In terms of portfolio construction, Neff is not an advocate of diversification. His investing approach relies on uncovering hidden value in downtrodden stocks and on a willingness to back decisions with exceptionally large bets.[32] In 1992, his top ten holdings in the Windsor Fund often accounted for approximately

39 percent of the total holdings of the fund, and not one of those stocks was one of the 50 companies with the largest market capitalization.[33] This is remarkable for a fund the size of the Windsor Fund.

Like Klarman, Neff is not averse to holding large cash positions when he believes the market, in general, is overvalued. In a 1992 interview, he discussed his cash position, which at the time was 16.5 percent and very high historically for the Windsor Fund. "The market has created low P/E opportunities more sparingly" was his explanation.[34]

As a contrarian, Neff ignores the crowd and seeks investments in companies and industries that are out of favor in the markets. In fact, unfavorable news draws Neff's attention to firms. He feels that markets frequently overreact and discount worst-case scenarios into stock prices. The release of bad news can represent a unique buying opportunity for a contrarian like Neff.

Unlike Buffett, who has stated that his preferred holding period is forever, Neff does not express such a sentiment and is much more willing to sell securities after a very short holding period if market valuations dictate. In his book, Neff cites examples of positions that he held (and realized a profit with) in a few weeks.[35]

TWEEDY, BROWNE COMPANY LLC

While the other value investors profiled are all individuals, Tweedy, Browne Company LLC is a venerable money management firm with roots in Ben Graham's value investing school. Tweedy, Browne Partners, a predecessor organization to Tweedy, Browne Company LLC, was featured in Warren Buffett's piece entitled *The Superinvestors of Graham-and-Doddsville*.[36] Buffett had worked with Tom Knapp, one of the founders of Tweedy, Browne Partners at Graham-Newman. As of June 30, 2012, the firm managed approximately $13.9 billion for individuals, institutions, partnerships, off-shore funds, and four mutual funds of a registered investment company. Tweedy, Browne is currently owned by its four managing directors, William H. Browne, Thomas H. Shrager, John D. Spears, and Robert Q. Wyckoff. A fifth managing director, Christopher Browne, who wrote *The Little Book of Value Investing*, passed away in 2009.

In an explicit statement of its investment philosophy, Tweedy, Browne states that "We do not attempt to be all things to all people, but instead pursue a value-oriented approach to investment management first pioneered by Benjamin Graham."[37] Much of their approach has been described as deep value. In a 1998 interview, when asked why some value investors fail, Christopher Browne stated "To buy deep value takes a lot of courage, because it looks really ugly. The companies are cheap because there are a lot of bad stories out there." His brother, William Browne, added, "It's like looking for the ugliest spouse because she will love you the most."[38]

But, the firm doesn't limit its investments to the deep value sector. They view themselves as somewhat of a hybrid between Graham's cigar butts and Buffett's franchise value investments. Robert Q. Wyckoff described the Tweedy,

Browne holdings as "Our portfolios today are a mix of high-quality, Buffett-type businesses and Ben Graham-type bargains."[39]

In contrast to Buffett or Ruane, Tweedy, Browne does not take large positions in individual companies but instead builds a portfolio with very wide diversification. The firm follows a strict discipline of investing a small percentage of its portfolios, about 4 percent, into any one company. It also limits its exposure to 15 percent for any one industry.[40]

Tweedy, Browne distinguishes itself from the other value investors profiled in this chapter by applying the principles of value investing globally as well as within the United States. The firm entered the global investment arena relatively early, in 1983. It has found a great deal of success in international investing and was named winner of Morningstar's 2011 International-Stock Manager of the Year Award.[41] It should be noted that it hedges its currency exposure. "We want to earn our returns from the stocks and not from the currencies," says portfolio manager Bob Wyckoff.[42]

As with several of the other value investment managers profiled in this chapter, when Tweedy, Browne's portfolio managers can't find stocks to buy, they aren't afraid to hold cash. The fund currently has 11 percent of assets in cash.[43]

WALLY WEITZ

Wally Weitz, CFA, is often referred to as the "other oracle of Omaha" and a "disciple of Warren Buffett," both titles that he readily embraces—and who wouldn't? His firm, Wallace R. Weitz & Co., manages over $4 billion for the Weitz Funds. Since its inception in 1983, the Weitz Value Fund has compiled an enviable record, returning 12.3 percent compounded annually compared to 10.3 percent in the S&P 500. In an interview with Morningstar, Weitz describes how his investment philosophy relates to Buffett's:

> The idea that I picked up from him 30 plus years ago is that you are really buying little pieces of a real business. So, as other people either misperceive what the business is about or act on much shorter term considerations . . . the price of the stock can get way above or way below that business valuation.[44]

Weitz's approach to value investing has evolved over the years. It combines Graham's price sensitivity and insistence on a "margin of safety" with a conviction that qualitative factors that allow companies to have some control over their own destinies can be more important than statistical measurements, such as historical book value or reported earnings.[45] Weitz looks for firms that generate cash—cash beyond what is needed to maintain the business—in industries that he understands. Thus, he maintains a very focused investing strategy, choosing more concentrated positions in fewer names than most mutual fund managers. While the average mutual fund will have well over 100 positions, Weitz maintains fewer than 50 positions in each of his three funds. Like Klarman, Weitz is not afraid to hold large cash positions at any one time. As of August 2012, the Weitz Value Fund had over 20 percent in cash.

Weitz has stated that "stock prices are a combination of the value of the business and the valuation that people put on that business. As cash leaves chasing some other, more interesting investment opportunity, the valuation part shrinks [and the stock becomes attractive.]"[46] He looks for firms that sell at a deep discount: in excess of a 40 percent discount to his estimate of value.[47]

Unlike most of the other value investors profiled in this chapter, Weitz considers companies of all capitalization sizes, sells stocks short, and uses a limited amount of leverage. In a *Bloomberg Business Week* article, Weitz explained what he referred to as a "defensive short." It involves identifying a group of stocks, or a sector, that seems fully valued or overpriced and shorting it to buy more of his favorite stocks on the long side. For example, when Weitz felt that small caps became more popular than large caps, he shorted some small caps and invested the proceeds in large caps. This strategy allows him to take bigger positions in his best ideas.[48]

CHARLES BRANDES

Charles Brandes, CFA, is chairman of Brandes Investment Partners, a California-based money management firm founded in 1974 with nearly $30 billion under management as of the end of June 2012. Brandes is closely linked to Ben Graham, whom he met in the early 1970s when Mr. Graham retired to La Jolla, California.[49] Brandes's firm "applies the value investing approach, pioneered by Benjamin Graham, to security selection and was among the first investment firms to bring a global perspective to value investing."[50] The firm has been so successful that Charles Brandes appears on the Forbes 400 list of wealthiest Americans.

Brandes believes in long-term investing and long holding periods. In fact, he defines speculation in two ways. First, any contemplated holding period shorter than a normal business cycle of three to five years is speculation. He also believes that any purchase based on anticipated market movements or forecasting is also speculation.[51]

He is a very patient investor. Like Buffett, Brandes uses a sports analogy to describe this patience. Buffett often describes investing like a baseball batter who can wait indefinitely for the right pitch to hit. In other words, it isn't three strikes and you are out, and there are certainly no called strikes. Similarly, Brandes states that there is no 24-second clock in the investment business. In professional basketball, if a team doesn't shoot within 24 seconds they lose the ball. "In the investment business you can dribble and pass the ball around until you get the shot you want."[52]

Like many of the value investors profiled in this chapter, Brandes emphasizes the basic concept of margin of safety. He is a self-proclaimed deep value specialist and looks for firms with a particularly large margin of safety. Brandes believes that you can use margin of safety to estimate the level of the market and the values that may exist. In a 2011 interview, Brandes indicated that in 2006 and 2007, the margins of safety in his portfolio were getting particularly low, around 20 percent. Conversely, in 2009, he was seeing 50 and 60 percent, and in some instances 70 and 80 percent discounts from intrinsic value at the bottom of the market. These were the biggest discounts he had seen in his career.[53]

His firm developed expertise in small capitalization and international equity sectors. By the very nature of this strategy—concentrating in small capitalization issues—Brandes manages a highly diversified portfolio. These firms have limited market capitalization. Brandes must limit exposure to any specific holding in order to not move markets with substantial purchases or sales.[54] Consistent with a strategy requiring many holdings, he doesn't believe in site visits, as they make more sense for investors who take large positions.[55]

Brandes doesn't make any decisions based on top-down or external considerations. He doesn't attempt to forecast the direction of the market or take into account specific macroeconomic events. Instead, like Buffett, he looks at investing as buying part ownership in a business and focuses on the performance of firms internally.[56] While he looks for deep value investments throughout the world, he doesn't attempt to forecast currencies and considers that speculation.[57]

Like Buffett, Brandes is not a fan of gold as an investment. He believes that gold does not create wealth. It can be a store of wealth, especially in periods where you have governments printing money, but not a wealth producer.[58]

BILL MILLER

The final investor profiled in the chapter, Bill Miller, CFA, is a cautionary tale. Miller was the long-time manager of the Legg Mason Capital Management Value Trust and compiled an unparalleled record by beating the S&P 500 over a period of 15 straight years from 1991 through 2005. He was widely hailed as an investment genius and one of the top mutual fund managers of all time, garnering numerous awards from *Money* magazine, Morningstar, and *Barron's* for his investment prowess. In fact, he was the subject of a popular book written by well-known financial journalist Janet Lowe entitled *The Man Who Beats the S&P*.[59] Reminiscent of a Dickens novel, however, the period from 2006 through 2011 really was a "Tale of Two Cities"—it was the best of times, it was the worst of times—when compared to the early years of his tenure at Legg Mason Capital Value Trust. The fund underperformed the S&P 500 by such a substantial margin from 2006 through 2011 that investors who held throughout the entire time period saw their gains reduced to merely average performance over that 20-year period. In 2008 alone, the fund declined in value by over 55 percent, while the S&P 500 fell by 38.49 percent. Miller stepped down as the manager of the fund at the end of 2011.

Over the entire time that Miller was lead manager of the fund (from 1990 through 2011), after expenses, the fund gained an average of 9.39 percent annually, versus 9.14 percent for the S&P 500.[60] The underperformance in the later years was devastating to his fund, as assets under management fell from a high of $20.8 billion in 2006 to $2.8 billion at the end of 2011.[61] Of course, investors who chased performance and invested in the fund after Miller had established his enviable record actually suffered substantial losses. In fairness to Bill Miller, only a handful of mutual fund managers can claim to match or slightly exceed the performance of the S&P 500 over 21 years, but the precipitous fall from grace cannot go without mention and evaluation.

Before discussing the reasons for the dramatic turn in performance, we briefly describe Miller's investment philosophy. Janet Lowe summarized Miller's investment style in six bullet points. They are a composite of many of the elements of the styles from investors we described earlier in this chapter. In brief, Miller:

- doesn't attempt to predict the direction of the market.

- looks for franchise value.

- is willing to provide forecasts when determining value, but doesn't believe that the numbers tell him everything.

- looks for investment ideas everywhere.

- looks for a margin of safety.

- doesn't trade frequently.[62]

So, given his investment philosophy, why was there such a disparity between his performance from 1991 to 2005 compared to his performance from 2006 to 2011? We believe this is directly attributable to four factors: willingness to invest in the technology sector, his philosophy on probability, taking concentrated positions in specific industries, and overconfidence.

Unlike most value investors, Miller embraced investing in the technology sector. His holdings were dramatically different from the typical value investor's and included large positions in firms such as America Online, Google, Dell, and Amazon. In fact, he purchased Google in the initial public offering.[63] Critics claimed that Miller was operating as a growth investor and was a value investor in name only. Jim Cramer wrote in a column on theStreet.com that investing in these types of firms and claiming a value style was "a masquerade."[64] Suffice it to say, most value investors did not have positions in these types of firms, and the strong performance of technology firms relative to the market prior to the bursting of the Internet bubble definitely accounted for some of Miller's outperformance. His timing in the technology sector was impeccable, as Miller exited many of these positions just prior to the crash of the sector in 2001.[65]

Miller also had an interesting take on the concept of winners and losers and probability. Much like Peter Lynch's concept of a "tenbagger" (a stock in which you have made ten times your money),[66] Miller believed in big winners driving his portfolio performance. Janet Lowe describes this philosophy as "Miller fully expects to be wrong a certain number of times, but he expects to be so spectacularly right enough times that he will achieve a high level of performance."[67] In fact, Miller was wrong more often than most money managers on picking winners, but his winners were, on average, bigger winners and drove his outperformance for a large portion of his tenure at Legg Mason Value Trust. For example, Miller had a 3,500 percent gain in Dell by 1999.[68] Such a spectacular return on one stock can certainly make up for a large number of investment missteps.

For this idea of probability and the law of large numbers to work, the individual stock bets have to be independent or at least not highly correlated with each other. The fact that Miller made concentrated bets in out-of-favor industries that continued to suffer was a critical element in his substantial underperformance over the past few years of his tenure. As noted above, Miller successfully took concentrated positions in technology stocks and rode them higher before the technology crash of 1999. But, in the midst of the financial crisis, Miller not only retained his positions in financial stocks but also increased positions in Fannie Mae, Freddie Mac, AIG, and other stocks in the sector. In early September 2008, while Fannie and Freddie were dropping precipitously, Miller disclosed that Legg Mason had purchased 30 million additional shares in one week.[69] Although his timing in technology stocks during the Internet bubble was flawless, Miller was effectively undone by his poor timing in financial stocks around the recent financial crisis.

Confidence is a positive quality in an investment manager. On the other hand, overconfidence can be lethal. Value investors often see falling prices as buying opportunities. If you like the stock at $30 per share, then you should love it at $20 per share. Miller underestimated the depth of the financial crisis and kept purchasing shares of financial stocks as prices continued to weaken. This overconfidence was exemplified by his remark that "the only way he would stop buying more when a stock's price fell was when we can no longer get a quote."[70] Making oversized bets on specific situations has led to the undoing of many investors.

CONCLUSION

This chapter has introduced some of the most prominent value investors and their unique value investing styles. As you can see, there is no universal value investing approach, but each of the approaches presented in this chapter do have common features; namely, buying good companies at depressed prices. This strategy provides these investors with a healthy margin of safety. If you embrace these tenets, then you can vary your investment style and do well relative to the broad markets on a risk-adjusted basis.

CHAPTER THIRTEEN

CHOOSING THE RIGHT STYLE AND VALUATION MODEL

Success in investing doesn't correlate with I.Q. once you're above the level of 125. Once you have ordinary intelligence, what you need is the temperament to control the urges that get other people into trouble in investing.

—Warren Buffett

We saw in Chapter 12 that there are multitudes of successful value investing styles with substantive variations. The iconic investors profiled in the previous chapter adapted elements of value investing styles to fit their individual circumstances and personalities. In developing your own unique style, you should consider your psychological makeup (that is, your intellectual and emotional strengths and weaknesses), attitude toward risk, income needs, and tax situation. Recognize that few of us are purely rational investors bereft of emotional and cognitive biases. We urge you to select a style that is consistent with your personality and personal circumstances.

Your chosen style will also dictate which of the valuation models presented in this book you will rely on. Some styles are consistent with dividend discount models, and other styles are consistent with free cash flow models, for instance. Whatever style you adopt, you will do well to heed the advice of the old saying, "Don't try and fit a square peg in a round hole." That is why ice cream manufacturers make both chocolate and vanilla, and that is also why there is no one "best" investment method for everyone.

YOUR PSYCHOLOGICAL MAKEUP

We are all wired a little differently, so recognition of our fundamental differences is key when developing an investment style. While you can certainly work to address some of your psychological limitations—most notably, patience—there are other aspects of our personalities that are more hardwired into us and are more difficult to modify. As indicated in the quote preceding this chapter, Warren

Buffett believes that these psychological limitations, not lack of intelligence, are the downfall of many investors.

An honest assessment of your own personality is critical in developing a style that is both intellectually and psychologically consistent with your makeup. You don't want to try to adopt a style that is inconsistent with your personality, as you will be in constant conflict with yourself. In this section, we address patience, regret aversion, and attitude toward risk as key elements that investors need to honestly assess when developing an investment style. Do you have what it takes to control the urges that get other people into trouble when investing?

Patience

We have all heard the adage that patience is a virtue. By its very nature, successful value investing demands a large degree of patience. Due to the inherent contrarian nature of a value investing strategy, this strategy can underperform a growth or momentum strategy for large periods of time. This is especially true if the market is being driven by sentiment, as was the case in the dot.com bubble of the late twentieth century.

Figure 13-1 shows the relative performance of the Russell 2000 Value Index versus the Russell 2000 Index from 1980 through 2011.[1] The Russell 2000 Index measures the performance of the small-cap segment of the U.S. equity universe. It includes those Russell 2000 Index companies with lower price-to-book ratios and lower forecasted growth values. Over this period, the arithmetic average annual return on the Russell 2000 Value Index was 14.0 percent versus 12.1 percent for the Russell 2000 Index. Although, on average, the value index beat the broader index, there are three periods where the Russell 2000 Value Index underperformed the Russell 2000 Index: 1989 through 1991, 1998 and 1999, and 2009 through 2011.

FIGURE 13-1

Russell Value minus Russell 2000.

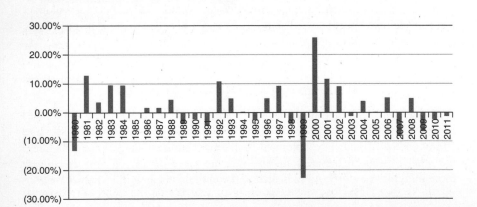

Like clockwork, during the time periods of underperformance you will see financial stories with headlines proclaiming that value investing is dead. These headlines appeared right before the bursting of the tech bubble in 2000 and appeared again in the latter half of 2012. It seems that, periodically, some market observers will claim that there is a new paradigm in the markets and that the tried-and-true methods of value investing are passé. Although technological advances have indeed improved our lives, the absurd valuations the market was placing on nascent technology companies during the late 1990s were not sustainable: The intrinsic value of a firm is still related to earning power. As detailed in earlier chapters, perhaps the four most dangerous words in the English language are "This time it's different." No matter what people try to tell you, in the long run, the value of a firm is related to its ability to generate earnings and cash flow.

It is psychologically very difficult to remain true to your value investing convictions when day after day, it seems, investors speculating in the latest fad are being rewarded. Indeed, this often happens during extended periods in the investment markets. Successful value investors have to have a psychological makeup that will allow them to withstand these extended periods of underperformance and have the courage of their convictions that they will eventually be vindicated in the long run.

Even the world's greatest investor has been, at times, criticized for adhering to his value investing principles. A *Barron's* cover story entitled "What's Wrong, Warren?" appeared at year-end 1999. The article contains quotes deriding Buffett and states, "[He] hasn't been able to make the next leap forward and adapt to the current technology-driven bull market. The reason: Technology isn't in Buffett's 'circle of competence,' and thus he doesn't feel comfortable seeking long-term winners in the sector."[2] Berkshire Hathaway shareholders are pretty pleased that Buffett wasn't able to "advance his thinking" and that he stuck with his old-fashioned tried-and-true investment style. It seems like his circle of competence is sufficient.

Value investors must understand that Buffett's "Mr. Market" does not correct misevaluations overnight. There are many tales of prominent value investors who were absolutely correct in the long run, but never got to realize that success because their investors were impatient and withdrew funds from them. This was particularly true in the technology bubble. In what could be a repeat of the tech bubble on a different scale, some investors today are wondering if the high market multiples placed on firms such as Facebook and LinkedIn are warranted. Most value investors would agree that these firms are not typical value-type opportunities and wonder if the emperor has any clothes.

One of the wonderful aspects about managing your own portfolio is that you don't have to answer to anyone but yourself. If the market hasn't recognized that you are correct yet, you aren't forced to change strategies because you aren't competing with other money managers for assets and aren't being judged on your performance from quarter to quarter. In this way, amateur investors have a big "staying power" advantage over many professional investors. Professional investors, unfortunately, need to be concerned with short-term performance and performance relative to their peers in order to attract cash inflows and discourage cash outflows from those increasingly fickle investors who chase performance and the latest investing fad.[3]

One of the tests you can perform on yourself to see if you are cut out to be a value investor involves how often you check your investment statements and how you react to the inevitable fluctuations in value. If you are someone who constantly monitors the value of your investment holdings and whose mood changes depending upon the vagaries of the market, then you may simply not be cut out to be a value investor. Will you be able to stay true to your convictions when the market rewards other strategies for extended periods of time? Or will you capitulate and believe the value investing naysayers who claim that this time the world has indeed changed?

A second test involves your reaction to price changes immediately after a purchase or sale. Although it's doubtful that many people are pleased to see a stock they purchase immediately decline in value, if your reaction is that you must have made a mistake, you may not be well-suited to being a value investor or may need to change your attitude toward market vicissitudes. A true value investor greets a price decline as an opportunity, if appropriate, to increase a position in that stock, recognizing that, in essence, Mr. Market has put the stock on the clearance-sale rack.

Regret Aversion

Closely aligned with patience is regret aversion. Regret aversion is a behavioral finance principle that leads investors to make poor decisions. It is also a psychological theory that posits that some people have regrets when they see that their decisions turn out to be wrong even if they appeared correct with the information available to them at the time they made the decision. In the context of investing, regret aversion is based on the desire of investors to avoid experiencing painful regret as a result of bad investment decisions.

Regret aversion can have dimensions related to actions that people have taken, as well as actions that they *could* have taken.[4] Regret from an action taken is an error of commission, and regret from an action not taken is an error of omission. The iconic value investors certainly don't beat themselves up over errors of omission, or they would have a strong propensity to invest cash sooner rather than later. As in Buffett's baseball analogy, Buffett doesn't regret not swinging at a pitch that is in his strike zone and is willing to wait for an even better pitch to hit.

In the previous chapter we saw that nearly all of the investors profiled were willing to hold large positions in cash at times when they didn't see appropriate value in the market. Buffett went a step further in 1969 when he liquidated the Buffett Limited Partnership because he was unable to find good value investments in a richly priced market in which the so-called nifty fifty[5] stocks traded at astronomical P/E multiples:

I would continue to operate the Partnership in 1970, or even 1971, if I had some really first class ideas. Not because I want to, but simply because I would so much rather end with a good year than a poor one. However, I just don't see anything available that gives any reasonable hope of delivering such a good year and I have no desire to grope around, hoping to 'get lucky' with other people's money. I am not attuned to this market environment, and I don't want to spoil a decent record by trying to play a game that I don't understand just so I can go out a hero.[6]

If you would suffer substantial regret from an advancing market that you weren't invested in, it is extremely difficult to hold a large position in cash. Imagine having a 20, 30, or even 50 percent cash position and watching the market—or even a segment of the market—advance substantially. Do you have the psychological makeup to stick to your value investing convictions, or would you capitulate and follow the herd? The compounding factor is that investors who "switch horses" from value to growth generally do so late in the cycle. They miss much of the positive performance in the growth area, and, once value stocks turn around, they miss the positive performance in the value arena. This explains why most individual investors underperform index averages. Staying true to your investment style during market periods in which it appears to be out of favor takes a great deal of intestinal fortitude. But the patient investors are the ones that are handsomely rewarded.

Regret aversion also manifests itself in errors of commission—again, from actions taken. Many investors avoid selling stocks in which they have unrealized losses because they rationalize that until they close the position they haven't really incurred the loss. Investors are much more willing to sell stocks that have gained in value because they get to savor the realization of the gain. This propensity is buttressed by the old investment adage, "You can't go broke by taking a profit." Taken to the extreme, such a strategy of selling winners and riding losers would result in an investor holding a portfolio of only losers.[7] From a tax perspective, just the opposite strategy makes sense. Selling stocks at a gain incurs the payment of a tax on the capital gain, while selling stocks at a loss allows the investor to realize a capital loss that can be used to offset gains and reduce taxes. Recognize that the nature of investing is that you will make some mistakes: Even the great investors take positions that turn out to be unprofitable. Be careful, however, what you classify as a mistake. If a stock goes down, that doesn't mean you made a mistake. If you believe that the market is undervaluing a particular stock, a falling stock price may actually represent a better buying opportunity. A mistake is when you realize that either circumstances have changed, or you underestimated the difficulties encountered by a firm—for instance, realization that a firm's losses from derivatives exposure were larger than anticipated.

The value investor must attempt to assess his degree of regret aversion. Trying to follow an investment style that is inconsistent with your psychological character is destined to fail. It is better that you recognize your emotional biases and build a strategy that is consistent with them rather than fight them. Be true to yourself is an axiom worth following in the investment arena.

Attitude Toward Risk

One of the themes of this book is that, if done correctly, value investing effectively reduces risk. Specifically, if you purchase securities with a large margin of safety, you have effectively reduced the risk of incurring losses on that position. Having said that, all broad classes of stock are certainly not created equally when it comes to risk. As we pointed out in Chapter 2, both the risk and return of broad value strategies versus broad growth strategies are dramatically different. We showed how, over time, value stocks outperform growth stocks, and small stocks outperform large stocks. That is, there is a value stock premium and additionally a small stock premium. See Figure 13-2.

But the outperformance of both value stocks over growth stocks and small stocks over large stocks comes at a price, and that price is risk. If you define risk as variability in returns—and most investors do—you find that value stocks tend to have greater variability in returns than growth stocks, and small stocks have greater variability in returns than large stocks.

What does this mean for the aspiring value investor? It means that the value investor must be willing to endure—that's where patience and intestinal fortitude come into play—more variability over time in returns to reap the rewards of a value investing strategy. It also means that some value investing strategies are more volatile than others. For instance, if you focus your energies on smaller capitalization value stocks and concentrate your holdings there, your returns (both annual and monthly) are likely to exhibit more variability than other investors who may adopt a growth strategy or a blended (growth and value) strategy.

When determining what style to adopt, both your *ability* and *willingness* to bear risk must be considered. Ability to bear risk is a quality that lends itself more to a rational, quantitative analysis. It is determined by an investor's financial goals relative to his resources and the time frame in which the goals must be met. If the investor has very modest goals relative to the size of the investment portfolio, he has greater ability to bear risk: that is, the ability to withstand short-term volatility and incur negative short-term returns. Simply put, a young professional with a high-paying job who is saving for a retirement that is decades in the future has

FIGURE 13-2

Historical annual return characteristics, 1926–2012.

Style	Geometric Average Returns	Standard Deviation of Returns
Large Value	11.2%	27.5%
Small Value	14.2%	32.4%
Large Growth	9.2%	20.4%
Small Growth	9.3%	32.9%

Source: Based on Kenneth French's Data Library.

a greater ability to bear risk than someone with an underfunded retirement plan who is quickly approaching retirement age and is underemployed. A crude rule of thumb used by many financial planners (and shown in Box 13-1) attempts to capture the ability to bear risk via the "100 minus your age rule."

Box 13-1 The 100 Minus Your Age Rule of Thumb for Asset Allocation

For many years, the financial planning community has used a crude asset allocation rule based solely on age. One of the biggest decisions that investors make is the allocation of investments across asset classes. The "100 minus your age rule" simply states that if you are 30 years old, you should allocate 100 minus 30, or 70 percent, of your investable assets in stocks and the other 30 percent in bonds. On the other hand, if you are 65 years of age, you should allocate 100 minus 65, or 35 percent, of your investable assets in stocks and the majority, or 65 percent, of your portfolio in bonds. This rule clearly implies that over time, as investors age, they should reallocate assets from the generally riskier equity class to the less risky bond class.

Although we don't advocate that investors adhere to the "100 minus your age rule," the rule illustrates that, in general, the ability to bear risk is related to investment horizon, in addition to your accumulated asset base. Specifically, the longer your investment horizon, the more ability you have to bear risk. Realize that investment horizon is not solely related to age. For instance, if you are funding your child's college fund, the investment horizon is much longer if the child is in nursery school rather than in high school.

Ability to bear risk is certainly related to the magnitude of your asset base. If you have accumulated a large nest egg, you have more ability to bear risk than someone who has not accumulated an adequate financial base.

The greater your ability to bear risk, the wider the scope of consideration you can give to different value investing strategies. For instance, someone with a higher ability to bear risk could consider a value investing strategy concentrated in small capitalization stocks. Further, such an investor can afford to devote a larger portion of their portfolio to such a strategy. On the other hand, people with less ability to bear risk may wish to concentrate a smaller portion of their portfolio and employ a less risky large capitalization value strategy.

While ability to bear risk can be quantified, willingness to bear risk is more qualitative and can only be subjectively assessed. Two investors can have the same ability to bear risk and be dramatically different when it comes to their willingness to bear risk. One way to gauge a person's willingness to bear risk is to simply ask this question: If your portfolio suddenly declined in value by X percent, would you lose sleep over it and suffer substantial regret? If the answer switches from yes to no when X is 10 percent, then the individual has very little willingness to bear risk, and quite frankly, has limited investment options unless that attitude can change. If the answer switches from yes to no when X is 30 percent, then the individual has a high willingness to bear risk.

Meir Statman, a behavioral economist at Santa Clara University, developed an interesting way to measure willingness to take risk. He asked survey respondents to answer the question:

> Suppose your portfolio is currently invested in cash and you have an opportunity to invest it such that you have a 50/50 chance to increase its value by 50 percent. However, the investment strategy also has a 50/50 chance to reduce the portfolio's value by X percent. What is the maximum X percent value loss you are willing to accept?[8]

The more value you are willing to lose, the more willing you are to accept risk. Investors in China and Vietnam are willing to place 16 percent to 17 percent of their wealth at risk, on average, for a 50-50 chance for a 50 percent gain. Investors in Brazil and Tunisia, on the other hand, are only willing to put about 10 percent of their capital at risk for a 50 percent upside. U.S. investors are willing to put about 12.6 percent of their wealth at risk, on average. You might think about using your answer to this question and the averages from these countries to gauge your willingness.[9]

It is also true that an individual's willingness to bear risk is not constant: It often changes through time and with investing experience. It is much easier to proclaim that you are willing to bear hypothetical losses than to incur actual losses. People's willingness to bear risk often changes with life experiences. There is no direct correlation between age and willingness to bear risk, but many young people are more willing to bear risk because they often have little to lose or have not experienced the pain of loss. Ironically, young people frequently choose an asset allocation that is much too conservative for their station in life when they are first enrolling in a retirement program. And, this decision can and does have significant ramifications on their standard of living in their retirement years.

Willingness to bear risk is also often dependent on the current economic outlook. During the height of a bull market many people generally feel bold and proclaim that they have a strong appetite to bear risk. And, why not? During bull markets, aggressive asset allocations and strategies are generally rewarded. However, during the depths of a bear market many people are afraid and say that they don't have much tolerance for risk. They often "pull their chips off the table" just when the market has reached its nadir. If you think that this sounds like the opposite of Buffett's advice ("Be greedy when people are fearful and fearful when people are greedy"), you are correct. If somehow you can convince yourself to be willing to bear more risk when others are not doing so, you will find that more value investing opportunities will present themselves. Similarly, when it seems like people's appetites for risk are insatiable, it is likely time to become more risk averse yourself. Value investors don't believe in the wisdom of crowds and instead speak of the madness of crowds. Just remember that, in investing, the phenomenon of regression to the mean has been fairly consistent through time.

The bottom line is that attitude toward risk is a function of both an individual's ability to bear risk and willingness to bear risk. A person's ability to bear risk is a function of age and station in life and can be quantitatively determined. A person's willingness to bear risk is more subjective, and, while you can rationally determine that you should be more willing to bear risk, it may simply be that you are not psychologically wired to do so. Realize that that's OK. Being unwilling to bear risk is not a weakness. Choose an investment style that is consistent with your unique psychological profile.

DIVERSIFICATION

One of the key elements of your investment style concerns the degree of concentration or diversification of your holdings. Do you want to emulate Buffett and Ruane and hold more concentrated portfolios, or is more diversification as practiced by Brandes and Tweedy, Browne your style?

How many separate holdings does it take to be diversified? A classic study from the early 1970s showed that dramatic diversification benefits were achieved by increasing the number of holdings to 10.[10] Figure 13-3 shows that the risk of portfolios of a given number of stocks declines as more stocks are added. Beyond 10 stocks, the diversification gains were shown to be minimal. Every introductory investments textbook, it seems, provides a graph showing that the lion's share of the diversification benefit (as measured by standard deviation of the portfolio's returns), or approximately 90 percent, is achieved by holding 10 securities and that nearly full diversification can be realized with as few as 30 holdings.[11] Be aware, however, that in order to be diversified a 10- or 20-stock portfolio needs to be diversified across industries.

FIGURE 13-3

Portfolio risk as function of number of stocks.

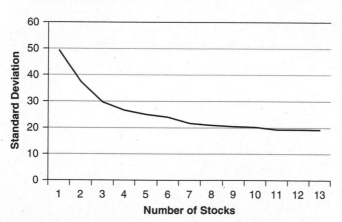

An individual investor who is managing his own investment portfolio cannot properly monitor 30 or more holdings. To be sure, one can over diversify and end up with a menagerie instead of a portfolio. At that point, the investor would be wise to simply adopt an indexing strategy and accept the return on the market instead of attempting to tailor a portfolio to his or her own unique circumstances. You can still be a value investor using index funds or other pooled funds by choosing the right funds, as we will discuss in Chapter 15.

So, how diversified or concentrated should your portfolio be? There is something intellectually appealing about concentrating your investments into only your best ideas. Hasn't every investor at one time said something like, "Why didn't I just put all of my money in Green Mountain Coffee Roasters or Panera Bread, stocks of companies that are well-known consumer brands and have increased in value by 9,210 percent and 1,628 percent, respectively, in the first decade of the twenty-first century?" Had you done so, your money worries would have been over. Peter Lynch famously wrote in 1989, "Who would have suspected that if you'd bought the Subaru stock along with the Subaru car, (in the early 1970s) you'd be a millionaire today."[12]

Maintaining the courage of your convictions sounds like a noble premise and a motto to live by. In his 1978 letter to shareholders, Warren Buffett said:

> Our policy is to concentrate holdings. We try to avoid buying a little of this or that when we are only lukewarm about the business or its price. When we are convinced as to attractiveness, we believe in buying worthwhile amounts.[13]

To buttress his point, Buffett likens wide diversification to Noah building the ark:

> Buy two of everything in sight and end up with a zoo instead of a portfolio.[14]

One of the authors of this book, Bob Johnson, often wonders why he didn't put a sizeable portion or even all of his wealth in Berkshire Hathaway or Ameritrade, two Omaha-based companies that he has had interactions with for many years. In fact, he knows the iconic principals of each firm, Warren Buffett and Joe Ricketts, quite well. In 1980, when Dr. Johnson was receiving his undergraduate degree, Berkshire Hathaway A shares (the only Berkshire shares available at the time) could have been purchased for around $340 per share. At the time of the writing of this book, the shares were selling for nearly $160,000. Such an investment would have returned 46,958 percent over that 32-year time period. That represents a compound annual return of over 21 percent!

Dr. Johnson actually briefly served on the advisory board of TransTerra Corporation, the precursor organization to Ameritrade.[15] Ameritrade went public at an initial split-adjusted offering price of $1.25 per share in March of 1997. With the price of Ameritrade at the time of the writing of this book at around $17 per share, ignoring dividends, the return over that 15-year period is 1,260 percent, or around 19 percent compounded annually!

Yet, even the two firms Dr. Johnson was very familiar with (Berkshire Hathaway and Ameritrade) are fundamentally dissimilar. Berkshire Hathaway, by its very nature, is already quite diversified whereas Ameritrade is much more of a pure play. An investor who owns Berkshire Hathaway actually owns a stake in publicly traded companies Coca-Cola, American Express, Anheuser-Busch, Procter & Gamble, and IBM, among others. In addition, the firm wholly owns GEICO, See's Candies, Nebraska Furniture Mart, and Dairy Queen, plus many other unique and profitable businesses. Clearly, Berkshire Hathaway is already well diversified. Thus, an investor with a sizeable stake in Berkshire Hathaway is much more diversified than a person with an equal stake in a less diversified firm.

Ameritrade, on the other hand, is much more focused on the online discount brokerage firm arena. An investor concentrating his wealth in Ameritrade would be subject to the vagaries of that specific industry, and his wealth would be at risk accordingly.

While courage of your convictions is laudable, recognition of your fallibility is also a positive quality in an investor. While Green Mountain Roasters has been a tremendous investment over a long period of time, the price has been extremely volatile. In September 2011, the stock reached a high of $115.98. Less than a year later, in mid-2012, the stock price had fallen by over 85 percent from its highs. An investor holding a concentrated position in that stock would have experienced a great decline in paper wealth.

For a variety of reasons, investors often choose to concentrate their wealth in the stock of their employer. There are many reasons for this phenomenon, but both overconfidence and the existence of employer matches in pension plans can largely explain this behavior. Frequently, employees have an overly optimistic outlook concerning their own firm's prospects and that translates into concentrating investment in the firm. Allocating your financial assets to the stock of the company you work for results in a highly concentrated portfolio of both your financial capital and your human capital.[16]

One has to look no further than Enron, the most notorious bankruptcy in U.S. history, to realize the danger of compounding risk by investing your financial assets in your employer's firm. An investor who invested in Enron stock in 1985 would have earned a return of over 2,500 percent through the beginning of 2001 when the stock reached a high of over $90 per share.[17] One year later, the shares were essentially worthless. When asked by an ABC news correspondent why he had his wealth so concentrated, an Enron employee said, "Enron continued to be very, very strong during that time. Why should I put something in money markets at 2 or 3 percent when I can have Enron?"[18] When taken to the extreme, standing your ground can lead you to ruin.

It is worth noting that looking at simply the number of holdings does not completely tell the diversification story. An investor can put together a portfolio with many holdings, yet be very concentrated. For example, a portfolio of 10 oil companies would not be nearly as diversified as a portfolio of 10 companies drawn from the broader energy sector. Likewise, a portfolio of 10 companies drawn from a broad spectrum of sectors—energy, service, consumer staples, consumer discretionary, financial, and the like—would be much more diversified than a portfolio drawn simply from the energy sector or any single sector. As noted in the previous chapter, Bill Miller built his enviable record by concentrating his holdings in technology stocks—companies that many other value investors chose to neglect. His undoing was concentrating holdings in financial firms during the height of the recent financial crisis.

When it comes to concentrating holdings, you win some and you lose some. The moral of the diversification story is that unless you are willing to accept the risk of financial ruin—and very few of us are—some diversification is a prudent strategy. Recognize that to achieve financial success the concentrated investor has to make two sound decisions: when to buy and when to sell. In retrospect, Enron was an excellent investment from 1985 to the beginning of 2001. The investor selling in early 2001 was handsomely rewarded, while the investor selling in late 2001 was wiped out. Similarly, Green Mountain Coffee Roasters was a terrific investment from 2000 to 2009, but from late 2011 to mid 2012, it was an unmitigated disaster.

Our recommendation is that whatever value investing style you adopt, some diversification of your holdings is warranted. The amount of that diversification will be a function of your appetite for risk. Investment pundits have suggested that the decision to diversify is the answer to the question, "Do you want to sleep well or eat well?" The implication is that if you have a high-risk portfolio, you eat well because there is a possibility of a large return and a more prosperous lifestyle. On the other hand, an investor with a lower-risk portfolio can sleep well because he or she doesn't need to worry about the possibility of losing one's entire investment.

As with most things in life, moderation is the answer. We can have extreme confidence yet not bet the farm on our single best idea. Even Warren Buffett doesn't make those kinds of bets. Each of the three authors of this book holds a portfolio that is well diversified. We all are certainly comfortable with our degree of investment knowledge, having chosen to dedicate our careers to financial education. Yet we also realize that we are not willing to stake our standard of living on beliefs that can look valid before the fact, yet later could be proven invalid by factors beyond our control.

NEED FOR INCOME

Your choice of investment style may also be influenced by your need (or desire) for current income versus capital appreciation. If you are counting on current income from your investment portfolio to cover your living expenses or support your lifestyle, then you may want to focus on identifying value stocks with high dividend yields. You would certainly rely more on the dividend discount model of valuation if you were to choose this investment style.

Some experts would say that you don't need to concern yourself with dividend yields, as you can simply create your own dividend by periodically selling off shares of stock when you need cash. The periodic selling of shares to raise cash to supplement income is often referred to as a homemade dividend. While in theory this line of reasoning is valid, the tactic requires a great deal of discipline. Many investors who have income requirements prefer to hold a portfolio that has a yield sufficient to provide the income they require. They prefer not to be concerned with making decisions about which holdings to sell to create the homemade dividend.

While investors can sell a portion of their holdings and in effect create their own dividends, the reverse is not true without having the tax authorities take a portion of the dividend payout. In other words, if you hold stocks that pay a dividend, and you don't need that dividend to supplement your income (in fact, you simply turn around and reinvest those dividends in the market), you incur tax liabilities and Uncle Sam takes a portion of your wealth. This results in you having a smaller portfolio than you would have had if the dividend weren't paid. Essentially, this is why Berkshire Hathaway doesn't pay a dividend and doesn't plan on doing so.

If you don't need income and don't want to incur tax liabilities from current income, then you might look for value investments that have little or no dividend yield. From a pure tax standpoint, that philosophy is an efficient method of accumulating wealth.

TAX STATUS

Often investors have holdings in both taxable and nontaxable accounts. For instance, investors often have nontaxable 401(k) or IRA accounts in which they can accumulate wealth tax free and only incur taxes when funds are withdrawn from the accounts. It certainly makes sense for investors to hold positions in dividend-paying stocks in the nontaxable accounts and nondividend paying stocks in taxable accounts, all else equal.

It also makes sense for investors to place investments in their core, long-term holdings in a taxable account and more transitory (or trading) holdings in a nontaxable account. While most value investors have a long time horizon and plan to hold assets for an extended period of time, they have other holdings that they consider more temporary and transitory in nature. For instance, if I consider Berkshire Hathaway to be one of my core long-term holdings, I would want to hold it in my taxable account because it does not pay any dividends and I don't plan to sell it and incur capital gains. On the other hand, suppose that I believe that Companhia Siderurgica Nacional (ticker symbol SID), a Brazilian-based steel company, is undervalued. In that case, I may want to hold it in my nontaxable account, for two reasons: 1) it has a dividend yield of approximately 2.5 percent and 2) I don't plan on holding it over the long term, but will sell it when the market recognizes the undervaluation.

We realize that such a division between taxable and nontaxable accounts cannot always be accommodated. The point of the discussion is to indicate that, when possible, such a distinction helps the investor make their investing more tax efficient.

WHICH VALUATION MODEL TO USE?

Once investors determine which value investing style they want to follow, they need to choose an investment model (or models) to use. Chapters 7 through 11 presented the five primary valuation models: dividend discount, free cash flow, asset based, residual income, and a variety of relative methods. As we described in the individual chapters, some models are more applicable for specific firm and industry types. The following represents a discussion of the broad classes of stocks and industries that each model is best suited.

Dividend Discount Models

Dividend discount models are generally the first models that students are introduced to in undergraduate and graduate investment courses. The appeal of these models is their simplicity. One simply takes the current dividend, estimates a future growth rate (or growth rates), and arrives at a value by assuming a specific required rate of return. Dividend discount models have been around since the 1950s, when Myron Gordon published his version of the constant growth dividend model. Since that time many variations have appeared and have been applied by a multitude of investors, both professional and amateur.

While intellectually appealing, the dividend discount model is limited to valuing firms that actually pay cash dividends. This was once the majority of firms, but not anymore. The percentage of firms in developed markets that pay dividends has been in a long-term decline. Eugene Fama and Kenneth French found that 66.5 percent of U.S. stocks paid dividends in 1978, while only 20.8 percent did so in 1999.[19] Thus, overall, one can conclude that the dividend discount models are less applicable today than they were several decades ago. In fact, it would seem that these models would only apply to about 1 in 5 potential stock investments.

While it is true that the overall percentage of dividend paying stocks has declined dramatically, in certain segments of the market, it is still the norm for a stock to pay a dividend. For example, in the large capitalization sector of the market, the vast majority of firms still pay dividends. As of the writing of this book, 410 of the firms in the S&P 500 paid dividends. Figure 13-4 shows that there was a secular decline in the number of firms in the S&P 500 that paid dividends, but that trend seems to be reversing. All 30 firms in the Dow Jones Industrial Average pay dividends; only 52 in the tech-heavy NASDAQ 100 are dividend payers.

Thus, investors pursuing a large capitalization value investing strategy are likely to find the dividend discount model to be a good fit for their investment style. Still, relying on the dividend discount model will bias the investor's universe for some stock sectors and against other sectors. Table 13-1 is excerpted from Ashwath Damodaran's website. It lists sectors with the highest dividend yields from the *Value Line* universe of 6,177 stocks.

FIGURE 13-4

Percent of S&P 500 companies paying dividends.

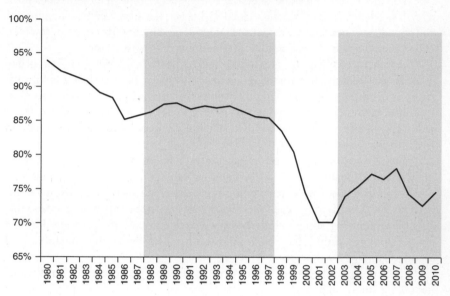

TABLE 13-1

Dividend Fundamentals by Sector as of January 2013 (Value Line)

Sector	Dividend Yield	Dividend Payout Ratio	N
Beverage	2.46%	49.30%	35
Drug	3.13%	48.28%	223
Electric Utility (Central)	4.28%	60.93%	20
Electric Utility (East)	4.17%	66.01%	17
Electric Utility (West)	3.84%	59.16%	15
Food Processing	2.69%	49.55%	119
Household Products	3.06%	53.76%	27
Natural Gas Utility	3.14%	76.95%	27
Pipeline MLPs	5.79%	69.72%	53
Real Estate Investment Trusts	7.90%	76.79%	127
Tobacco	4.17%	72.59%	11
Total	2.20%	36.10%	6177

Source: http://people.stern.nyu.edu/adamodar/New_Home_Page/datafile/divfund.htm

As you can see, the sectors with the highest dividend yields are utilities, real estate investment trusts (REITs), and consumer staples, including household products, food processors, beverage, and drug companies. Although they are not shown here, the sectors with negligible dividend yields are, not surprisingly, e-commerce, educational services, entertainment technology, health care information, Internet, investment companies, retail automotive, and wireless networking.

Another consideration is whether the company's dividend is appropriate given its profitability. If a company continues to pay a high dividend but profitability is declining, then you should consider another valuation model. The dividend discount model is appropriate when the company's dividend policy is linked with its profitability—in other words, when the company's dividend is supported by earnings.

Investors pursuing a large capitalization value investing style who rely on the dividend discount model as their preferred valuation model will find that their universe of potential investments will emphasize some sectors and exclude others. This isn't necessarily a bad thing. Such investors need only to understand this situation. Excluding some industries from consideration—for instance, Internet and e-commerce firms—may be a good thing, given the frothy valuations and volatile nature of those sectors.

The dividend discount model is certainly less appropriate for an investor pursuing a small capitalization value strategy. Only about 40 percent of firms in the small capitalization Russell 2000 index even pay dividends, and at the time of this writing the dividend yield on the index was a paltry 1.38 percent, compared to 2.03 percent on the S&P 500. Suffice it to say, the dividend discount model is biased in favor of larger, more well-established firms.

Free Cash Flow Models

As indicated in Chapter 8, the free cash flow models—free cash flow to equity (FCFE) and free cash flow to the firm (FCFF)—are applicable to a wide variety of firms and can be employed whether the firm pays a dividend or not. The free cash flow models are most appropriate where dividends are not available or in cases where investors are attempting to value an initial public offering or a private company. These models are also appropriate for dividend-paying firms in which the free cash flow to equity is substantially different than dividends paid, as in the case of Apple. Remember, Apple pays a dividend, but the dividend is substantially less than what it could pay given the enormous free cash flow it is generating. The same could be said for a firm that is temporarily paying out significantly higher dividends than free cash flow to equity would justify in the long run.

The use of FCFE versus FCFF is somewhat nuanced, but the big advantage of FCFF is that it is appropriate if the level of leverage in the firm is expected to change dramatically. For instance, in a leveraged buyout situation, analysts would use FCFF because the firm would become highly leveraged.

Free cash flow models are much more demanding of the user than the dividend discount models. Since the free cash flow models do not rely on readily available data, the analyst needs to compute these quantities based on various assumptions and forecasts. These models demand that the investor understand the firm's financial statements, operations, industry, and financing in much more detail than in the dividend discount model. Professional analysts consider these models much more useful than the dividend discount models.

Asset-Based Approaches

We believe that asset-based approaches are typically the exception rather than the rule. In other words, we recommend that you don't adopt a steady diet of valuing firms via the asset-based approach, but rather consider this approach in unique circumstances. This method is particularly valuable for valuing firms in which you believe that management is underutilizing its asset base and in which a change of control might unleash the earning power of the assets. Asset-based approaches are often appropriate in identifying potential takeover or spin-off targets.

Asset-based approaches are also often appropriate for valuing firms with large holdings in natural resources. For instance, if timber prices are depressed, a timber company may decide to reduce harvesting in a recessionary period or in a period in which commodity prices are depressed. Employing a dividend or free cash flow approach might dramatically understate the value of the underlying assets and also understate the firm's future earning potential.

Note that asset-based approaches are not limited to those firms that you feel are underperforming. There certainly are some high-performing firms that, for whatever reason, the market simply undervalues. In Chapter 9 we presented an example of an asset-based approach valuing Berkshire Hathaway suggesting that it is undervalued with a margin of safety of roughly 12 percent. I doubt that many commentators would posit that Berkshire Hathaway is an underperforming or mismanaged firm.

As with free cash flow models, asset-based approaches require you to do some digging in order to identify these kinds of special situations. The application of asset-based models is not as straightforward as dividend discount or free cash flow models.

Residual Income Models

As detailed in Chapter 10, residual income models are most appropriate for firms that generate cash flow in a manner that is fundamentally different from other companies. As was illustrated, banks do not operate in the same manner as most manufacturing companies, retailers, and other standard firms. On the contrary, banks essentially earn a spread on the difference in interest rates between borrowed and lent funds. Thus, operating cash flow can be difficult to determine and impossible to forecast. The residual income model is effective for valuing many companies. However, this is particularly the case with those companies whose book value and earnings are a major driver of profitability, such as those in the financial industry. The residual income model can be used when cash flows are unpredictable but earnings are relatively stable. The residual income model should not be used when you have concerns about the quality of the company's earnings (you suspect they are playing accounting games).

Relative Valuation

From its very name, you realize that relative valuation models are not absolute valuation models because you are valuing a firm on metrics relative to another, hopefully comparable, firm or set of firms. As such, we suggest using this set of models as a first pass and then employing one or more of the other valuation models to determine whether an investment truly represents a value investing opportunity. In other words, if you simply purchase a stock because it is the most attractively priced relative to some group, you may be making a mistake for a couple of reasons. First, the stock may be the most attractively priced for good reason—that is, its future prospects might be poor. Secondly, the entire group might be overvalued and not worthy of consideration. Bill Miller made the latter mistake when he took large positions in the financial industry during the initial stages of the financial crises. These firms may have been inexpensive on a relative value basis, but the entire industry was poised for a downfall.

Which multiples to use, varies greatly by sector. As illustrated in Chapter 11, price-to-book is commonly used in the financial sector: that is, for banking, insurance, and other financial firms. The reason that price-to-book predominates in the financial sector is that book equity is what capital ratios are based upon and it determines, in effect, the amount of leverage the firm can employ. On the other hand, in retailing, price-to-book is not used. Typically, what retail analysts focus on are sales and, in particular, same store sales. In fact, what often causes changes in the price of retailers is the release of same store sales data. Thus, in retailing, many analysts use the price-to-book metric as a relative valuation tool.

One of the sectors we haven't emphasized thus far is technology. This sector has been primarily valued on growth prospects, and thus variations of the PEG ratio described in Chapter 11 are helpful in performing relative valuations on technology firms.

Finally, price-to–cash flow is frequently used to perform relative valuations on firms in industries that are big cash generators, such as REITs and utilities. The bottom line with any of these relative valuation metrics is that they must be defined consistently across firms and used for truly comparable firms.

CONCLUSION

The beauty of value investing is that there is no single prescription to define the school of thought. As Warren Buffett has said, "There's more than one way to get to heaven," indicating that various methods can produce good investment results. You can develop a unique style that is consistent with your psychological makeup, attitude toward risk, income needs, tax situation, and other unique circumstances, and you don't have to blindly adhere to some orthodoxy. Which investment valuation model you select will, to some extent, be dictated by your investment style. Many value investors have a preferred valuation method but are not averse to employing other methods as circumstances dictate.

CHAPTER FOURTEEN

DISTRESSED INVESTING

I prefer to believe the opposite—that there is always an indestructible beauty at the heart of darkness.

—Mary Balogh, *A Secret Affair*

In Chapter 12, we discussed several different styles of value investing through the lenses of nine famed value investors. Seth Klarman is among those who doesn't mind sitting on liquidity to serve as "one-stop shopping for an urgent seller" and sees value in many types of assets not just equity and debt. In this chapter, we will explore this notion of distressed investing and how the strategic value investor can apply fundamental principles to spot hidden opportunities and avoid disaster.

Be warned, however, distressed investing is not for the faint of heart. That it is sometimes pejoratively referred to as vulture investing reflects the cold analytical skills and steely fortitude one must have to sift through the remains of corporate road kill. As the opening quote suggests, distressed investing requires the ability to discern the beauty at the heart of darkness. OK, perhaps that's a bit melodramatic! The point remains that, even more than the discipline of value investing itself, distressed investing requires one to go against the grain and to buck conventional wisdom about a company or security. We outlined barriers to successful value investing in Chapter 4 and the titanium spine it requires. This is even more the case with distressed investing.

DISTRESS VERSUS BANKRUPTCY

Many people associate financial distress or distressed securities with bankruptcy. That is entirely understandable because the firms that enter bankruptcy are indeed financially distressed and the securities that finance those firms are therefore distressed, as well. However, firms can be financially distressed without having filed for bankruptcy. In fact, most firms that ultimately file for bankruptcy are financially distressed long before they do so.

Moreover, the notion of distressed securities exists outside the formal realm of bankruptcy. Many mortgage-backed securities (MBS) or collateralized mortgage obligations (CMO), for example, were considered distressed securities in the depths of the financial crisis even though the MBS itself doesn't go to bankruptcy.[1]

BANKRUPTCY

Because most people equate financial distress with bankruptcy, let's begin there. Bankruptcy is simply the legal process that governs the disposition of assets for insolvent firms. The process determines how much security holders and other stakeholders will receive in the event of liquidation, or it determines their rights and legal claims in the event of reorganization.[2]

Bankruptcy comes in several forms. In the United States, Chapter 7 bankruptcy refers to the part of the Bankruptcy Code that governs the liquidation process associated with insolvent firms (i.e., those no longer able to pay their creditors).

The more common bankruptcy filing in the United States is for Chapter 11 protection, described in Box 14-1, which allows a firm to continue operating while it renegotiates the terms of its debts to its creditors. Sometimes that involves extending the repayment period while the firm sells assets or executes a cost-cutting program. Other times, creditors are asked to accept a fraction of what is owed while the firm reorganizes itself. Why would creditors accept less than what is owed them or extend repayment options? The answer is simple. The alternative to restructuring might be receiving much less or perhaps nothing at all. Whatever plan worked out between the company and its creditors needs to be approved by a bankruptcy court to ensure that the terms are balanced against the claims of other stakeholders, such as employees, pensioners, vendors, or other litigants. At that point, the firm "emerges" from bankruptcy.

Insolvency versus Illiquidity

There is a fundamental difference between insolvency and illiquidity. The debts of an insolvent firm are greater than its assets. In other words, it has negative equity. Insolvency is therefore a balance-sheet concept.

An illiquid firm, by contrast, has insufficient cash flow to meet its current debt service obligations. Illiquidity is therefore an income statement or cash flow concept. For example, Bear Stearns, which was purchased by JPMorgan in 2008 in a sale arranged by the government in an effort to avoid bankruptcy and thereby avoid triggering a cascade of financial firm bankruptcies, was not insolvent. It was unable to meet its short-term and refinancing obligations because it was illiquid. Specifically, it lost access to the capital markets and was unable to refinance its short-term obligations.

Likewise, a firm can be insolvent, but liquid (at least for a period of time). Many pension funds are insolvent but liquid. They have insufficient assets to meet long-term obligations they have accrued over time, but they are able to generate enough current cash flow to meet the obligations for current pensioners. Ultimately, the day of reckoning will approach for many pension funds who do not have enough assets (or prospects to get enough assets) to meet obligations in the long term.

Box 14-1 Is Chapter 11 Good for the Economy?

The idea behind Chapter 11 bankruptcy protection is to provide an option for firms that are temporarily insolvent to continue operating. This allows them to work through a tough time rather than shutting their doors completely and transferring the assets to some other entity; thus incurring the costs associated with losing the value of the firm as a going operation. Stuart Gilson of Harvard University believes that Chapter 11 bankruptcy provisions are critical to a healthy economy and are largely responsible for the ability of the United States to recover from the recent financial crisis while much of Europe has not. Elizabeth Warren, the former Harvard Law school professor and Obama appointee for the Consumer Financial Protection Bureau, agrees.[3] According to Gilson, $3.5 trillion of corporate debt was distressed or in default between 2008 and 2011. About one-half of that amount entered Chapter 11 bankruptcy protection, which is almost 20 times what was seen during the prior two years. Much of the U.S. corporate debt that defaulted during this time period has been managed down without massive liquidations.

Not everyone agrees about the benefits of Chapter 11 protection. One study shows that Chapter 11 has a long-term adverse effect on industry peers, who underperform the market by 7 percent in the year following a firm's emergence from bankruptcy.[4] In contrast, the reorganized firm outperforms the market by 25 to 140 percent.[5]

It is important to understand that assets don't just evaporate in bankruptcy. So, if bankruptcy destroys value, it's not because assets disappear. The assets are simply transferred from equity holders to creditors or sold to another owner, and the proceeds are used to satisfy as much of the creditors' claims as possible. Creditors, in effect, become the new shareholders. Value destruction in bankruptcy results from the direct costs associated with the process itself (e.g., court fees and lawyers) and indirect costs associated with distress (e.g., lost sales from customers' lack of confidence, loss of trade credit, and damage to a brand name).

In a strict sense, shareholders should get nothing in bankruptcy unless and until creditors get everything owed to them because creditors have a priority claim. Secured creditors (who are protected by a claim on particular assets) would have priority over senior unsecured creditors who would have priority over unsecured junior creditors. Employees and others that have provided trade credit in the normal operations of the firm (e.g., suppliers) typically have priority over creditors. In practice, this hierarchy of claims is usually not adhered to strictly because claim holders petition the court, laying out their case for why their claim should have priority. So, the process is usually not black and white.

Consider the example of the General Motors Chapter 11 reorganization during the financial crisis in 2009. In 2007, the union lent money to GM as an unsecured creditor to maintain retiree health benefits under the auspices of the union umbrella that GM was having difficulty sustaining without additional financing. The union, an unsecured creditor, was given priority over other unsecured creditors; understandably dismayed, the other unsecured creditors argued that a fundamental principle of bankruptcy law is that creditors with like claims should receive similar treatment. The union received 17.5 percent of the newly issued GM stock (the old stuff became worthless) and $9 billion in preferred stock and debt, while other unsecured creditors received 10 percent of the stock of the "new" GM and warrants to purchase 15 percent more at preferred prices.[6] If it had received treatment like other unsecured creditors, the union would have gained $5.6 billion rather than the $17.8 billion it actually got (by some accounts). That's a dramatic difference.[7]

Most countries have some form of Chapter 7 and Chapter 11 bankruptcy provisions. Prepackaged bankruptcy is a variation on a theme in which the firm in distress negotiates new terms with creditors before filing for bankruptcy under Chapter 5 of the code. Courts are asked to affirm the reorganization plan. If accepted, the plan becomes binding on all parties, even if they did not participate in or voted against the plan; however, a requisite number of creditors and stockholders need to be involved. In a similar arrangement, called prenegotiated Chapter 11 bankruptcy, firms ask key creditors to sign an agreement promising to vote for a restructuring plan once the firm is in Chapter 11, rather than formally soliciting votes.

Another less common option is out-of-court restructuring, otherwise known as a workout, in which a firm in distress negotiates with its creditors to reduce its obligations by swapping new securities (e.g., debt, equity, or convertible securities) for the distressed debt. A workout can be an easier and less expensive alternative to bankruptcy, but it is usually effective only if there are a relatively small number of creditors. Negotiations across multiple stakeholders can be cumbersome, and it is more difficult to reach an agreement. The recent sovereign debt restructurings in southern Europe are examples.

Box 14-2 Application: Now That's a Sweet Deal!

Hostess Brands, Inc., struggled with financial distress for many years. Their stock fell to $2.05 in 2004 from an all-time high of $34 per share. It filed for bankruptcy in 2004 (as Interstate Bakeries) and emerged in 2009 as a private company. The bankruptcy process was notable because it was the longest in

U.S. history at the time. Throughout the process, the firm fought off multiple takeover bids.

By August 2011, Hostess Brands was in trouble again. The company stopped paying future pension benefits after August 2011, which understandably upset the employees' union, and the firm filed for bankruptcy again in January 2012. Talks with the Teamsters Union to renegotiate wage and pension benefits looked promising for a while, but broke down in the summer of 2012. In short order, after workers went on strike in November 2012, Hostess laid off all its workers and put all its assets up for sale. The court approved the liquidation a week later.

The assets of different product lines went to different bidders. If you are wondering who got the Twinkies line, it was Apollo Global Management, an American private equity firm that specializes in purchasing distressed securities involving corporate restructurings and other special situations.

In some sense, distressed investing principles are no different from the strategic value investing principles we have outlined in this book. In another sense, distressed investing often constitutes betting on binary outcomes that do not exhibit typical investment-like characteristics. For example, the value of distressed securities is often wholly determined by whether a judge approves a restructuring plan, whether the sale of assets is ultimately consummated, or whether union workers are able to win political support to protect their claims.

Many times, the result of a Chapter 11 bankruptcy proceeding is a merger or acquisition. In 2013, for example, American Airlines won court approval to combine with US Airways to form the world's biggest airline after having initially filed for bankruptcy protection in November 2011. Over that time, its share price increased tenfold from a low of around 40 cents per share to over four dollars per share. In another example, Sears Roebuck merged with the new Kmart in November 2004 after it emerged from bankruptcy in May of the previous year. So how do we distinguish between speculative situations that have little hope of recovery from those truly momentous investment opportunities that present themselves only rarely?

ARE FIRMS EMERGING FROM BANKRUPTCY GOOD INVESTMENTS?

Distressed investing is contrarian to the extreme. You must be willing to buy when literally everyone else is selling and saying, "There is no way out of this!" This is often on the heels of a dramatic upswing when everyone is saying, "This time it's different!" Howard Marks is known for patiently biding his time with pools of liquidity waiting for these opportunities, which are marked by dramatic shifts in market sentiments.

It bears emphasizing that securities (particularly senior and secured debt) do not become valueless when a borrower defaults on principal or interest payments and files for Chapter 11. As mentioned above, the assets do not evaporate, and the firm does not cease operating. Lenders typically recover some portion of what is owed them. How much depends on their priority, whether they are secured, the maturity of the issue in relation to Chapter 11 filing, as well as a host of other factors.

Whether securities associated with Chapter 11 reorganization bankruptcy are viable investment opportunities depends largely on how likely firms that enter Chapter 11 reorganization successfully emerge from it. Measuring investment success, however, is an elusive concept. We could determine success, for example, by whether or not such a firm refiles for bankruptcy. But if that's the case, what is the appropriate time frame? Two years? Three years? Five years? Perhaps a better measure is asset or sales growth or profitability. But, if so, what levels of growth or profitability are sufficient to warrant success?

If we are able to develop a meaningful definition of success, are we able to determine which firms entering the bankruptcy process are more likely to emerge successfully? An important predictor of success is whether creditors are willing and able to propose a reorganization plan to the courts prior to filing. Firms that do this are more than twice as likely (72 percent versus 33 percent) to have a plan confirmed by the court.

Box 14-3 Application: What Goes Around Comes Around

Apple was on the brink of bankruptcy in 1997. Its stock was trading at about $4.50 per share. At the time, Michael Dell quipped that Apple should liquidate and return whatever money was left over to shareholders. Since then, Apple reached a high of over $700 per share for a return of—wait for it— over 15,000 percent. At the time of this writing, Apple was trading at about $450 per share, or 36 percent off its high. A 36 percent loss doesn't sound great, but it still represents a 9,900 percent return from the point that Michael Dell suggested hanging it up.

Recently, Apple issued the largest bond offering ever at $17 billion. So, it seems that distressed investing can have its merits. Interestingly, about the same time Apple issued its record-breaking bond offering, Dell was struggling and in the middle of a high-profile battle to go private, in an effort to return the firm to its former glory. It seems the shoe is now on other foot.

According to one study, 40 percent of firms who have filed for bankruptcy continue to experience operating losses three years after bankruptcy, and two-thirds file for bankruptcy a second time. These firms also underperform their peers and significantly and consistently fall short of the expectations and projections laid out in their reorganization plan. Several factors seem to influence post-bankruptcy performance. One of the most compelling is whether or not the management that led the firm into distress continues to manage the firm out of bankruptcy, which is not the usual case. If so, the firm is more likely to experience poor performance after bankruptcy.[8] It seems that the old saying "Fool me once, shame on you; fool me twice shame on me" applies here.

Factors that have been shown to improve post–Chapter 11 performance are:[9]

1. New management
2. Being incorporated in the state of Delaware (a state that encourages takeover bids, which are the second most likely outcome of emerging from Chapter 11)
3. A prepackaged bankruptcy
4. A long duration of the bankruptcy process (if it is not prepackaged)
5. Equity retained by pre–Chapter 11 shareholders

Some of these factors are intuitive; others are not. On one hand, it makes sense that replacing the management that oversaw a firm's slide into distress bodes well for the future. On the other hand, there's no guarantee that new management will have as much firm and industry expertise. Restructuring costs are quite high. So high, in fact, that an unduly drawn out reorganization process runs the risk of depleting the firm's dwindling resources, at least for small firms.

Also counterintuitive is the observation that firms under Chapter 11 protection typically have better access to capital when they enter or even when they emerge than before entering the process. Chapter 11 allows firms to suspend payments to existing claim holders and even issue securities senior to their claims. Certain types of securities, like warrants and convertible bonds, can also help provide access pre– and post–Chapter 11.

THE ROLE OF WARRANTS AND CONVERTIBLES

Lack of access to the capital markets is a common cause for otherwise viable firms to run into liquidity problems and hence financial distress. Distressed firms have been known to use warrants or convertible bonds either as part of a voluntary restructuring of swapping one set of securities for another, Chapter 11 reorganization, or simply as a technique to stave off one of these two outcomes. Warrants and convertible bonds have certain characteristics that make them particularly useful in this regard.

Warrants are like long-term call options issued by a firm. They entitle the warrant holder to buy shares of common stock from the issuing firm at a fixed price, known as the strike price. For example, if warrants have a strike price of $10 per share and the stock price goes up to $25 per share, then warrant holders benefit to the tune of $15 per share because they would exercise their warrants and pay $10 for shares worth $25. If the stock price is anywhere between $0 and $10, they would not bother exercising their warrants, but they are not out any extra money. Warrant holders are no worse off if the stock price is $3 per share than if it is $8.

They simply let the warrant expire worthless in either case. As a result, their downside risk is limited. The difference between warrants and traditional call options is that warrants are issued by the firm, and the firm issues additional shares if the warrants are exercised, resulting in dilution of the existing share base.

Convertible bonds are similar to traditional bonds, but they give the bondholder the right to exchange their bonds for common stock at a fixed ratio. Convertible bondholders would want to do this if the stock price increases. In this sense, convertible bonds are a lot like traditional nonconvertible bonds with warrants attached. In fact, a similar financing technique in distressed situations is to issue traditional debt with warrants attached, rather than bundling them together in the form of a convertible bond.

Why might these types of securities be useful for both investors and issuers of distressed securities? Distressed firms typically need financing to continue their ongoing operations as the existing securities in their capital structure come to maturity and need to be refinanced. The problem is that investors are reluctant to lend to distressed firms because the risks are so high. And if the firm pulls through and is successful, most of the gains will accrue to the stockholders. Therefore, warrants and convertible bonds are ways to give potential investors some upside potential and limit their downside risk.

Interestingly, unlike most securities, such as debt, a warrant's value increases as the risk of the underlying asset increases because the investor's downside risk is limited. Volatility does not hurt on the downside because the worst that can happen is that warrants expire worthless, but volatility really helps on the upside.

Why would a firm give away the upside? If they are in a distressed situation, they may not have much choice. But there is another reason. Suppose a distressed firm is able to pull themselves from the brink and their prospects improve. They will likely need additional financing down the road as their prospects improve. Convertible bonds have a built-in mechanism to accommodate this good fortune. As the stock price increases, convertible bond holders will gladly trade their bonds for the more valuable equity, thereby removing the debt from the firm's balance sheet without having to repay it. Moreover, the additional equity shores up the firm's balance sheet and positions it well for further financing.

So, if you are investing in distressed situations, do not discount the valuable role that warrants and convertible bonds can play in helping an otherwise well-run firm recover from financial exigency.

VALUING DISTRESSED SECURITIES

Much debate has occurred over the last 40 years about whether financial markets are efficient. That is, do security prices represent an unbiased view of all available information? Are securities priced accurately, making investment analysis futile? For decades, economists have passionately argued both sides of this question. Whether or not markets are efficient, almost all economists agree that mispricing (if it's to occur) is most likely to take place in situations characterized by illiquidity, complexity, uninformed investors, lack of analysts following, and intense fear or greed. Distressed investing features all these characteristics.

In these situations, the strategic value investor looks for nuggets of gold in the mud. To do so, requires an understanding of the various possible phases of the distressed security. Distressed debt is likely to be in one of four basic stages:

1. Remain a performing loan
2. Become part of the voluntary restructuring
3. Be subject to the terms of a Chapter 11 reorganization plan
4. Chapter 7 liquidation

Evaluating a distressed security involves estimating the likelihood that it will be in one of these stages, as well as its anticipated recovery if it is in one of those stages.

Remain Performing Loan

Short-term securities have the best chance of recovery if a company is going to avoid Chapter 11 reorganization because the firm needs to meet those obligations in order to avoid filing. Whitman and Diz (2009) illustrate this notion using the senior unsecured notes of General Motors Acceptance Corporation (GMAC) during the distress of October 2008. Cerberus Capital Management owns 51 percent of GMAC common stock. They offered holders of the 7¾ percent coupon senior unsecured notes maturing in January 2010 an exchange offer, including warrants and stock that represented a substantial discount from what was owed them. The note holders had little incentive to accept the offer: Cerberus was unlikely to file for Chapter 11 because it holds a 51 percent stake in the common stock, which likely would become worthless if they filed Chapter 11.

An important question: What kind of return is required to entice investors into these distressed waters? For debt that was likely to remain performing, Whitman and Diz were seeking a minimum 25 percent yield-to-maturity in 2008. For securities that were likely to participate in a voluntary reorganization (next paragraph), they were demanding internal rates of return well in excess of 30 percent at the time.

Voluntary Restructuring

Debt restructuring is not necessarily a cataclysmic event. Even in a restructuring, some senior creditors can be reinstated, never missing a contracted payment. On the other hand, some junior creditors may be wiped out, receiving nothing. Creditors with claims in between may receive a new package of securities or cash.

One factor that can induce creditors to agree to a voluntary exchange is the threat of having their claim subordinated by those credit holders participating in an exchange offer. Even if the original bond indenture prohibits this kind of subordination, new securities exchanged for distressed securities can be granted seniority over nonexchanging debt instruments. This kind of brinksmanship is common in voluntary restructurings.

Chapter 11 Reorganization

Failing the payment of all agreed-upon cash flows, and failing the possibility of an attractive voluntary restructuring or exchange of securities, many debt holders are likely to recover something in a Chapter 11 reorganization. Again, senior and secured debt holders are likely to recover a portion of what is owed them, while junior and unsecured debt holders are likely to receive little or nothing. According to Whitman and Diz (2009), "Chapter 11 bankruptcy is not the end of the game but the beginning of the game."

Chapter 7 Liquidation

If a voluntary restructuring and Chapter 11 reorganization fail, then a company enters Chapter 7 bankruptcy, and the assets are liquidated. The proceeds are used to satisfy the claimants in order of their priority. An analyst can judge the potential liquidation value by estimating the recovery rate for the different categories of the firm's assets and adapting provisions for priority claim holders. This allows the analyst to see which securities are likely to be paid in such a scenario and which are not. Box 14-4, 14-5, and 14-6 demonstrate different stages of a liquidation analysis.

Box 14-4 Liquidation Analysis

Thompson Robbins, Inc., is a firm with over $15 billion of assets, according to their book values listed on the balance sheet. It has claims, including debt and accounts payable, of $7.6 billion. On the surface the firm appears solvent; however it no longer has access to the capital markets that would allow it to roll over its short-term unsecured debt. The firm is therefore in financial distress and has failed to develop a viable reorganization plan in Chapter 11 bankruptcy. It is now, consequently, in Chapter 7 liquidation.

Amount in millions of dollars				
	Book Value	Estimated Recovery Rate	Estimated Liquidation Value	Residual Distribution	Estimated Recovery
Cash	50	100%	50		
Accounts Receivable	2,000	70%	1,400		
Inventory	1,000	50%	500		

Pre-paid Expenses	500	0%	–		
Property, Plant, and Equipment					
Land and Buildings	1,200	120%	1,440		
Machinery	300	50%	150		
Goodwill	10,000	0%	–		
Total Assets	15,050		3,540		
Deductions:					
Liquidation Costs			800	2,740	100%
Tax Claims			200	2,540	100%
Employee Claims			100	2,440	100%
Secured Debt			500	1,940	100%
Senior Unsecured Debt			2,500	(560)	78%
Junior Unsecured Debt			3,500	(4,060)	0%

Unfortunately, book values are often poor proxies for liquidation values, especially in financial distress situations. Although the firm may recover all or most of its cash holdings and value of the accounts receivable, its inventory will likely be liquidated at a fraction of its book value, in this case 50 percent. By contrast, some property plant and equipment (like land and buildings) are likely carried on the balance sheet at below market value even in the distressed situation. In this case, suppose that the land and buildings can be liquidated for 120 percent of book value, but that the machinery can be liquidated for only 50 percent of book value.

By multiplying the recovery rates by the book value for each type of asset (note that we could become much more specific about the asset categories), we see that the estimated liquidation value is a little over $3.5 billion. Of this amount, liquidation costs will consume $800 million, and $200 million will be taken for tax claims. These obligations, along with the $100 million owed to employees, must be paid before any of the security holders are paid, leaving $2.44 billion to satisfy their claims.

If this is the case, the secured debt holders will receive everything owed them. The senior unsecured debt holders, however, will receive only $1.94 billion of the $2.5 billion that is owed them for a recovery rate of 78 percent. The junior unsecured debt holders will receive nothing.

(Continued)

> This type of analysis allows the investor to estimate the probability of recovery as well as perform sensitivity analysis by changing the estimated recovery rates for each of the different asset categories.

If we can estimate the likelihood that each of these four stages will govern a security's payoff and an estimate of the recovery rate each of these four stages, then we can develop an expected payoff for a distressed security.

Box 14-5 Expected Recovery

Thompson Robbins, Inc., is in distress but has not yet filed for Chapter 11 bankruptcy. It is in the process of contemplating a voluntary reorganization. You are looking at the junior unsecured debt and feel that the probability that the debt remains conforming is 20 percent, but there is a 50 percent likelihood of a voluntarily restructuring. There is also a 20 percent and 10 percent probability of a Chapter 11 reorganization and a Chapter 7 liquidation, respectively.

	Likelihood	Estimated Recovery Rate	Expected Recovery
Remain Performing	20%	100%	20%
Voluntary Restructuring	50%	70%	35%
Chapter 11 Reorganization	20%	30%	6%
Chapter 7 Liquidation	10%	0%	0%
			61%

The recovery rates in each of these four scenarios are 100, 70, 30, and 0 percent, respectively. By multiplying the likelihood by the recovery rate under each scenario and summing the products across the four scenarios, you estimate that the junior unsecured debt has an expected recovery rate of 61 percent. Applying a 30 percent margin of safety to this expectation would imply a justified purchase price of about $0.36 on the dollar for the strategic value investor.

Distressed investing is different from traditional value investing in part because security payoffs are often determined by unpredictable, idiosyncratic events, such as the whims of bankruptcy court or the posturing of various stakeholders, rather than general economic trends. That makes forecasting fundamentally different, as well as more difficult. For example, a bankruptcy court can unexpectedly alter the priority of payments. Alternatively, the collateral underlying secured debt could become unexpectedly compromised. An anticipated government bailout or corporate merger could unexpectedly fail to materialize. For these reasons, the strategic value investor should demand large margins of safety in distressed situations.

VALUATION MULTIPLES

In Chapter 11, we discussed valuation multiples at some length, focusing on the common equity multiples, such as the price-to-earnings and price-to-book ratios. These metrics relate the market price of the equity to an accounting measure of equity. In distressed investing situations, an appropriate relative valuation measure is an enterprise value approach because the equity by itself is likely to have little or no value.

Enterprise value (EV) equals the value of a company's debt plus the value of its equity. A commonly used earnings proxy is earnings before interest, taxes, depreciation, and amortization (EBITDA). The EV-to-EBITDA ratio equals:

$$Enterprise\ Value\text{–}to\text{-}EBITDA = \frac{Value\ of\ Debt + Value\ of\ Equity}{EBITDA}$$

A shortcoming of EBITDA is that it ignores the capital expenditures required to maintain the value of the assets going forward. It therefore overestimates the free cash flow that would be available to security holders over the long term. Free cash flow to the firm (FCFF) can be a better measure of the net sustainable cash flow to the firm. To estimate FCFF, it is necessary to deduct capital expenditures required to maintain the capital stock.[10]

$$Enterprise\ Value\text{–}to\text{-}FCFF = \frac{Value\ of\ Debt + Value\ of\ Equity}{EBITDA - Capital\ Expeditures}$$

In many cases, the depreciation recorded by a firm over, say, five years or more approximately equals the capital expenditures over the same period of time. If we can credibly make that assumption, then depreciation and capital expenditures should cancel each other out, and we can use a more simple measure of enterprise value–to–EBIT. EBIT is earnings before interest and tax, otherwise known as operating income.

$$Enterprise\ Value\text{–}to\text{–}Operating\ Income = \frac{Value\ of\ Debt + Value\ of\ Equity}{EBIT}$$

No matter which measure of cash flow or income we choose for the denominator, we want to be sure to make adjustments for nonrecurring noncash charges, such as restructuring charges. For example, when a company closes a production facility and lays off workers, they often take a one-time charge that recognizes the costs associated with that decision. If these charges are unlikely to recur, the analyst can add them back in to EBIT or EBITDA or add back the amortized value of these charges over the period to which they pertain. Noncash charges, such as write-downs of inventory or bad debt expense, should also be added back into earnings on a forward-looking basis.

Box 14-6 Valuation Multiples

Thompson Robbins, Inc., from the previous example, has an enterprise value of $3.54 billion, which is the expected liquidation value of its assets. (Recall that assets equal debt plus equity.) The firm's most recent income statement follows:

Sales	9,000
Cost of Goods Sold	5,000
Gross Margin	4,000
Operating Expenses	1,000
Depreciation	500
EBIT	2,500
Interest Expense	300
EBT	2,200
Tax Expense	880
Net Income	1,320

The firm's EBITDA is equal to $3 billion ($2.5 billion of EBIT plus $500 million of depreciation). Therefore, the enterprise value–to-EBITDA ratio is equal to $3.54 billion/$3 billion, or 1.18.

If its capital expenditures are equal to $400 million, then the enterprise value–to-FCFF ratio is equal to $3.54 billion/$2.6 billion, or 1.36. If capital expenditures and depreciation are likely to offset each other over the medium to long term, then the enterprise value–to–operating income ratio would provide a reasonable valuation relative to free cash flow to the firm and be equal to $3.54 billion/$2.5 billion, or 1.42.

Each of these valuation metrics can then be compared to other similar distressed situations. All else equal, lower valuation ratios are more attractive than higher ones. You can also use nondistressed companies in a similar industry as benchmarks, making a substantial margin of safety adjustment, such as 40 to 50 percent.

DEEP VALUE INVESTING

In Chapter 9, we introduced the concept of deep value investing. Deep value investors look for situations with a profound undervaluation, which often represent distressed situations. In these types of circumstances in which fear overwhelms greed, the share price may sometimes be less than the company's net working capital alone, after deducting all debt. Benjamin Graham discussed this in his seminal book, *The Intelligent Investor.*[11] These firms are selling at a price that enables the investor to pay essentially nothing for the fixed assets (any buildings, machinery, land, etc.) and any goodwill items that appear on the balance sheet. The metric sometimes used is the price-to-net working capital, or:

Price-to–Net Working Capital Ratio

$$= \frac{Price}{Current\ Assets - Current\ Liabilities - Long\text{-}Term\ Debt}$$

A firm is trading at a deep value if this ratio is less than one. An even deeper value situation occurs when the net cash ratio is less than one. Price-to–net cash ratio equals:

$$Price\text{-}to\text{-}Net\ Cash\ Ratio = \frac{Price}{Cash - Current\ Liabilities - Long\text{-}Term\ Debt}$$

Box 14-7 Application: Firms Selling at Less Than Net Working Capital Less Long-Term Debt

Although finding instances in which either of these ratios is less than one is certainly rare, it does indeed happen. In Chapter 9, we show that there were nine cases in 2012 in which firms were selling for less than their net working capital per share less debt.

	As of January 27, 2012					
Ticker	Name	Net Working Capital Per Share	Long-Term Debt Per Share	Short-Term Debt Per Share	NWC – LTD Per Share	Market Price
BSHI	Boss Holdings, Inc.	11.90	0.50	1.10	10.30	8.00
CXS	Crexus Investment Corp.	12.00	00.0	00.0	12.00	11.06
FLXS	Flexsteel Industries, Inc.	14.10	00.0	00.0	14.10	14.03
GENC	Gencor Industries, Inc.	9.40	00.0	00.0	9.40	7.17
MRINA	McRae Industries	14.80	00.0	00.0	14.80	13.05
MPAD	Micropac Industries, Inc.	6.50	00.0	00.0	6.50	5.10
OPST	OPT-Sciences Corp.	13.50	00.0	00.0	13.50	11.80
PARF	Paradise, Inc.	26.00	00.0	1.10	24.90	14.60
TNRK	TNR Technical, Inc.	12.70	00.0	00.0	12.70	10.79

Source: American Association of Individual Investors, Stock Investor Pro Database, February 28, 2012.

(*Continued*)

> As of this writing, those nine stocks had an average return of more than 25.5 percent over the subsequent 17 months—almost exactly equal to the return on the S&P 500 over the same time.

Tweedy, Browne; Wally Weitz; and Charles Brandes, who were profiled in Chapter 12, consider themselves deep value investors. Weitz doesn't necessarily look for firms that sell for less than net cash values, but rather looks for firms that sell at a deep discount: in excess of a 40 percent discount to his estimate of value.[12] Brandes uses margin of safety to measure market sentiment. In 2006 and 2007, he saw margins of safety of around 20 percent, which he views as relatively slim. In 2009, he saw margins of safety around 50 to 60 percent (sometimes as high as 80 percent), which were the highest that he had seen in his career.

Having a large margin of safety is critical for the average investor, who must make investments without the benefit of having control. Through his holding company, Berkshire Hathaway, Warren Buffett is a control investor who can afford to buy good companies at a good price. You, on the other hand, do not have the benefit of control and must manage your risk by demanding large margins of safety. Even with the luxury of control, Buffett strikes himself some pretty good deals.

WARREN BUFFETT AND "WEAPONS OF MASS DESTRUCTION"

In the Berkshire Hathaway 2002 annual report, Warren Buffett labeled options contracts "weapons of mass destruction," a quote that garnered a lot of attention at the time. Among other things, he said, "I view derivatives as time bombs, both for the parties that deal in them and the economic system."

Buffett was specifically worried about systemic economic risks associated with counterparty risk (e.g., the chance that one party to the contract defaults on their obligations) and the cascading effect it would have throughout the financial system. His comments were in some sense prescient.

Buffett's comments became all the more noteworthy after the onset of the global financial crisis in 2007 when he disclosed in the 2008 Berkshire Hathaway annual report that the firm sold $4.2 billion worth of put options on stock indices, including the S&P 500 and three international indices, with expiration dates between 2009 and 2027.

The buyer of a put option has the right to sell an asset to the seller of the put option at a specific price at some future date.[13] In this case, the asset is equivalent to a portfolio of stocks composing the S&P 500 or other stock index. Buyers of put options are often motivated by the desire to create "portfolio insurance." By buying the right to sell a portfolio of S&P 500 stocks for a specific price, they have guaranteed a minimum selling price for their portfolio in the event of a market crash.

The seller, on the other hand, is providing the insurance and will suffer a loss if the market price declines below the agreed-upon fixed price. If stock prices increase above the agreed-upon fixed-price, the seller of the put options pockets the premium that the buyer paid for the insurance. It's like purchasing homeowners insurance. If your house does not burn down, the insurance company keeps the premium without having to pay a claim.

In 2008, Buffett decided to use put options as a way to take advantage of the distressed investing environment rather than buying stocks outright. At the time, investors were reeling from the consequences of the financial crisis and worried about the stability of the financial system at large, and in March 2009 the S&P 500 hit a 10-year low. Buffett took advantage of this environment of fear by selling portfolio insurance (i.e., put options) to investors worried about purchasing downside protection for their portfolios.

Buffett justified the strategy of selling long-dated put options by arguing that the effects of inflation alone will tend to increase stock prices over such a long time frame. At an inflation rate of 2 percent over 100 years, one dollar grows to $7.24. Add to that the prospect that economic conditions were likely to improve at some point, and he concluded that there was less than a 1 percent chance that the put options would be exercised against him (i.e., obligate Berkshire Hathaway to reimburse the buyers of the put options for investment losses). In the meantime, he would have the $4.2 billion of option premiums to invest as he and Charlie Munger saw fit.

Since March 2009, the S&P 500 returned almost 150 percent, allowing Berkshire Hathaway to record a profit of $1.25 billion in 2012 alone. There are several things that make Buffett's put option play different from the distressed investment techniques we have discussed up to this point. First, Warren Buffett made a play on the distress in equity markets as a whole rather than on a single stock. In a sense, that is a much bolder move because Warren was making a statement about mispricing in the market as a whole rather than individual stock. Second, rather than an investment in high-yield or restructured debt of the reorganized company, Buffett used the equity markets.

Box 14-8 Application: Brilliance Is More Brilliant in Hindsight

Although it may seem obvious at the time of this writing (and most probably as of your reading) that selling portfolio insurance on stock market indexes in 2008 was an obviously brilliant call, bear in mind that the path to riches is almost never straight. That is as true for Warren Buffett as it is for the rest of us mere mortals.

(Continued)

At the end of 2008, Berkshire Hathaway recorded a $1.7 billion loss in their options positions. This fact highlights once again the difficulty not only of being a strategic value investor, but even more so of being an investor in distressed securities. Mispriced securities can often become more mispriced before they return to fundamental value. This truism makes it very difficult to execute a distressed investing strategy successfully.

Not only was Buffett a little bit early on his call about overall stock market levels, he was also early in predicting the rebound of the real estate market and as a result suffered interim losses for number of years before the real estate market began to return to health.

WARREN BUFFETT AND MORE "WEAPONS OF MASS DESTRUCTION"

Buffett developed other types of distressed investing strategies during the financial crisis, as well. In 2007, he began writing insurance on mortgage-backed securities (MBS). MBS are pools of mortgages. Like mutual fund investors, investors in MBS purchase a portion of the mortgage pool and receive cash flow as the mortgages are paid back. By pooling mortgages into a single security, investors diversify their credit risk over many borrowers, rather than being subject to the credit risk of a single borrower.

Real estate mortgages were obviously at the heart of the financial crisis in 2007. Although the repayment of many of these mortgages was insured by companies that accepted an insurance premium in exchange for reimbursing investors in the case of default, many of those insurers became financially unstable as a result of the many claims that were being made on their resources. Berkshire Hathaway stepped in to become a sort of insurer of last resort, ensuring repayment in the case of default if the primary insurer became sufficiently insolvent to do so themselves.

Buffett also invested indirectly in real estate by purchasing financial stocks, such as Wells Fargo and U.S. Bancorp, during the financial crisis. The loan portfolios of firms like these are more complicated than that of MBS, but Buffett saw opportunity in financial crisis carnage.

THE MIRROR IMAGE OF DISTRESS

Value investors not only buy solid underpriced assets with good fundamentals but they also sell short overpriced assets with poor fundamentals. This is the opposite of distressed investing but is founded on the same principles. Again, Buffett provides an example.

Since the onset of the financial crisis, investors have poured into fixed income securities with minimal credit risk, thereby pushing up the price and driving down the yields of these securities. The Federal Reserve and other central banks across the globe have exacerbated this situation by encouraging investors to invest in riskier assets by driving down the yields on government securities. As a result, government bonds have become very expensive, and government borrowing rates are at historic lows. In essence, the upside for government bonds is very low, and the downside is quite high. As a result, many investors view government bonds as fundamentally overvalued.

In May 2013, Berkshire Hathaway issued $1 billion of 5-year and 30-year debt as a way to short the bond market and sold a combined $2.5 billion since May 2012. Issuing bonds is the opposite of buying bonds. If one is inclined to buy bonds when yields are high, he or she should be inclined to sell bonds when yields are low.

John Paulson, founder of New York-based hedge fund Paulson & Co., famously shorted the housing market in the years leading up to the financial crisis. Although he was convinced that the housing market, and more specifically the subprime mortgage market, was grossly inflated, he was unsure how to develop an investment strategy to capitalize on it. It is not possible, for example, to short sell residential real estate.

He, too, lost millions of dollars initially before the wisdom of his analysis was borne out. Gregory Zuckerman even wrote a book on it, called *The Greatest Trade Ever.* Interestingly, the travails of the real estate market since then have caused him to take the opposite position in 2013. Somewhat like Buffett, he made substantial investments in several mortgage-backed securities insurers, such as MGIC Investment Corp, Radian Group, and Genworth Financial.

Box 14-9 Application: Brilliance Is Sometimes Less Clear in Hindsight

Lest you think that distressed investing is easy, John Paulson made distressed investments in Bank of America and Citigroup during 2011. These investments did not pay off. The value of his flagship hedge fund, Paulson Advantage Fund, fell by 40 percent in the year ended September 2011. Fortunately for him, he invested his personal wealth in gold and made $3.1 billion during that timeframe.

Buffett, on the other hand, has always viewed gold as a speculative investment, arguing that it has little underlying fundamental value because it does not generate any future cash flows other than the prospect of potential price appreciation. Buffett makes his point this way. The world's gold stock is about 170,000 metric tons which, if all melded together, would create a cube of about 68 feet per side worth $9.6 trillion. For that much money, one could buy all the cropland in the United States, 16 Exxon Mobils (the world's most profitable company), and have about $1 trillion of "walking-around money" left over. Which would you rather have, all that or a giant cube of metal?

As compelling is that argument is, Buffett has watched the price of gold rise from approximately $400 per ounce to a high of about $1,900 per ounce over a 10-year period. As of this writing, gold is trading at about $1,400 per ounce.

CONCLUSION

Christopher Browne of Tweedy, Browne sums up distressed investing well, saying "To buy deep value takes a lot of courage, because it looks really ugly. The companies are cheap because there are a lot of bad stories out there."[14]

Many of the principles are the same as value investing generally. However, distressed value investing takes stronger resolve, and there are some significant differences. For example, the outcomes are often based on idiosyncratic decisions of individuals or bankruptcy courts rather than long-term trends. In those situations, distressed investing can be more akin to speculation than investing. The disciplined investor who is willing to buck conventional wisdom and rely on the weight of his or her analysis, however, stands to profit handsomely.

CHAPTER FIFTEEN

APPLYING VALUE INVESTING TO THE MARKET

Investors with no knowledge of (or concern for) profits, dividends, valuation or the conduct of business simply cannot possess the resolve needed to do the right thing at the right time.

—Howard Marks

Throughout this book we have included many examples of how value investing is applied in practice. We have discussed why you should embrace value investing; how to evaluate economies, industries, and companies; how to value stocks of those companies; and how to define your unique personal value investing style and select valuation models that are appropriate to that style. In this chapter we take these applications a bit further by addressing how you can identify value stocks that fit your style or the style of a particular well-known value investor you admire and wish to emulate. For investors who prefer to use pooled investment vehicles, we also show how you can apply the principles in this book to mutual funds, ETFs, and investments in separately managed accounts. We also summarize the major steps involved in strategic value investing.

IDENTIFYING VALUE STOCKS

There are tens of thousands of potential stock investments available to investors. No investor has time to evaluate all of them, so you need to have methods of identifying small numbers of potentially good value stocks for which you can perform the necessary due diligence and valuation. Recall from Chapter 4 that there are both top-down and bottom-up approaches to analysis. In the top-down approach, you first forecast the economy, and then select industries which will likely perform well, and finally select the best value companies in the industry. In a bottom-up approach, you first identify the individual securities of interest, and then evaluate how they are expected to perform in the future economy. There are three common methods of identifying potential value stocks whether you start with a top-down or bottom-up approach. You can choose to peruse financial publications for stocks that appear to be good companies trading at good prices, for example, reviewing publications like *Barron's* each week. The April 20, 2013 edition of *Barron's* featured an article titled "Chiquita Brands Has Appeal," documenting that Chiquita Brands' stock is down 40 percent yet is forecasted to produce $30 million in free cash flow going forward. This is a stock for which you can pull the financial statements, analyze them, and perform your own independent valuation using the techniques presented in this book.

Cover stories are commonly believed to be a contrarian indicator. A 2007 study in the *Financial Analysts Journal* looked at the investment performance of stocks that were the subject of cover stories from *BusinessWeek*, *Fortune*, and *Forbes* over a 20-year period from 1983 to 2002. Although positive cover stories follow periods of positive performance, and negative cover stories follow periods of negative performance, performance following publication (after adjusting for market movements, size, and industry effects) tends to be normal, for the most part.[1] That said, there is some evidence that companies that secure naming rights for major league sports stadiums exhibit poor subsequent performance. (Think Enron, MCI WorldCom, TWA, and US Airways).

Another option is to look at well-known value investors to see what they are buying (and selling) and perform your own due diligence on those stocks. Lastly, you can subscribe to a financial database or use an online service to screen large numbers of stocks to identify those that have characteristics of value stocks on which you can perform due diligence. Realize that these three methods outlined here are not mutually exclusive, but, in fact, are complementary.

Recall in Chapter 12 that we provided the value investing styles of some prominent and successful value investors. Table 15-1 summarizes some of the factors these investors focus on. This list provides a good starting point for factors to use when reading financial publications or screening databases for attractive stocks.

TABLE 15-1

Factors of Interest for Successful Value Investors

Value Investor	Factors of Interest
Ben Graham	Large companies, high liquidity, low debt, positive and stable earnings, moderate P/E (15 or less), moderate P/B (1.5 or less).
Warren Buffett	Large companies, high-quality management, economic pricing power. Buffett holds a more concentrated portfolio than many.
Seth Klarman	Often holds large amounts of cash and invests in value securities of all types (not just stocks), looks for large margin of safety (significant discounts).

Bill Ruane	Companies in sectors with strong revenue growth and improving margins, large companies, strong management, quality at the right price.
John Neff	Low P/E ratio (40 to 60 percent below the market), earnings growth over 7 percent (but below 20 percent to avoid risk), good dividend yield desirable, total return (dividend yield plus earnings growth) double the P/E ratio, solid companies in growing fields, strong fundamentals (cash flow, ROE, etc.).
Tweedy, Browne Company LLC	Holds a widely diversified portfolio, limits individual companies to 4 percent of portfolio, limits each industry to 15 percent of portfolio.
Wally Weitz	Strong cash generation (free cash flow), deep discounts (40 percent to intrinsic value), all capitalizations.
Charles Brandes	Deep value, small capitalization companies, strong performance.
Bill Miller	Strong franchise value, good margin of safety.

MONITORING VALUE INVESTOR ACTIVITY

Finding value stocks held by prominent value investors is relatively easy. Public companies and investment management companies are required to file periodic reports with regulators. For example, in the United States they are required to file reports with the Securities and Exchange Commission. Relevant filings include:

- Form 13F Quarterly Report of institutional money managers (managing over $100 million in securities) listing their holdings at that point in time.
- Form 13D or 13G Report required to be filed within 10 days by anyone who purchases more than 5 percent of a public company. Subsequently must also report any additional transactions aggregating 1 percent.
- Form 10K Annual Report required of any public company (for example, Berkshire Hathaway) that typically has a discussion of major purchases.
- Form 10Q Quarterly Report required of any public company.

These filings can be obtained in a search of the SEC's EDGAR database (http://www.sec.gov/edgar/searchedgar/webusers.htm).

For example, a search for Berkshire Hathaway filings on April 21, 2013, revealed the most recent form 13F filed on February 14, 2013. This form lists all of the holdings of Berkshire as of that date. This list can be perused for stocks you might consider investigating further. You can also compare this list to the previous 13F filing to identify any recent purchases or sales. The same search also turned up a Form 13D for Bill Gates and related entities on their significant holdings in Berkshire stock.

Rather than search the EDGAR database yourself, you can also subscribe to services that monitor SEC filings and present the information to you in an easily accessible manner.

Box 15-1 Application: Value Investor Database

GuruFocus (www.gurufocus.com) is an online subscription service that tracks the ownership, purchases, and sales of prominent value investors as well as company insiders. Suppose that you view the database on April 21, 2013, to obtain information on Tweedy, Browne. The database shows that Tweedy, Browne has 59 holdings and seven recent purchases. All holdings and purchases are listed. You note that its largest holding is Johnson & Johnson (JNJ) and their most recent purchase is UniFirst Corporation (UNF). You decide to perform your own due diligence on these two stocks. As a first pass, you can look at these companies on GuruFocus, which identifies other value investors who may also hold these stocks as well as any recent insider activity. You review UNF and find that it is also held by another prominent value investor, Joel Greenblatt of Gotham Capital, who also recently purchased it. Unfortunately, the same database indicates some recent sales of company stocks by insiders (including the CEO). Before proceeding further, you might investigate the reasons for these sales and what percent of their holdings were sold. In this case, the CEO sold two thousand shares out of his holdings of approximately three million shares, so it is likely that this sale was motivated by diversification reasons.

SCREENING FOR VALUE

Another method of identifying potential value stocks for further analysis is to screen databases for stocks with attractive features such as those listed in Table 15-1 above. If you are starting with a top-down approach, then you can limit your screens to stocks in those industries you expect to do well in the future economic environment. Online stock screeners are abundant—well-known and popular screeners include Yahoo! Finance, Google Finance, Morningstar, and Finviz. Some of these services are free, while others require a subscription. You can also subscribe to commercial databases through Bloomberg, Thomson Reuters, S&P, Capital IQ, and others. The commercial databases typically have many more search fields, such as historical ratios, rather than just being limited to current period ratios. Other databases are designed for individual investors, such as Stock Investor Pro from the American Association of Individual Investors or screeners available on GuruFocus (mentioned above). Some of these databases have predefined screens you can use; in addition to those you can create your own.

Box 15-2 Application: Predefined Value Screens— GuruFocus

GuruFocus has a predefined screen called the Buffett-Munger screener which screens for:

- Companies that have high predictability rank, that is, companies that can consistently grow revenue and earnings.
- Companies that have competitive advantages, that is, firms that can maintain or even expand profit margins while growing the business.
- Companies that incur little debt while growing business.
- Companies that are fairly valued or undervalued. They use PEPG as indicator. PEPG is the P/E ratio divided by the average growth rate of EBITDA over the past five years.

You can narrow down the screen by market capitalization. Running this screen on April 21, 2013, yields 18 S&P 500 stocks that meet the Buffett-Munger Screen. These include Apple, PetSmart, and Danaher Corporation, among others. This screen narrows down the universe of stocks to a manageable number for further detailed analysis.

Box 15-3 Predefined Value Screens: Stock Investor Pro

Stock Investor Pro has a wide variety of predefined screens. One is a Free Cash Flow screen that identifies stocks with positive free cash flow and low price-to–free cash flow multiples. Running this screen on April 21, 2013, yielded 221 stocks out of the database of over 9,000 stocks. Representative firms meeting this screen were Apple, ABM Industries, and Quest Diagnostics, among others. The Stock Investor Pro database also includes screens based on the techniques of well-known value investors such as Ben Graham and John Neff.

Some databases permit you to create both custom screens and custom ratios. You can use the ratios in this book to create your own stock screens to identify stocks for further analysis.

Box 15-4 Custom Value Screen: Stock Investor Pro

You subscribe to the Stock Investor Pro database and in mid 2013 create custom ratios and screens to search for companies with low forward P/E ratios (price/next year's earnings forecast of less than 10 times), high cash flow yield (cash flow yield of over 20 percent computed as average operating cash flow

(Continued)

divided by current price for one-, three-, and five-year periods), operating cash flow exceeds net income and dividend yield in excess of 3 percent. Your screen reveals eight stocks for further analysis:

Ticker	Company
AYR	Aircastle Limited
AM	American Greetings Corporation
CEL	Cellcom Israel Ltd.
IMKTA	Ingles Markets, Inc.
LXK	Lexmark International, Inc.
MFI	MicroFinancial Inc.
PBI	Pitney Bowes, Inc.
WCRX	Warner Chilcott Plc

AVOIDING VALUE TRAPS

Often companies trade at low prices because they deserve it. For example, a firm may be in a declining industry and future earnings and cash flow will likely decline. The current price may appear attractive based on past earnings or cash flow, but the firm may actually be overpriced due to estimated low future cash flows. Unfortunately, this may not become evident immediately. Such stocks are aptly named *value traps*, and many value investors are drawn to them because they appear to be inexpensive. The key to avoiding value traps is not to focus merely on cheap prices. As a strategic value investor, you want to find good companies selling at attractive prices; however, you do not want one without the other. Look for companies with sound fundamentals (strong earnings, cash flow, ROE, financial position, etc.; see Chapter 5) and good future prospects (good products in a sound industry that will likely perform well in the expected economic conditions; see Chapter 4). Then it is incumbent upon you to perform an independent valuation of the company given your future forecasts (see Chapters 6 through 11).

ASSET PRICE BUBBLES

Recall the discussion from Chapter 1 when we cautioned you on speculation versus investment. This book is about investing, not speculating; however, there are many investors who from time to time do speculate. Speculation, or simply extreme optimism, can result in assets, including stocks, increasing in price such that the market or some segment of the market sells at unreasonably high prices relative to fundamental values. In extreme cases, a speculative frenzy erupts, where each new investor wants to get in on the action so badly that he or she keeps paying ever higher prices and an asset bubble is created. Recall our tulipmania example from Chapter 1. Other notable bubbles include the South Sea Company bubble in the 1700s,[2] the railway mania in the 1840s, the roaring twenties stock-market bubble, the Internet bubble of the late 1990s, and the more recent U.S. real estate bubble. The inevitable result is that the asset bubble bursts and prices plummet. As a strategic value investor, you want to avoid participating in the frenzy, and, if possible, to position yourself to take advantage of any subsequent market correction or crash. If you see a bubble developing (very high market price multiples and very few, if any, value stocks to buy) you should consider trimming holdings that have increased in value and holding cash to purchase assets that become distressed.[3] After the recent market crash in real estate, banking, and mortgage-backed securities, Warren Buffett stepped in and put some of Berkshire's money to work, relying on his conviction that "you want to be greedy when others are fearful, you want to be fearful when others are greedy."

COMBINING TECHNICAL WITH FUNDAMENTAL ANALYSIS

In this book we have been primarily concerned with examining a company's fundamentals (earnings, cash flow, financial position, products, and the like) and determining the intrinsic value of a stock using various valuation methods. This is classic fundamental analysis as espoused by Ben Graham (adapted for modern analysis and valuation techniques). We view fundamental analysis as critically important and central to investing. Technical analysis primarily focuses on price and value data gleaned from stock trading activity. We advise you to consider technical analysis as an add-on or supplement to fundamental analysis. Technical analysis has its limitations and will certainly not help you determine intrinsic value, but it may help guide you about the market consensus regarding a security. As such, technical analysis can be used as a complement to fundamental analysis and can help you identify and avoid price bubbles, identify out of favor stocks, and time buy and sell decisions. While there are many technical indicators used by market technicians (some were discussed in Chapter 4), we will focus on a few technical patterns that may be helpful.

Support and Oversold Conditions

Support is a price level at which a stock seems to stop falling and pauses. Often the stock price rebounds from this level. What might cause this price behavior? Let's say you are an investor with a strong interest in a particular stock. The stock price falls to $10 per share from $14, and it is now trading at an attractive price. But, for whatever reason, you decide not to buy it. The price goes up a couple of dollars per share, and you regret not having bought it at $10. What might you do the next time it falls to $10? There is a pretty good chance you would step

F I G U R E   15-1

Technical chart of Microsoft.

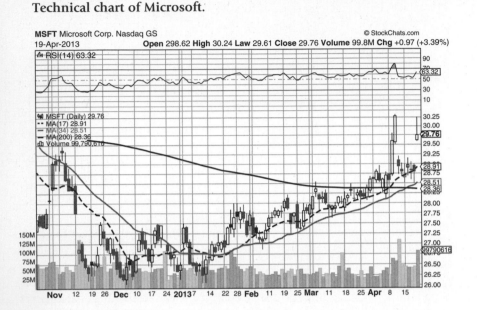

MSFT Microsoft Corp. Nasdaq GS   © StockChats.com
19-Apr-2013   **Open** 298.62 **High** 30.24 **Law** 29.61 **Close** 29.76 **Volume** 99.8M **Chg** +0.97 (+3.39%)

in and buy it if you still like the stock. The aggregate behavior of investors may create just such a price pattern. (See a recent chart of Microsoft as presented in Figure 15-1.) Figure 15-1 is a candlestick chart, with the price action in the middle, volume information and dates at the bottom, and a technical indicator (RSI) at the top.[4] Note that on several occasions Microsoft's stock price fell to approximately $26.25 and stopped or slightly rebounded. This appears to be an area of support for Microsoft's stock. Support levels can help a value investor identify entry points for a stock (at what price to buy).

Another feature of this chart is the RSI (Relative Strength Indicator). This is a momentum indicator that looks at the speed and rate of change of price movements. A value of 30 or below indicates a stock appears oversold and might be a buying opportunity. A value of 70 or above indicates the stock might be overbought and could be pulled back. Notice the RSI fell to 30 at about the same time Microsoft's stock fell to $26.25—another indication this may be an attractive entry point. Note the more recent price run up, when the price jumped to $30 and RSI spiked above 70. It appears the market got ahead of itself and pulled back.

If a firm releases news that does not meet or exceed market expectations, the market often reacts negatively and to a greater extent than necessary.[5] This is indicated by an oversold indication and a lower than justified price, which may be near a support level. These are often opportunities to buy good value stocks at reasonable (in effect, bargain) prices.

Resistance and Overbought Conditions

In technical terms, the opposite situation to support is resistance. This is a level at which a stock seems to stop rising and either stabilizes or retreats. We can see some resistance to Microsoft's price at $27.50 in the November to January time frame in the candlestick chart presented above. Each time the stock reached $27.50, it appeared to hit resistance and fall back. In February and March the stock seemed to test this resistance level and eventually broke through. Sometimes the former resistance level will become a support level. Note that there appears to be some new resistance at the $30 price level—the same level at which RSI signals an oversold condition.

If you are interested in buying a stock that appears to be at a resistance level, then you may want to watch the stock a bit before buying. If you own a stock that consistently hits a resistance level, then you should verify your valuation and your comfort that there is still a good margin of safety present. If these conditions don't hold, you might consider selling at these levels.

Similarly, an overbought indicator may be a sign that the market for stock has overheated. If this continues, a price bubble may form and you may want to stay away until a better buying opportunity presents itself.

We caution you about getting carried away with technical analysis. It is often the case that perusing charts will tell you a great deal about the past yet provide you with little information about the future.

PUTTING IT ALL TOGETHER

Strategic value investing is not just about finding inexpensive stocks, it is about being deliberate and calculated in identifying good companies selling at attractive prices. You need to approach value investing as if you were acquiring a business enterprise in its entirety, as essentially you are becoming an owner of an operating business. You should understand the business and evaluate how the business is expected to do in the current and future economic environment. The following are essential components of strategic value investing, although the order in which they are performed may differ depending upon your approach (for example top-down versus bottom-up):

- Identify potential value stocks (using a top-down approach, through financial publications, by monitoring other value investors, or through screening). Chapters 4, 12, 13, and 15.
- Analyze the state of the economy and its future trajectory and evaluate how the industry will likely perform in that economic environment. Chapters 4 and 6.
- Perform a fundamental analysis of the company. Chapters 5 and 6.

- Value the company, determining its intrinsic value and margin of safety. Chapters 7 through 11.
- Time your buys and sells based on market conditions for those companies that have a good margin of safety (the higher the margin of safety the less emphasis you have to place on timing; just buy). Chapter 15.

USING POOLED INVESTMENT VEHICLES

Selecting individual stocks is time-consuming. However, you can still be a value investor using pooled investment vehicles such as mutual funds and ETFs (exchange traded mutual funds). This permits you to capture the return on value stocks shown in earlier chapters and remain diversified. On the other hand, because you are subcontracting some of your work to others expect to pay for the work done for you by others. If you select index mutual funds or ETFs, the price you will pay can be quite small, while actively managed funds will be priced to compensate active managers for their time and effort.

Index Funds

There has been quite a proliferation of index funds (both mutual funds and exchanged traded funds) these days and they come in a variety of flavors. You can invest in an overall index (of varying capitalization sizes), an industry, the growth segment of an index, the value segment of the index, and virtually any other slice of an index. As a value investor, you want to go for the value slice of an index or the industry slice you view as the most attractive value. Cost matters, and what might seem a low expense ratio can cost you significantly over a long period of time, so pay particular attention to the expenses embedded within a fund. Fortunately, the market for index funds has become quite competitive these days, and expense ratios have declined significantly over time.

Box 15-5 Application: Selecting Index Funds

You would like to invest in large capitalization equities and want to take a value approach. You examine several funds offered by Vanguard, the location of your retirement account (we could have just as easily selected Fidelity, another good choice for index funds). The following are two of the many funds available to your retirement account:

Fund	Vanguard 500 Index Fund Signal	Vanguard Value Index Signal
Ticker	VIFSX	VVISX
Target	S&P 500 Index (Large-Cap)	Large-Cap Value

1-Year Return	13.93%	16.87%
3-Year Average Return	12.65%	12.11%
5-Year Average Return	5.83%	4.75%
10-Year Average Return	NA	NA
Expense Ratio	0.05%	0.10%
P/E Ratio (Underlying Stocks)	13.25	11.83
P/B Ratio	2.02	1.45
P/S Ratio	1.31	1.08
P/CF Ratio	7.12	5.64
Dividend Yield	2.26%	2.92%

Data from Morningstar as of April 27, 2013

These two funds have been around for more than five years but less than 10, hence a 10-year history is not available. The value fund selects those large-cap stocks trading at the lowest multiples in the index, a very mechanical process. The fund does not perform other fundamental analysis or screening; nor is it designed to, as it is an index fund. Although for the five-year period the value fund slightly underperformed the overall index, this is not unexpected (as noted throughout this book, value investors must be patient, as the value strategy often underperforms the market and other strategies during various time periods).

In using value index funds, you can limit your economic analysis to whether you feel the environment is attractive for stocks. If you are willing to delve further and analyze which industries are likely to do well in the current economic environment, you can take a value approach to investing in sector funds.

Box 15-6 Application: Selecting Sector ETFs

You have an interest in finding funds or sectors that are undervalued relative to the S&P 500 index and plan to invest using iShares ETFs. You collect the following information from the iShares website.

ETF Ticker	IVV	IVE	IYE
Focus	S&P 500	S&P 500 Value	U.S. Energy
Largest Industry	Information Tech – 17.4%	Financials – 23.1%	NA
Second-Largest Industry	Financials 16.07%	Energy – 14.91%	NA
1-Year Return	13.90%	16.43%	10.53%

(Continued)

3-Year Average	12.58%	11.92%	12.47%
5-Year Average	5.76%	3.95%	2.58%
10-Year Average	8.46%	8.72%	14.65%
P/E Ratio	21.09	19.38	16.98
P/B Ratio	3.99	2.94	2.38
Expense Ratio	0.07%	0.18%	0.47%

Here we see with 10 years of data, the value slice of the S&P 500 slightly outperformed the entire S&P 500 (after expenses). You could invest in the value fund, but notice this fund has over weighted energy stocks. So, you pull up the iShares energy ETF and find that sector is indeed undervalued relative to the broader index. However, the energy fund has a higher expense ratio and would be less diversified. As with any investment, you should carefully review the economic environment, particularly when looking at an industry focused fund.

Active Funds

Another approach is to select an active manager who follows a value philosophy. These managers may run mutual funds or may operate separately managed accounts for individual investors. Active management is time consuming because you, the manager, must perform all of the fundamental analysis and valuation you would otherwise be doing yourself. In selecting value managers you should seek those that have a long history of strong performance and who charge reasonable expense ratios. You can find such managers by screening databases such as Morningstar. Learn as much as you can about the manager and, if possible, interview a manager to learn his or her value investing philosophy and processes using the techniques described in this book to make sure this style reflects your own beliefs and that his or her processes are sound. Investigate the manager's experience, education, and professional certifications, such as the CFA (Chartered Financial Analyst) designation. Studies have shown that all these factors tend to be positively correlated with manager skill and positively related to performance.

Box 15-7 Application: Selecting Active Value Managers

You examine the Morningstar database for some of the prominent value investors mentioned in this book and find two funds. Data from Morningstar is extracted below with an S&P 500 Index fund for comparison.

Fund	Fidelity Spartan 500	Weitz Value Fund	Tweedy Browne Value
Ticker	FUSEX	WVALX	TWEBX
Target	S&P 500 Index	Large-Cap Blend	Large-Cap Blend
1-Year Return	13.88%	17.20%	17.24%
3-Year Average Return	12.59%	14.01%	9.61%
5-Year Average Return	5.76%	7.13%	6.86%
10-Year Average Return	8.46%	7.35%	8.00%
15-Year Average Return	4.17%	6.58%	4.90%
Expense Ratio	0.03%	1.00%	1.25%
P/E Ratio	13.86	16.89	12.52
P/B Ratio	1.98	2.32	1.60
P/S Ratio	1.32	1.32	1.06
P/CF Ratio	6.70	6.96	7.57
Dividend Yield	2.29%	1.21%	2.38%

Data from Morningstar as of April 27, 2013

Note that over the longest time frame (15 years) both value managers have outperformed the S&P 500. Interestingly, Morningstar classified both of these funds as blends between value and growth. This seems quite appropriate for the Weitz fund given the higher multiples relative to the S&P 500. Remember, though, a low multiple is not the only indicator of a value approach. You are looking for good companies selling at discounts to their intrinsic value. Sometimes these stocks might be trading at multiples that make them look like growth stocks (growth at a reasonable price).

CONCLUSION

Early in this book we showed why you should be a value investor: Over the long term, value wins. You can improve your performance by not being merely a value investor who buys inexpensive stocks but by being a strategic value investor who seeks to find good companies in industries expected to do well that are selling at discounts to their intrinsic value. There are no shortcuts or magic formulas in strategic value investing. You need to do your homework to evaluate the fundamentals of the company, its business, and industry. You also need to make many judgments about the future and use these judgments as inputs into a valuation model to assess the intrinsic value and margin of safety for every investment you make. Above all, you need to have confidence in your convictions and remain patient. Value investors often will lose the battle (the short run) but win the war (the long run). Happy hunting!

N O T E S

CHAPTER 1

1. That said, a relatively recent study by controversial *Freakonomics* author Steven Levitt and Thomas Miles refutes the argument that winners and losers in poker are determined purely by chance. Levitt and Miles demonstrate that poker players that have done well in previous poker tournaments tend to do well in subsequent poker tournaments, earning a 30.5 percent return on investment versus a 15.6 percent loss for ordinary players. We know of no study that documents this kind of systematic performance differential among mutual fund managers.

2. Graham's vision would ultimately happen in the form of the Chartered Financial Analyst (CFA) designation—the gold standard of credentials in the investment profession and a program in which the authors have been intimately involved.

CHAPTER 2

1. Arbitrage is the practice of simultaneously buying an asset at a relatively low price in one market and selling the same or a very similar asset at a relatively higher price in another market, with the expectation that the two prices will converge. An arbitrageur, who executes these trades, hopes to profit by the amount of the price differential.

2. Technically, Fama and French look at the book-to-market (BE/ME) value of equity, which is the inverse of P/B. We just reverse the interpretation of the figures. The motivation for using BE/ME is to make sense of firms with negative or zero book values. In these cases, P/B has no meaning, but BE/ME retains its meaning. We discuss the concept using P/B because it is more intuitive and more consistent with the vernacular of investment professionals.

3. If we start off with $100 and lose 50 percent, we have $50 after one year. If we earn a positive 50 percent return on the $50 in the second year, then we only have $75 after the second year for a –25 percent two-year return. The arithmetic expression is $100(1 - 0.50) \times (1 + 0.50) = \$75$. We need a 100 percent return in the second year to get back to even.

4. The statistical term for a return distribution with relatively "fat tails" is *platokurtotic*.

5. The statistical term for a return distribution with relatively "thin tails" is *mesokurtotic*.

6. Because the time period under study here is so much shorter and the figures so much more modest, we use a traditional scale on the Y-axis rather than a logarithmic scale.

7. Interestingly, there is a similar difference among small-cap value and growth stocks in that year using definitions proposed by Ibbotson Associates. But the numbers are quite different. This highlights that our definition of value and growth can produce very different results. We will discuss this more fully in Chapter 5.

8. The concept of beta was first developed in the early- to mid-1960s and occupies a central place in modern portfolio theory.

CHAPTER 3

1. See Remolona, Kleiman, and Grunstein (1997) and Boyer and Zheng (2009).

2. For example, Kim (2010).

3. For example, Chevalier and Ellison (1997) and Sirri and Tufano (1998).

4. Bailey, Kumar, and Ng (2011).

5. Odean (1999).

6. For example, Del Guercio and Tkac (2002), Geotzmann, Ingersoll, and Ross (2003), Agarawal, Daniel, and Naik (2004), Baquero and Verbeek (2009), Ding, Getmansky, Liang, and Wermers (2009), Kaplan and Schoar (2005), Robinson and Sensoy (2013), Phalippou (2010), Hanson and Sunderman (2013).

7. For example, Bailey, Kumar, and Ng (2011).

8. For example, Barber and Odean (2001).

9. Arnold, Earl, and North (2007).

10. Both sides of the trade need not be profitable for arbitrage strategy to be successful. If the fair value of the two similar securities decreases below the purchase price of the long position, the arbitrageur will lose money on the long position. This loss will be more than offset by the profit on the short position. Similarly, if the fair value of the two similar securities increases above the selling price of the short position, the arbitrageur will lose money on the short position. This loss will be more than offset by the profit on the long position, however.

11. This implication is what gives this situation the name "negative-stub-value."

12. Shleifer and Vishny (1997) develop a model that shows that arbitrage can become ineffective when prices diverge far from fundamental value.

13. §404(a)(1)(b) of ERISA.

14. In case you are wondering, the girlfriend never really bought into the sunk cost idea. The relationship didn't last long after that.

15. Zweig (2007) and Peterson (2007).

16. Kahneman (2011).

17. Kahneman (2011) and Adler (2009).

18. Barber and Odean (2000).

CHAPTER 4

1. Warren Buffett, Letter to Berkshire Hathaway shareholders, February 28, 2005, p. 4.

2. Warren Buffett, Letter to Berkshire Hathaway shareholders, February 27, 2009, p. 5.

3. www.cboe.com.

4. David B. Bostian Jr., "The Nature of Effective Forecasts," in *Improving the Investment Decision Process Better Use of Economic Inputs in Securities Analysis and Portfolio Management*, Association for Investment Management and Research, 1992, pp. 5–12.

5. Michael E. Porter, "How Competitive Forces Shape Strategy," *Harvard Business Review*, March/April 1979. A concise summary of Porter's five competitive forces can be found at Michael E. Porter, "The Five Competitive Forces That Shape Strategy," *Harvard Business Review*, January 2008, pp. 78–93.

6. Benjamin Graham and Jason Zweig, *The Intelligent Investor: The Definitive Book on Value Investing*, New York: Collins Business Essentials, 2003, p. 7.

7. Elizabeth Collins, Paul Larson, and Warren Miller, "Introducing a New Source of Economic Moats: Efficient Scale," Morningstar, 2011.

CHAPTER 5

1. Portions of this chapter were adapted from *Financial Statement Analysis: A Global Approach*, Thomas R. Robinson, Paul Munter, and Julia Grant, 2003, with permission.

2. To quote Everett Dirksen: "A billion here, a billion there, and pretty soon you're talking about real money."

3. Hey, you knew those footnotes were there for a reason.

4. EBITDA is calculated as EBIT + Depreciation + Amortization.

5. For more on this topic see Howard Schilit and Jeremy Perler, *Financial Shenanigans*, New York: McGraw-Hill, 2010.

CHAPTER 6

1. Gerald E. Pinto, Elaine Henry, Thomas R. Robinson, and John D. Stowe, *Equity Asset Valuation* 2nd ed., CFA Institute, Hoboken, NJ: Wiley, 2010.

2. The great American philosopher and Hall of Fame baseball player Yogi Berra once said, "You better cut the pizza in four pieces because I'm not hungry enough to eat six." This same analysis applies to a company's decision to enact stock splits. If a company splits the stock 2 for 1, each investor still owns the same percentage of the company. They have, in effect, more slices, but their percentage of the pie is identical before and after the split.

3. Recognize, however, that stocks could be in the 95th percentile because their earnings are uncharacteristically low for the past 12 months. For example, a firm could have an unusually high P/E ratio because nonrecurring losses were realized.

4. Some firms, such as Berkshire Hathaway, have never paid a dividend. And Berkshire shareholders are happy that Buffett has retained the earnings and not made dividend payments.

5. One example of many is the case of EasyLink Services Corporation, which entered into barter arrangements for advertising on its websites. In exchanging advertising, the value of which could be overstated, the company showed higher revenue (and higher expenses) and touted the increasing revenue in its press releases. EasyLink was subject to enforcement action by the U.S. Securities and Exchange Commission for these activities.

CHAPTER 7

1. Gordon was professor emeritus of finance at the Rotman School of Management, University of Toronto.

2. The model was actually developed independently by Sharpe, Jack Treynor, Jan Mossin, and John Lintner. Sharpe is generally given the credit for the model, as he did the most to develop its applications.

3. Markowitz is the father of modern portfolio theory and was the first to quantitatively demonstrate the diversification benefits of holding assets in a portfolio and how risk is properly measured in a portfolio context and not in isolation.

4. Alternatively, some would argue that the market risk premium should be determined by using the return on short-term U.S. Treasury bills as the appropriate risk-free rate. If one used the T-bill as the risk-free proxy, the market risk premium would be 8.2 percent (11.9–3.7). Again, there is no "right" or "wrong" method, simply variations on a theme.

5. P. Brett Hammond, Jr. and Martin L. Leibowitz, "Rethinking the Equity Risk Premium: An Overview and Some New Ideas," pp. 1–17 in *Rethinking the Equity Risk Premium*, edited by P. Brett Hammond Jr., Martin L. Leibowitz, and Laurence B. Siegel, Charlotte, VA: Research Foundation of CFA Institute, 2011.

6. The calculation methodology for determining the β of a stock is regression analysis, most commonly performed by using monthly data over a three- or five-year period. There are many different calculations of β, but most estimates are very similar. Suffice it to say, one does not need to understand how a β is calculated to use it in determining an appropriate discount rate.

CHAPTER 8

1. Future free cash flow not distributed to shareholders increases future share price (assuming the market believes that management will not frivolously waste it in other ways).

CHAPTER 9

1. See Jim Rinehart, "U.S. Timberland Post-Recession: Is It the Same Asset?" *R&A Investment Forestry*, 2010.

2. "Canadian Regulators Order Sino-Forest Executives to Resign," *New York Times Deal Book*, August 26, 2011.

3. See Ye Xie and Nikolaj Gammeltoft, "Muddy Waters Losing Support in Stock Market," *Bloomberg News*, February 28, 2012.

4. Sometimes you will see this referred to as a price-to-book (P/B) ratio or market value–to-book (MV/BV) ratio. Don't be confused, as this is simply the reciprocal of the BV/MV ratio. In the case of price-to-book, a value investor would look for firms selling at relatively low P/B ratios.

5. It is quite interesting that Dr. Fama developed the efficient market hypothesis and then proceeded to publish numerous academic studies that provided evidence refuting the theory. In fact, the EMH has spawned an entire cottage industry of academic articles and practitioner-oriented money management processes that rely on so-called EMH anomalies.

6. Fama and French also provided evidence in support of the so-called "small firm effect." That is, even after controlling for differential risk levels, small firms outperform large firms.

7. An additional screen of a selling price of at least $5/share was added to eliminate the inclusion of any "penny stocks."

8. See Tobin (1969).

9. Available at http://www.federalreserve.gov/releases/z1/. Note that historical data needed to estimate Tobin's q is also available on the St. Louis FRED website.

10. Chart available at Vectorgrader.com.

11. Charles Mead and Andrew Frye, "Paulson's Math Seen Failing as Hartford Financial Weighs Breakup: Real M&A," *Bloomberg News*, February 17, 2012.

12. As an aside, investment bankers made money by combining the firms and then breaking them up. Nice work if you can get it.

13. An interview with Tom Gayner is in the June 30, 2011 issue of *Value Investor Insight*.

14. Buffett himself has said that "The business schools reward difficult complex behavior more than simple behavior, but simple behavior is more effective."

15. See http://gregspeicher.com/?p=2891.

16. Benjamin Graham, *The Intelligent Investor*, 4th rev. ed., New York: Harper & Row, 1973, p. 85.

17. This analysis also included a requirement that the equity be selling for at least $5/share. This eliminates penny stocks from the analysis.

CHAPTER 10

1. Residual income is also sometimes referred to as economic profit or by commercial terms such as economic value added (EVA®).

2. A perpetuity is a constant stream of identical cash flows without end. The value of a perpetuity is easy to determine. The annual cash flow is simply divided by the appropriate discount rate.

CHAPTER 11

1. This approach is called a cross-sectional comparison.

2. This approach is called a time series comparison.

3. The perils of forecasting have been opined by many, but our favorite quote is by the esteemed American baseball playing philosopher Yogi Berra who once said, "It's tough to make predictions, especially about the future."

4. Global Industry Classification Standard (GICS) is an industry standard for defining industries to varying levels of detail. The more digits in the code, the more specific the description. GICS contains 10 sectors (2 digits), 24 industry groups (4 digits), 68 industries (6 digits), and 154 subindustries (8 digits). Standard & Poor's and Morgan Stanley assign firms into this GICS framework. The more digits that line up, the more precise the peer match—in theory.

5. There is nothing magical or theoretical about dividing the P/E ratio by the growth rate. It is simply an ad hoc adjustment to accommodate growth differentials. Although it lacks a crisp theoretical motivation, it is, like most of the other measures we discuss, a useful tool.

CHAPTER 12

1. A terrific book documenting Graham's contribution to the investing profession is *Benjamin Graham: Building a Profession*, edited by Jason Zweig and Rodney N. Sullivan, New York: McGraw-Hill, 2010.

2. John Train, *The Money Masters,* New York: Harper Business, *2000*.

3. Roger Lowenstein, *Buffett: The Making of an American Capitalist*, New York: Random House, 1995, p. 46.

4. Robert R. Johnson, *Meeting with Warren Buffett*, Class Notes, October 1992.

5. Warren Buffett, Berkshire Hathaway Chairman's Letter, 2010.

6. Warren Buffett, Berkshire Hathaway Chairman's Letter, 2009.

7. Ibid.

8. Financial Crisis Inquiry Commission Staff Audiotape of Interview with Warren Buffett, Berkshire Hathaway, May 26, 2010.

9. Ibid.

10. Gerald S. Martin and John Puthenpurackal, "Imitation Is the Sincerest Form of Flattery: Warren Buffett and Berkshire Hathaway," Working paper, April 15, 2008, http://ssrn.com/abstract=806246, http://dx.doi.org/10.2139/ssrn.806246.

11. Warren Buffett, Berkshire Hathaway Chairman's Letter, 1993.

12. Ibid.

13. "Seth Klarman: The Oracle of Boston," *The Economist*, July 7, 2012.

14. "Baupost's Klarman Sees Poor Outlook for Stocks," *Reuters*, May 18, 2010.

15. Johnson, Class Notes, October 1992.

16. Seth Klarman, *Margin of Safety: Risk-Averse Value Investing Strategies for the Thoughtful Investor*, New York: Harper Business, 1991, p. 84.

17. Ibid, p. 88.

18. "Seth Klarman: The Oracle of Boston," *The Economist*, July 7, 2012.

19. "Baupost's Klarman Sees Poor Outlook for Stocks," *Reuters*, May 18, 2010.

20. Jason Zweig, "Legendary Investor Is More Worried than Ever," *Wall Street Journal*, May 22, 2010.

21. "Seth Klarman: The Oracle of Boston," *The Economist*, July 7, 2012.

22. Ibid.

23. Johnson, Class Notes, May 1993.

24. Tom Lauricella, "Sticking to What Works: Reopened After a 26-Year Closure, Sequoia Hews to a Time-Tested Approach," *Wall Street Journal*, July 6, 2010.

25. "Money Men: The Graham and Dodders," *Forbes.com*, February 23, 2009.

26. Tom Lauricella, "Sticking to What Works: Reopened After a 26-Year Closure, Sequoia Hews to a time-tested approach," *Wall Street Journal*, July 6, 2010.

27. John Neff with S. L. Mintz, *John Neff on Investing*. New York: John Wiley & Sons, 1999, p. xviii.

28. This section draws heavily from Chapter 7 (pp. 61–82) of John Neff with S.L. Mintz, *John Neff on Investing*. New York: Wiley, 1999.

29. John Reese, "John Neff's Total Return P/E Approach," *Forbes.com*, June 1, 2010.

30. Robert D. Hershey Jr., "Mutual Funds Quarterly Review: Vanguard's Ace Stock Picker Is Back on Top," *New York Times*, July 5, 1994.

31. In Windsor Fund financial statements, common stock investments were broken down into four main categories—recognized growth companies, less-recognized growth companies, moderate growth companies, and cyclical growth companies. In the Appendix to *John Neff on Investing*, the breakdowns by category for October 1981 are presented. At this time, Windsor had only 9 percent of assets in recognized growth companies, 25 percent in

less-recognized growth companies, 31.5 percent in moderate growth companies, and 33.1 percent in cyclical growth companies. Cash represented the remainder.

32. Robert D. Hershey Jr., "Mutual Funds Quarterly Review: Vanguard's Ace Stock Picker Is Back on Top," *New York Times*, July 5, 1994.

33. Floyd Norris, "Market Place: Power Behind the Windsor Fund," *New York Times*, March 6, 1992.

34. Ibid.

35. John Neff, *Neff on Investing*, pp. 116–117.

36. Warren Buffett, "The Superinvestors of Graham-and-Doddsville," *Hermes, the Columbia Business School Magazine*, Fall 1984, pp. 4–15.

37. About Tweedy, Browne, http://www.tweedy.com/about/

38. Carole Gould, "Investing with Tweedy, Browne & Co.," *New York Times*, December 20, 1998.

39. "The Money Men: The Graham & Dodders," *Forbes*, February 23, 2009.

40. Ibid.

41. Bridget B. Hughes, "Tweedy, Browne: Temperament One of Investors' Biggest Foes," *Morningstar.com*, January 4, 2012.

42. "Tweedy, Browne Shields Investors from Downturn," Forbes.com, March 1, 2012.

43. Ibid.

44. *Advice from a Buffett-Style Investor*, Morningstar Video, June 28, 2007.

45. Seekingalpha.com

46. *Advice from a Buffett-Style Investor*, Morningstar Video, June 28, 2007.

47. "The Other Oracle of Omaha," *Kiplinger's Personal Finance*, August 2012.

48. "The Other Oracle of Omaha Speaks," *Bloomberg Businessweek*, September 23, 2010.

49. Don Bauder, "Brandes Defies Market, Buys Stocks of Dailies," *San Diego Reader,* December 13, 2007.

50. "About Us," www.Brandes.com.

51. Charles H. Brandes, *Value Investing Today*. Homewood, IL: Dow Jones-Irwin, 1989, p. 5.

52. Ibid, p. 32.

53. Bosco Lujan, "The Value Investing Philosophy: An Interview with Charles H. Brandes, Chairman of Brandes Investment Partners," *Rady Business Journal,* 2011.

54. Tom Stabile, "When Doing Right by Clients Backfires," *FT.com,* June 3, 2012.

55. Charles H. Brandes, *Value Investing Today*. Homewood, IL: Dow Jones-Irwin, 1989, p. 67.

56. Ibid, p. 24.

57. Bosco Lujan, "The Value Investing Philosophy: An Interview with Charles H. Brandes, Chairman of Brandes Investment Partners," *Rady Business Journal,* 2011.

58. Ibid.

59. Janet Lowe, *The Man Who Beats the S&P*, New York: Wiley, 2002.

60. Ibid.

61. Ibid.

62. Lowe, pp. 14–15.

63. Jason Zweig, "The Long Climb and Steep Descent of Legg Mason's Top Stock Picker," *Wall Street Journal,* November 18, 2011.

64. Ibid., p. 10.

65. Patrick McGeehan, "A Manager's Fight to Keep a Winning Streak Alive," *New York Times*, January 7, 2001.

66. Peter Lynch with John Rothchild, *One Up On Wall Street.* New York: Simon and Schuster, 1989, p. 15.

67. Lowe, p. 9.

68. Lowe, p. 6.

69. Joe Nocera, "Bill Miller's Really Bad Bet," *New York Times*, September 8, 2011.

70. Jason Zweig, "The Long Climb and Steep Descent of Legg Mason's Top Stock Picker," *Wall Street Journal,* November 18, 2011.

CHAPTER 13

1. The Russell 2000 and Russell 2000 Value Indexes are simply used for illustrative purposes. While the Russell 2000 Value is a crude measure of the performance of a typical value investing strategy, the differential over a long period of time between the Russell 2000 Value and Russell 2000 Index is meaningful.

2. Andrew Bary, "What's Wrong, Warren?" *Barron's,* December 27, 1999.

3. The excess use of leverage is another factor that could force a value investor to abandon an otherwise successful strategy before it has a chance to play out.

4. "Reading 8: The Behavioral Biases of Individuals," *Behavioral Finance, Individual Investors and Institutional Investors*, CFA Program Curriculum, Level III, 2012, vol. 2, p. 84.

5. The nifty fifty was the late 1960s to early 1970s version of the dot.com bubble. These large-cap stocks of quality firms were considered very solid long-term investments. The P/E multiples of the nifty fifty were driven up to 40, 50, even 80. The bear market of the mid to late 1970s was largely driven by the performance

of these firms. The lesson for investors is that bubbles can occur in any sector or asset class.

6. Warren Buffett, "Letter to Limited Partners," May 29, 1969.

7. Behavioral economists have dubbed this the disposition effect. Research has shown that such a strategy leads to dramatically lower returns.

8. Paraphrasing from Meir Statman "Countries and Culture in Behavioral Finance" CFA Institute Conference Proceedings, September 2008, pp. 38–44.

9. Statman also developed questions to measure regret, happiness, and trust.

10. E. J. Elton and M. J. Gruber, "Risk Reduction and Portfolio Size: An Analytic Solution," *Journal of Business*, October 1977, pp. 415–437.

11. Realize that by full diversification, we are not referring to the elimination of risk. Full diversification will reduce unsystematic risk. But the investor is still **left** holding systematic or market risk. Correlations today are higher than they were in the 1970s, so full diversification is likely to take a larger number of individual securities.

12. Peter Lynch, *One Up on Wall Street*. New York: Simon and Schuster, 1989, p. 16.

13. Warren Buffett, Berkshire Hathaway Chairman's Letter, 1979.

14. Jay Steele, *Warren Buffett: Master of the Market*, Dresden, TN: Avon, 1999, p. 154.

15. TransTerra Corporation became Ameritrade Holdings in November 1996.

16. Human capital is simply the current value of one's earning power over one's lifetime. For a young professional, human capital is an extremely high percentage of his or her total assets. For an older, retired individual, human capital may not exist.

17. Chris Higson, "Did Enron's Investors Fool Themselves?" *Business Strategy Review*, 2001, vol. 12, no. 4, pp. 1–6.

18. Catherine Valenti, "Enron Losses May Inspire 401(k) Reforms," *ABCNews.com*, December 4, 2001.

19. See Eugene F. Fama and Kenneth R. French, "Disappearing Dividends: Changing Firm Characteristics or Lower Propensity to Pay?" *Journal of Financial Economics*, 2001, vol. 60, no. 1, pp. 3–43.

CHAPTER 14

1. Some of the firms that sponsored and packaged MBS and CMO did enter bankruptcy proceedings, however, and some distressed investors gobbled up their shares, including Warren Buffett and Berkshire Hathaway.

2. Bankruptcy applies to individuals, municipalities, not-for-profits, and other legal entities as well.

3. See Elizabeth Warren and Jay Lawrence Westbrook, "The Success of Chapter 11: A Challenge to the Critics," *Michigan Law Review*, 2008, vol. 107, no. 4, pp. 604–642.

4. Gaiyan Zhang, "Emerging from Chapter 11 Bankruptcy: Is It Good News or Bad News for Industry Competitors?" *Financial Management*, 2010 (Winter), pp. 1719–1742.

5. A. C. Eberhart, E. I. Altman, and R. Aggarwal, "The Equity Performance of Firms Emerging from Bankruptcy," *Journal of Finance*, 1999, vol. 54, pp. 1855–1868.

6. We discuss warrants more fully below.

7. James Sherk and Todd Zywicki, "Obama's United Auto Workers Bailout," *The Wall Street Journal*, June 13, 2012.

8. Edith Schwalb Hotckiss, "Postbankruptcy Performance and Management Turnover," *Journal of Finance*, 1995, vol. 50, no.1, pp. 3–21.

9. Surendranath R. Jory and Jeff Madura, "The Long-Run Performance of Firms Emerging from Chapter 11 Bankruptcy," *Applied Financial Economics*, 2010, vol. 20, no. 14, pp. 1145–1161.

10. This is an approximation. You can measure FCFF more precisely by using information from the cash flow statement as detailed in Chapter 8.

11. Benjamin Graham, *The Intelligent Investor*, 4th rev. ed., New York: Harper & Row, 1973, p. 85.

12. "The Other Oracle of Omaha," *Kiplinger's Personal Finance*, August 2012.

13. It is the opposite of a warrant, which we discussed earlier in this chapter.

14. Carole Gould, "Investing with Tweedy, Browne & Co.," *New York Times*, December 20, 1998.

CHAPTER 15

1. Tom Arnold, John H. Earl, and David S. North, "Are Cover Stories Effective Contrarian Indicators?" *Financial Analysts Journal*, 2007, vol. 63, no. 2, pp. 70–75.

2. One of the greatest financial market quotations of all time came as a result of the South Sea bubble. When asked to explain how he lost over 20,000 British pounds investing in the South Sea Company, Sir Isaac Newton was quoted as saying, "I can calculate the movement of the stars, but not the madness of men."

3. Many market participants recognize that an asset bubble is forming, yet continue to purchase assets because they don't want to miss making further profits. We are reminded of the quote from Chuck Prince, CEO of Citigroup, in July 2007: "As long as the music is playing, you've got to get up and dance. We're still dancing." This statement was in reference to the mortgage securitization bubble that played a major role in precipitating the recent financial crisis. We advise you to stop dancing long before the music stops.

4. It is referred to as a candlestick chart because the daily entries often resemble a candle's wax pillar and wick. If you study technical analysis, then you will find some very colorful descriptors of charts and techniques. A good resource for, and

introduction to, technical analysis is *Technical Analysis: The Complete Resource for Financial Market Technicians*, by Charles D. Kirkpatrick II and Julie R. Dahlquist, Upper Saddle River, NJ: FT Press.

5. There is a great deal of academic research suggesting that the market overreacts to both positive and negative news, implying that Mr. Market is a bit manic-depressive.

RESOURCES

CHAPTER 1

Buffett, Warren, 1996, "An Owner's Manual," Berkshire Hathaway Website. Accessed September 13, 2013, http://www.berkshirehathaway.com/owners.html.

Buffett, Warren, 1984, "The Superinvestors of Graham-and-Doddsville," *Hermes, the Columbia Business School Magazine*, Fall.

Fisher, Philip, 2003, *Common Stocks and Uncommon Profits and Other Writings*, with a new introduction by Ken Fisher, Hoboken, New Jersey: Wiley Investment Classics.

Graham, Benjamin, 2003, *The Intelligent Investor*, revised edition with contributions by Warren Buffett and Jason Zweig, New York: Collins Business.

Graham, Benjamin, 2010, *The Memoirs of the Dean of Wall Street*, New York: McGraw-Hill.

Graham, Benjamin, and David Dodd, 2008, *Security Analysis*, 6th ed. with new contributions from many prominent value investors, New York: McGraw-Hill.

Levitt, Stephen D., and Thomas J. Miles, 2012, "The Role of Skill Versus Luck in Poker: Evidence from the World Series of Poker," working paper, University of Chicago.

Zweig, Jason and Rodney Sullivan, 2010, *Benjamin Graham: Building a Profession*, New York: McGraw-Hill and CFA Institute.

CHAPTER 2

Chui, Andy C. W., Sheridan Titman, and K.C. John Wei, 2010, "Individualism and Momentum Around the World," *Journal of Finance*, vol. 65, no. 1 (February), pp. 361–391.

DeBondt, Werner F. M. and Richard H. Thaler, 1985, "Does the Stock Market Overreact?" *Journal of Finance* , vol. 51, no. 3, pp. 793–805.

Fama, Eugene, and Kenneth French, 1992, "The Cross-Section of Expected Stock Returns," *Journal of Finance* , vol. 47, no. 2, pp. 427–466.

Fama, Eugene, and Kenneth French, 1993, "Common Risk Factors in the Returns of Stocks and Bonds," *Journal of Financial Economics* , vol. 33, no. 1, pp. 3–56.

Fama, Eugene, and Kenneth French, 1996, "Multifactor Explanations of Asset Pricing Anomalies," *Journal of Finance* , vol. 51, no. 1, pp. 55–84.

Foerster, Stephen, 2013, "Double Then Nothing: Why Stock Investments Relying on Simply Heuristics May Disappoint," *Review of Behavioral Finance*, vol. 3, no. 2 (November), pp. 115–140.

Jegadeesh, Narasimhan, and Sheridan Titman, 1993, "Returns to Buying Winners and Selling Losers: Implications for Stock Market Efficiency," *Journal of Finance*, vol. 48, no. 1 (March), pp. 65–91.

Jegadeesh, Narasimhan, and Sheridan Titman, 2001, "Profitability of Momentum Strategies: An Evaluation of Alternative Explanations," *Journal of Finance*, vol. 56, no. 2 (April), pp. 699–720.

Lakonishok, Josef, Andrei Shleifer, and Robert W. Vishny, 1994, "Contrarian Investment, Extrapolation, and Risk," *Journal of Finance,* vol. 40, no. 5 (December), pp. 1541–1578.

Yan, Zhipeng, and Yan Zhao, 2011, "When Two Anomalies Meet: The Post-Earnings Announcement Drift and the Value-Glamour Anomaly," *Financial Analysts Journal*, vol. 67, no. 6 (November/December), pp. 46–60.

CHAPTER 3

Adler, David E., 2009, *Snap Judgment*, Upper Saddle River, NJ: FT Press.

Agarwal, Vikas, Daniel Naveen, and Narayan Naik, 2004, "Role of Managerial Incentives and Discretion in Hedge Fund Performance," *Journal of Finance*, vol. 64, no. 5, pp. 2221–2256.

Arnold, Tom, John H. Earl, and David S. North, 2007, "Are Cover Stories Effective Contrarian Indicators?" *Financial Analysts Journal,* vol. 63, no. 2 (March/April), pp. 70–75.

Bailey, W., A. Kumar, and D. Ng, 2011, "Behavioral Biases of Mutual Fund Investors," *Journal of Financial Economics,* vol. 102, no. 1, pp. 1–27.

Baquero, G. and Marno Verbeek, 2009, "A Portrait of Hedge Fund Investors: Flows, Performance and Smart Money," working paper, Erasmus University, Rotterdam.

Barber, B. M., and Terrance Odean, 2000, "Trading Is Hazardous to Your Wealth: The Common Stock Investment Performance of Individual Investors," *Journal of Finance,* vol. 55, no. 2 (April), pp. 773–806.

Barber, B. M., and Terrance Odean, 2001, "Boys Will Be Boys: Gender, Overconfidence, and Common Stock Investment," *Quarterly Journal of Economics*, vol. 116, no. 1 (February), pp. 261–292.

Barber, B. M., and Terrance Odean, 2013, "The Behaviour of Individual Investors," in *The Handbook of the Economics of Finance,* edited by George M. Constantinidies, Milton Harris, and Rene M. Stultz, Amsterdam: Elsevier, B.V., vol. 2, Part B., pp. 1533–1570.

Boyer, Brian, and Lu Zheng, 2009, "Investor Flows and Stock Market Returns," *Journal of Empirical Finance*, vol. 16, no. 1, pp. 87–100.

Byrne, Alistair, and Mike Brooks, 2008, *Behavioral Finance: Theories and Evidence*, Charlottesville, VA: Research Foundation of CFA Institute.

Chevalier, Judith, and Glenn Ellison, 1997, "Risk Taking by Mutual Funds as a Response to Incentives," *Journal of Political Economy,* vol. 105, pp. 1167–1200.

Davies, Greg B., and Arnaud de Servigny, 2012, *Behavioral Investment Management: An Efficient Alternative to Modern Portfolio Theory*, New York: McGraw-Hill.

Del Guercio, D., and P. Tkac, 2002, "The Determinants of the Flow of Funds of Managed Portfolios: Mutual Funds versus Pension Funds," *Journal of Financial and Quantitative Analysis,* vol. 37, pp. 523–558.

Ding, Bill, Mila Getmansky, Bing Liang, and Russ Wermers, working paper, 2009, "Share Restrictions and Investor Flows in the Hedge Fund Industry."

Evensky, Harold, Stephen M. Horan, and Thomas R. Robinson, 2011, *The New Wealth Management*: *The Financial Advisors Guide to Managing and Investing Client Assets*, New York: Wiley.

Frazzini, Andrea, and Owen A. Lamont, 2008, "Dumb Money: Mutual Fund Flows and the Cross-Section of Stock Returns," *Journal of Financial Economics*, vol. 88, no. 2, pp. 299–322.

Goetzmann, William, Jonathan Ingersoll, and Stephen Ross, 2003, "High-Water Marks and Hedge Fund Management Contracts," *Journal of Finance*, vol. 58, no. 4, pp. 1685–1717.

Graham, Benjamin, and David L. Dodd, 1934, *Security Analysis*. New York: McGraw-Hill.

Hanson, Samuel G., and Adi Sunderam, 2013, "The Growth and Limits of Arbitrage: Evidence from Short Interest," *Review of Financial Studies*, forthcoming.

Horan, Stephen M., 1998, "A Comparison of Indexing and Beta among Pension and Non-Pension Assets," *Journal of Financial Research*, vol. 21, no. 3, pp. 255–275.

Kahneman, Daniel, 2011, *Thinking, Fast and Slow*, New York: Farrar, Straus and Giroux.

Kahneman, Daniel, Paul Slovic, and Amos Tversky, eds., 1982, *Judgment Under Uncertainty*. New York: Cambridge University Press.

Kahneman, Daniel, and Amos Tversky, 1979, "Prospect Theory: An Analysis of Decisions Under Risk." *Econometrica*, vol. 47, no. 2 (March), pp. 263–291.

Kaplan, Steve, and Antoinette Schoar, 2005, "Private Equity Performance: Returns, Persistence and Capital," *Journal of Finance,* vol. 60 no. 4 (August), pp. 1791–1823.

Kim, Jaebeom, 2010, "Stock Returns and Aggregate Mutual Fund Flows: A System Approach," *Applied Financial Economics*, vol. 20, no. 19, pp. 1493–1498.

Klement, Joachim, 2010, "The Flaws in Our Financial Memory," *Journal of Financial Planning,* vol. 23, no. 8 (August), pp. 54–60.

Mitchell, Mark, T. Pulvino, and Erik Stafford, 2002, "Limited Arbitrage in Equity Markets," *Journal of Finance*, vol. 57, no. 2 (April), pp. 551–584.

Nofsinger, John R., 2005, *The Psychology of Investing*, 2nd ed. Upper Saddle River, NJ: Pearson Prentice Hall.

Odean, T., 1999, "Do Investors Trade Too Much?" *American Economic Review*, vol. 89, no. 5 (December), pp. 1279–1298.

Peterson, Richard, 2007, *Inside the Investor's Brain: The Power of Mind Over Money*. Hoboken, NJ: John Wiley & Sons.

Phalippou, Ludovic, 2010, "Venture Capital Funds: Performance Persistence and Flow-Performance Relation," *Journal of Banking and Finance*, vol. 34, pp. 568–577.

Remolona, Eli M., Paul Kleiman, and Debbie Gruenstein, 1997, "Market Returns and Mutual Fund Flows," *FRBNY Economic Policy Review*, (July), pp. 35–52.

Robinson, David T., and Berk Sensoy, 2013, "Do Private Equity Fund Managers Earn Their Fees? Compensation, Ownership and Cash Flow Performance," *Review of Financial Studies*, vol. 26, no. 11 (November), pp. 2760–2797.

Shefrin, Hersh, and Meir Statman, 1995, "Making Sense of Beta, Size, and Book-to-Market," *Journal of Portfolio Management*, vol. 21, no. 2 (Winter), pp. 26–34.

Shiller, Robert J., and George A. Akerlof, 2009, *Animal Spirits: How Human Psychology Drives the Economy, and Why It Matters for Global Capitalism*. Princeton, NJ: Princeton University Press.

Shleifer, Andrei, and Vishny, Robert W., 1997, "The Limits of Arbitrage," *The Journal of Finance*, vol. 52, no.1 (March), pp. 35–55.

Sirri, Erik, and Peter Tufano, 1998, "Costly Search and Mutual Fund Flows," *Journal of Finance*, vol. 53, pp. 1589–1622.

Thaler, Richard H., and Cass R. Sunstein, 2008, *Nudge: Improving Decisions about Health, Wealth, and Happiness*. New Haven, CT: Yale University Press.

Wood, Arnie, ed., 1995, *Behavioral Finance and Decision Theory in Investment Management*. Charlottesville, VA: CFA Institute.

Zarowin, Stanley, 1987, "Investing Psychology Winners and Losers," *Sylvia Porter's Personal Finance*, (July–August), pp. 50–55.

Zweig, Jason, 2007, *Your Money and Your Brain*. New York: Simon & Schuster.

CHAPTER 4

Bostian, David B., Jr., 1992, "The Nature of Effective Forecasts," in *Improving the Investment Decision Process: Better Use of Economic Inputs in Securities Analysis and Portfolio Management*, Charlottesville, VA: Association for Investment Management and Research.

Brilliant, Heather and Elizabeth Collins, 2014, *Why Moats Matter: The Morningstar Approach to Stock Investing*, Wiley, forthcoming.

Buffett, Warren, February 28, 2005, Letter to Berkshire Hathaway shareholders.

Buffett, Warren, February 27, 2009, Letter to Berkshire Hathaway shareholders.

Collins, Elizabeth, Paul Larson, and Warren Miller, 2011, "Introducing a New Source of Economic Moats: Efficient Scale," *Morningstar*.

Graham, Benjamin, and Jason Zweig, 2003, *The Intelligent Investor: The Definitive Book on Value Investing*, New York: Collins Business Essentials.

Porter, Michael E., 1979, "How Competitive Forces Shape Strategy," *Harvard Business Review*, (March/April), pp. 137–145.

Porter, Michael E., 2008, "The Five Competitive Forces That Shape Strategy," *Harvard Business Review*, (January), pp. 78–93.

CHAPTER 5

Robinson, Thomas, Hennie van Greuning, Elaine Henry, and Michael Broihahn, 2009, *International Financial Statement Analysis*, CFA Institute Investment Series, Wiley.

Schilit, Howard M., and Jeremy Perler, 2010, *Financial Shenanigans: How to Detect Accounting Gimmicks and Fraud in Financial Reports*, 3rd ed. New York: McGraw-Hill.

CHAPTER 6

Fama, Eugene, and Kenneth French, 1992, "The Cross-Section of Expected Stock Returns," *Journal of Finance*, vol. 47, no. 2, pp. 427–466.

Fama, Eugene, and Kenneth French, 1993, "Common Risk Factors in the Returns of Stocks and Bonds," *Journal of Financial Economics*, vol. 33, no. 1, pp. 3–56.

Ibbotson Associates, 2012, *SBBI Classic Yearbook*. Chicago: Ibbotson Associates.

Pinto, Gerald E., Elaine Henry, Thomas R. Robinson, John D. Stowe, 2010, *Equity Asset Valuation*, 2nd ed., CFA Institute, Hoboken, NJ: Wiley.

CHAPTER 7

Fisher, Irving, 1907, *The Rate of Interest: Its Nature, Determination and Relation to Economic Phenomena.* New York: Macmillan.

Fisher, Irving, 1930, *The Theory of Interest, As Determined by Impatience to Spend Income and Opportunity to Invest It.* New York: Macmillan.

Gordon, Myron J., 1959, "Dividends, Earnings and Stock Prices," *Review of Economics and Statistics,* vol. 41, no. 2, pp. 99–105.

Sharpe, William F., 1964, "Capital Asset Prices: A Theory of Market Equilibrium Under Conditions of Risk," *Journal of Finance,* vol. 19, no. 3, pp. 425–442.

CHAPTER 8

Koller, Tim, Marc Goedhart, and David Wessels, 2010, *Valuation: Measuring the Value of Companies,* 5th ed., New York: Wiley.

Larrabee, David, and Jason Voss, 2013, *Valuation Techniques: Discounted Cash Flow, Earnings Quality, Measures of Value Added, and Real Options,* CFA Institute Investment Perspectives, New York: Wiley.

Pinto, Jerald, Elaine Henry, Thomas Robinson, and John Stowe, 2010, *Equity Asset Valuation,* CFA Institute Investment Series, New York: Wiley.

CHAPTER 9

Anslinger, Patricia L., Steven J. Klepper, and Somu Subramaniam, 1999, "Breaking Up Is Good to Do," *McKinsey Quarterly,* no. 1, pp. 16–27.

Cusatis, Patrick J., James A. Miles, and J. Randall Woolridge, 1993, "Restructuring Through Spinoffs: The Stock Market Evidence," *Journal of Financial Economics,* vol. 33, no. 3 (June), pp. 293–311.

Fama, Eugene F., and Kenneth R. French, 1992, "The Cross Section of Expected Stock Returns," *Journal of Finance,* vol. 47, no. 2 (June), pp. 427–465.

Fama, Eugene F., and Kenneth R. French, 1998, "Value versus Growth: The International Evidence," *Journal of Finance,* vol. 53, no. 6 (December), pp. 1975–1999.

Haugen, Robert, 1995, *The New Finance: The Case against Efficient Markets,* Englewood Cliffs, NJ: Prentice Hall.

Hite, G., and J. E. Owers, 1983. "Security Price Reactions Around Corporate Spin-Off Announcements," *Journal of Financial Economics,* vol. 12, no. 4 (December), pp. 409–36.

Lakonishok, Josef, Andrei Shleifer, and Robert W. Vishny, 1994, "Contrarian Investment, Extrapolation, and Risk," *Journal of Finance,* vol. 49, no. 5 (December), pp. 1541–1578.

McConnell, John. J., and Alexei V. Ovtchinnikov, 2004, "Predictibilty of Long-Term Spin-Off Returns," *Journal of Investment Management,* vol. 2, no. 3 (Third Quarter), pp. 35–44.

Miles, James A., and James D. Rosenfeld, 1983. "The Effect of Voluntary Spin-Off Announcements on Shareholder Wealth," *The Journal of Finance,* vol. 38 (December), pp. 1597–1607.

Rosenberg, Barr, Kenneth Reid, and Ronald Lanstein, 1985, "Persuasive Evidence of Market Inefficiency," *Journal of Portfolio Management,* vol. 11, no. 3, pp. 9–17.

Schipper, Katherine, and Abbie Smith, 1983. "Effects of Reconstructing on Shareholder Wealth," *Journal of Financial Economics,* vol. 12, pp. 437–467.

Schipper, Katherine, and Abbie Smith, 1986. "A Comparison of Equity Carve-outs and Seasoned Equity Offerings," *Journal of Financial Economics,* vol. 15, pp. 153–186.

Tobin, James, 1969, "A General Equilibrium Approach to Monetary Theory," *Journal of Money, Credit and Banking*, vol. 1, no. 1, pp. 15–29.

Van der Hart, Jaap, Erica Slagter, and Dick van Dijk, 2003, "Stock Selection Strategies in Emerging Markets," *Journal of Empirical Finance*, vol. 10, no. 1–2, pp. 105–132.

CHAPTER 10

Larrabee, David, and Jason Voss, 2013, *Valuation Techniques: Discounted Cash Flow, Earnings Quality, Measures of Value Added, and Real Options*, CFA Institute Investment Perspectives, New York: Wiley.

Pinto, Jerald, Elaine Henry, Thomas Robinson, and John Stowe, 2010, *Equity Asset Valuation*, CFA Institute Investment Series, New York, Wiley.

Stewart, Bennett, 2013, *Best-Practice EVA: The Definitive Guide to Measuring and Maximizing Shareholder Value*, New York: Wiley.

CHAPTER 11

Pinto, Jerald, Elaine Henry, Thomas Robinson, and John Stowe, 2010, *Equity Asset Valuation*, CFA Institute Investment Series, New York: Wiley.

Schilit, Howard M., 1993, *Financial Shenanigans: How to Detect Accounting Gimmicks and Fraud in Financial Reports*, New York: McGraw-Hill.

Robinson, Thomas, Hennie van Greuning, Elaine Henry, and Michael Broihahn, 2009, *International Financial Statement Analysis*, CFA Institute Investment Series, New York: Wiley.

CHAPTER 12

Klarman, Seth, 1991, *Margin of Safety: Risk-Averse Value Investing Strategies for the Thoughtful Investor*, New York: Harper Business.

Lowenstein, Roger, 1995, *Buffett: The Making of an American Capitalist*, New York: Random House.

Zweig, Jason, and Rodney N. Sullivan, eds., 2010, *Benjamin Graham: Building a Profession*, New York: McGraw-Hill.

CHAPTER 13

Elton, E. J., and Gruber, M. J., 1977, "Risk Reduction and Portfolio Size: An Analytic Solution," *Journal of Business*, (October), pp. 415–437.

Koller, Tim, Marc Goedhart, and David Wessels, 2010, *Valuation: Measuring the Value of Companies*, 5th ed., New York: Wiley.

Larrabee, David, and Jason Voss, 2013, "Valuation Techniques: Discounted Cash Flow, Earnings Quality, Measures of Value Added, and Real Options, *CFA Institute Investment Perspectives*, New York: Wiley.

Pinto, Jerald, Elaine Henry, Thomas Robinson, and John Stowe, 2010, *Equity Asset Valuation*, CFA Institute Investment Series, New York: Wiley.

Steele, Jay, 1999, *Warren Buffett: Master of the Market*, Dresden, TN: Avon.

CHAPTER 14

Eberhart, A. C., E. I. Altman, and R. Aggarwal, 1999, "The Euity Performance of Firms Emerging from Bankruptcy," *Journal of Finance,* vol. 54, pp. 1855–1868.

Edith Schwalb Hotckiss, 1995, "Postbankruptcy Performance and Management Turnover," *Journal of Finance*, vol. 50, no. 1, pp. 3–21.

Lehavy, Reuven, and Suneel Udpa, 2011, "Kmart: Predicting Bankruptcy, Fresh Start Reporting, and Valuation of Distressed Securities," *Issues in Accounting Education*, vol. 26, no. 2, pp. 391–419.

Warren, Elizabeth, and Jay Lawrence Westbrook, 2008, "The Success of Chapter 11: A Challenge to the Critics" *Michigan Law Review*, vol. 107, no. 4, pp. 603–642.

Whitman, Martin J., and Fernando Diz, 2009, *Distressed Investing*, New York: Wiley Finance.

Zhang, Gaiyan, 2010, "Emerging from Chapter 11 Bankruptcy: Is It Good News or Bad News for Industry Competitors?" *Financial Management*, (Winter), pp. 1719–1742.

Zuckerman, Gregory, 2010, *The Greatest Trade Ever*, New York: Crown Business.

CHAPTER 15

Kirkpatrick II, Charles D., and Julie R. Dahlquist, 2011, *Technical Analysis: The Complete Resource for Financial Market Technicians*, NJ: Pearson Education.

Murphy, John J., 1998, *Technical Analysis of the Financial Markets: A Comprehensive Guide to Trading Methods and Applications*, 2nd revised ed., New York: New York Institute of Finance.

INDEX

ABOUT THE AUTHORS

STEPHEN M. HORAN

Stephen M. Horan is managing director and co-lead of education activities at CFA Institute, the leading global credentialing and professional membership association for investment professionals with over 115,000 CFA charterholders and 125,000 members, providing vision and leadership for its educational programs and publications. Prior to joining CFA Institute, Dr Horan was a principal of Alesco Advisors, LLC, a financial analyst and forensic economist in private practice providing expert witness testimony and conducting economic impact studies, and a professor of finance at St. Bonaventure University. He publishes regularly on a variety of investment topics, authoring or coauthoring dozens of peer-reviewed articles in academic and professional journals as well as many books. His work is widely recognized and he has received numerous research grants and awards, including the prestigious Graham and Dodd Readers' Choice Award. He is quoted regularly in the financial and popular press, including the *Wall Street Journal*, the *New York Times*, the *Financial Times*, *Barron's*, and *Forbes*. Dr Horan holds the Chartered Financial Analyst (CFA) designation, the Certificate in Investment Performance Measurement (CIPM), and a PhD in finance from the State University of New York at Buffalo.

ROBERT R. JOHNSON

Robert R. Johnson is a professor of finance in the Heider College of Business at Creighton University. He teaches in the Master of Security Analysis and Portfolio Management Program and serves as the editor for the *Quarterly Journal of Finance and Accounting*. Bob also serves on the board of RS Investments, a San Francisco-based investment management firm that is majority-owned by The Guardian Life Insurance Company. He was formerly deputy CEO at CFA Institute and was responsible for all aspects of the CFA Program for the majority of his 15-year tenure at CFA Institute. He received the Alfred C. "Pete" Morley Distinguished Service Award from CFA Institute in appreciation of his leadership, stewardship, and outstanding service. Prior to joining CFA Institute, Bob was a professor of finance at Creighton University and won several teaching awards including the university-wide Robert F. Kennedy Award for Teaching Excellence. Bob has over 60 refereed articles in leading finance and investment journals and has authored several books. He has extensive media relations experience and has been quoted in the *Wall Street Journal*, the *Financial Times*, *Barron's*, and *Forbes*, among others. He has appeared numerous times on *ABC World News*, Bloomberg TV, and CNN, among others. Bob is a CFA charterholder and a Chartered Alternative Investment Analyst (CAIA). He holds a bachelor's degree in business administration from the University of Nebraska-Omaha, a master's degree from Creighton University, and a doctorate from the University of Nebraska-Lincoln.

THOMAS R. ROBINSON

Tom Robinson is managing director of the Americas at CFA Institute, leading a cross-functional team that participates in developing global strategy, implements the global strategy regionally, and engages with stakeholders regionally. Previously Tom served as managing director of education at CFA Institute, providing vision and leadership for a 100-member global team producing and delivering educational content for candidates, members, and other investment professionals. Prior to joining CFA Institute, Tom had a 25-year career in financial services and education, having served as a tenured faculty member at the University of Miami, managing director of a private wealth investment advisory firm, and director of tax and consulting services at a public accounting firm. Tom has published regularly in academic and professional journals and has authored or coauthored many books on financial analysis valuation and wealth management. Tom is a CFA charterholder, a Certified Public Accountant (CPA) (Ohio), a Certified Financial Planner (CFP®), and a Chartered Alternative Investment Analyst (CAIA). He holds a bachelor's degree in economics from the University of Pennsylvania, and a master's and doctorate from Case Western Reserve University.